THE NEW LATIN AMERICAN LEFT

Transnational Institute

Founded in 1974, the Transnational Institute (TNI) is an international network of activist-scholars committed to critical analyses of the global problems of today and tomorrow, with a view to providing intellectual support to those movements concerned to steer the world in a democratic, equitable and environmentally sustainable direction. In the spirit of public scholarship, and aligned to no political party, TNI seeks to create and promote international co-operation in analysing and finding possible solutions to such global problems as militarism and conflict, poverty and marginalisation, social injustice and environmental degradation.

Email: tni@tni.org
Website: www.tni.org
Telephone + 31 20 662 66 08
Fax + 31 20 675 71 76

De Wittenstraat 25
1052 AK Amsterdam
The Netherlands

The New Latin American Left

Utopia Reborn

Edited by Patrick Barrett, Daniel Chavez
and César Rodríguez-Garavito

PLUTO PRESS
www.plutobooks.com

First published 2008 by Pluto Press
345 Archway Road, London N6 5AA

www.plutobooks.com

Copyright © Patrick Barrett, Daniel Chavez and César Rodríguez-Garavito 2008

The right of the individual contributors to be identified as the authors of this work has been asserted by them in accordance with the Copyright, Designs and Patents Act 1988.

British Library Cataloguing in Publication Data
A catalogue record for this book is available from the British Library

ISBN 978 0 7453 2639 9 Hardback
ISBN 978 0 7453 2677 1 Paperback

Library of Congress Cataloging in Publication Data applied for

This book is printed on paper suitable for recycling and made from fully managed and sustained forest sources. Logging, pulping and manufacturing processes are expected to conform to the environmental standards of the country of origin. The paper may contain up to 70 per cent post-consumer waste.

10 9 8 7 6 5 4 3 2 1

Designed and produced for Pluto Press by
Curran Publishing Services, Norwich
Printed and bound in the European Union by
CPI Antony Rowe, Chippenham and Eastbourne

CONTENTS

ACRONYMS AND OTHER TERMS

AD	Acción Democrática (Democratic Action, Venezuela)
AD–M-19	Alianza Democrática M-19 (M-19 Democratic Alliance, Colombia)
ADN	Acción Democrática Nacionalista party (Nationalist Democratic Action, Bolivia)
ALBA	Alternativa Bolivariana para la América (Bolivarian Alternative for the Americas)
ANAPO	Alianza Nacional Popular (National Popular Alliance, Colombia)
APC	Alianza Patriótica para el Cambio (Patriotic Alliance for Change, Paraguay)
ARENA	Aliança Renovadora Nacional (National Renovation Alliance, Brazil)
CARICOM	Caribbean Community
CCC	Corriente Clasista y Combativa (Militant and Class-based Current, Argentina)
CCZ	Centro Comunal Zonal (District Communal Centre, Uruguay)
CGT	Confederação Geral do Trabalho (General Labour Confederation, Brazil); Confederación General del Trabajo (General Workers' Confederation, Argentina)
CND	Convención Nacional Democrática (National Democratic Convention, Mexico)
CNI	Congreso Nacional Indígena (National Indigenous Congress, Mexico)
CNTE	Coordinadora Nacional de Trabajadores de la Educación (National Co-ordinator of Education Workers, Mexico)
Cocopa	Comision de Concordia y Pacificación (Commission of Concordance and Peace, Mexico)
CONAIE	Confederation of Indigenous Nationalities (Ecuador)

Conamup — Coordinadora Nacional del Movimiento Urbano Popular (National Coordinator of Popular Urban Movements, Mexico)

COPEI — Comité de Organización Política Electoral Independiente (Committee of Independent Electoral Political Organisations, Venezuela)

CNDAV — Comisión Nacional en Defensa. del Agua y de la Vida. (National Commission in Defence of Water and Life, Uruguay)

CNPA — Coordinadora Nacional del Plan Ayala (National Co-ordinator of the Ayala Plan, Mexico)

COB — Central Obrera Boliviana (Bolivian Workers' Confederation)

CR — Causa R (Radical Cause, Venezuela)

CSUTCB — Confederación Sindical Única de Trabajadores Campesinos de Bolivia (Confederation of Peasant Workers' Unions of Bolivia)

CTA — Central de Trabajadores Argentinos (Confederation of Argentine Workers)

CTV — Confederación de Trabajadores de Venezuela (Confederation of Venezuelan Workers)

CUT — Central Unica dos Trabalhadores (Unified Workers' Confederation, Brazil,); Central Unitaria de Trabajadores (Unitary Workers' Confederation; Colombia)

EBR 200 — Ejército Bolivariano Revolucionario (Revolutionary Bolivarian Army 200)

ELN — Ejército de Liberación Nacional (Army of National Liberation, Colombia)

EP — Encuentro Progresista (Progressive Encounter, Uruguay)

EP-FA/NM — Encuentro Progresista-Frente Amplio/Nueva Mayoría (Progressive Encounter-Broad Front/New Majority, Uruguay)

EPL — Ejército Popular de Liberación (People's Army of Liberation, Colombia)

ERP — Ejército Revolucionario del Pueblo (People's Revolutionary Army, Argentina)

EU — European Union

EZLN — Ejército Zapatista de Liberación Nacional (Zapatista National Liberation Army, Mexico)

[ix]

FA	Frente Amplio (Broad Front, Uruguay)
FAR	Fuerzas Armadas Revolucionarias (Armed Revolutionary Forces, Argentina)
FARC	Fuerzas Armadas Revolucionarias de Colombia (Revolutionary Armed Forces of Colombia)
FDN	Frente Democrático Nacional (National Democratic Front, Mexico)
FEDECAMARAS	Federación de Cámaras de Comercio y Producción (Federation of Chambers of Commerce and of Production, Venezuela)
FHC	Fernando Henrique Cardoso
FNAP	Frente Nacional de Acción Popular (National Front for Popular Action, Mexico)
FNT	Fórum Nacional do Trabalho (National Labour Forum, Brazil)
FORA	Federación Obrera Regional Argentina (Regional Workers Federation of Argentina)
FREPASO	Frente País Solidario (Front for a Country of Solidarity, Argentina)
FSLN	Frente Sandinista de Liberación Nacional (Sandinista National Liberation Front, Nicaragua)
FSP	Frente Social y Político (Social and Political Front, Colombia)
FTA	free trade agreement
FTAA	Free Trade Area of the Americas
FTV	Federación por la Tierra, la Vivienda y el Hábitat (Land, Housing and Habitat Federation, Argentina)
FV	Frente para la Victoria (Front for Victory, Argentina)
FZLN	Frente Zapatista de Liberación Nacional (Zapatista National Liberation Front, Mexico)
IADB	Inter-American Development Bank
IBGE	Brazilian Institute for Geography and Statistics
IMF	International Monetary Fund
IU	Izquierda Unida (United Left, Argentina)
M-19	Movimiento 19 de Abril (19 April Movement, Colombia)
MAS	Movimiento al Socialismo (Movement Towards Socialism, Bolivia, Venezuela, Argentina)
MDB	Movimento Democrático Brasileiro (Brazilian Democratic Movement, Brazil)

MEP	Movimiento Electoral del Pueblo (People's Electoral Movement, Venezuela)
MERCOSUR	the Common Market of the South
Mides	Ministry for Social Development (Uruguay)
MIR	Movimiento de Izquierda Revolucionaria (Movement of the Revolutionary Left, Bolivia, Venezuela)
MITKA	Movimiento Indio Tupak Katari (Tupak Katari Indian Movement, Bolivia)
MLN-T	Movimiento de Liberación Nacional-Tupamaros (National Liberation Movement-Tupamaros, Uruguay)
MNR-I	Movimiento Nacionalista Revolucionario de Izquierda (Nationalist Revolutionary Movement of the Left, Bolivia)
MOIR	Movimiento Obrero Independiente y Revolucionario (Independent and Revolutionary Workers Movement, Colombia)
MPP	Movimiento de Participation Popular (Popular Participation Movement, Uruguay)
MRB 200	Movimiento Revolucionario Bolivariano (Bolivarian Revolutionary Movement, Venezuela)
MRTK	Movimiento Revolucionario Tupak Katari (Tupak Katari Revolutionary Movement, Bolivia)
MST	Movimento dos Trabalhadores Rurais Sem Terra (Landless Peasants' Movement, Brazil)
MTD	Movimiento de Trabajadores Desocupados (Unemployed Worker's Movement, Argentina)
MVR	Movimiento Quinta República (Fifth Republic Movement, Venezuela)
NAFTA	North American Free Trade Agreement
NM	Nueva Mayoría (New Majority, Uruguay)
OAS	Organisation of American States
OPEC	Organisation of Petroleum Exporting Countries
OPP	Planning and Budget Office (Uruguay)
PAN	Partido Acción Nacional (National Action Party, Mexico)
Panes	welfare programme for the poorest (Uruguay)
PC	Partido Colorado (Crimson Party, Uruguay); Partido Comunista (Communist Party, Argentina)
PCB	Partido Comunista Brasileiro (Brazilian Communist

	Party); Partido Comunista de Bolivia (Bolivian Communist Party)
PCdoB	Partido Comunista do Brasil (Communist Party of Brazil)
PCM	Partido Comunista Mexicano (Mexican Communist Party)
PCR	Partido Comunista Revolucionario (Revolutionary Communist Party, Argentina)
PCU	Partido Comunista del Uruguay (Communist Party of Uruguay)
PCV	Partido Comunista de Venezuela (Communist Party of Venezuela)
PD	Polo Democrático (Democratic Pole, Colombia)
PDA	Polo Democrático Alternativo (Alternative Democratic Pole, Colombia)
PDC	Partido Demócrata Cristiano (Christian Democratic Party, Uruguay)
PDI	Polo Democrático Independiente (Independent Democratic Pole, Colombia)
PDT	Partido Democratico Trabalhista (Democratic Labour Party, Brazil)
PDVSA	Petroleos de Venezuela (Venezuela's state-owned oil company)
PI	Partido Intransigente (Intransigent Party, Argentina)
PJ	Partido Justicialista (Justice Party, Argentina)
PL	Partido Liberal (Liberal Party, Brazil)
PMDB	Partido do Movimento Democrático Brasileiro (Party of the Brazilian Democratic Movement)
PMS	Partido Mexicano Socialista (Mexican Socialist Party)
PN	Partido Nacional or Blanco (National or White Party, Uruguay)
PNDA	National Household Sampling Survey (Brazil)
PODEMOS	Poder Democrático y Social (Democratic and Social Power, Bolivia)
POR	Partido Obrero Revolucionario (Revolutionary Workers' Party, Bolivia)
PP	Polo Patriótico (Patriotic Pole, Venezuela)
PPPs	public–private partnerships
PPT	Patria Para Todos (Homeland for All, Venezuela)

PPS	Partido Popular Socialista (Popular Socialist Party, Brazil)
PRD	Partido de la Revolución Democrática (Party of the Democratic Revolution, Mexico)
PRT	Partido Revolucionario de los Trabajadores (Revolutionary Workers' Party, Colombia)
PRI	Partido Revolucionario Institucional (Institutional Revolutionary Party, Mexico)
PS	Partido Socialista (Socialist Party, Argentina, Bolivia, Uruguay)
PSB	Partido Socialista Brasileiro (Brazilian Socialist Party)
PSDB	Partido da Social Democracia Brasileira (Brazilian Social Democracy Party)
PSOL	Partido Socialismo e Liberdade Socialism (Socialism and Liberty Party, Brazil)
PST	Partido Socialista de los Trabajadores (Socialist Workers' Party, Mexico)
PSTU	Partido Socialista dos Trabalhadores Unificado (Unified Socialist Workers' Party, Brazil)
PT	Partido de los Trabajadores (Workers' Party, Brazil)
PSUM	Partido Socialista Unificado de México (Unified Socialist Party of Mexico)
PV	Partido Verde (Green Party, Brazil)
TCP	Tratado de Comercio de los Pueblos (Peoples' Trade Agreement, proposed by the Bolivian government)
TIFA	trade and investment framework agreement
TNI	Transnational Institute
UCR	Unión Cívica Radical (Radical Civic Union, Argentina)
UDP	Unidad Democrática Popular (Popular and Democratic Union, Bolivia)
UN	United Nations
UNIR	Unión Nacional de Izquierda Revolucionaria (National Union of the Revolutionary Left, Colombia)
UP	Unión Patriótica (Patriotic Union, Colombia)
USAID	US Agency for International Development
WSF	World Social Forum
WTO	World Trade Organisation

ahorrista	saver
altiplano	highlands plateau
asambleas	assemblies
cacerolazo	collective mobilisation accompanied by the banging of pots
campesino	farmer, farmworker
Cardenismo	stemming from the radical reformism of Mexican President Lázaro Cárdenas in the 1930s
Carupanazo	armed uprising in Venezuela in the early 1960s
Caracazo	social explosion of February 1989, Venezuela
cocaleros	coca leaf growers
Consejos Comunales	communal councils, Venezuela
Cordobazo	strike in the city of Cordoba, Argentine, in 1969
coordinadora	network of social movements
encuentro	gathering of activist organisations
focistas	Adherents of Ché Guevara's *Foco* theory of revolutionary guerrilla warfare
Fome Zero	welfare programme for the poorest (Brazil)
Katarismo	an Aymara Indian political movement, Bolivia
misiones	programmes to expand and improve basic public services (Venezuela)
mutualista	community-based mutual aid society
Panes	welfare programme for the poorest (Uruguay)
Petista	member of Brazil's PT, or Worker's Party
piquetero	from *piquete*, to block a road or street to demonstrate or call attention to grievances; in Argentina, movement of unemployed workers
Porteñazo	armed uprising in Venezuela in the early 1960s
puntofijismo	democratic period in Venezuela following overthrow of Jiménez dictatorship in 1958
Uribismo	support for President Álvaro Uribe of Colombia

PREFACE AND ACKNOWLEDGEMENTS

In the last few years, there has been a resurgence of social movements and left parties in Latin America with a strength and power unparalleled in the recent history of the region. Left and left-of-centre political forces with different historical trajectories and ideological nuances have achieved first municipal power and later national office in several Latin American countries. At the same time, social movements – from indigenous and peasant movements in Bolivia, Ecuador and Mexico to the *piquetero* movement in Argentina – have become central forces in the political life of those countries, to the point of decisively shaping the profile and rhythm of change of local and national governments.

The most recent and visible example of the advance of the left is the election of Fernando Lugo as President of Paraguay, a country with a very long tradition of rule by the right and ultra-right. The victory by the Catholic Bishop and leader of the Alianza Patriótica para el Cambio (APC, Patriotic Alliance for Change) put an end to 61 years of authoritarian and corrupt administration by the Colorado Party (PC), the same party that had sustained the brutal dictatorship of Alfredo Stroessner. In statements recorded by the Spanish newspaper *El País*, Lugo declared that the electoral results of 20 April 2008 amounted to 'a victory for the new Latin American left' and that his government would be based on a 'preferential option for the poor'.

This resurgence has taken social and political analysts by surprise, and their work is thus yet to take systematic account of them. As for the few analyses that do exist – thoroughly reviewed in Chapter 1 – two gaps are discernible. One is a lack of comparative or regional perspective. The other is the lack of an overview of the left that includes parties, governments and social movements, and the relationships between these three types of political actors, as work to date has tended to concentrate only on either partisan politics or on grassroots mobilisation.

This book is a product of the realisation that there is a gap to bridge between recent political trends and actual research-based knowledge about them. In an effort to provide such a bridge, we organised a three-year study on the emergence and consolidation of a *new* Latin American left. Due to the breadth and the explicitly comparative character of the project, we invited a group of Latin American political and social analysts with outstanding academic track records to examine the past, present and future of the left in their countries of origin. On the basis of a common research agenda and the collective discussion of drafts, authors analysed parties, governments and social movements in ten countries: Argentina, Bolivia, Brazil, Colombia, Ecuador, El Salvador, Mexico, Nicaragua, Uruguay and Venezuela. Seven case studies were finally included in this volume, with those on Ecuador, El Salvador and Nicaragua being excluded for strictly editorial reasons. The country studies are complemented by an introductory text and two essays taking a broader look at the *new left* in Latin America.

The original studies were presented at an international conference on The New Latin American Left: Origins and Future Trajectory, held in Madison on 29 April 29 to 2 May 2004 and jointly organised by the A.E. Havens Center for the Study of Social Structure and Social Change at the University of Wisconsin-Madison and the Amsterdam-based Transnational Institute (TNI). The conference offered an unprecedented space for constructive, critical dialogue involving both activists and analysts, authors of the case studies as well as political and social leaders of the left in ten countries. The participation of social and political leaders enriched not only the quality and depth of debate at the meeting, but also the subsequent exchanges around the case studies resulting in this book. Participants included Axel Andrés Castellanos (Movimiento de Trabajadores Desocupados, Argentina), Rodrigo Chávez (Círculos Bolivarianos, Venezuela), Daniel García-Peña (Polo Democrático Independiente, Colombia), Carlos Gaviria Díaz (Frente Social y Político, Colombia), Julio Marín (Partido de los Trabalhadores, Brazil), Lorena Martínez (Asociación de Comunidades Rurales por el Desarrollo, El Salvador), Germán Rodas Chavez (Partido Socialista, Ecuador), Óscar Olivera (Coordinadora por el Agua y por la Vida de Cochabamba, Bolivia) and Mónica Xavier (Frente Amplio, Uruguay). Other Latin American and international analysts attending the conference were María Helena Alves (Viva Río, Brazil), Patrick Bond (Witwatersrand University, South Africa), Sylvie Mayer (Espaces Marx, France), José Luis Rocha (Universidad Centroamericana, Nicaragua) and Hilary Wainwright (TNI).

A first version of this book was published in Spanish in April 2005: *La Nueva Izquierda en América Latina: Sus Orígenes y Trayectoria Futura* (Bogota: Grupo Editorial Norma). Given the rapid succession of developments in Latin America since the previous edition's publication – in which history appears to be advancing at a much more accelerated pace than in other regions of the world – all the texts of the original version were revised and updated by the authors through May 2007 (with some subsequent corrections).

As with any other academic and editorial project of such significance and scope, this book would not have been possible without the invaluable support of organisations and people that have accompanied it in its different phases. First, we would like to thank the research institutions we belong to, the Havens Center and the Transnational Institute. Our two organisations jointly undertook this project, drawing on long histories of rigorous, critical and politically committed study of Latin American and global political processes to make the Madison meeting the success it proved to be. Furthermore, the dynamic produced not only this impressive volume but the *Madison Dialogue*: an ongoing, open and horizontal space for knowledge building and exchange among scholars and activists about political changes in Latin America. We are also grateful for the financial support of TNI and the Anonymous Fund, the Nave Fund and the Office of International Studies and Programs at the University of Wisconsin-Madison, which made the project financially possible.

Among those that were engaged in the first stages of this initiative, we would like to show our deepest gratitude to one person in particular, Luis Carlos Arenas, former researcher at the Instituto Latinoamericano de Servicios Legales Alternativos (ILSA, Colombia) and current Director of the Wisconsin Coordinating Council for Nicaragua. Luis Carlos had a role as active as the three editors of the book throughout the project. As always, he shared his vast knowledge of politics and society in Latin America with a generosity unusual in the academic world, as he offered his essential support without asking for anything in return.

If Luis Carlos's support was indispensable for the conception and execution of the project, that of five more people was fundamental to turning it into a book. Fiona Dove and Oscar Reyes, at TNI in Amsterdam, made possible the complex co-ordination of tasks throughout (and predictably, after) the editorial process. Liza Figueroa-Clarke, Kate Wilson and Patrick Barrett rose admirably to the challenge of translating the texts submitted in Spanish by very tight deadlines, sacrificing sleep and putting on hold other personal and professional responsibilities.

Last, but not least, we would like to pay tribute to all the anonymous men and women who continue to work so tenaciously for the transformation of the unequal political and social realities of Latin America.

Patrick S. Barrett
Daniel Chavez
César Rodríguez-Garavito
May 2008

1 UTOPIA REBORN?
Introduction to the Study of the New Latin American Left
César Rodríguez-Garavito, Patrick Barrett and Daniel Chavez

At the beginning of the 1990s, the Mexican political scientist Jorge Castañeda (1993:3) opened his well-known book on the Latin American left with this unequivocal judgement:

> The Cold War is over and Communism and the socialist bloc have collapsed. The United States and capitalism have won, and in few areas of the globe is that victory so clear-cut, sweet, and spectacular as in Latin America. Democracy, free-market economics, and pro-American outpourings of sentiment and policy dot the landscape of a region where until recently left–right confrontation and the potential for social revolution and progressive reform were widespread. Today conservative, pro-business, often democratically elected and pro-US technocrats hold office around the hemisphere. The United States spent nearly 30 years combating nationalist Marxist revolutionaries where the left was active, influential, and sometimes in control, and where it is now on the run or on the ropes.

Viewed a decade and a half later, it is striking that Castañeda's declaration of the end of a historical cycle for the left was as correct as his diagnosis and future predictions were mistaken. We now know that, in effect, the end of *really existing socialism* marked the end of an era for the Latin American left, one which was defined by the milestones of the Cuban revolution in January 1959, the Popular Unity government of Salvador Allende in Chile (1970–73), the victory of the Sandinista revolution in Nicaragua in

1979 and Daniel Ortega's electoral defeat in 1990 (Sader, 2001). Despite the survival of the Cuban revolution and the Colombian guerrilla movement into the new millennium, since the fall of the Sandinistas and the demobilisation of the Guatemalan and Salvadorian guerrillas, the dominant tendency on the Latin American left turned from armed revolution to reform through elections and popular protest.

In this way, beginning with the Zapatista uprising of January 1994, events quickly invalidated the premature diagnosis of the triumph of neoliberalism, liberal democracy and the close alignment of Latin America with the United States, as well as the prognosis of a left on the defensive, limited to exploring familiar variations on the market economy and representative democracy. As the chapters in this book abundantly illustrate, the region is witnessing the multiplication and consolidation of leftist movements, parties, and local and national governments that question every one of the elements of this diagnosis. Today, parties and political figures representing self-styled leftist or 'progressive' tendencies govern in Argentina, Bolivia, Brazil, Cuba, Chile, Ecuador, Nicaragua, Uruguay and Venezuela, as well as many of the most important cities in the region, from Bogotá and Mexico City to Montevideo, Caracas, Rosario, San Salvador and Belo Horizonte. At the same time, diverse social movements of the left have become fundamental political forces in different countries, as demonstrated, among other examples, by the decisive influence of indigenous movements in Bolivia, Ecuador and Mexico, the mobilisation of Brazilian landless rural workers, and the activism of unemployed workers and *piqueteros* in Argentina.

Similarly, the new forms of social mobilisation and the proposals and experiments offered by contemporary progressive governments go beyond the narrow confines of classic modifications of the market economy and representative democracy. An example is the system of participatory budgeting introduced by the Partido de los Trabajadores (Workers' Party, PT) government in Porto Alegre in 1990, which combines an innovative redistribution policy with a radicalisation of democracy through direct citizen participation. This has been reproduced, to varying degrees and with various nuances, by many other leftist municipal administrations (see Goldfrank, 2006).

In this way, the programmes offered by the 'new' left go beyond the specific issues of economic equality and democracy. As numerous analysts have shown, a good part of what is original about the *new* Latin American left can be found in the way these traditional concerns have been expanded to include many different agendas related to ethnicity, gender, race and other sources of inequality (see Lechner, 1988; Dagnino, 1998; Sader, 2001 and 2002; Wallerstein, 2003; Santos, 2005). To cite only the most obvious example, the demand for the rights to cultural difference and self-determination has become a central part of the left's agenda as a result of the mobilisation of indigenous peoples in Ecuador, Bolivia and Mexico over the past two decades.

This book offers a systematic and explicitly comparative analysis of the origins, characteristics, dilemmas and possible future trajectories of the various manifestations of the new Latin American left. Towards that end, and in accordance with the methodology and the process of discussions and meetings described in the preface, each of the seven case studies refers to a common set of themes, based on a detailed analysis of the most relevant leftist – or *progressive* – parties, movements or governments in the country in question. The central objective of this introductory chapter is therefore to present the general themes that structure the empirical analysis contained in the case studies, emphasising the connections, similarities and differences between them. In this way, in the pages that follow, we seek to offer an overall view of the forest of the Latin American left that complements the detailed examination of the trees (the movements, parties and governments) presented in the empirical chapters. This comparative and general overview makes it possible not only to offer a more precise definition of what is 'new' and what is 'left', but also to emphasise the central issues, actors and dilemmas involved.

Although this book is the first attempt at a comprehensive analysis of this phenomenon, in recent years an extremely interesting and copious body of literature has emerged that includes incisive debates aimed at renovating the theory and political strategy of the Latin American and international left.[1] In view of this, an additional aim of this introductory chapter is to situate the central themes and case studies presented in the book within that growing body of literature and those burgeoning regional and international debates. In Chapters 9 and 10, Atilio Boron and Boaventura de Sousa Santos present general commentaries that point towards that same objective.

In order to gain a full understanding of the nature of this book, it is worth clarifying what it is *not*. First, the book does not aim to be a conclusive and definitive evaluation of new left formations. As several of the authors emphasise, it might be too early to know with any certainty the contours, limitations or likely future outcomes of left forces whose rise dates barely to the last few years, or in some cases months. Nevertheless, this does not imply that it is not possible to trace their antecedents and historical roots; examine their composition, possibilities, limitations and dilemmas; establish the connections among different segments of the left within each country, and between them and others in the region and the world; and identify the factors that may determine their future. These are the central tasks of this volume, to contribute to the emerging academic and political discussion about the new left. In this sense, the text leaves the question regarding the future trajectory of the new left unanswered – hence the question mark following the possibility of a 'utopia reborn' in the title of this introductory chapter.

Second, the book does not present a unified and comprehensive theoretical synthesis or proposal regarding the new left. This is not only because of the nature of the project of open and pluralistic dialogue that gave rise to the book, but also because of the very nature of the new left itself. As political theorists who have examined the topic in the region have emphasised (Dagnino, 1998; Holloway, 2001, 2004), and as Bartra, Schuster, Santos and Boron argue convincingly in this volume, the variety of actors and issues that comprise the contemporary Latin American left does not fit easily within the dominant unitary leftist theories of previous decades, based on an orthodox reading of Marxism, or more precisely, of Marxism-Leninism. This does not mean that, in addition to conducting careful empirical case studies, the authors do not engage in theoretical analysis based on what they observe in their countries and the region as a whole. Several of the case studies are, in fact, original and incisive contributions to the theoretical debates about the left, and the final chapters by Boron and Santos were written with this specific end in mind. Nevertheless, neither this introduction, nor any of the contributions, is searching for a definitive theoretical synthesis.

Finally, in keeping with the above, the book is not a prescriptive or strategic manual on the left, of the sort that proliferated in past decades in the academic literature on the topic, and to which some analysts continue to dedicate their efforts even today (see for example Petras, 1999; Petras and Veltmeyer, 2006). This does not mean that it does not draw general conclusions about the political actors and strategies of the new left forces in the region. The methodology used to reach these conclusions, however, is more inductive than deductive; that is, it is based on a meticulous empirical examination and a rigorous analysis of the experiences of each country, rather than an exercise in applying a uniform theoretical or political model to the realities of different movements, parties, and governments of the left.

SIGNIFICANCE AND ORIGINS OF THE 'NEW' LEFT

The demise of the old left and the significance of the new

Given that the title of this book and several of the chapters employ the concept of the *new left*, it is important to begin with a definition of this expression. As César Rodríguez-Garavito explains in his chapter on Colombia, the adjective *new* is used here in a descriptive, rather than evaluative, sense. Hence, it refers to the fact that the left formations under consideration are of recent origin or in recent years have strengthened their capacity for mass mobilisation (in the case of movements), for competing in the electoral arena (in the case of political parties), or for governing (in the case of local and national administrations).

Although each of the political forces has followed its own timeline, in general the developments analysed in this book have taken place in the 1990s and in the first half of the current decade: that is, in the years following certain global and regional events – such as the fall of the Berlin wall in 1989, or the end of the Sandinista revolution in 1990 – that are widely recognised as the end of an era for the left and the beginning of a new one. For the purposes of this book, therefore, the *new left* is new because it is recent, and not because it is better or worse than what came before it.

To describe something as new is, of course, only meaningful in relation to that which preceded it in time. In order to characterise the new left, it is therefore necessary to specify not only the elements of continuity with the old left (that is, those elements that make it possible to describe both as of the left), but also the characteristics that differentiate it from the latter. With respect to the first task, for the specific purposes of this introduction, we draw on Norberto Bobbio's (1995) now classic distinction between right and left, according to which the former advances a positive view of social hierarchies in order to defend the economic and political virtues of inequality, while the latter promotes equality between individuals and groups (whether classes, genders, racial/ethnic groups, etcetera), inspired by a horizontal vision of society.

As Bobbio himself and many other commentators have noted, the criterion of equality, even understood in this broad sense, is not sufficient to characterise the subtleties and historic tendencies of the right or the left, nor does it encompass the totality of the agendas of either. In the case of the left, for example, the defence of equality has been accompanied by various demands for radical democracy, international solidarity, anti-imperialism and other aims. We will return to this later, in the context of the debate over the values of equality, difference and democracy within the contemporary Latin American left. For now, however, Bobbio's distinction serves as a preliminary criterion for distinguishing between left and right-wing positions, and for underscoring the continuity between the 'old' and 'new' lefts, both of which – despite their considerable differences in strategy, theoretical framework and programmes – are concerned with the promotion of equality.

Reference to the new naturally emphasises its contrast with the old. For this reason, and in order to make the concept of the *new Latin American left* descriptively and analytically useful, it is necessary briefly to examine the differences between the old left and the contemporary left, as well as the point of historical inflection between the two. Today, when analysts and political actors speak of the new left, the historical left they have in mind is the collection of political parties, social movements and guerrilla organisations that comprised the spectrum of the left between 1959 (with the victory of the Cuban revolution) and 1990 (with the end of the 'second revolutionary wave'). The high points of this second wave were the advances of guerrilla forces in El Salvador, Guatemala and, above all, Nicaragua, between the 1970s and 1980s, and it ended, as mentioned above, with the electoral defeat of the Sandinistas in 1990 (see Pearce, 1999).

The organisations that comprised the left during this period can be classified into five groups:

- Communist parties, almost all formed in the second decade of the last century, which came to defend the 'peaceful road to power' and maintained close ties to the Soviet Union.
- The nationalist, or *popular* left, which included such figures as Juan ·Domingo Perón (in Argentina), Getulio Vargas (in Brazil) and Lázaro Cárdenas (in Mexico).[2]
- The guerrilla organisations of varying ideology, strategic orientation and social extraction that multiplied during the two revolutionary waves initiated by the Cuban and Nicaraguan revolutions.
- The reformist parties, which focused on competing in elections and pursuing change 'within the system', and were more distant from the Soviet Union and Cuba.
- The social left, which included trade unions, *campesino* leagues, ecclesiastical base communities, human rights organisations, and other rural and urban movements.

As Emir Sader (2001) has explained, towards the end of the 1980s and the beginning of the 1990s, each of these groups went through a period of decline or transformation that marked the twilight of the left of the previous three decades and its point of inflection towards a new left. As communist parties went into crisis following the collapse of 'really existing socialism' in the Soviet Union and the so-called socialist camp, the Cuban revolution entered a 'defensive phase', and armed struggle was extinguished across practically the entire region with the Sandinista defeat, the demobilisation of the remaining guerrilla movements, and the growing political isolation of those that survived in Colombia and Peru.

The reformist and national-popular parties suffered equally profound transformations. With their social and ideological bases weakened and prematurely seduced by the neo-liberal wave that swept the region in the 1980s, they moved rapidly towards the centre and adopted some variation of the 'third way'. The shift was evident in the neo-liberal policies applied by social-democratic and national-popular parties and coalitions during the 1990s, ranging from those of the PRI under Salinas in Mexico, to those of Peronism under Menem in Argentina, and those implemented by the *Concertación* governments in Chile. The so-called *Buenos Aires Consensus* bears witness to the spirit of the time. This well-known document, authored by Roberto Unger and Jorge Castañeda in 1997 on the basis of discussions with Latin American political figures from the centre and the left, attempted to offer a creole version of the 'third way' (or a 'tropical Blairism', as Sader called it) in the face of the rising tide of neo-liberalism.[3]

Finally, the effects of neo-liberalism on the social left were equally profound, insofar as they weakened the predominant organisational form of social mobilisation of the past century: the trade unions. As Federico Schuster demonstrates in his chapter on Argentina, the combined effect of rising unemployment, privatisations, the 'flexibilisation' of labour regulations, rural bankruptcies and mass migrations to the cities, the growth of the informal economy, and financial crises undermined the social bases of trade unionism. In the place of the formal work positions that had been lost in the public and private sectors, enormous populations of chronically unemployed, informal and migrant workers emerged (Portes, 2003), forming a dispersed *pobretariado* very distinct from the organised proletariat that had sustained trade unionism for decades.

The destabilisation of the social bases, ideologies and strategies of the various manifestations of the Latin American left was the regional expression of the crisis of the so-called old international left. Beyond the specifics of Latin America, this crisis within the international left – as Immanuel Wallerstein has shown (2003) – consisted of two components, symbolised by the decline of the progressive traditions of two of the great modern revolutions. The theoretical component of the crisis is symbolised by the extinction of the legacy of the French Revolution, with its faith in the linear course of history, progress (which guaranteed a 'happy ending') and the fundamental rationality of humanity. The leftist version of this tradition – historical materialism – offered not only a comprehensive theory of society and history, but also the certainty for leftist movements and parties that the outcome of history would be on the side of the oppressed. The growing critique within left-wing intellectual circles of this social and historical vision – which in Latin America was heavily influenced by Gramsci's critique of the orthodox reading of Marx (Dagnino, 1998) – marked the gradual transition to new interpretations of the left's theoretical traditions and the formulation of new theories (more on this below).

The other component of the crisis of the old international left relates to its political strategy, and is symbolised by the decline of the Leninist canon that emerged from the Russian Revolution. Leninism's contribution to the Marxist theory of history was to highlight a privileged historical subject – the party, or the party-state – which was responsible for guiding and realising the revolutionary potential of the proletariat. The political strategy illustrated by the Russian Revolution and the centralised states that emerged from it helped to solidify the belief within a significant part of the international left that the most effective political actions were those based on hierarchical, centralised structures and directed toward taking state power. Nevertheless, with decades of Soviet authoritarianism contributing to a deepening disenchantment with statism and centralism among many sectors of the international left, the fall of the Soviet Union dealt the *coup de grâce* to the Leninist vanguardist model. As we shall see shortly, this 'crisis of the Leninist subject' (Tischler, 2001) generated a profound revision of strategies and theoretical frameworks at the heart of the parties and movements that came to form the contemporary left.

The emergence of the new left

Following the historical trajectory briefly outlined in the previous section, the final decade of the past century found the Latin American and international left in an openly defensive position, immersed in a deep internal critique of the strategies and ideas that had guided it throughout the century. From the other end of the political spectrum, the 'liberal economic creed' (Polanyi, 1995), dominant during the second half of the nineteenth century and the first decades of the twentieth, re-emerged in the form of neo-liberalism (Sader and Gentili, 1999; Blyth, 2002). The rise of neo-liberalism and its rapid diffusion from the governments of Augusto Pinochet, Ronald Reagan and Margaret Thatcher was so vertiginous that the political and intellectual right was able to declare the end of ideology and the impossibility of any alternative.

In the midst of this climate of retreat on the left and the consolidation of the right's *pensée unique*, what factors can explain the subsequent emergence of a new left in Latin America? We refer the reader to Atilio Boron's essay in Chapter 9, which offers an incisive and detailed response to this question. For the purposes of this introduction, we limit ourselves to mentioning the four main points of Boron's diagnosis and linking them to the case studies contained in the chapters that follow.

First, by the beginning of the 1990s, the ravages of the unconditional opening of the region's economies to the flow of goods, services and capital were beginning to be clearly felt. As has been amply documented, the negative impact of neo-liberalism on growth, inequality and poverty was particularly evident in those countries which, as a result of being exceptionally hard hit by the 1982 debt crisis, had adopted shock therapy as part of structural adjustment programmes promoted by multilateral financial agencies (see Hubert and Solt, 2004). It is therefore no accident that the event that symbolises the emergence of the new Latin American left – the Zapatista uprising in Chiapas – took place in Mexico on 1 January 1994, the date on which the North American Free Trade Agreement (NAFTA) came into effect.

As Armando Bartra describes in Chapter 7, the unconditional opening of the Mexican economy required by NAFTA served not only to consolidate neo-liberalism, but also to increase popular discontent with the structural adjustment measures. According to Bartra's eloquent account, the bankrupting of the countryside and the resulting exodus of millions of *campesinos* and unemployed Mexicans to the United States reveals NAFTA's 'heads I win, tails you lose' business deal: 'exporting bankrupted farmers and importing agricultural products'. It is for this reason that the Zapatista uprising, and their call in 1996 for a 'Conference for Humanity and Against Neo-liberalism' in Chiapas, generated such resonance.

As the economic crises and corruption scandals linked to structural adjustment reforms multiplied throughout the region, leftist movements and parties opposed to neo-liberalism emerged or gained strength. President Fernando Henrique Cardoso's decision to privatise Brazil's public services and state-owned enterprises engendered generalised discontent

[9]

with neo-liberalism, swelling the PT's electoral following and carrying Lula da Silva to the presidency in 2002 (see Chapter 2).

The Argentine collapse in December 2001 marked the death foretold of the region's most radical neo-liberal experiment of the 1990s, and opened the way for Néstor Kirchner's government (see Chapter 6). The regressive effects of the drastic reforms in Bolivia and Ecuador in the 1980s and 1990s triggered social protests by *campesinos*, indigenous peoples and urban workers, and the rise of powerful social movements and leftist parties (see Chapter 8). Venezuela's 'dual society', fed by structural adjustment policies, intensified the reaction of the majority of the population that had been denied access to the country's considerable riches. This reaction was channelled by Hugo Chávez's Movimiento Quinta República (Fifth Republic Movement, MVR), and helps to explain the solid electoral support that popular sectors have given to the Chávez government in ten consecutive local and national elections (see Chapter 3).

Although the Colombian transition to neo-liberalism was more gradual than in most countries in the region, the economic crisis came suddenly in 1999, and with it the rapid deterioration of social indicators under the neo-liberal era became apparent. This created the space for the left to restore a defence of 'the social' and thereby win elective office, including the mayoralty of Bogotá as well as other important political positions. Moreover, in the presidential elections of May 2006, it achieved the largest vote for a progressive party in Colombian history, with more than 2,600,000 votes, or 22 per cent of the electorate (see Chapter 5).

In Uruguay, the alarming economic and social deterioration caused by structural reforms not only contributed to the victory of the Frente Amplio (Broad Front) in the 2004 presidential elections. It also led to two popular referenda that were internationally unprecedented, the first (in 1992) blocking the privatisation of state-owned enterprises, and the second (in 2004) establishing a constitutional prohibition on the privatisation of water (see Chapter 4).

The second factor that helps to explain the rise of the new left is the emergence of new political actors that have served to compensate for the decline of the trade unions. Although unions continue to be a central part of the left – as is demonstrated by the fact that two of the parties that have come to govern cities and countries in the region, the PT in Brazil and the Colombian Polo Democrático Alternativo (Alternative Democratic Pole, PDA), have their roots in trade union initiatives – a large part of the left's organisational and ideological novelty comes from recent indigenous movements, *campesino* organisations, movements of the unemployed, mobilisations of landless rural workers, afro-descendent organisations, feminist movements and other forms of social mobilisation (Álvarez et al., 1998). In fact, as we will argue below, this variety and plurality of actors is one of the central characteristics of the new Latin American left. This is evident in all the case studies in this book, from the indigenous and *campesino* coalitions in Bolivia, Mexico and Ecuador, and the 'broad fronts' of social movements, to the various parties in Uruguay, Brazil and Colombia.

Third, the diminished legitimacy and internal crises of traditional parties, which until recently were firmly rooted in the political systems of the entire region, have created political opportunities which the new left formations have succeeded in exploiting. Following the transition to democracy almost everywhere in the region, it became clear that most of the traditional parties or factions lacked the capacity or the political resolve to convert the popular will into government policies. This explains why political parties continually rank among the least respected institutions in national public opinion polls, and why, in a recent regional study of political attitudes, only 58 per cent of those surveyed stated that democracy is preferable to other forms of government (Corporación Latinobarómetro, 2006).

In some contexts, such as Argentina in 2001 or Ecuador until recently, all types of parties, whether new or old, have been the targets of citizens' discontent. This is the source of the slogan made famous during the protests that brought down Argentine President Fernando de la Rúa: *que se vayan todos, que no quede ni uno solo* ('throw them all out, every last one'). In other cases, the main focus of citizens' frustration has been the parties controlling rigid two-party systems that closed off the political system during much of the previous century, such as AD and COPEI in Venezuela, the Liberal and Conservative parties in Colombia, and the Blanco and Colorado parties in Uruguay. In one or the other situation, social movements and progressive parties – independently or together – filled part of the space left by the decline of these traditional parties.

Finally, the new Latin American left has been strengthened by the revitalisation of the international left following the 1999 protests in Seattle and the emergence of a global movement against neo-liberalism and war. As Boaventura de Sousa Santos argues in Chapter 10, this is a very diverse and decentralised international left, whose nexus is the World Social Forum (WSF) and whose manifestations can be found in a growing number of national and regional gatherings, protests in cities around the world, and movements and organisations promoting progressive economic and political programmes. The fact that the WSF was born in 2001 in Porto Alegre, Brazil – the city that was, at the time, the symbol of the PT's political success – shows that the Latin American left has had considerable political and symbolic influence on this movement, which at the same time serves as a space for interaction and a source of support for the movements and NGOs (and to a lesser extent, the parties) that compose it.

CHARACTERISTICS OF THE NEW LATIN AMERICAN LEFT

As the chapters that follow clearly demonstrate, the recent experiences of the left are very diverse. They include the radical grassroots mobilisation of *campesinos*, indigenous peoples, women, students, environmentalists, people of African descent, unemployed and landless rural workers, not always articulated (indeed, at times in explicit confrontation) with the platforms of left parties, as well as the centre-left parties that have won local and national office, and organisations of the historic left – such as trade unions and communist parties – that continue to mobilise and integrate themselves into the new cycles of protest and various newly formed party coalitions. This does not mean that it is not possible to detect certain common characteristics of the new left. Based on the case studies contained in this volume, we highlight below a (non-exhaustive) list of five characteristics that are present in the majority of the political forces under study and that contrast with the characteristics of the historic left described above.

Plurality of strategies and articulation of decentralised forms of organisation

By contrast with the left that preceded it – which, as we saw, emphasised theoretical unity and strategic centralisation – the new left is distinguished by a marked plurality. With respect to organisational strategies, in place of the Leninist unitary political subject – the vanguard party or party-state – the predominant forms are 'broad fronts' of parties and movements, *coordinadoras* (networks) of social movements, or *encuentros* (gatherings) of activist organisations.

In all cases, we see coalitions or networks whose participant organisations contribute to common political purposes – for example, an election, a campaign or a cycle of protests – without losing their organisational autonomy.[4] The Uruguayan Broad Front (FA) and the PT in Brazil are the paradigmatic cases of the first type of coalition between parties and leftist movements, a model that sectors of the Colombian left have attempted to reproduce via the creation of the Social and Political Front and the Alternative Democratic Pole. The Coalition in Defence of Water and Life in Cochabamba – internationally renowned for having prevented the privatisation of the city's water – is the most visible example of articulation between social movements (Olivera, 2004). With respect to gatherings of activists and NGOs with left-wing agendas, the innumerable encounters that led to the growth of the feminist movement (Álvarez, 1998; Vargas, 2003) and the regional indigenous movement (Ceceña, 1999; Brysk, 2000; Bartra, 2004; Rodríguez-Garavito and Arenas, 2005; Escárzaga and Gutiérrez, 2005) stand out.

The same plurality is reflected in the strategic political objectives of the contemporary left. Winning government office and the democratic reform of the state remain central objectives for many of the new political forces. Alongside these, however, a significant group of social movements promotes an anti-party, anti-state position, based on civil resistance and self-management. Among these, Holloway (2001) and Zibechi (2003) have highlighted the Zapatistas in Mexico and the *piqueteros* in Argentina. This strategic position and the reaction it has provoked among analysts have given rise to some of the most intense academic and political debates about the new left, as we shall see at the end of this introduction. For now, however, we want to emphasise that, when viewed as a whole, the strategy of the forces of the contemporary left is as distant from the old Leninist obsession with taking national power as it is from the extreme vision of authors such as Hardt and Negri (2002, 2004), according to which the new left consists of a hyper-decentralised international network of local organisations that seek global forms of co-ordination, rather than the reform of the state or seizing national power.

Between these two poles, one can find a wide range of strategies that includes, in addition to competing in elections for local and national power, the construction of what Nancy Fraser (1993) has called *multiple public spheres*, which are set in contrast to the Habermasian idea of a unitary public sphere as a counterpart to the state. The multiple public spheres include spaces of community self-government – such as the *campesino* councils and the committees of Bolivian farmers organised around irrigation rights (see Chapter 8), the Zapatista *Juntas de Buen Gobierno* ('good government committees') and autonomous municipalities (see Chapter 7), and the Argentine neighbourhood assemblies (see Chapter 6) – as well as citizen forums for democratic deliberation that are linked to the state, such as the Brazilian and Uruguayan participatory budget assemblies (see Chapters 2 and 4) and the Venezuelan grassroots committees (see Chapter 3).

Multiplicity of social bases and political agendas

A second characteristic, directly related to the first, is the broadening of the social bases and political agendas of the left. The economic, political and social changes that eroded the political primacy of trade unions and the monopoly of the struggle against class inequality within the heart of the left – and the resulting emergence of 'new social movements'– have been extensively analysed by social scientists (see Melucci, 1996).

The same shift is obvious in the Latin American left. In fact, some of the most effective forms of popular mobilisation involve actors whose agendas are based as much on the classic demands for social equality as they are on demanding respect for difference. The paradigmatic example of this type of mobilisation is the new continental *indianismo* that has expanded since the indigenous peoples rising organised around Ecuador's Confederation of Indigenous Nationalities (CONAIE) in 1990. Today this forms the main social base of the Movimiento al Socialismo (Movement Towards Socialism, MAS) in Bolivia and – to a lesser extent – of Rafael Correa's new government in Ecuador, and it is a social and political force on the rise in Colombia and Mexico as well.

The inclusion in the new left agenda of the right to difference, on a par with the right to equality – or the extension of the classic objective of promoting equality to include the struggles against forms of discrimination based on ethnicity/race, gender, sexuality and the like – contrasts with the historical trajectory of the left in the last century. As Luis Tapia demonstrates in his analysis of Bolivia, the response of the historic left to the cause of multiculturalism was unenthusiastic at best, and in the worst case was openly hostile. This kind of response was demonstrated before by the repression of the Miskito autonomous indigenous movement by the Sandinista government in the 1980s. Although the history of the Latin American left shows the persistence of profound internal tensions within the left around this theme – for example, between the historic left and the CONAIE in Ecuador (see Dávalos, 2005) – the dominant tendency is towards what Norbert Lechner (1988) has called the *logic of politics* (as opposed to the exclusionary logic of war), which imposes mutual recognition on the different actors on the left.

In order to capture the plurality of agendas, strategies and social bases of new left forces, Schuster and Bartra propose in their chapters that we speak of *lefts* in the plural. In the same vein, in Chapter 10, Santos argues eloquently that the new left's possibilities for cohesion will depend on the creation of 'depolarised pluralities' – that is, on a labour of translation and mutual intelligibility among the parties, movements and organisations that from different angles are opposing neo-liberalism, imperialism and other sources of inequality and domination. The international movement for an alternative form of globalisation, articulated through the WSF, is striving for the same type of co-ordination of plurality (Seoane and Taddei, 2001; Sader, 2002; Sen et al., 2004; Santos, 2005).

Prominence of civil society

A recurring theme among contemporary left forces is the defence of civil society as a space for political action. This new addition to the left's ideology and programmes can be explained as much by the fact that civil society was the focal point of resistance to the region's right-wing military dictatorships as by the rejection of traditional Leninist statism mentioned above.

According to Francisco Weffort, 'the discovery that there was more to politics than the state' (1984:93) began for the Latin American left with the experience of the solidarity of the Catholic Church, human rights organisations and other members of civil society during the period of authoritarian military rule, and continued in the two decades that followed with the multiplication of progressive NGOs and autonomous spaces for citizens' deliberation, such as the Mexican and Brazilian neighbourhood associations in the 1990s (Avritzer, 2002). The international left has taken the same path, as demonstrated by the dominance of social organisations within the WSF and the explosion of theoretical and empirical analyses of civil society.

The prominence given to civil society has generated intense internal tensions and debates within the left. In his chapter, Atilio Boron emphasises the ambiguity of the concept and the risks it poses for the left when the term is understood as the condensation of political virtues, in opposition to the state. In the same vein, Emir Sader (2002) has criticised the international left's concentration on civil society, and its consequent abandonment of the task of transforming the state, which would thereby remain in the hands of neo-liberal reformers. Álvarez (1998) and Pearce and Howell (2001) – among other analysts – have warned of the risks of *NGO-isation* of social movements: that is to say, the possible domination by NGOs of social activist agendas and forms of action.

Some of the case studies confirm the dangers identified by these analysts – for example, the Argentine neighbourhood assemblies analysed by Schuster, which, in the absence of an articulation with the state, dissolved as the diverse interests that they accommodated moved in opposing directions. However, other cases illustrate the vitality of civil society as a space for mobilisation on the left – for example, the Bolivian indigenous and *campesino* councils for self-government. Meanwhile, a third group of experiences clearly exhibit an articulation of society and the state – for example, the local participatory budgeting programmes in Brazil and Uruguay – and, in this way, have contributed to the democratisation of both the state and civil society. We will return to these issues in the final section of this chapter.

Reformism

For the reasons outlined in the previous section, the fundamental dichotomy of the left in the past century, *revolution or reform*, was resolved in favour of the latter with the end of the second wave of armed revolutions in Nicaragua in 1990. Reform, either through institutional means or through non-violent extra-institutional mobilisation, appears to be the dominant path taken by the contemporary left. The fact that the new left is 'reformist' nevertheless has distinct implications and effects for political actors and analysts situated in different locations on the ideological and political spectrum than the left of previous decades.

For the social-democratic parties and other variants of reformism, the closure of the revolutionary path implied a welcome vindication of their historic position and the disappearance of the counterweight that separated them from the centre. Thus, as noted above, many of these – such as the Argentine Peronists, the Mexican PRI-ists, and the Chilean Socialists – quickly gravitated towards the centre and developed some form of 'tropical Blairism'. By contrast, among those searching for more radical social and economic ruptures prior to 1990, the triumph of reformism has generated the dilemma of how to promote 'non-reformist reforms' (Gorz, 1964). In this last group, we find the majority of the movements and parties that have positioned themselves or remained explicitly on the left or centre-left.

Whatever the level of enthusiasm that has met the triumph of reformism, it has had at least two implications for the Latin American left. On the one hand, in political terms it has meant a distancing from armed struggle as the path to social transformation and access to power. For example, the unprecedented success of the left-wing parties in Colombia – the Social and Political Front, the PDI and more recently the PDA – has been marked by an explicit break with guerrilla groups and with the historic Colombian left's 'combination of all forms of struggle' (see Chapter 5). The same posture can be seen at a regional and a global level, as is demonstrated by the fact that one of the guiding principles of the WSF is non-violence, which has led to the exclusion of armed organisations of the left.

On the other hand, in economic terms, reformism has meant the abandonment of models of centralised socialism – though not, as we shall see, of all appeals to socialism. In their place, the proposals and economic programmes of the new left have combined the market with more or less profound forms of state intervention, income redistribution and democratic planning. Given that economic reformism concerns one of the central problems of the new left – the construction of alternatives to neoliberalism – we will explore this issue in greater detail in the following section.

Deepening democracy

The final characteristic common to the political forces studied in this book is the centrality of democracy. As we saw, one of the motives behind the resurgence of the left in Latin America is the generalised disaffection with 'really existing democracy'. In this context, it is therefore not surprising that the left has placed great emphasis on the deepening and expansion of the democratic canon, via proposals and practices that combine representative democracy with the radicalisation of participatory democracy. Given the prominence of this issue on the agendas of contemporary leftist parties and movements, and its contrast with the programme of much of the historical left, we examine it more closely in the section that follows.

BETWEEN NEO-LIBERALISM AND DEMOCRACY

Against the backdrop of this general overview of the origin and characteristics of the new left, we are now in a position to focus on two issues that illustrate with particular clarity both its advances and possibilities, as well as its main dilemmas and tensions: (1) the search for alternatives to neoliberalism and capitalism, and (2) the democratisation of Latin American politics and societies, including the democratisation of the forces of the left themselves.

As the following chapters demonstrate, these two themes are not only present in all the national case studies, but have also given rise to the most intense internal debates within the left. The discussions are especially acute in relation to the promises and limitations of leftist local and national governments, and have been particularly evident in the cases of the Lula government in Brazil – whose leftist critics accuse it of having continued the neo-liberal policies of its predecessors (Oliveira, 2004, 2006) – and the Chávez government in Venezuela, which has provoked distrust among some sectors of the regional left, who brand it as authoritarian and populist and contrast it with the pragmatic left of Lula (Villalobos, 2004). Francisco Panizza (2005) refers to Brazil's Workers' Party and Uruguay's Broad Front, together with Chile's Socialist Party, as the clearest examples of 'the social-democratisation of the Latin American Left'. Identical dilemmas appear in other prominent examples of the contemporary left, as illustrated by the discussions about the political, social and economic orientation of the Kirchner government in Argentina and the Vásquez government in Uruguay.

Variations on the 'two lefts' thesis have become increasingly commonplace in Latin American academic and political circles. Jorge Castañeda (2006), for example, contrasts those governments and parties that pursue 'pragmatic, sensible, and realistic paths' (such as the PT in Brazil, the Socialist Party in Chile and the Broad Front in Uruguay), with those that 'emerge from a purely nationalist and populist past, with few ideological foundations' (such as those headed by Chávez in Venezuela, Kirchner in Argentina, and López Obrador in Mexico City). Similarly, the former communist leader and current ideologue of the Venezuelan opposition, Teodoro Petkoff (2005), distinguishes between the 'advanced reformist left' and what he calls the 'Bourbon left' (alluding to the European tradition of authoritarian monarchs). Offering a less polarising but still bipolar viewpoint, Carlos Vilas (2005) has emphasised the differences between the 'old' left and a 'new' left – purportedly those parties and movements that have dropped 'infantile leftism', internalised democratic values, and acknowledged the need for 'responsible' macroeconomic policies. Finally, from an over-simplistic perspective and lacking analytical rigour, Plinio Mendoza, Carlos Montaner and Álvaro Vargas Llosa (2007) establish a distinction between a 'carnivorous' left – represented by Ricardo Lagos, Michelle Bachelet, Lula da Silva, Tabaré Vásquez, Alan García and Daniel Ortega – and a 'vegetarian' left – represented by Fidel Castro, Hugo Chávez and Evo Morales.

In contrast to the proponents of the 'two lefts' thesis, in this book we speak of *the left* in general, not only because the boundary between these two poles is far from clear and continues to be the object of debate, but also because, in contrast to Castañeda and other analysts, we include within the cast of actors on the left not only parties and governments, but also social movements. The breadth and diversity of the left understood in this way thus makes a categorical distinction between two lefts impossible, to the extent that, to be descriptively accurate, it is necessary to speak of a variety of *lefts*.[5]

Beyond neo-liberalism: the problem of alternatives

As governments and social movements have discovered in recent years, it is one thing to mobilise and channel generalised discontent with neo-liberalism, and quite another to build alternatives that translate that discontent into local experiences and national policies that promote equality in the short term and are sustainable in the medium and long term. The clearest example of this difficulty is the tensions afflicting left-wing parties that have won local and national office. The dilemma is as much economic as it is political. Subjected, on the one hand, to the pressures of global markets and the demands for economic orthodoxy of international financial institutions and, on the other hand, to the scrutiny of electors who voted for them in order to change the course of the economy, various governments on the left have continued the programmes of their neo-liberal predecessors – and have even introduced reforms that the latter had been unable to consolidate due to the opposition of the very left-wing parties now in power. As Danilo Astori declared upon being named Uruguay's minister of economy and finances following the left victory in the October 2004 presidential elections, the Broad Front government 'will have to do things that we ourselves have criticised. Exactly the same will happen here as in Brazil' (Rother, 2004:A8).

The political cost of this transformation is potentially very high. As Eduardo Galeano recalled, on celebrating Tabaré Vázquez's electoral victory in his country, given that 'sins against hope are the only ones that attain neither forgiveness nor redemption' (2004:6), the survival of the left as a viable political option depends in large part on resolving the dilemma between deepening neo-liberalism or implementing feasible alternatives to it. It is very possible that the results of the 2004 Brazilian municipal elections – in which the PT lost control of two cities that were of fundamental political and symbolic importance (São Paulo and Porto Alegre) – were the early signs of the costs of the orthodox management of the economy during the first half of the Lula government (see Sader, 2005).

The terrain on which this dilemma takes place is defined by the national and international constraints confronting governments of the left. With respect to the latter, the irony for these governments lies in the fact that the circumstances that facilitated their electoral victories significantly limit their room for manoeuvre. In effect, the same economic crises that swung voters to the left in countries like Brazil, Venezuela and Uruguay, left a legacy in their wake – including high fiscal and balance of payments deficits, vulnerability to attacks by speculative capital, excessive dependence on the international prices for basic goods – that present formidable obstacles for changing the course of fiscal, monetary and social policy.

To continue with the paradigmatic example of Brazil, the mere prospect of Lula's electoral victory in 2002 was enough to prompt international financial actors to withdraw their short-term capital from the country and cause the risk rating for Brazilian debt to skyrocket. Given that short-term capital controls had been dismantled as part of the structural adjustment package, only a few months after the election Brazil faced the possibility of an economic collapse similar to that experienced by Argentina a few months earlier.

The International Monetary Fund (IMF) responded to the emergency loan request of Lula's predecessor, Fernando Henrique Cardoso, with a condition that left no doubt about its power to intervene in national policy-making: of the total financial assistance authorised, only a fraction would arrive before the elections. The rest would depend on the promise of all the candidates – including Lula – that if elected they would continue and deepen the neo-liberal policies, including an increase in the primary fiscal surplus that would severely limit the future government's capacity for social spending. Faced with this ultimatum, the PT issued its *Letter to the Brazilian people*, in which it submitted to the IMF conditions – to the relief of investors, the disappointment of its traditional bases, and the satisfaction of the middle-class voters who finally voted for Lula (see Chapter 2). This episode left the power of the international financial community absolutely clear: although it does not vote, it does veto in order to maintain the rules of the global economic game.

The national obstacles to changing economic course are also significant. One of the fundamental reasons that neo-liberalism has been able to resist the rise of the left and popular discontent is the inertia of institutions and economic cadres formed during the neo-liberal era. As Sánchez, Machado Borges Neto and Marques demonstrate in Chapter 2, monetarist economists and other neo-liberal reformers are firmly entrenched within the Central Bank, the Ministry of Economics, and the Finance Ministry of Brazil. It is for this reason that the Lula government has maintained an orthodox monetary and fiscal policy that sets these members of the so-called *economic team* against members of the PT's *political team*, who occupy other positions in the government and the party, and who prefer (or preferred) a decided shift away from neo-liberalism.

In this way, in Pierre Bourdieu's terms (1999), the legacy of neo-liberalism in the region is felt today in the tension between a 'right hand' of the state, charged with maintaining economic orthodoxy, and a 'left hand', generally represented by the ministries of education, health, labour and social welfare, seeking to push policy in a post-neo-liberal direction.

The Venezuelan case, as Edgardo Lander demonstrates in Chapter 3, vividly illustrates both the presence of these national and international restrictions and how circumstances can make them less restrictive. Lander points out that Chávez's Fifth Republic Movement government has generated an unprecedented increase in social spending, channelled primarily through the so-called *misiones*: programmes to expand the coverage, and improve the quality, of basic public services (health, education, infant nutrition, etcetera) in poor areas. This social policy – whose popularity has been evident in the many elections in which marginalised classes have consistently voted for Chávez, including a recall referendum (see López Maya, 2004) – was made possible by the reorientation toward social spending of Venezuela's oil revenue, which has been exceptionally high in recent years and is without parallel in other countries of the region. This extraordinary source of foreign exchange has diminished the influence of international financial institutions and the restrictions burdening other leftist governments that are dependent on international capital. At the same time, the Venezuelan experience illustrates the tight restrictions produced by national resistance to changes in economic policy. The redirection of oil income towards social investment took place only after a prolonged strike by the Venezuelan business class, who were joined by the personnel of the state-owned oil company.

While these and other obstacles are recognised by the parties, governments and movements of the new left, there are profound debates and divisions over the possible room for manoeuvre within the indicated limits, and the capacity of governments, whether on their own or with the support of social movements, to go beyond those limits and increase the possible range of economic policies. As Daniel Chavez asks in his chapter on Uruguay, to what extent are the narrow margins for manoeuvre a product of the decisions of the governments themselves? To what extent are these governments being more 'fundist' than the International Monetary Fund? Judging by the intense controversy surrounding the

Lula government, both internal and external to the PT – which even led to the December 2003 expulsion of PT members of Congress who had criticised the government – these questions trace deep lines of division within the new left.[6] While the government and the PT leadership contend that prudence and orthodoxy are necessary conditions for opening space for post-neo-liberal policies, their critics call for a change of course and assert that the imperatives of macroeconomic stability are equivalent to a permanent conversion to neo-liberalism.

This state of things might lead one to conclude that there is, in effect, 'no alternative' to neo-liberalism, as Margaret Thatcher proclaimed two decades ago. Nevertheless, the chapters in this book show that the problem lies more in the question than in the response regarding the existence of an alternative. If the question is whether the new Latin American left has a fully developed and clear alternative to the neo-liberal model, the answer is clearly *no*. Instead, what we find in the case studies are multiple local or national initiatives with diverse degrees of effectiveness and originality.

The path followed by several 'progressive' governments suggests that the reconstitution of the Latin American left is no longer defined by radical changes in institutional politics and macroeconomic policies, but by the implementation of social reforms. This apparent new left 'agenda' takes for granted the basic principles of market economics, while promoting reforms such as the implementation of welfare programmes for the poorest members of society (such as the *Fome Zero* in Brazil or the *Panes* in Uruguay), a renewed concern for public security, a more active role for the state as regulator and mediator between capital and labour, the expansion and improvement of public services, and the introduction of a more progressive tax regime.[7] Despite making a positive difference in the lives of the citizens affected by these policies, they do not add up to a comprehensive alternative model to neo-liberalism. Moreover, these and other post-neo-liberal experiences are far from consolidated, and the political actors themselves promote them in an atmosphere of considerably greater uncertainty than that which drove the ideology and programmes of the old left.

Indeed, it bears noting that in all the countries governed by the left, we observe the existence of actors that are not simply anti-neo-liberal but also anti-capitalist and have thus positioned themselves to the left of the progressive parties in government. This implies growing pressure from both sides of the political spectrum and a much more complex equilibrium than the bipolar left–right contradiction hegemonic throughout the region. In this context, we see the left both *in* government and *against* the government, with the line separating supporters and opponents not always clear.

[22]

As seen in Brazil and Venezuela with the re-election of Lula and Chávez, the poor tend to support the government, whereas those with higher levels of formal education tend to adopt a more critical stance. At the same time, the economic policies implemented by some of the progressive governments analysed in this volume are endorsed by social and economic sectors that not long ago were at the forefront of resistance to the left. In short, the very same governments are seen by some critics as 'sold out to market forces' and neo-capitalists, whilst others perceive them as not market-friendly enough. For all these reasons, Latin America is at this moment a privileged laboratory for analysing the identity and future evolution of the left and progressive left politics in and beyond the region.

In one important respect, the uncertainty characterising the contemporary Latin American left may be seen as an advance over the old left. Indeed, as Atilio Boron contends in Chapter 9, the construction of economic and social alternatives never proceeds in accordance with a manual or a pre-conceived model. Rather, it is a historical, dialectical and ultimately unpredictable process with multiple possible outcomes.[8] The inflexible pursuit of a pre-conceived model is therefore more likely to serve as a hindrance to the construction of an alternative than as a reliable guide. Similarly, in an essay exploring the problems of the transition to socialism, Erik Olin Wright (2004:17) contends that such a transition is best conceived as moving in a general *direction*, rather than toward a specific institutional *destination*. This approach, he asserts, is like:

> leaving for a voyage without a map of the journey, or a description of the destination, but simply a navigation rule that tells us if we are going in the right direction and how far we have travelled. This is obviously less satisfactory than a comprehensive roadmap, but it is better than a map whose destinations are constructed through wishful thinking and which give a false sense of certainty about where we are headed.

From this broader perspective, an extensive range of proposals, programmes and experiments becomes visible, and it becomes possible to analyse and evaluate the extent to which the actors on the left today offer alternatives to neo-liberalism. Thus, rather than a fixed destination, a more useful analytical criterion consists of determining to what extent these economic initiatives go in the direction of the values widely recognised by the left itself, such as decreasing inequality between classes and countries, economic democracy and environmental sustainability. In other words, these aspirations constitute the essential points of reference on the left's navigation rule.

But to continue with Wright's metaphor a bit further, it is also essential to understand the left's point of departure and – perhaps even more crucially – the specific set of obstacles it is likely to confront as it embarks on the pursuit of those aspirations. As the above discussion strongly suggests, this is particularly relevant to Latin America, given the enormous unmet needs of the region's population, its structurally disadvantageous position in the hemispheric and global economy, and perhaps most importantly the fierce opposition of domestic and foreign elites to progressive social and economic change. This implies that in assessing the policies advanced by the new left, it is necessary to consider not only their success in producing real improvements in people's lives, but also their capacity to alter the structural relations of power. It is the relationship between these two objectives that is of course at the heart of the long-standing debate between revolution and reform. As Atilio Boron notes, several decades ago Rosa Luxemburg warned that as genuine as reforms may be they do not alter the prevailing social and political order, and indeed will in the end serve to strengthen it by demobilising progressive social and political forces. For Luxemburg, therefore, the only really viable option was a direct assault on the power of elites – in a word, the revolutionary 'conquest of political power'. This is obviously not the hegemonic approach within the contemporary Latin American left.

For a variety of historical reasons, revolution no longer occupies a prominent place on the agenda of the contemporary Latin American left and, almost by default, there has been a return to reformism. Yet, Luxemburg's warnings about the power implications of reformism are as relevant today as ever. Does this mean that the left faces an irresolvable dilemma, or is there an alternative to the seemingly equally unpromising options of reform and revolution? An answer may be found in André Gorz's concept of 'non-reformist reforms', to which we alluded above, or what Armando Bartra refers to in Chapter 7 as 'revolutionary reforms'. Such reforms seek not only to produce immediate and genuine improvements in people's lives, but also to build popular political capacity and thereby lay the foundation for further advances at subsequent stages of political struggle. In other words, popular political power is not only deployed to bring about short-term changes; the changes themselves are selected with the specific strategic goal of augmenting that power. Thus, rather than simply ends in themselves, non-reformist reforms are a means to an end, the first step in a process of ongoing and sustained transformation in the relations of social and political power between dominant and subordinate groups.

The successful design and implementation of such reforms is, of course, a tricky proposition. For it is precisely because elites often perceive even quite minor changes as the first step on a slippery slope to an eventual erosion of their power that they have often been violently opposed to any change whatsoever. Still, the history of social and political struggle demonstrates that elites have on many occasions been forced to accept rather significant change, typically after concluding that suppressing change posed a far greater threat to their power and privilege than acquiescing to it. Again, in most cases, the outcome of this struggle is unpredictable, and the resulting change rarely what any of the participants intended. As we shall discuss in greater detail below, this is as much the product of the tensions and contradictions internal to the left itself, most importantly, between social movements, parties and governments.

Finally, it bears noting that following Hugo Chávez's open call for the construction of a 'socialism for the twenty-first century' in Venezuela and beyond, the new Latin American left's option for 'reform' over 'revolution' no longer appears as unanimous as it once did. Immediately after his re-election in December 2006, Chávez called on his followers to dissolve their existing parties and to form a new and revolutionary United Socialist Party of Venezuela as the means to 'construct socialism from below'. In his chapter, Edgardo Lander contends that there is no possibility of building a democratic alternative to the capitalist order, of pursuing a revolutionary project, without first having a profound debate about the historical experience of 'really existing socialism'.

It is therefore impossible to assess how many of the policies being implemented today in Latin America could be characterised as 'non-reformist' or 'revolutionary' reforms. As we shall see, the authors of the chapters that follow highlight numerous examples of policies and initiatives that offer diverse types of policies, whose depth and radicalism vary significantly, depending on the economic and social context in which they are taking place. Some look for the immediate relief of basic needs left unsatisfied by neo-liberal programmes; for this reason they frequently operate as complements to such programmes. The social policies aimed at the poorest sectors – for example, the programmes to fight hunger – are examples of this kind of alternative. Other initiatives – such as the initial renegotiation of the Argentine debt under the Kirchner government – imply a break with some of the pillars of neo-liberalism. A third group of policies – such as the direct management of public companies by consumers and citizens as an alternative to privatisation – have post-capitalist characteristics, insofar as they are based on community control of production and management of productive units (see Olivera, 2004; García Linera, 2004; Chavez, 2007).

At a local level, leftist governments in cities such as Bogotá, Porto Alegre, Montevideo, Mexico City, São Paulo and Caracas have revived the issue of *the social*, which had been marginalised during the neo-liberal era, and consequently have introduced important changes in municipal social and fiscal policy. The conversion of the PT's participatory budget into an icon for left-wing local governments, and the interest that this model has inspired in international theory and political science, can be explained by the fact that by combining heightened social spending, increased tax collection, income redistribution, administrative efficiency and the empowerment of the citizenry in general and the poorer sectors in particular, it is possibly the clearest successful example of non-reformist reforms undertaken by leftist administrations (Fung and Wright, 2003; Baiocchi, 2003). As the evolution of the participatory budget of Porto Alegre illustrates, this kind of reform faces serious resistance from economic and political elites, to the extent that its success has resided in displacing its decision-making power toward popular organisations and organised civil society, always with the guidance and co-ordination of a proactive state apparatus (Baierle, 1998).

Also at the local level, several important experiences created by social movements stand out, among them the aforementioned community management of water in Cochabamba, Bolivia, the co-operative management of 'recovered' firms by unemployed workers and *piqueteros* following the massive wave of bankruptcies in Argentina in 2001, the sustainable management of natural resources in indigenous territories, and diverse experiences of the international 'fair trade' movement (which involve communities of small farmers and unions from the region working with international networks of activists and consumers).

At the national level, early signs of post-neo-liberalism were also expected in some of the PT's social policies: the Lula government's educational, agrarian and urban reforms were supposed to be heading in this direction but, as Chapter 2 shows, the current path of such policies is not always an alternative to neo-liberalism. A more open break with neo-liberalism, motivated by the profound nature of the Argentine crisis, was exhibited by the Kirchner government, as demonstrated by its decision to delay paying international creditors in order to give priority to social spending and the reactivation of the domestic economy, thereby openly contradicting the recommendations of international financial institutions following the crisis.[9] In Venezuela, the restructuring of the management of oil revenue and the considerable expansion of social programmes also goes against the Washington Consensus and the policies of previous governments.

Whatever the eventual outcome of these and other governments, the initial signs already reveal that just as there is no single variety of capitalism or neo-liberalism, the emerging alternatives are equally diverse. Given their distinct starting points, levels of economic development, positions in the global economy and institutional structures, the countries that have turned to the left follow different routes, the results of which are not possible to predict in advance. This last point is illustrated by the recent economic performance of Argentina and Brazil. Despite the initial predictions by the international financial press of the success of Lula's more orthodox route and the certain failure of the heterodox route chosen by Kirchner, growth has been fairly positive in both countries under the two governments, and especially vigorous in Argentina, which bounced back from the crisis thanks to an annual growth rate of over 7 per cent in recent years.

Finally, at the regional and global levels, the highlights include Lula, Kirchner, Morales and fundamentally Chávez's proactive foreign policy of promoting South–South regional and global blocks in order to alter the international economic rules of the game. Among the regional initiatives, we can find the Brazilian opposition to the initial proposal for a Free Trade Area of the Americas (FTAA), the terms of which were unfavourable to Latin American countries, proposals for strengthening MERCOSUR (the Common Market of the South) and the promotion of a wide range of alternatives to the Washington Consensus's recipes for trade liberalisation. More recently, we can observe the construction of proposals based on solidarity, justice and complementarity between nations, such as the Bolivarian Alternative for the Americas (ALBA) or the Bank of the South. Lastly, efforts are underway at a global level to strengthen the negotiating power of the Global South in the World Trade Organization (WTO), via alliances like the one attempted at the ministerial conferences in Cancun in 2003 and Hong Kong in 2005.

The new left and democracy

The corruption scandals and deterioration in economic and social conditions that have taken place across the length and breadth of the region during the last two decades generated a crisis of legitimacy of the region's new and old democracies. One result of the crisis was the weakening of the age-old parties that had dominated electoral systems until the 1990s: the Institutional Revolutionary Party (PRI) in Mexico, the Democratic Alliance and COPEI in Venezuela, and the Liberal and Conservative parties in Colombia.

The political space thereby opened to new left movements and parties – whose popular protests and electoral strategies were decisive in the creation of that space – once again placed on the agenda of progressive forces a problem that had caused profound divisions within the old left: *democracy*. On the one hand, the confluence of ideas drawn from Marx, Gramsci and Luxemburg had contributed to the formation of a radical democratic tradition in Latin America that inspired agendas of free and egalitarian participation, in both the political and the economic spheres. On the other hand, the widespread acceptance of Leninist vanguardism and the demonstration effect of the Stalinist experience had given rise to a rejection of so-called 'bourgeois democracy' or 'strictly formal democracy' by influential sectors of the old left. In their view, as Luis Tapia notes in Chapter 8 in relation to the dominant attitude within the Bolivian left until the 1970s, liberal democracy was either a form of political organisation of the capitalist class, or a stage along the road to socialism.

At the end of the last century, two historic events changed the balance of forces within the left in favour of the radical democratic tradition. The first, mentioned above, was the end of 'really existing socialism' and the demise of the revolutionary path. This served to reinforce the shift initiated in the 1980s toward replacing the idea of revolution with that of democracy as the central concept of the left's political ideology (Weffort, 1984; Lechner, 1988). The second was the experience of opposition to the right-wing military dictatorships in various countries, in which leftist parties and activists played a leading role. In fact, some of the most consolidated parties of the new left, such as the Brazilian PT and the Uruguayan FA, have their roots in the struggle against authoritarian rule, which was initiated by their activists from exile or from within local human rights organisations, trade unions, guerrilla groups or intellectual circles (see Chapters 2 and 4).

As the return to democracy became the source of political and ideological cohesion within the left, the theories and programmes of the social movements and parties that would come to form the new left extended the critique of right-wing authoritarianism to a critique of authoritarianism in general. Even after the transition to liberal democracy in nearly the entire continent, the legacy of this shift by the left is evident in its defence of

[28]

civil rights vis-à-vis governments with authoritarian leanings. For example, the new Colombian left has been the visible leader of the opposition to the multiple attempts by the Uribe government to suspend or weaken the individual rights consecrated in the 1991 constitution (see Chapter 5).

In theory at least, the implications of this embrace of democracy by the left can be understood on two levels. On the one hand, it can be seen as providing a means to an end, offering the politico-institutional openings necessary for the realisation of the left's central aspirations. This is not a new discovery, of course, as historically it has been those who have had the most to gain from democracy (namely, subordinate classes and labour in particular) that have fought hardest for it (Rueschemeyer et al., 1992). On the other hand, democracy can also be understood as an end in itself, not only because of the traumatic experience of authoritarianism that has led to a deeper appreciation for basic civil liberties, but also because democracy itself can become the object of change. That is to say that one of the changes that democracy makes possible is a deepening of democracy. Put somewhat differently, democracy is an obvious arena for the pursuit of non-reformist reforms – making use of existing democratic openings to institute reforms that deepen and expand democratic practices and procedures, including those that are outside formal political institutions. In this sense, it may be more appropriate to speak of *democratisation* as an ongoing, dynamic process than of *democracy* as a final end state.

In practice, the shift towards deepening democracy has developed on two fronts. In relation to representative democracy, the rise of various parties has been linked to their role as promoters and guarantors of the democratic rules of the game. The PT, for example, went from being a minority local party to being a powerful electoral force at the national level thanks in large part to the leading role it played in removing Fernando Collor de Mello from office for corruption in the early 1990s. The Mexican Partido de la Revolución Democrática (Party of the Democratic Revolution, PRD) also opened the way for the reform of the Mexican electoral system following the scandal produced by the 1988 presidential elections, in which the PRI stole the election from the victorious PRD candidate, Cuahutémoc Cárdenas. Today, even those parties frequently accused of being 'anti-democratic' (such as Hugo Chávez's Fifth Republic Movement, or Evo Morales' Movement Towards Socialism) routinely participate in elections, and in that way – according to Lander and Tapia in their respective chapters – have sustained electoral systems that could otherwise have collapsed under the weight of the traditional parties' loss of legitimacy.

The second front concerns the experiences and proposals in the area of participatory democracy, which has become a central theme in the ideology and programmes of numerous left movements and parties (Santos, 1999 and 2003a). In effect, within the theories and institutions of participatory democracy, one can see a convergence between the deepening of democracy and another distinctive characteristic of the new left: the revitalisation of civil society and its articulation with the state.

We have already mentioned the ways in which the participatory budgets and other forms of citizen involvement in municipal administration demonstrate these characteristics. Other experiments and proposals illustrate the same tendency. Some are firmly established – for example, the good government committees in the Zapatista territories and the community councils in the Cochabamba region of Bolivia – while others are more tentative or fleeting, such as the popular assemblies that channelled the discontent of Argentines toward the formal system of political representation. In either case, it involves experiences that take place at a local level, given the logistical limitations of direct citizen participation. Thus, in addition to the promotion of radical democracy, an emerging front on the agenda of the left is the articulation between local participatory democracy and representative democracy at the national level, as illustrated by the campaign initiated by Bolivia's social movements and the MAS to hold a Constituent Assembly aimed at establishing a new institutional map that would integrate elements of both (see Chapter 8).

The incorporation of democracy into the programmes of the left is, nevertheless, far from being unanimous and peaceful. Three points of tension and controversy are evident in the case studies. First, several of the most prominent social movements have deep reservations about the transformative potential of the institutions of representative democracy. In Ecuador, for example, the indigenous movement exhibits a deep distrust toward the existing channels of representation, which on many occasions – particularly the 1998 Constituent Assembly and the 'betrayal' by Lucio Gutiérrez in 2002 – ended up reinforcing the power of political, ethnic and economic elites. Similar reservations can be detected in the Bolivian *campesino* and indigenous movements, whose recent experience shows that mobilisation and direct democracy have been more effective than the attempts to reform the institutions of political representation.

Second, the application of democratic principles to the structures of left parties and organisations themselves has been uneven. While a few parties, such as the Uruguayan Broad Front, choose their candidates in democratic primary elections, most continue to be dominated by vanguards or figures reminiscent of the old left. For example, the weakening and (until 2006) repeated electoral defeats of the Sandinista National Liberation Front (FSLN) in Nicaragua, one-time icon of the Latin American left, can to a large extent be explained by the absence of internal democracy and renewal, linked to the domination of the party by the historic figure of Daniel Ortega (Rocha, 2004; Torres Rivas, 2007). With respect to social movements, we have already referred to the risks of 'NGO-isation', with the consequent dominance of professional staff over the grassroots in the making of fundamental strategic decisions.

Finally, the question of respect for democratic institutions predominates in the intense controversy, both inside and outside the left, over the 'Bolivarian revolution' in Venezuela. As Fernando Coronil (2004) indicates, there are two perspectives on the issue in contemporary Venezuela: while for supporters of the government, democracy began with the Chávez 'revolution', after decades of institutional manipulation on the part of the traditional parties, in the view of its detractors, the government put an end to democratic checks and balances in order to institute an authoritarian state. In Chapter 3, Edgardo Lander documents this 'cognitive break' between the two sectors and offers an analysis that questions the leading role played by the armed forces in the government, while at the same time refuting the image of the Bolivarian process as a break with democratic institutions (see also López Maya, 2004).

THE ACTORS ON THE NEW LEFT:
MOVEMENTS, PARTIES AND GOVERNMENTS

Following an examination of the meaning, origin, characteristics and central tensions of the new left, we move now to a brief discussion of the three principal types of actors examined in the empirical chapters: the social movements, parties and governments to which they now have access.[10] Given that throughout the preceding pages, we have referred to all three and have illustrated their initiatives and programmes in the countries under consideration, in what follows we concentrate on the task of examining the relationships among these three political forms, each of which plays a distinct but crucial role in a complex and often contradictory division of labour within the left. In this way, we attempt to break the general category of the new left into its component parts and to demonstrate how their distinct political logics and the national contexts in which they operate give rise to complementary or contradictory relationships, which in turn help to explain the characteristics and perspectives of the left in each country.

Of these, social movements might be considered the most essential. For social movements not only serve as the single most important counterbalance to the social forces of oppression (on the basis of class, race, ethnicity, gender, for example); they also provide the primary impetus for social and political change. Indeed, social movements are the principal novelty of the new left in several of the countries analysed. As Federico Schuster demonstrates, the renewal of the Argentine left following the shift from Peronism to neo-liberalism under Menem can be attributed to the mobilisation of *piqueteros*, popular assembly participants, trade unionists, middle-class people who had lost their life savings, and ordinary citizens who took to the streets to protest, deliberate and demand that every last politician be thrown out of office. In Mexico, in the words of Armando Bartra, the most promising left is in the streets – that is, in the protests of indebted farmers, bankrupted *campesinos*, the chronically unemployed and surviving trade unionists. The most robust and organised social movements in the region can be found in Bolivia, where they have been capable of exercising direct pressure on the course of governments and the economy, while in Ecuador the power of the indigenous movement has been demonstrated by the ousting of two presidents. Even in those cases where political parties dominate the left, grassroots pressure has been decisive, as demonstrated by the central role of Brazilian trade unionism in the rise of the PT and the party's historic relations with the Landless Peasants' Movement (MST).

Beyond the details of the national experiences, for the purposes of this section we highlight four characteristics common to the different case studies. First, as Atilio Boron asserts in Chapter 9, Latin American political and economic structures are extremely unyielding and have only ceded ground when faced with the reality or immanent possibility of massive popular mobilisation. This explains why most analysts had argued in the late 1990s that the outlook for the left was most promising in those countries with strong social movements – such as Bolivia or Brazil – and why it was more uncertain in countries where, for historical reasons, social movements have proved more fragile, such as Colombia. Such predictions were somehow off-target, as the crisis of the PT and the whole of the Brazilian left would indicate. However, the proven capacity of elites to influence the Brazilian government would seem to confirm Boron's argument about the unyielding character of the region's economic and political foundations. The Brazilian experience also suggests that strong social movements are a necessary but hardly sufficient condition for a sustained process of change, a point to which we will return below.

Second, there is a notable convergence in the evolution of the demands of social movements in different countries. In general, this involves a change from demands for privileges for specific groups (for example, industrial trade unions, *campesinos*, truck drivers) to more universal demands based on the concept of citizenship or the defence of fundamental rights. Among other cases, this tendency can be observed in Argentina, where Schuster documents the transition from protests based on the demands of trade unions to those based on citizenship rights; Brazil, where the same transition has taken place toward the defence of citizenship (Dagnino, 1998); and Colombia, where, despite the violence against members of social movements, the latter have advanced in the same direction and have attained an unprecedented level of visibility in recent years (see Rodríguez-Garavito in this volume; Archila, 2004).

Third, the region's movements have experienced a prolonged 'protest cycle' (Tarrow, 1998), which began with the mobilisations against privatisation at the beginning of the 1990s and continued with the mobilisations of *ahorristas*, unemployed workers and sectors of the middle class affected by the second wave of structural adjustment programmes at the beginning of this century. Initially directed against neo-liberal reforms, the cycle of protests has widened to include mobilisation against the traditional political actors responsible for those reforms, as illustrated with particular clarity by the explosion of protests in Argentina over the past ten years.

Finally, as we already indicated, the social bases of the old and new movements have diversified. Together with the strengthening of movements of the indigenous, people of African descent and landless rural workers, among others, another novelty of recent social protest lies in the fact that class-based movements have included sectors that were not traditionally included within trade unionism, such as the unemployed and workers in the informal sector (see Chapter 6).

Beyond the details of specific cases, the relationships between movements on the one hand, and parties and governments on the other, have been one of the most dynamic focal points of internal political and theoretical discussion within the new left. Some movements and political theories, inspired by the Zapatista experience, have developed a grassroots position, centred on local self-management that declares itself anti-political in that it does not seek to take state power. As John Holloway has insisted, from this point of view, the novelty of the contemporary left would reside in 'the project of changing the world without taking power' (2001:174). This implies a strategy that 'goes beyond the state illusion ... the paradigm that has dominated thought on the left for more than a century [and] that places the state at the centre of the concept of radical change' (Holloway, 2000:46). Instead of party competition and attaining government office, the political and theoretical focus of this aspect of the new left can be found in the permanent mobilisation of the grassroots, without connection to electoral politics. The privileged actor of this left, therefore, is the autonomous and rebellious social movement, capable of pressuring for change from below. These movements, moreover, would be directly articulated with their international counterparts, which together would constitute a network of global resistance that avoids the intermediation of national states (Hardt and Negri, 2004).

There are also those who, while in agreement with the new left's critique of statism, nonetheless underscore the importance of state power for the advance of the left's programmes (Boron, 2001; Bartra, 2003a). They note the parallels between the anti-politics that stresses local self-management and mobilisation, and the neo-liberal proposal to minimise the state. Such a position would surrender the terrain of the electoral arena and the state to the agendas of the right. From an alternative perspective, parties and governments are as important as they have ever been, and they are at least on an equal footing with the social movements in making up the new left.

With respect to the state, its key attribute is its capacity to intervene in social and economic relations. Although this capacity is most often used to reproduce or deepen social and economic inequalities, it is also essential to mitigating them and thus to enabling social movements to realise their fullest potential. In the words of Santos in Chapter 10, 'while the state can sometimes be an enemy, it can also be a precious ally, particularly in peripheral or semi-peripheral countries.' This is not to say that the state is a passive instrument of social and political forces (let alone a neutral agent or an autonomous subject). Rather, it can be understood as an 'institutional complex of forms of intervention and representation' with changing institutional boundaries and asymmetrical effects on the nature of social and political forces and their capacity to pursue their interests (Jessop, 1990). In other words, consistent with the tensions within the Brazilian state discussed in Chapter 2 and Santos' description of the state as a contradictory social relation in Chapter 10, it should be seen as a 'strategic terrain' upon which contending social and political forces struggle to give the individual or collective activities of its different branches a specific strategic direction.

Social movements are therefore not limited simply to blocking state action or 'pressuring from below'. They are also capable of transforming the state, both by redirecting its modes of intervention (in order to lessen social and economic inequalities and thus alter the balance of social forces) and by transforming its forms of representation (in order to make it more accessible and thus more susceptible to pressure from below). Thus, building on the concepts of non-reformist reforms and democracy as an object of change discussed above, the relationship between social movements and the state should be understood as a dialectical one. For the manner in which social movements engage the state will be crucial to determining not only the latter's institutional capacities and strategic direction, but also their own power and capacity for constructing an alternative society.

Similarly, political parties can play a critical role in advancing the cause of a viable left alternative. More specifically, they perform three fundamental tasks related to this objective. First, a political party (or parties) of the left can serve as the political arm of social movements, enabling them to project their social power and express their demands in the political arena and providing them with a necessary means for gaining access to the state. Second, a political party is uniquely positioned to promote a broadly conceived socio-political project capable of integrating diverse social actors and movements and can thus play a key role in providing an overarching vision and point of connection for social movements with distinct 'sectoral' concerns.[11] Finally, organised political force in the form of parties is of great importance to giving the diverse activities of the state's various agencies a specific strategic direction and providing the political support necessary to sustain it (see Boix, 1998).

While political parties are uniquely positioned to carry out these tasks, their essentially electoral logic very often works in direct conflict with the logic of social movements. As Adam Przeworski (1985) argued in his classic work, the imperative of winning elections forces leftist parties to offer a programme that appeals not only to their primary base among subordinate classes, but also to centrist voters among the middle and even upper classes. As a result, not only are the demands of social movements at risk of being marginalised, they are also under enormous pressure to refrain from making use of their principal power resource (social mobilisation), particularly if it involves acts of disruption.[12] This tension only becomes intensified if the party proves victorious and assumes office. Schuster's account (Chapter 6) of the Kirchner government's effort to demobilise the social movements that helped bring him to power provides a clear illustration of this tension, as well as its potential long-term consequences. As Schuster notes, if Kirchner succeeds in this effort, he will probably gain a degree of political stability, a goal to which all governments aspire. But it is likely to come at the cost of diminishing the government's power (and room for manoeuvre) vis-à-vis Argentina's dominant classes, and thus its capacity to undertake more significant reforms.

Thus, the balancing act of the left parties consists of carrying out the promised programmes that mark the difference between them and the centre or the right, but within the economic, political, national and international restrictions that tend to cause them to gravitate towards the centre. Several of the case studies demonstrate that, in practice, the parties of the left have followed a common path to building their political capacity and mitigating the dilemmas that they face. It involves a multi-level strategy that proceeds from advances at the local and provincial levels to electoral victories at the national level. As students of left-wing local governments have documented, the latter have invariably been the launch pads for national candidates and political platforms (Stolowicz, 1999; Chavez and Goldfrank, 2004). The most prominent examples are, once again, the Broad Front, which built its national prestige on 15 years of governing Montevideo prior to its rise to national power in 2005, and the PT, which rose to the presidency after more than a decade of success in municipal administration in cities like Porto Alegre, Belo Horizonte, Fortaleza and São Paulo.

The distinct logics driving movements, parties and governments can thus give rise to diverse relationships of collaboration or confrontation. An ideal scenario for the left would consist of the presence of, and dynamic articulation among, strong popular movements, parties and governments, thereby maximising the left's overall capacity to build and sustain a viable alternative. Under this scenario, the first provide the grassroots demands and pressure necessary for the second to carry out their programmes and fulfil their responsibilities as instances of ideological and strategic articulation, and for the governments to drive the (non-reformist) reforms that comply with the programmes and create the possibilities for even more profound change, including the further strengthening of social movements and the deepening of democracy.

At the beginning of the Lula presidency, the Brazilian left was the closest to this complex model. However, in practice, the first two years of government were marked by scant social mobilisation and the consequent timidity of the PT in the execution of its government programmes. Given the strength of Bolivian social movements and their growing articulation with an ascendant leftist political party (MAS) currently in government, it is possible that Bolivia will come closer to this model in the near future. The opposing scenario is made up of fragile movements, and of weak parties that lack the capacity to govern. Of course, the majority of the cases are situated somewhere between these two scenarios, ranging from those dominated by political parties (such as Colombia) to those dominated by movements (such as Ecuador).

The debate over the relative importance of movements, parties and governments runs throughout the new Latin American and international lefts and continues to produce contrasts between grassroots movement theories and organisations – such as Zibechi (2003) on the *piqueteros* – and party-centric or state-centric perspectives and organisations (see, for example, Mertes, 2002). The chapters by Bartra, Santos and Boron contribute to this discussion, and we refer the reader to them. From our perspective, the empirical evidence found in the case studies suggests that the majority of leftist actors and analysts assume a pragmatic position that views the relationships among movements, parties and governments as variables that depend on the political context and historical experience of each country. In this sense, as Santos argues in Chapter 10, framing the debate in terms of a categorical choice between institutional and extra-institutional action, or between parties and movements, or between state power and community power as the aims of social struggle, is frequently a pseudo-debate. It is for this reason that the chapters that follow give equal emphasis to governments, parties and movements.

STRUCTURE OF THE BOOK

In keeping with the aims, issues and central actors described in this chapter, the remainder of the book is organised into three parts. The first focuses on parties and examines the four most prominent contemporary experiences of leftist national and local government in the region. In Chapter 2, Félix Sánchez, João Machado Borges Neto and Rosa Maria Marques trace the Brazilian left's climb to national office in 2002 and analyse the economic and social policies of the PT-led government.

In Chapter 3, after documenting the historical roots of the crisis of the Venezuelan two-party system and the rise to power of the Fifth Republic Movement, Edgardo Lander explains the connection between that political and social trajectory and popular-sector support for the government of Hugo Chávez. Lander also examines the extent to which the policies and institutional changes initiated by the Chávez government have offered an alternative to neo-liberalism, as well as the deep and growing social and political polarisation that they have provoked. The author concludes his chapter with some critical reflections on the prospects of a unified socialist party in Venezuela.

In Chapter 4, Daniel Chavez goes back to the origins of the Broad Front at the beginning of the 1970s, and discusses its role in the resistance to the military dictatorship of 1973–84 and its subsequent political consolidation and rise to power in Montevideo in 1989. After briefly reviewing the coalition's performance in governing the capital city, he examines the road to national office, and the dilemmas and tensions that being in government has generated for the Uruguayan left.

In Chapter 5, César Rodríguez-Garavito analyses the political, economic and social factors that explain the emergence and electoral rise of a new left in Colombia since the end of the 1990s. Rodríguez-Garavito then turns to a study of the composition, perspectives and proposals of the new left. In so doing, he analyses the particularities of the Colombian context, namely the way in which the country's internal armed conflict has contributed to the polarisation of Colombian politics, the crisis of the traditional party system, and the emergence of successful political blocs on both the left and the right of the ideological spectrum

The second part of the book focuses on social movements, examining three countries that have been characterised by a continuous and dynamic process of social mobilisation since the 1990s. In Chapter 6, after reviewing the history of the Argentine left during the past century, Federico Schuster focuses on the cycle of protests that erupted during the economic crisis at the end of 2001. Schuster examines the composition and agendas of the new Argentine social movements and the influence they have exerted on the Kirchner government.

In Chapter 7, Armando Bartra begins by briefly tracing the singular history of the institutionalisation of the Mexican left since the revolution of 1910, summarising its major ups and downs over the course of the past century. Bartra then turns to an examination of the Zapatista, indigenous and *campesino* movements, as well as the principal political formation of the new Mexican left, the Revolutionary Democratic Party (PRD).

In Chapter 8, Luis Tapia studies the transformation of the Bolivian left and shows how, since the 1970s, democracy and the defence of indigenous cultural and political autonomy have become central to its agenda. Tapia emphasises the leading role and growing capacity for social mobilisation of the *campesino* and coca growers syndicates, as well as their articulation in the so-called 'water war' in Cochabamba and in electoral campaigns that have led to the rapid growth of leftist parties (most importantly, the MAS), culminating in the victory of Evo Morales in the 2005 presidential elections.

Finally, the third part balances the empirical focus of the case studies contained in the first two parts with two essays that offer a more general and theoretical perspective on the new Latin American left. In Chapter 9, Atilio Boron seeks to explain the resurgence of the left across the region, and devotes particular attention to two central problems confronting the new left that were mentioned above: the formulation of alternatives to neo-liberalism, and the relationship between the left and democracy. In Chapter 10, Boaventura de Sousa Santos concludes the book with a general reflection on the new Latin American and international left. Among other issues, Santos examines the need for a new connection between theory and practice in the contemporary left, the productive versus unproductive debates relevant to the pursuit of that connection, the points of contact among the various movements and parties, and the role of the World Social Forum as a gathering space for the international left.

NOTES

1. On the Latin American left see, among others: Álvarez et al. (1998); Boron (2001); Holloway (2001, 2004); Tischler (2001); Sader (2001, 2002); Munck (2003); Chavez and Goldfrank (2004); Rodríguez-Garavito et al. (2005); Elías (2006); Laclau (2006); Touraine (2006).

   On the international left, see, among many others: Bobbio (1995, 1996); Bosetti (1996); Kagarlitsky (2000); Hardt and Negri (2002, 2004); Wallerstein (2003); Sen et al. (2004); Wainwright (2005); Santos (2005).

2. Despite its inclusion within the broader framework of the left, we should be aware that the regimes led by Perón, Vargas and Cárdenas incorporated clear authoritarian features (in the role assigned to the national leadership, the relationship with the opposition and its own social base, and the internal structure of the ruling political force) that nowadays we would characterise as neo-fascist. Their social agenda, however, was undoubtedly progressive.

3. The text of the *Buenos Aires Consensus* can be viewed at <www.robertounger.com/alternative.htm>.

4. The same sort of coalitions and networks predominates in the left in other latitudes, as is shown by the initiatives – mostly failed – aimed at building a 'plural left' in France, and a 'rainbow coalition' in the United States (see Wallerstein, 2003).

5. This view is shared by Ramírez Gallegos (2006), who argues that the left has

acquired a specific form in each country, based on the legacy of neo-liberalism, the role and place of social movements, and the historic evolution of progressive parties. Hence, from this perspective, there would be many more than just 'two lefts', and all progressive forces would have as a common characteristic the will to strengthen the role of the state and improve social indicators beyond the political and institutional agenda of neo-liberalism.

6.   The importance of (and the controversy generated by) this topic is reflected in a large and growing bibliography on Brazil. See, for example, Knoop (2003); Carvalho (2003); Tavares (2003); Dowbor (2003); Costa (2003); Gonzaga (2003); Baiocchi (2004); Sader (2004); Oliveira (2004, 2006).

7.   In this sense, with the apparent exception of Chávez's Bolivarian transition to socialism, the new Latin American left seems to have embraced *post-neo-liberalism* as proposed by thinkers such as Joseph Stiglitz (2002, 2006), who propose a 'humanisation' of capitalism without altering the basic economic and political structures of capitalist societies.

8.   In fact, as Mark Blyth (2002) documented in his genealogy of neo-liberalism, the latter emerged gradually from a process of the convergence of diverse theories and political platforms that took more than three decades to crystallise before becoming the dominant model of the 1980s.

9.   This trend was later contradicted by the Argentine government's decision of January 2006, when $9,600 million were used to cancel the country's IMF debt in advance. To some analysts and political activists, this marked the 'independence' of the country vis-à-vis international financial institutions, while the radical left, social movements and the Nobel laureate Adolfo Pérez Esquivel criticised the payment of a debt which they regarded as immoral and illegal (Calloni, 2006).

10.   These three types of actors do not, of course, constitute an exhaustive list of political actors on the Latin American left. The latter also includes a range of additional actors – for example, progressive NGOs, left-wing intellectuals – that are not affiliated to any particular party, government or movement. Nevertheless, we concentrate on the latter in this section, given that they are the protagonists in the accounts presented in the case studies.

11.   This role, moreover, cannot be performed by corporatist institutions alone. Even in 'liberal corporatist' systems, where corporatist policy-making has tended to diminish the importance of parliamentary government mediated through parties, the party system has not been supplanted since it continues to manage many of the antagonistic issues that would overwhelm the consensus-building capacity of corporatist institutions (Lehmbruch, 1979, 1984). In the words of Bourke, 'involved in a party is social space in its totality. A party undertakes not only the promotion of specific, multiple, and heterogeneous interests, but also the reproduction of the totality of the social formation. In it unfolds the whole domain of hegemony, alliances, and compromises' (quoted in Leys, 1989:179).

12. This process was clearly evident during the transition from military to civilian rule in Chile, where the centre-left opposition to the Pinochet regime abandoned the social mobilisation strategy initiated in the wake of the 1983 protests in favour of an electoral one, thereby marginalising popular movements that had played a central role in the protests, most importantly the labour movement (see Barrett, 2000, 2001, 2002).

2 BRAZIL

Lula's Government: A Critical Appraisal

Félix Sánchez, João Machado Borges Neto and Rosa Maria Marques

A quick glance at Latin America at the beginning of the century confirms the deep changes taking place in the region, as well as the extent and depth of the social devastation wrought by neo-liberalism during the past two decades. Latin America and Brazil have changed, due in large part to the severe damage that neo-liberal policies have produced and their effect in reshaping the Latin American political landscape. Viewed from this perspective, the recent evolution of the Partido dos Trabalhadores (Workers' Party, PT) and of the government of Luís Inácio Lula da Silva demonstrates, on the one hand, the capacity of neo-liberal thinking to maintain its presence and influence in Latin America, and on the other, the demise of a party and its project for a different kind of society.

In Brazil, from a struggle for the expansion of rights and universal access to social, economic and political goods and services, the trajectory of the Lula government has evidenced, simultaneously, the priority of maintaining the privileges of the financial sector as well as an attempt to reach out to poor and marginalised sectors of society through the mediation of the traditional sectors of Brazilian politics. This would explain, for example, the virtual abandonment by the Lula government of the concern, previously central to the PT programme, for developing the participatory budget and adopting institutional mechanisms of participatory democracy and citizen participation in public policy-making (see Baiocchi, 2003; Gaspar et al., 2006). Rather than an expansion of a culture of rights, what we observe is a relationship with the poorest sectors of society based on the culture of subordination that has historically characterised the political action of the dominant classes in Brazilian society.

The commitment given to development based on a conception of sustainability and respect for the environment has frequently come into conflict with the hegemony of agribusiness and the government's option to prioritise the interests of this sector and of the national and multinational corporations, with investments in those sectors most implicated in the destruction of the environment. Without a doubt, a landmark in this trajectory was the government's approval of a law authorising genetically modified agricultural products, along with the numerous actions of the Movimento dos Trabalhadores Rurais Sem Terra (MST, Landless Peasants' Movement) and other rural social movements in favour of agrarian reform that have brought them into direct conflict with the interests of big agricultural capital, under the passive gaze of the government.[1]

In this sense, the difficulty that the PT has exhibited as a political party in meeting the challenge of becoming a government of change serves as flagrant proof of its inability to influence and coherently lead its own government in the effective application of a project of social transformation. In the same vein, there are growing indications that the nucleus in charge of the government may have abandoned that project and is instead adhering to the central tenets of neo-liberal thinking, especially in regard to the subordination of political action to the dictates of mercantile logic and the renunciation of the effort to salvage the social state and social mobilisation as the driving impulses of that alternative project (see Oliveira, 2006).

THE RISE OF THE PT TO GOVERNMENT

The presidential election of 1989 was exceptional by Brazilian and Latin American standards. In its first electoral contest, a political party openly defined as socialist, and with a candidate – Lula – who did not just claim to represent the working class but who was a worker himself, received more than 11 million votes, over 16 per cent of the electorate. The participation of the Workers' Party in Brazilian politics developed even further over the next decade. By the turn of the century the PT was in charge of 187 municipalities and three state governments. After three failed attempts (in 1989, 1994 and 1998), the PT finally won the 2002 presidential elections with the highest number of votes ever cast for a Brazilian politician.

Similar to the foundation of the FA in Uruguay (see Daniel Chavez's chapter in this volume) more than a decade earlier, the creation of the PT in Brazil took place in a context of growing popular mobilisation against authoritarianism. The party's creation can only be understood in relation to the broader process of mass organisation and activism that had developed in Brazil during the 1970s. The party was conceived as the new political actor that would express the autonomous interests of Brazilian workers in the institutional sphere.

From the beginning, the ideological identity of the PT has been different from that of other Brazilian left parties. It originally developed as an internally pluralistic party, with a popular-socialist ideology based on the concrete demands and proposals of the country's grassroots (particularly the unionised workers), rather than on theoretical inputs closely related to other existing or utopian models. In this sense, unlike many other left parties in Brazil and Latin America, the PT was never 'pro-Soviet', 'pro-Chinese' or 'pro-Albanian' (like one of the two traditional communist parties of Brazil), and did not follow the powerful populist tradition deeply rooted in the country since the times of Getulio Vargas.

Since its foundation, the PT has been closely linked with the country's main labour confederation, the Central Unica dos Trabalhadores (Unified Workers' Confederation, CUT), as well as with a wide range of community-based urban social movements. The proposals for the construction of a 'new citizenship from below' are rooted in the vision of grassroots activists and in a sound analytical critique of the historical elitism of Brazilian politics.

The main precedent for the creation of a new workers' party was the emergence of an autonomous labour movement in São Paulo and other major cities. The new unionism of the late 1970s and early 1980s was autonomous in relation to: (1) the state, (2) the traditional co-optation 'from above,' and (3) the Partido Comunista Brasileiro (Brazilian Communist Party, PCB). When the new labour confederation was created in 1983, the majority of its members were also *Petista* (PT) cadres. The CUT attracted the more militant sectors of the working class, and distinguished itself by its readiness to resort to strike tactics. It also assumed an ideological definition clearly different from the positions traditionally upheld by the Confederação Geral do Trabalho (General Labour Confederation, CGT), which was prone to less radical strategies and tactics (Moreira, 1998).

The Brazilian Communist Party, which had been heavily repressed by the military but was traditionally inclined to negotiate resolutions to political disputes, questioned the foundation of the new confederation and declared that the CUT represented the interests of a labour aristocracy, such as the auto and metalworkers of Greater São Paulo. Not surprisingly, the PCB had also repudiated the foundation of the PT some years earlier.[2]

The foundation of the PT in 1980 had to do with the broader changes in the cultural and social profile of the Brazilian labour force throughout the post-war period, as a result of the intertwined processes of industrialisation, urbanisation and literacy. In particular, the developmental policies implemented by the military during the late 1960s had favoured industrial growth, resulting in a significant expansion of the urban working class. The growing radicalisation of the workers' movement that led to the creation of the PT in the early 1980s should be understood in the context of the end of the cycle of economic expansion that began in the 1960s.

In Brazil, the left did not have to displace any 'traditional' party. Unlike Uruguay (see Chavez's chapter in this volume), Brazil had been characterised traditionally by fragile and weak parties and the constant renovation of the political spectrum. In 1930, Getulio Vargas terminated the evolution of the pre-existing liberal and elitist parties. The second reorganisation of political identities was determined by the coup of 1964, and was along the lines of the only two parties allowed by the military: the Aliança Renovadora Nacional (National Renovation Alliance, ARENA), the political arm of the dictatorship; and the Partido do Movimento Democrático Brasileiro (Party of the Brazilian Democratic Movement, PMDB), which represented the opposition to the regime.

The third reorganisation of Brazilian parties during the past century started during the democratic transition in the late 1970s and continued for over two decades. Between 1982 and 2000, a total of 78 parties participated in nation-wide electoral politics, ranging between five parties in 1982 and 30 in the 1998 elections (Marconi Nicolau, 2001). Most of the parties, however, did not have significant influence in national electoral contestations.

In 1994, Lula was the main adversary of Fernando Henrique Cardoso, who won the election backed by his own Partido da Social Democracia Brasileira (Brazilian Social Democracy Party, PSDB) and other centre-right and right-wing parties. By then, the leftist coalition led by the PT had broadened to include the Partido Socialista Brasileiro (Brazilian Socialist Party, PSB), the Partido Comunista do Brasil (Communist Party of Brazil, PcdoB), the newly-created Partido Popular Socialista (Popular Socialist Party, PPS, created by former members of the pro-Soviet PCB), the Partido Verde (Green Party, PV) and the Partido Socialista dos Trabalhadores Unificado (Unified Socialist Workers' Party, PSTU). In 1998, Lula was once again the main challenger to Cardoso (or FHC, as he is popularly known in Brazil), with the PT leading a centre-left coalition that included the two old partners, the PCdoB and the PSB, and the by then large Partido Democratico Trabalhista (Democratic Labour Party, PDT).

In the 2002 elections, Lula's candidacy in the second round was supported by a broad range of parties, from the small and neo-conservative Partido Liberal (Liberal Party, PL) to practically the whole spectrum of the left.

Throughout the 1990s, the highest concentration of *Petista* votes was found in the economically dynamic southern and south-east regions. This fact would suggest a correlation between higher degrees of industrialisation and urbanisation and the rise of the PT. In 2002, however, the PT lost the government of the emblematic state of Rio Grande do Sul – of which Porto Alegre, the hometown of participatory budgeting, is the capital city – after practically all the other parties united in an electoral front against the PT candidate. In 2004, the PT suffered an even more symbolic defeat, when the municipal government of the so-called world capital of participatory democracy, Porto Alegre, went to a coalition of centre-right parties united against the left (see Chavez, 2004).

Lula's victory in the 2002 presidential elections undoubtedly represented one of the most important landmarks in the development of the Latin American left. In addition to the fact that the PT had long been considered one of the main leftist parties (if not the leading leftist party) in the region, the characteristics of the president-elect himself – a former migrant from Brazil's impoverished north-east, metallurgical worker, and trade union leader – suggested that a legitimate representative of the Brazilian people had come to power, or at least to occupy the country's highest government office. There were therefore many reasons to regard the new government as an authentically popular one.

From the beginning of the 1990s, however, the PT went through a process of change, such that its more radical characteristics were significantly diminished. Lula made an enormous effort to gain the acceptance of the business community. A particularly strong step in this direction took place during the 2002 election campaign itself, with the PT's decision to form an alliance with the PL and the alliance's selection of businessman and then Senator José Alencar as its vice-presidential candidate. Nevertheless, these moves were not enough to make Lula an acceptable presidential candidate in the eyes of the business community. As his election became increasingly likely, a process of capital flight and speculation against the Brazilian currency ensued. The 'markets' were demonstrating their anxiety.

In this context, in July 2002, Lula released a document entitled *A Letter to the Brazilian People*, in which he reaffirmed his commitment to the changes sought by the population, while at the same time announcing 'respect for business contracts' and guaranteeing that any change would be the 'product of a broad national negotiation'. Since this document came to be considered a sort of synthesis of Lula's government programme, it is worth citing a few of the more important phrases that summarise its general orientation:

> The PT and its partners are fully aware that moving away from the existing model, as society is so emphatically demanding, will not occur magically overnight. ... There will have to be a clear and cautious transition between what we have today and that which society is demanding. Whatever was done or undone in eight years will not be compensated for in eight days. The new model cannot be a product of unilateral government decisions, as we see today, nor will it be implemented by decree, in a voluntaristic manner. It will be the fruit of a broad national negotiation, which must lead to an authentic alliance for the country, to a new social contract capable of ensuring growth with stability. The premise of this transition will naturally consist of respect for business contracts and the country's obligations. The recent financial market turbulence must be understood in the context of the fragility of the current model and the popular demand to overcome it.

In this letter, Lula does not claim to be 'leftist', nor a representative of the workers or the people, in opposition to the dominant classes. On the contrary, he seeks to speak explicitly for society as a whole, trumpeting a broad national negotiation that would lead to a 'new social contract'. He speaks, in particular, for the uneasy 'markets', which is why the central theme of the *Letter* is his guarantee that, if elected, he would respect all contracts.

It bears asking how much of this synthesis of the candidate's intentions retains what can be characterised as 'leftist' ideas. Two aspects stand out here: the emphasis on the need for change (he mentions the changes 'desired by society'), and his continued criticism of the government of Fernando Henrique Cardoso. Neither of these is, in itself, 'leftist'. But in the context in which they were announced, and bearing in mind the criticisms that Lula and the PT had been making of the Cardoso government up until that moment, the 'change' appeared to signal the abandonment of a neo-liberal model in favour of a resumed national development. If nothing in the *Letter* – or in anything that Lula and the PT said during the 2002 campaign – pointed to an effort to build a socialist society (the meaning usually given to a leftist proposal), there was, on the other hand, an indication that a 'developmentalist' model would be sought.

Moreover, while the candidate's speeches did not refer even remotely to the idea of a government of the poor against the rich – quite the opposite, since the candidate always appeared as *Lulinha Paz e Amor* ('Lula for Peace and Love'), making it clear that he would not endorse any social conflict – they did indicate that the candidate would govern for society as a whole. This was set in contrast to the government of Fernando Henrique Cardoso, regarded as a government for the rich, and implied that there would be special concern for the poor and social inclusion, which would bring about a reduction in social inequality.

Thus, the basic ideas of the campaign could be summarised as follows:

- the abandonment of the neo-liberal economic model of the Cardoso government
- the implementation of a developmentalist model
- the establishment of a government for society as a whole, with special concern for the most poor, which would seek to reduce social inequalities.

The official campaign documents (particularly the 'Lula for President' Coalition Programme, 'One Brazil for Everyone') also reinforced this interpretation. In the prevailing international context, this 'social developmentalism' could have been considered by many as enough to characterise his platform as (moderately) 'leftist', or at least as 'progressive'. The *Letter to the Brazilian People* can therefore be regarded as the declaration of the general direction of the programme and of a strategy for government: the idea that the proposed changes would be undertaken gradually, and on the basis of negotiations, in a 'transition' between the existing model and the desired new one.

LULA'S ECONOMICS

The composition of Lula's economic team illustrates the predictable subsequent evolution of the leftist government. If during the campaign Lula had promoted the idea of a gradual process of changes, once his official cabinet was assembled this perspective began to wane. The new economic team was marked by the presence of ideologues from the

Cardoso government or linked to his party, the PSDB, thus indicating a tendency toward continuity rather than change, even if such change were to be gradual.

Henrique Meirelles, the former international president of the Bank of Boston and a recently elected PSDB congressman, was named President of the Central Bank. In addition to praising the Bank's performance under Lula's predecessor, Meirelles retained the institution's entire executive management. Similarly, several key players in the new Finance Ministry had strong connections to the previous government or were identified with its policies, while the other two ministries with major roles in economic policy-making (Development and Agriculture) were assigned to big businessmen with ties to the PSDB.

Furthermore, the new Minister of Finance, Antônio Palocci, though a long-standing member of the PT, revealed on his first day in office his strong identification with orthodox economic principles. During his inaugural speech as Minister, he explicitly discarded the idea that there would be a process of transition to a new economic model, stating that:

> The subject of transition created some anxiety as to what would happen after this transitional phase, leading to speculation about the end to primary budget surpluses, the end to anti-inflation goals and the floating exchange rate regime, as well as the adoption of unconventional and creative measures for conducting macroeconomic policy. To these legitimate questions our reply is unequivocal: the new regime is under way; sound public-sector management demands fiscal responsibility and economic stability. The government that left office yesterday deserves credit on this point, and we are not ashamed to acknowledge it. However, this was not their exclusive patrimony, nor will it be ours. ... Thus, the transition from the model that we have and to that which the country is demanding is [designed] to overcome short-term difficulties.

From the very beginning, there were criticisms of the government's economic policy orientation, directed especially at the Central Bank and Minister Palocci, and coming mainly from the left wing of the PT and some other parties of the governing coalition, such as the PCdoB and the PSB. However, it was the debate over Lula's project to reform the public-sector pension system that revealed the high level of dissatisfaction present among a substantial part of his supporters. The centre-left

PDT and the PPS, which were not original members of the coalition, having supported Lula's candidacy only during the second round of voting, would break with the governmnet, citing disagreements over economic policy as one of the reasons.

The government's pension reform proposal was seen by many, including political analysts connected to the PT itself, as being guided by neo-liberal principles. There was active and radical opposition from a part of the union movement, and a more formal and limited opposition from the leadership of the CUT, the PT-led labour confederation. The latter approved a recommendation to vote against the proposed reform, but in truth this was merely formal in character, since the majority of the CUT leadership made it clear they were not expecting even those members of Congress most closely connected to the union movement to follow the recommendation. As a result of the ensuing conflict, the PT lost the support of public-sector employees and suffered a rupture: a senator and three congressmen were expelled from the party, and hundreds of party activists abandoned it. Although insignificant in numerical terms, the rupture represented a radical expression of the discontent that had taken hold of a much broader segment of the forces supporting the Lula government.

From the outset, the economic policy of the Lula government generated frustration among its supporters. In the first two years, 2003 and 2004, the most left-wing segments of the PT and the PCdoB, as well as the country's main social movements, contended that the government's economic policy had retained the neo-liberal tinge of the previous Cardoso administration, and they spoke quite often of the need to change it. The PSB, the PDT and part of the PPS offered opinions along these same lines, and even the National Directorate of the PT itself expressed its discomfort with this policy. Among supporters, many among the more left-wing sectors believed that 'the government was up for grabs', and therefore considered it a priority to defeat the neo-liberal sectors that existed within the administration.

In the following two years, the debate over economic policy among pro-government forces diminished in intensity, although it never disappeared. In spite of this, a new rupture occurred in the PT in 2005 following the party's internal elections, sparked by differences over the orientation of the government – particularly with respect to economic policy – and also by the campaign finance scandal (the *mensalão*) that had engulfed the party since June (see Wainwright and Branford, 2006). Still, the majority of those sectors within the PT and the social movements that had criticised the government's economic policy during its first two years in office began to do so with less intensity.

The fundamental reason behind this change in posture was the fact that it had become evident that the economic policy, when evaluated according to its own objectives, was relatively successful. Since 2003, inflation had been contained and currency speculation controlled. Moreover, beginning in the second half of that year, a process of economic recovery took place, producing a growth in GDP of 4.9 per cent in 2004 (compared to only 0.53 per cent in 2003 – that is, below the rate of population growth). During this period, the level of employment also experienced a recovery.

In 2005, the growth rate was much more modest (2.28 per cent), and the prospect for 2006 would also be a frustrating one (approximately 3 per cent). But the growth of exports, increasing trade and current account surpluses, and some recovery in employment served to offset the modest growth in GDP. The realisation of the current account surplus in particular encouraged some economists and government officials to claim that Brazil had reduced, or even overcome, its external vulnerability.

Although the favourable economic data (control of inflation, economic growth and improved income distribution) were subject to different interpretations, the claim that the government's economic policy had succeeded in reducing inequalities gained credibility. Thus, a majority of those within the PT (and the other pro-government parties) who had previously recognised the limitations of the government's policies began to speak of the Lula government as a very successful one. The economic policy's relative success even paved the way in 2006 for a re-election campaign based on a comparison of the results of the Lula government and those of the Cardoso government.

On the other hand, this stance of defending the results of the government's economic policy implied the near total abandonment of its earlier campaign discourse. The discussion about a change in the economic model and the transition to a new one all but disappeared, replaced by a simple comparison of the results obtained under previous governments. Implicitly, the Lula government had begun to present itself increasingly as a government that did a better job – and with greater 'social sensitivity' – of implementing the same economic policy that had been applied under its predecessors.[3]

Nevertheless, even putting aside the campaign commitments regarding a change in the economic model, the 'success' of Lula's economic policy can be questioned. In order to make a proper comparison between the results of the Lula government and those of his predecessor, it is necessary to take into account the international situation and the results achieved by other countries. From this perspective, the PT-led government can be seen as one of the worst in terms of growth performance, with the great majority of countries exhibiting far better results. Furthermore, it is clear that the economic performance of the Lula government is primarily a consequence of the international situation, rather than of the government's policies. This view has been supported by numerous economists, including those tied to the PT such as Márcio Pochmann, Labour Policy Secretary in the administration of Mayor Martha Suplicy of São Paulo. In a statement to the press on 17 October 2006, Pochmann declared that he could not identify 'any explicit public policy for creating employment in the country', and that Brazil had been living through a 'fortunate conjuncture' during the previous three years.

In relation to public services and state-owned enterprises, the Lula government made no changes with regard to the companies that had been previously privatised. Despite the PT's earlier questions about how the privatisations had been conducted, and its proposals for an official examination of that process, no progress was made. In other words, there was no deeper analysis – much less a reversal – of the privatisations that had been carried out under Lula's predecessors. Nevertheless, there was to be no new privatisation programme. The large enterprises that remained part of the state apparatus (such as Petrobrás, the powerful state-owned oil company) were left as they were, and according to the government, there is no intention to privatise them. With regard to the public–private partnerships (PPPs), considered to be a new and important means for the government to encourage private investment, the PPP law was only approved by Congress at the end of 2004. By September 2006, only two partnership projects had gotten under way, involving renovations of two stretches of the BR-116 and the BR-324, both in the state of Bahia.

From the government's perspective, it is argued that the 'reduction in fiscal fragility' was the result of 'a containment and stabilisation of the public debt', 'a reduction in the public deficit' and a 'deceleration in the growth of the tax burden'. So as to illustrate the 'reduction and control of inflation', it notes that the inflation targets have been met.

Four observations are in order. First, all of the above is true. Second, this clearly does not represent any change in the direction of macroeconomic policy. On the contrary, it is evident that these achievements correspond closely with the objectives and instruments (for example, the inflation target system and increased fiscal surplus) already established by the outgoing Cardoso administration. Third, the bottom line is that these advances did not depend on the merits of the Lula government's economic policy. In part, they followed a tendency inherited from the previous government. They represented the triumph over the crisis of 2002 – the result, to a large extent, of speculation against the Brazilian currency based on the market's fear that the opposition candidate would get elected. And they can be partly explained by an extremely favourable international situation. The fourth observation is perhaps the most important. These results have to be evaluated in light of the negative consequences of fiscal and monetary policies evident in other areas, which constitute (or should constitute) central objectives of any government – such as economic growth and income distribution.

Given all of the above, it is no surprise that the economic policies of the Lula government have enjoyed a great deal of support from the political representatives of the former government, as well as representatives of the financial sector, international financial institutions (the IMF and World Bank), and the governments of powerful foreign countries (among them, the United States). In fact, before being forced to leave office for reasons that had nothing to do with his management of the Finance Ministry, Antônio Palocci received strong praise from all these sectors. Meanwhile, the leaders of the economy's major productive sectors – that is, the large capitalists in manufacturing and agriculture – alternated between praising the overall seriousness of the economic policy and criticising its conservatism (especially the allegedly 'conservative' monetary policy). On several occasions, they demanded accelerated reductions in interest rates.

On the other hand, the representatives of the social movements – the traditional base of Lula and the PT – were generally critical of the direction of the government's macroeconomic policy and on several occasions demanded change. The majority supported President Lula's campaign for re-election, but have called for changes during his second term in office.

AGRARIAN AND SOCIAL POLICIES

With respect to the agrarian problem, the rural social movements – most importantly, the MST – understand that the Lula government has pursued an agricultural policy through a subordinate alliance between the large capitalist landowners and transnational corporations that control international agricultural trade and the production and distribution of seeds, fertilisers and pesticides. This means that priority has been given to huge farms with extensive tracts of land that make intensive use of chemical fertilisers and pesticides, and which are devoted to the production of monocultural export crops. These farms cultivate only 60 million of Brazil's 360 million arable hectares, and 85 per cent of the area under exploitation is used for sugarcane, soybeans and coffee (Stedile, 2007).

By contrast, the rural social movements, church support groups, environmentalists and the 45 entities that make up the National Forum for Agrarian Reform, among others, advocate the implementation of an alternative model based on family and peasant agriculture. This model envisages the organisation of the land in small and medium-size settlements, aimed at ensuring the viability of the 5 million family farmers with insufficient land, while implementing an agrarian reform that guarantees land for 4 million landless families. In addition, the model involves the following characteristics:

- polyculture as a means of making better use of the potential of the soil and climate while preserving biodiversity
- the production of pesticide-free foods
- agriculture that absorbs labour, creates jobs and guarantees income to those working in the countryside
- the use of farming techniques that respect the environment
- the adoption of conventional seeds that are already adapted to Brazil (and therefore have not been genetically modified).

With respect to social policies, the Lula government can be characterised by three axes: the development of the *Bolsa Familia* (the Family Grant programme), the reform of the public employee pension fund and the constant attacks on the social security funds. The family grant, created to combat misery and social exclusion and to encourage the emancipation of the poorest families, unified already existing programmes dedicated to families with income below the poverty line (school grants, food grants, food cards and cooking gas allowances), but went much further, with respect to both coverage and the benefits it granted. In October 2006, the programme was implemented in every Brazilian municipality, benefiting over 11 million families and 47,042,537 people, equivalent to 25 per cent of Brazil's estimated population. In exchange, the benefiting families with children under 15 years of age must enrol their children in school and guarantee their attendance, keep their vaccinations up to date, seek prenatal care and participate in educational programmes on breast feeding and nutrition.

The family grant benefit is not a right. As the name implies, it is a programme initiated by the federal government. On average, the benefit represents 21 per cent of the household budget, and in October 2006 it helped to raise family incomes by up to 39.58 per cent. In several Brazilian municipalities, the benefits are the main source of income, far outstripping not only municipal tax revenue, but also constitutional transfers and public resources dedicated to public health, among other indicators. There are municipalities where almost half the population benefits from this programme, especially in the north-eastern region of the country. All surveys indicate that the families use the funds to purchase food, thereby stimulating local markets.

The family grant programme, considered by the Lula government itself to be its greatest social policy achievement, earned it a new and solid social base of support, which was to be confirmed by pre-election voter opinion surveys and by the election results themselves in 2006. In 2004, the results of the first poll on the impact of this programme indicated that it would expand Lula's base of support among the least fortunate and least organised sectors of Brazilian society. The income transfer programme has thus led to a peculiar relationship with the president, one that has been described as 'new populism under a neo-liberal agenda' (Marques and Mendes, 2006). Increasing family incomes by up to 40 per cent enables the beneficiaries to rise above the absolute poverty line, but since it is not a right it falls within the restricted field of social assistance policies, and could be terminated at any moment. In addition, the implementation of this programme was not accompanied by policies that addressed the causes of poverty in Brazil, such as access to land or privileging propertied and wealthy classes in the tax system. Hence, Brazil continues to be one of the most unequal societies in the world.

As of 2005, the results of the social assistance programmes began to be disclosed. In terms of the personal distribution of income, calculated by the IBGE (Brazilian Institute for Geography and Statistics) using the National Household Sampling Survey (PNDA), the information concerning the first two years of Lula's government show that, at the same time, the income appropriated by the richest 1 per cent of the population increased as did that of the poor (20 per cent and 50 per cent poorest), while the income of the richest 10 per cent of the population showed a slight reduction. The improvement in the relative position of the poorest segment of the population is consistent with the evolution observed in the Gini and T. de Theil indexes, which fell from 0.596 to 0.576 and from 0.727 to 0.665, respectively, between 2001 and 2004. In addition, the percentage of the population living in extreme poverty declined from 15.2 per cent to 13.1 per cent, even though the family grant programme, the centrepiece of the government's social policy, had only been precariously established in Brazil in 2004. The percentage of the population living below the poverty line rose during the first year of the new government, when GDP grew by only 0.5 per cent, but registered some reduction in 2004. In 2001, 35.1 per cent of the population lived below the poverty line; in 2004, this percentage had fallen to 33.6 per cent. Nonetheless, the absolute number of people living in poverty during that period rose from 58.1 million to 59.4 million, illustrating the country's perverse economic and social dynamic.

With respect to labour policy, there are three areas in which the Lula government's performance can be analysed. The first of these involves the minimum salary. The second was the initiative to establish the National Labour Forum (FNT), and the third concerns labour legislation. Regarding the minimum salary, although the government has not upheld its campaign promise to double its real value, it did bring about a 40 per cent increase in purchasing power (comparing the situation in December 2002 with that of December 2006). However, it should be noted that this recovery began during the Cardoso government. Thus if we compare 2004 with 1995, we observe a 97 per cent increase in real terms over that period. In fact, during the first two years of the Lula government, the process of recovery actually decelerated, before picking up again in 2005 and 2006.

In his government programme, Lula had committed to establishing the FNT as a formal tripartite dialogue among employers, workers and the government aimed at discussing and advancing reforms of Brazil's union structure and labour code. The work of the FNT got under way in August 2003. However, the results were practically restricted to discussing and drawing up a proposal for union reform, even though its explicit objectives were to:

> promote the democratisation of labour relations through the adoption of a union organisation model based on freedom and autonomy and to bring the labour code up to date, making it more

compatible with the new demands of national development, in such as way as to create a favourable environment for creating jobs and income.

As for the controversial issue of pension funds, during its first year in office, the government initiated a reform of the public employee pension system. This reform eliminated the rights of public servants, establishing a ceiling on the value of the pension benefit (previously, the value of the pension was linked to that of the salary, with no reductions). In addition, the government introduced a pension contribution for public employees and private-sector workers insured by the general social security system. This contribution, which violates the pension fund principle of reciprocity, is only levied after the employee reaches a certain pension benefit level. The introduction of a maximum value for retirement pensions has been associated with the creation of pension funds, which in a similar fashion to those of private-sector workers, can be organised and managed by unions and union confederations. To date, however, these have not been regulated, since the necessary legislation has not yet been submitted for discussion and approval.

With regard to public health, the government's principal initiative occurred during the drafting of its budget proposal. Every year, the government has attempted to introduce items that are not considered health expenditures into the Health Ministry budget. Among others, these items include interest payments and expenses related to the retirement pensions of former ministry employees. Although these attempts were supported by the government's economic team, they did not prevail, as the government's health agencies and the Parliamentary Health Caucus rapidly mobilised and forced the government to retreat.

With respect to social security in general, which consists of pensions, social assistance and health, the government demonstrated a firm intention to alter the constitutional provision that regulates and earmarks the social security budget. This intention was expressed for the first time in a May 2003 communication by the Finance Minister, Antônio Palocci, to the director of the International Monetary Fund, Horst Köhler. Currently, the government has control over the allocation of 20 per cent of these funds. This 'flexibility' in the constitutional provision was introduced during the Cardoso government, and contrary to expectations, the Lula government has vigorously maintained it, subject to review in 2007. As that date draws closer, there is talk of increasing this percentage to 40 per cent.

BRAZIL'S INSERTION INTO THE GLOBALISED ECONOMY

Under Lula's predecessors, Brazilian foreign policy was completely submissive to the world's dominant powers. Free trade agreements were negotiated with Northern countries, mainly the United States, and with very little attempt to gain effective benefits, though at times there were efforts to reach reciprocal agreements with other countries considered 'medium-sized powers', such as Russia or India. The official discourse was that the country's basic aim was the re-establishment of its credibility as a democracy with proper respect for human rights, and recognition of its peripheral position on the international stage. In the context of ascendant neo-liberalism and the politics of the Washington Consensus, this submissive foreign policy reduced the country's already limited international role and intensified its vulnerability.

With respect to the creation of the Free Trade Area of the Americas (FTAA), despite having repeatedly stressed the need to implement adjustments aimed at 'softening' the US-driven proposal, the Brazilian government was very satisfied with it. The main argument in defence of the accord was the fact that it represented an 'opening of new markets' at a moment when countries should unquestioningly adapt themselves to the internationalisation of capital. Very strong internal opposition to the project led the government to postpone the negotiations for as long as it could, but in general it condemned the criticisms as childish and based on an 'ideological approach' to relations with the United States.

The Common Market of the South (MERCOSUR), in turn, had also adopted a completely free market approach based on the same argument that countries that did not open up to foreign investment would be internationally isolated. Beyond the growing fragility of the trade block, caused by the strong incursion by US capital into its principal member countries (Argentina and Brazil), there were attempts as of 1999 to establish a free trade zone between MERCOSUR and the European Union (EU), although government officials and business leaders were aware that there was little difference between the United States and the EU as far as trade policy was concerned.

Because of its adoption of a so-called 'realistic' foreign policy orientation, its approach to the field of international relations is considered one of the Lula government's major accomplishments. Based on the theory of 'sovereign insertion in the globalisation process', Brazil would no longer be content with a submissive role in international negotiations, but would instead take advantage of its status as a 'medium-size power' in the region in order to attain a stronger position in matters regarded as strategic. In comparison with the previous government, its posture was in fact more incisive, and Brazilian diplomacy played an active role in harmonising positions and/or projects of other developing nations. However, due to a supposedly pragmatic analysis of the international context, its performance would remain timid, lacking in a strong network of multilateral connections, and vacillating, thereby permitting it, on the one hand, to criticise the protectionism of the great powers and defend MERCOSUR, and on the other, to pursue a more 'attractive' FTAA with the United States.

Brazil's foreign relations have unquestionably become more multilateral. In addition to the traditional partnerships with developed countries, the Brazilian government has sought to create and strengthen agreements with developing countries, particularly Argentina, China, India and Russia, and has attempted to strengthen its ties with Africa (principally South Africa and Portuguese-speaking Africa) and the Middle East (for example, Brasilia was host to the 2005 Latin American and Arab Nations Summit). As noted above, however, the limitation of these initiatives is that they are not particularly comprehensive, or more precisely, are confined to trade liberalisation for a few sectors of the economy and/or the co-ordination of policy positions in relation to narrowly defined issues within the international system.

In the multilateral sphere, Brazil stood out for its political performance at the United Nations (UN), projecting itself as an active mediator between core and peripheral nations. The objective of this policy was to obtain a permanent seat on the Security Council, albeit without veto power, which would thereby enable Brazil to introduce topics related to the fight against hunger and poverty on the global agenda, as well to demand that the UN Millennium Development Goals be accomplished within the anticipated timeframe. While this policy of 'protagonism' permitted the use of idealistic rhetoric in the formulation of a social agenda, it also revealed its limitations insofar as it obliged the country to participate in an arena dominated by great powers. This led Brazil to conduct, as military leader of the United Nations Stabilisation Mission in Haiti (MINUSTAH), the disastrous UN intervention which, in addition to incurring significant military and economic costs with no guarantee of concrete diplomatic returns, exposed the truly ambiguous nature of the country's foreign policy and its claims to respect the sovereignty of peoples and to place a priority on South–South relations.

In the World Trade Organization (WTO), Brazil won important victories related to farm subsidies, as in the cases of cotton and sugar. Nevertheless, the focal point of its policy in this multilateral institution was its role as one of the key players in a political group of more than 20 developing countries, the G-20, which opposed the limited concessions made by the United States and the European Union in the area of agricultural trade at the September 2003 WTO meeting in Cancún. Although several Latin American countries withdrew from the group under pressure from the United States following the Cancún meeting, the central nucleus – South Africa, Argentina, Brazil, China and India – remain united. As regards multilateral trade negotiations, more specifically the Doha Round, this alliance is very opportune, since it creates the politico-diplomatic conditions necessary for an organised and effective defence of the common interests of countries in similar conditions on the international stage.

With respect to the FTAA, the Lula government questioned certain essential aspects of its format, with the alleged purpose of obtaining greater balance in the negotiating agenda. The Brazilian proposal, articulated with MERCOSUR, was to reduce tariffs on farm and industrial goods, with safeguard clauses for infant industries, without however dealing with more 'strategic' topics, such as government purchases, investment, services and intellectual property. The decision of the United States to negotiate within the WTO on those matters that directly affected the Brazilian oligarchies interested in the accord, such as agriculture and anti-dumping, led Brazil –together with MERCOSUR – to be open to negotiating topics of particular interest to the United States within/under the multilateral organism. Although at the November 2003 meeting in Miami, the United States briefly retreated by apparently accepting MERCOSUR's proposal to establish an FTAA 'light', it resumed a more aggressive posture at the August 2005 Puebla meeting by opposing the proposals put forward with the support of 13 other countries. There were other attempts at reconciliation on the part of MERCOSUR, but the United States and the other G-14 countries (such as Mexico, Canada, Chile, Costa Rica) had no intention of yielding on any front. The FTAA negotiations stagnated at Mar del Plata in December 2005, when Venezuela and MERCOSUR stated definitively their lack of interest in implementing the original accord.

It is worth noting that in order to justify the negotiation of a treaty which the PT had traditionally opposed, Lula's former principal economic adviser, Aloízio Mercadante, resorted once again to the old argument used by the PSDB about the necessity of hemispheric integration free of ideological influence: 'This [hemispheric integration] should not be seen as an ideological question, or as a position for or against the United States, but rather as an instrument that may or may not serve Brazil's strategic interests' (*Valor Econômico*, 15 July 2002).

Given the failure of the FTAA, the current politico-economic strategy of the United States is bilateral negotiation of free trade agreements with individual Latin American countries. Rather than aggressively opposing this new project, the Lula government has invested in a limited South American Community of Nations, without any well-defined methods or timelines. At present, the most significant initiatives of co-operation between Brazil and South America relate to the development of physical infrastructure.

Even before Lula, MERCOSUR had been used as a forum for articulating projects and positions, and was seen by Brazil as a defensive fortress for negotiations with the United States and the European Union. The government had put forward proposals whose real intention was to reinvigorate the accord, which had been weakened during the 1990s; these included completing the customs union (and even developing the basis for the creation of a common market), implementing a new agenda with respect to the technological development and integration of productive bases, and institutionalising the accord. It is also worth recalling the compensatory measures that were established among the countries of the region, as well as several proposals in the area of social policies.

The main problem is that MERCOSUR has not overcome the main obstacle to its consolidation as an effective regional union: breaking with its essential class nature. By representing the political and economic interests of the economic oligarchies of its member-countries, its greatest contribution, as already noted, has been to engage in negotiations with the United States and the European Union. In this sense, its strength should be celebrated, particularly in the context of the current neo-liberal environment. However, it must be recognised that its capacity to bring about greater integration is limited by the very battles that these regional oligarchic groups are waging amongst themselves. Perhaps Venezuela's entry into the bloc will lead it to acquire a more social character (see Edgardo Lander's chapter in this volume).

Confronted by this context, the Lula government has achieved significant trade surpluses, but based on a very limited range of exports, and with very disappointing growth in the productivity of more technologically intensive sectors.

THE RESULTS OF THE 2006 ELECTIONS AND BEYOND

In the second round of the 2006 presidential elections, held on 29 October, Lula was re-elected with 58.3 million votes (60.8 per cent), defeating the PSDB candidate, Geraldo Alckmin. After a campaign in which both the rightist and leftist opposition focused on the growing revelations of corruption within the government and the PT, and in which the media gave concerted and historically unprecedented support to the opposition candidate (Alckmin), Lula was re-elected to a second four-year term of office as President of Brazil.

In percentage terms, Lula's re-election represented a slight drop from his first victory in the second round of the 2002 elections, when he obtained 61.27 per cent of the vote. However, given the climate surrounding his government, continually threatened by accusations of corruption to the point that several of the most prominent members of the government were removed from office, this was a surprising result. In terms of the distribution of votes, taking into account the geographical location of the states, the income of voters and the size of the municipalities, the election revealed a divided country, with Lula winning in 20 of the 27 states, including all those in the north-east (the country's poorest region), all but one in the north (the country's second poorest), three in the south-east and two in the central-west, including the Federal District where the nation's capital is located. On the other hand, he lost in all of the states in the south. In addition, the polls all demonstrated that the smaller and poorer the municipality, and the lower the income of the voter, the stronger was his support. The election also revealed a new fact of Brazilian reality – the poorest segments of the population paid no heed to the views of so-called opinion makers, especially those expressed via the press and television.

Among those who backed Lula in the second round, the MST and the majority of the Brazilian left, principally intellectuals, were of particular importance. However, it should be noted that a significant part of the Brazilian left did not support Lula in the second round. This was the case of the Frente de Esquerda (Leftist Front), a coalition backing the presidential campaign of Senator Heloísa Helena that included the Partido Socialismo e Liberdade Socialism (Socialism and Liberty Party, PSOL; created by PT dissidents), the PSTU, the PCB and the PDT.[4]

What might have motivated the Brazilian people to re-elect Lula, despite his economic policies and the accusations of corruption? In attempting to answer this question, and keeping in mind the demographic profile of his electorate, it is important to recall that Lula had increased the purchasing power of the minimum salary by 40 per cent during his first term. The government also transferred income to 11.1 million families using the family grant programme, benefiting more than 47 million people (25 per cent of the estimated population) and increasing by up to 39.58 per cent the income of the families that received the benefits. In addition, the government made abundant credit available to poor families, created a grant concession programme for university studies at private institutions (benefiting more than 200,000 students) and reduced taxes on basic necessities and building materials for popular housing, among other additional measures. Finally, the unemployment rate in September 2006, though still high, was almost two percentage points below that of September 2002, when Fernando Henrique Cardoso was president.

Thus, there is little doubt that for the immense majority of the people who voted for Lula, the determining factor was the fact that their situation was better than in the recent past, without taking into account whether the measures that led to this would endure or not. The prospect of Lula pushing through the labour and union reforms and further advancing the pension system reform during his second term was of little or no concern to them. This is partly explained by the fact that the majority of the unions, as well as practically the country's entire media, are in favour of these reforms.

With respect to unions, in 2007 one can expect to see discussion of the government's proposed constitutional amendment, which among other provisions foresees state intervention and mandatory affiliation with a workers' confederation. In the field of labour relations, the draft project includes: (1) the elimination of provisions in the current legislation that establish the precedence of the law in relation to that which is negotiated, whenever this is more favourable to the worker; (2) provisions for the negotiation and conclusion of agreements by higher-level entities without consulting the unions' grassroots in general assemblies, and which may not be modified by the member union even if the workers are against the conditions of the agreement; (3) the right of the employer to hire replacement workers during strikes, should the union itself not agree to designate workers who would continue to carry out their duties during the strike.

With respect to the pension system, the government is expected to introduce even tighter restrictions on access to pensions, reduce the range between the lowest and highest pensions, and disconnect the minimum pension from the minimum salary. With regard to the social security system in general, it is discussing the elimination of the prohibition on the use of social security revenues for other purposes and/or an increase in the percentage of revenue made available to the National Treasury (presently 20 per cent, based on a measure introduced by Fernando Henrique Cardoso in 1994).

Finally, with regard to economic policy, although the Central Bank has in recent months continued to reduce the basic interest rate (13.25 per cent in November 2006), there is no sign of any change. The priorities continue to be to honour the obligations to financial capital and the development of agribusiness.

LULA'S GOVERNMENT: A LEFTIST GOVERNMENT?

In conclusion, it is interesting to resume the discussion as to what would justify characterising Lula's first government as a *leftist* – or at least, *progressive* – government. The justification for characterising it as a government of transformation derives principally from its performance in three policy areas: foreign policy, which is regarded as progressive; income transfer policies, which seek to reduce inequalities; and the minimum wage policy, which demonstrates the government's 'social sensitivity'. In addition, those who consider the Lula government leftist also point to his decision not to criminalise the social movements and his dialogue with those movements.

It is fundamentally these reasons, in fact, that were invoked by certain sectors of the left that have been critical of the government to justify their support for Lula in the second round of the 2006 presidential elections. Perhaps the most important example is the MST, whose principal leader, João Pedro Stedile, declared the following on 5 October 2006:

Alckmin would mean the return of the hegemony of the United States government over Latin America. Right now, the continent is in a process of transition, and in practically every election, the people have voted for anti-neo-liberal candidates. This has created three groups of governments: a leftist group (Venezuela, Bolivia and Cuba); a group of moderate governments, which are in transition from neo-liberalism and stand up to American policy on an ad-hoc basis (Brazil, Argentina, Uruguay, Peru and Ecuador); and the group of countries who have become faithful allies of the Americans (Chile, Paraguay and Colombia). An Alckmin victory would tip the balance in favour of the United States, with Brazil joining the group of servile allies.

A week later, an 11 October editorial in *Brasil de Fato*, a weekly publication over which the MST has a major influence, emphasised the Lula government's respect for democratic institutions, arguing that Lula should be re-elected in spite of the 'disappointing results for the working class' of his first term, and despite the likelihood that his second term would 'be even more committed to a neo-liberal agenda':

> An analysis of the four years of President Lula's first term in office leads to a disappointing balance for the working class, above all with respect to the economy. Moreover, bearing in mind the new composition of the National Congress and the alliances in play during the first term, the likely tendency is for the second Lula government to be even more committed to the neo-liberal agenda, especially should the decline of popular and mass struggles persist or accelerate. We all know that. Nevertheless, it must be made clear that at no time did the forces who support him become public nor did they insinuate the use of force and the destruction of existing democratic institutions, which (while weak and limited) enable us to organise and gather our forces in order to make further advances and bring about the structural changes that the working class and the people need.

The editorial went on to remind readers of the history of struggle of the Brazilian working class, including the sacrifices required to win the political freedoms they enjoy today. It called on readers to 'abandon this economistic discussion of the present conjuncture, and properly distinguish between our principal enemy, our adversaries and our allies. Whenever we get this wrong, we end up defeated.' It asserted that the principal enemy presently confronting the Brazilian working class were those forces behind the Geraldo Alckmin candidacy. It therefore claimed that he was the one who must be defeated in the 2006 elections. 'Thus, to vote for Lula, even with no illusions about his economic policy, is the duty of all of us who constitute the working class and the Brazilian people.'

Let us consider, first, the policies aimed at reducing inequalities. The income distribution results during Lula's first term are, at the very least, ambiguous. At the same time as they benefited the poorest, they failed to alter the imbalance whereby those in the lowest strata relied primarily on wages for income, as opposed to the rents or profits available to the richer classes, at a time of substantial growth in financial profits (as will be explored below). Moreover, the critics of the Lula government make a convincing comparison between the cost of programmes like the family grant and the cost of public-sector interest (expenses which constitute an income concentration factor). The interest paid by the public sector taken as a whole has amounted to approximately 8 per cent of GDP, similar to the level incurred during the last three years of Cardoso's second term of office. One would also have to take into account the nature of the 'new populism under a neo-liberal agenda', which can be attributed to the family grant programme.

In the case of foreign policy, the discussion is even more complex. The Lula government has in fact remained close to, or has attempted to maintain good relations with, governments to its left – such as the Chávez government. It has also sought to develop an international relations policy in which relations with Latin America and countries of the Global South carry more weight. In addition, during the FTAA negotiations, it changed course by adopting a more critical position than that of the previous government, which has contributed in part to the current impasse in the negotiations. On the other hand, after a period in which it had assumed a more critical posture in the WTO negotiations, in alliance with India, China and other countries, Brazil has now moved to a policy more in accord with the great powers. João Pedro Stedile's characterisation of the Lula government as part of a 'moderate group', neither leftist nor a faithful ally of the United States, that is, a group of countries who face up to American policy in an ad-hoc manner, seems appropriate. However, there would appear to be insufficient reason for affirming that these countries – and in particular, Brazil under Lula – are in a process of 'transition from neo-liberalism'.

With regard to the Lula government's more democratic character, there is no doubt that not criminalising the social movements is a position that favours the left, without being an exactly leftist position. Nevertheless, in order to substantiate the claim that the Lula government is engaged in a real dialogue with social movements, it would be necessary to demonstrate that Lula has been sensitive to at least an important part of their demands. By contrast, it is not difficult to show that the PT-led government has been responsive to the basic demands of the financial markets and Brazil's dominant classes.

Taken as a whole, in order for the characterisation of 'leftist government' to hold up, the reasons indicated for justifying the characterisation of the Lula government as 'leftist' (with its limitations, and bearing in mind the possible differences of interpretation as to how its results were obtained) must be compared with the undeniably neo-liberal nature of the macroeconomic policies it has implemented, such as the social security reforms and the ongoing liberalisation of the financial sector.

Distancing itself from its social base, Lula's government, before and after the money-for-votes scandal, constituted itself as a consortium of the PT in Brazilian politics, moving into a terrain in which the corrupting power of money exercises its greatest influence. Despite all the efforts of the Lula government to place the blame for the ongoing crisis on the PT alone, the web of power responsible for the crisis – whatever degree of legality or illegality that characterises it – was and continues to be managed from the presidential palace in Brasilia. The elimination of some of those who were exposed by the investigations has done nothing to alter the nature of the government. The alliances and promiscuous relations it maintains with capital, as well as its current class commitments, are evidence that it is not correct to imagine the corruption problem is confined to the party, as if the government has played only a passive role in this degenerative process.

This project was founded on the idea of assuming control over part of the state apparatus in order to attempt to influence hegemonic thought at a time when the neo-liberal model is running out of steam. The methods that were used were developed with the aim of gaining control of the central government, and they crystallised with Lula's rise to the presidency. This option led the government and the party progressively to distance themselves from their historical roots. It was a divorce that obstructed the trajectory of the party and its entire previous history of fighting neo-liberalism. It was the option for building a project of power based on reducing political action to the traditional level of a society that had never experienced the participation of those 'with no opportunity and no voice', and which ended up prevailing before and after the allegations of the money-for-votes scandal with Lula's government.

Today, the PT exists as an amorphous party machine, a new PMDB that engages in a pragmatic dispute for government power, but which has turned its back on any intention of serving as a channel for the expression of popular demands for social and political change, for the construction of a nation or for socialist transformation. The proposal to 're-found' the PT, put forward by some leftist sectors within the government, is condemned to failure because of the disfigurement of the Lula government and the gap already established between the party, the government and the socialist left.

The course of the Lula government, along with the disfigurement of the PT as an instrument for progressive change, has opened the door to a profound political restructuring of the left – and in particular of the socialist left. This process will be necessarily unequal and, probably, prolonged, implying the reconstitution of political and social institutions, the reconstruction of a project for the country, the formulation of an alternative political direction and the recuperation of workers' capacity for initiative and confidence in their own strength. The task facing the socialists is to resume the process of independent organisation of the workers. This implies the necessity of undertaking a political and social process that is capable of confronting not only the present crisis, but also the changes in the class structure and in the political struggle caused by 15 years of neo-liberal globalisation and the changes in the relation between the national and international terrains of the socialist struggle. It is within this framework that it will be possible for the left to formulate a socialist project capable of confronting the challenges of our time.

NOTES

1. For an overview of the aims and evolution of the MST, see Stedile (2002).
2. Like many other Latin American countries, for many years Brazil had two communist parties, the pro-Soviet PCB and the pro-Chinese and later pro-Albanian PCdoB (Partido Comunista do Brasil). PT and CUT activists used to refer to the positions traditionally defended by the two communist parties as *peleguismo*, pointing to political positions characterised by the populist manipulation of workers' demands, the tendency to negotiate with the government and the business sector, and the bureaucratic control over the labour movement.
3. One of the clearest examples of this perspective is the book by Aloízio Mercadante, titled *Brazil, the First Half: A Comparative Analysis of Lula's Government* (Mercadante, 2006). The author is the leader of the government in the Brazilian Senate, and is in general considered one of the government's main spokespersons on economic matters. The book's preface was written by Lula himself.
4. Heloísa Helena received 6.8 per cent of the votes cast nationally in the first round. The PSOL, the Front's principal member, managed to elect only three congressmen, thereby reducing its previous representation when its delegation was composed of congressmen who had left the PT.

3 VENEZUELA
Populism and the Left:
Alternatives to Neo-Liberalism
Edgardo Lander

THE PACT OF PUNTO FIJO AND THE LEFT

Following the overthrow of the Marcos Pérez Jiménez dictatorship in 1958, the democratic period known as *puntofijismo* began in Venezuela. Headed by the country's two main political parties – Acción Democrática (Democratic Action, AD) and the Comité de Organización Política Electoral Independiente (Committee of Independent Electoral Political Organisations, COPEI) – the Pact of Punto Fijo had the backing of the armed forces, the Catholic Church hierarchy, the main trade union (the Confederación de Trabajadores de Venezuela – Confederation of Venezuelan Workers, CTV) and the largest business organisation (the Federación de Cámaras de Comercio y Producción – Federation of Chambers of Commerce and of Production, FEDECAMARAS) (López Maya and Gómez Calcaño, 1989). However, within a short period of time and in a highly polarised social climate, the confrontation between an exclusionary political regime that showed little tolerance for dissent, and an increasingly radicalised left became more acute. In 1960, constitutional guarantees were suspended, the newspapers of the left were shut down, and leftist union leaders were subjected to the CTV's disciplinary tribunal. Under the influence of the Cuban Revolution, an armed struggle began and the Partido Comunista de Venezuela (Communist Party of Venezuela, PCV) and the Movimiento de Izquierda Revolucionaria (Movement of the Revolutionary Left, MIR) were proscribed, marking the first breakaway from AD.

In 1962, after several years of rural and urban struggle that included military uprisings known as the *Carupanazo* and the *Porteñazo*, the armed left was defeated, with hundreds of people detained, tortured, disappeared or killed. In the meantime, the economy recovered, due in large part to a significant increase in oil revenue. Combined with vigorous public policies in the areas of industrialisation, employment, infrastructure, health and education, the economic recovery led to a major improvement in the quality of life of much of the population (measured by heightened access to schooling, health and other public services, increased life expectancy, reduced infant mortality, a growth in employment and other indicators). Conditions for upward social mobility also improved. Thus, despite the repression of the political opposition and struggles for social rights, as well as the persistence of deep inequalities, expectations of a better future were on the rise, the legitimacy of the democratic regime was strengthened and the two-party system was consolidated. The left's military defeat was compounded by its political isolation, as its decision to pursue armed struggle distanced it from the majority of the popular sectors, with the sole exception of students.

Following the Communist Party's decision to abandon armed struggle and to participate in the 1968 elections, and the so-called 'policy of pacification' of the Rafael Caldera government that emerged from those elections, various left organisations gradually began to return to legal activity. The defeat of armed struggle – within an international context of profound debate over 'really existing socialism' – generated a process of critical self-reflection and the emergence of new left political organisations. The most significant of these resulted from splits in the PCV: the Movimiento al Socialismo (Movement Towards Socialism, MAS) and Causa R (Radical Cause, CR). The MAS was inspired by euro-communism, with its strong critique of Soviet socialist and Leninist party models, and generated great expectations, especially within intellectual and student sectors. Their leader and most important theoretician was Teodoro Petkoff (Petkoff, 1969, 1970). As its central doctrinal proposals, CR assumed the radical democratic ideas of its leader (Alfredo Maneiro), as well as the concept of an open political organisation, in opposición to both Stalinism and the Leninist conception of the party (Maneiro, 1971). It carried out its most successful political work among the trade unions operating in the basic industries – especially the iron and steel industries of the Orinoco – in Ciudad Guayana (see López Maya, 1995).

The 1970s were nevertheless not a propitious decade for left politics in Venezuela. With the quadrupling of fiscal income resulting from the sharp rise in oil prices in 1973 – during the first Carlos Andrés Pérez administration – a collective delirium of 'Great Venezuela' set in, an image of a rich country that without much effort, would grow in a sustained manner towards a society of abundance. Any critical voices (Pérez Alfonzo, 1977; Equipo Proceso Político, 1978) were stifled in the ensuing oil rent feast.

The basis of what would later become the Movimiento Quinta República (Fifth Republic Movement, MVR) was established in December 1982 with the so-called Samán de Güere oath, between Hugo Chávez and two other military men, and the creation of the Ejército Bolivariano Revolucionario (Revolutionary Bolivarian Army 200, EBR 200). After ten years of political organising inside the armed forces throughout the entire country, the movement – renamed Movimiento Revolucionario Bolivariano (Bolivarian Revolutionary Movement, MRB 200) in 1989 – came to public attention during the attempted coup d'état of 4 February 1992. The coup failed militarily, but it represented a major political victory for the movement, as it exposed the existence of important divisions within the armed forces and the growing weakness of the government. Moreover, it converted Hugo Chávez overnight into a political figure of national significance. With the leaders detained, another coup attempt took place on 27 November of the same year, which also ended in failure. Chávez spent two years in prison where he concentrated on studying and establishing relations with civilian sectors that would later become political allies. Upon his release from prison in 1994, by order of the then President Rafael Caldera, he travelled throughout the country organising his political movement.

THE PROLONGED CRISIS OF *PUNTOFIJISMO*

The last two decades of the twentieth century constituted a period of uninterrupted economic and political decline in Venezuela. After more than two decades of sustained growth, significant improvement in the quality of life and a consolidation of the legitimacy of the democratic regime, in February 1983 the symbolic beginning of the end of the oil bonanza occurred when the government of Luis Herrera Campins decided to devalue the Bolívar after many years of fixed parity with the US dollar.

The crisis in Venezuela occurred later than those in most other Latin American countries. Nevertheless, given the expectations of sustained growth and improvement in the quality of life that had become part of the Venezuelan national self-image, the political and cultural impact of the decline was very profound. This was a very prolonged crisis, marked by a 20-year deterioration in the quality of life of the majority of the population.

In 1997, per capita income in Venezuela was 8 per cent lower than in 1970. During this same period, workers' income fell by approximately half. It has also been estimated that between 1984 and 1991, the poverty rate nearly doubled, rising from 36 per cent of the population to 68 per cent (Martel, 1993).

These processes of exclusion, segregation and fragmentation led to socioeconomic breakdown – especially in the cities – and the disintegration of the mechanisms and traditional forms of socialisation and social integration, in particular the family, the school and the workplace. They also led to the development of new models of socialisation, 'alternative socialisations', based primarily on the need to survive under conditions of extreme adversity (Pedrazzini and Sánchez, 1992). The benefits of the country's economic growth (health, education, housing, well-paid work and upward social mobility), which during the first decades of the democratic regime offered the promise of a better future to the country's popular sectors, now appeared inaccessible. Poverty and social exclusion were no longer seen as transitory phenomena in a 'developing' society, or as conditions that could be overcome through individual effort. Instead, they were increasingly seen as a permanent condition of society. It was not simply a matter of the exclusion of a minority, which in relation to society as a whole could be categorised as marginal, but rather the living conditions and cultural reproduction of the majority of the population.

In the face of the political system's accelerating loss of legitimacy, it became clear to the country's elites that it would be necessary to alter the centralised and presidentialist state, which had grown increasingly inefficient, corrupt and incapable of responding to the demands of an ever more diversified and complex society. The goals of modernisation and democratisation, the latter understood primarily as decentralisation of the state, gained broad support within the political class and became the central tasks promoted by the Presidential Commission on State Reform beginning in 1984 (COPRE, 1988). While society became increasingly divided, political debate was dominated by the idea of carrying out institutional changes in order to make the Venezuelan political system more decentralised, democratic and participatory.

Nevertheless, in an *apartheid* society that produced such severe economic exclusion with defined cultural boundaries and such radically differentiated individual and collective identities, institutional political reforms could make only a limited and partial contribution to the development of a democratic culture and to truly inclusive practices in the political system. From a legal and institutional point of view, the reforms created new mechanisms of incorporation and participation, steps toward the decentralisation of the state, the direct election of mayors and governors, and conditions for the emergence of local and regional leaderships that would diversify and breathe life into the political system (López Maya and Lander, 1996). However, the economic and cultural processes of exclusion were much more powerful than the potential democratising impact of these political reforms.

The apparent paradox of an increasingly divided society and a political debate centred on its democratisation can be explained through the conceptions of democracy, citizenship and participation that underlie it. When democracy is spoken of in this context, significant semantic shifts from the idea of democracy in the hegemonic discourse have already taken place. The social-democratic and Christian-democratic notions of the state, equality, citizenship and politics, which had been shared by the majority of the political spectrum for decades, were subjected to serious questioning and assigned new meanings by neo-liberal and neo-conservative ideological positions. In the media, an anti-political and anti-party discourse became predominant, one which established a Manichean opposition between the state (characterised as corrupt, inefficient and clientilistic) and a mythical 'civil society' (which included the media), understood as the synthesis of all virtues (creativity, initiative, efficiency, honesty and participation).

The paradigmatic new subject of the 'citizen democracy' that was to replace the 'party democracy' was the 'citizen-neighbour', conceived out of the experience of the urban neighbourhood organisations of the middle and upper middle class (Lander, 1996a). The main preoccupation of these organisations was the defence of property and protection from the threats posed by the excluded (Santana, 1989). The normative horizon of this idea of conservative democracy was one of an apolitical society, without ideological debates, in which the main tasks of government are concerned with the efficiency and honesty of management, and participation and democratic decision-making over collective life are strictly limited to local spheres. The economy must be vigorously protected from the 'demagogic and irresponsible' demands that are formulated in the name of democracy. All state social or redistributive policies are suspected of populism.

The social and political organisations (parties and trade unions), which in previous decades had been the main channels of expression of popular demands, not only enter into crisis, but also, in the new political discourse, tend to be regarded as illegitimate. In this model of citizenship, whose paradigmatic image is the middle or upper-middle-class neighbour (with their professional expertise, access to the media, personal political relations and the use of the Internet as an organisational tool), and in conditions in which all pubic policies of redistribution and most state-run social policies are viewed as increasingly illegitimate, there is little space for the articulation and expression of the interests of the country's poor majority. It concerns a political model, which, to paraphrase Bonfil Batalla (1990), could be called the *Imaginary Venezuela*, disconnected from the *Deep Venezuela* – that is, from the *life-world* of the majority of the population.

The terminal crisis that led to the exhaustion of the Punto Fijo political model occurred during the second government of Carlos Andrés Pérez. The profound division in Venezuelan society was manifest most clearly in the social explosion of February 1989, an event that came to be known as the *Caracazo*. Looting took place in the country's main cities on a scale never before seen in Venezuelan history. Following an initial period of confusion, the government responded by partially suspending constitutional guarantees. A curfew was declared and a brutal military repression was ordered, leaving more than 500 – and possibly many more – dead. Left-wing parties and organisations were as surprised by these events as was the government. The absence of a popular reaction in defence of the democratic system against the two coup attempts in 1992 confirmed the disintegration and increasing illegitimacy of a political system that had been considered exceptional, a showcase of democracy in Latin America.

The *Caracazo* coincided with the arrival in Venezuela of the rigorous conditions that international financial institutions had been imposing on the majority of the continent. In the context of a drastic reduction of international reserves, significant fiscal and balance of payment deficits, and an external debt that was impossible to pay under those conditions, the government of Carlos Andrés Pérez signed a 'letter of intent' with the International Monetary Fund (IMF). The agreement committed the government to implementing orthodox structural adjustment policies (Lander, 1996b), despite the fact that during his electoral campaign, Pérez had appealed to the image of abundance of his first government. These agreements were not put forward for parliamentary discussion and were only made known to the public after they were signed.

The application of structural adjustment policies brought to light two interrelated characteristics that Venezuelan democracy shared with those of other countries in the continent, and which oil revenue had partially concealed or attenuated: first, the elite nature of a political regime that was deeply exclusionary and insensitive to the demands of the majority of the population; and second, the severely limited nature of autonomous decision-making in the political system, due to the international economic and geopolitical conditions to which it was subjected. It was precisely these two issues that constituted the main axis around which the fundamental theme of Chávez's discourse was articulated: *popular concerns* and *national autonomy*. Perhaps this explains his immense popular support, and the strong resistance that his image and his government generate in other social sectors.

As yet another expression of the depth of the political crisis that the country was experiencing, Carlos Andrés Pérez did not manage to complete his second presidential term, as he was removed from office by Congress under accusations of corruption. The breakdown of the two-party system was demonstrated in the subsequent elections. Rafael Caldera abandoned the ranks of COPEI, a party he had founded and for which he had served as the main leader and ideologue for half a century. Once the decision was made to launch his candidacy, he organised the Convergencia Nacional (National Convergence) and created an electoral alliance of 16 political forces, which included the MAS, the Movimiento Electoral del Pueblo (People's Electoral Movement, MEP), the PCV and other small parties. Rejecting the policies of neo-liberal adjustment, he proposed the option of a 'Letter of intent to the people'. His electoral victory represented the first time since 1958 that a candidate who did not belong to either AD or COPEI won the presidency.

After surviving the deepest crisis of the financial system in the country's history during the first years of his term, and following a long period of indecision, Caldera ended up agreeing to a 'Letter of intent' with the IMF. Under the name *Agenda Venezuela*, he adopted the basic orientations of the neo-liberal agenda that he had previously rejected. The consequences of the Employment Law reform, which drastically reduced workers' social security benefits, and the liberalisation and internationalisation of the oil industry were particularly severe (Lander, 2003). The sustained deterioration of the population's living conditions continued, as did the deepening crisis of legitimacy of the political system, its parties and its leaders.

In 1997, the Fifth Republic Movement decided to participate in the 1998 presidential elections and registered itself as a party with the Supreme Electoral Council. By the time of the 1998 elections, it had become a fundamental point of reference for the entire Venezuelan left. The main organisations of the left – MAS, Patria Para Todos (Homeland for All, PPT), PCV, MEP – and other smaller organisations decided to support the MVR by forming the Polo Patriótico (Patriotic Pole, PP).[1] After AD and COPEI decided at the last minute to withdraw their support from their respective candidates (Irene Sáez and Luis Alfaro Ucero) and to support Henrique Salar Römer in a last-ditch attempt to prevent Chávez's victory, the latter assumed the presidency with 56.20 per cent of valid votes.

POPULISM AND THE LEFT IN THE *CHAVISTA* PROJECT

Chávez has repeatedly referred to his movement as *revolutionary*:

> That which is revolutionary is a way of life. Let us clarify what we mean by the term revolution: a radical, complete change of a model, of a society in the political, economic, social spheres, etcetera. It means conceiving of the necessary path for Venezuela via a total, radical change. It is a vision that must also confront everything, without evading anything. Here we find another quality of the revolutionary: it should not fail to confront any problem or contradiction. There cannot be a political revolution without a cultural revolution, a moral revolution. This is an integral concept in order for it to be truly revolutionary.
>
> (Blanco Muñoz, 1998:115)[2]

'In order to be revolutionary, [the movement] must confront [exploitation]. It should be an anti-exploitative, anti-imperialist movement' (Chávez, in Blanco Muñoz, 1998:81). Nevertheless, during the early years of his administration and in the period preceding the 1998 elections, Chávez's discourse advanced a concept of revolution that clearly distanced itself from a socialist project, from the forms in which the Latin American left had previously conceived of revolution. According to Chávez, the categories of left and right were no longer adequate to define the nature of the transformations required. He believed liberal, capitalist democracy to have failed as much as the paradigm of a classless communist society.

Although he recognised the importance of Marx's contribution, he stated that he did not consider himself either Marxist or anti-Marxist (Blanco Muñoz, 1998:116). He considered that given this absence of theories and ideologies suited to change under current conditions, the tough challenge facing revolutionaries in Venezuela and Latin America resides in constructing options for the transformation of society from their own history, their own roots and their own cultural traditions.

In the search for the construction of a national project based upon their own historical experience, the idea of the *tree of three roots* was formulated, in which the fundamental role of Simón Bolívar is complemented by that of Simón Rodríguez, the Liberator's teacher, and Ezequiel Zamora, hero of the Federal War. The initial definitions of the project of transformation as being Bolivarian and the reiterated references to this tree of three roots are more symbolic of integration, of the reconstruction of national and continental history, than part of a political and economic project for the country (see Müller Rojas, 2001).

When Chávez won the elections and became president, the government did not have a systematic, doctrinal or ideological body of thought, nor did it have clear guidelines about what a project for the country would look like, nor political organisations capable of responding adequately to these shortcomings. In terms of the classic distinctions between left and right, in its initial phases the project was heterogeneous and, even at its core, had positions that could be labelled as traditional conservative military nationalism.

It is this open character, subject to diverse and conflicting influences, this search for a home-grown project rooted in the popular and the national, with its prevailing charismatic leadership, together with the significant military component, that has led some analysts to characterise the *chavista* project as populist or radical populist (Parker, 2001, 2003; Ellner and Hellinger, 2003; Ellner, 2004).

To use the concept of populism to analyse the process of transformation in Venezuela requires us to rid it of the pejorative connotations with which it is usually associated in political debate. In both the Marxist and Liberal traditions, there is a marked (and strongly Eurocentric) tendency to underestimate the historical significance of populism in Latin America and the role that it has fulfilled in structural contexts characterised by extraordinary heterogeneity, hierarchical organisation and exclusion of the popular sectors. The notion of populism associated exclusively with demagogic and manipulative *caudillismo* does not allow for the recognition of the significant role these processes have played in incorporating broad sectors that were excluded both under oligarchic regimes and in liberal-democratic experiences.[3] The historical experience of populism in Latin America and the present theoretical-conceptual debate around it have provided useful tools for the analysis of aspects of the *chavista* experience. This entails a critical revision of the normal use of the word. In the words of Dick Parker (2001:14):

we do not identify it [populism], as the traditional left and current neo-liberal analyses do, with demagogy (although it can be demagogical); nor do we adopt the functionalist vision that presented it as a 'deviation' in the process of modernisation of the continent (Germani, 1965), nor do we accept as useful the type of analysis that restricts it to the historical period during which import substituting policies predominated.

This analyst argues that it is convenient to work with the line of thought that Ernesto Laclau put forward years ago, and which has been taken up by David Raby in order to analyse the current processes in the continent:

> Raby's starting points are Ernesto Laclau's initial writings (1978) regarding populist discourse as a mechanism of 'popular-democratic questioning,' which arises in situations of hegemonic crisis and which represents an attempt to resolve the crisis *one way or another* through the capture and mobilisation of the latent anti-oligarchic, anti-imperialist and anti-state feelings of the dominated classes. ... Raby also coincides with Laclau in indicating that this type of discourse is compatible with a wide range of political alternatives that range from fascism to revolutionary socialism.
>
> (Parker, 2001:14)

This characterisation, as a popular-democratic interrogation with anti-oligarchic and anti-imperialist features, in conditions of hegemonic crisis and with its particular style of 'leadership and a dynamic of organisationally fluid popular mobilisation', is a good starting point to analyse the current Venezuelan process. It is precisely this open character of programmatic positions, the extraordinary weight of Chávez's personal leadership, the until now limited capacity to construct consistent political-organisational instruments, and the nature of the social sectors that make up its most solid base of support (the most excluded sectors, traditionally the least organised sector of the population) that make it difficult to predict the future direction of the process of transformation in the country.

Whether or not the *chavista* project advances in the direction of changes in the relations of power and towards a more democratic and participatory society no longer mainly depends upon its original ideological content. Of greater importance will be the social and political struggles that are developing, the correlations of power between the forces of change and those of the opposition, the collective learning of the popular sectors and their capacity to generate their own organisational instruments, the extent to which the severe inefficiency of public administration can be overcome, the characteristics Chávez's leadership adopts in the future, the politico-organisational boundaries of the so-called forces of change and the establishment of more solid political organisations, as well as the Latin American and international context. In the very process of these struggles, the collective actors and their projects and political proposals will dynamically redefine and re-articulate themselves.

REPRESENTATIVE DEMOCRACY AND PARTICIPATORY DEMOCRACY

One essential axis of *chavismo*'s political proposal is the idea of participatory democracy. This idea lays claim to the notion of another democracy, distinct from liberal democracy, which it considers exhausted. According to Chávez, it is not just a question of the crisis of the two-party system or of the specific forms that democracy acquired in Venezuela:

> What they have called a democratic system in these last few years is not substantially different from what they call, for example, the dictatorship of Marcos Pérez Jiménez. ... I believe that deep down it is essentially the same pattern of domination with a different face, whether that of General Gómez or Doctor Rafael Caldera. But behind this figure, this *caudillo* with a beret or without one ... there exists the same pattern of domination in the economy, in politics, the same negation of the rights of peoples to be masters of their own destiny.
>
> (Blanco Muñoz, 1998:120)

The most consistently reiterated proposal of *chavismo*, both before and during the electoral process, was the need to convene a *constituent process* in order to 're-found the country', replace the *Fourth Republic* with the *Fifth Republic* and replace the liberal democratic representative model with a political model of participatory democracy in which the people would play a leading role. The Chávez government's first act, in January 1999, was a decree calling for a consultative referendum on whether or not to convene a National Constituent Assembly. In spite of stiff opposition from the old political class, the Supreme Court upheld the constitutionality of the

[79]

referendum, which was held in April that year. Chávez managed to garner the support of 87.75 per cent of the votes cast, albeit with an abstention rate of 62.35 per cent. He also received strong support for his candidates in the elections to the National Constituent Assembly, achieving an overwhelming majority, which allowed the government to design a constitutional model without the need for major negotiations with the opposition.

Despite the Assembly's radical critique of liberal and representative democracy, its insistence on the need to replace it with participatory democracy, and the prominence this issue had in the constituent debate, the new political model did not replace representative democracy, but rather complemented it with various methods of participation. The mechanisms for election and distribution of the majority of public positions retained their representative character. Similarly, the separation of powers characteristic of the liberal democratic tradition was preserved, but two new powers were added to the three traditional powers of executive, legislature and judiciary: the Citizen Power (constituted by the ombudsman, the attorney general and the comptroller general) and the Electoral Power. The president's powers were strengthened in certain critical areas (such as military promotions), the presidential period was lengthened to six years, and the possibility of immediate re-election was introduced.

The mechanisms of participation included in the new constitutional text are important and varied. In accordance with Article 62, all citizens 'have the right to participate freely in public affairs, either directly or through their elected representatives'. The broad range of forms of participation and involvement, both political and economic, are established in Article 70. The constitution also established popular referenda of a consultative nature in all spheres of political organisation, from the level of local parishes to the national level (Article 71). All popularly elected posts are subject to recall (Article 72). Likewise, bills under discussion in the National Assembly and international treaties and agreements may be subject to referenda (Article 73). National laws or presidential decrees with the force of law may also be totally or partially abrogated through popular referenda (Article 74).

In accord with Article 118, the state recognises the right of workers and the community to develop associations of a social and participatory nature, such as co-operatives: 'The state shall promote and protect these associations intended to improve the popular and alternative economy.' The political, cultural, linguistic, economic and territorial rights of indigenous peoples are widely protected (Articles 9 and 119–25). Based on the principle of progressivism, human rights are characterised as inalienable, indivisible and interdependent (Article 19). There is broad recognition of civil and political as well as economic, social and cultural rights. The state must guarantee free access to education, health and social security.

From the point of view of the aims of participatory democracy and control of public administration, the Bolivarian legislation regulates the participation of the people in the formulation, implementation and control of public administration. Contrary to other experiences of local participation in Latin America, such as the participatory budget in Porto Alegre, in which legal norms systematised the accumulated experience, in the Venezuelan case the norms preceded experience, because they are an expression of constitutional mandates and of the political will to promote them. Putting them into practice has been very uneven, with truly successful experiences occurring in only some of the country's municipalities. The technical water committees and the community water councils are possibly the best and most systematic experiences of a model of participatory public administration. These are the organisational instruments through which the country's (public) water companies, via their community management, stimulate the organisational processes in the communities, with the aim of converting them into fully public companies – that is, controlled and supervised by their owners, or the communities which they serve.

As with so many other issues, in the promotion of participatory democracy, the extent to which it can progress towards a more democratic society, with a more equitable distribution of power and economic resources, is not an issue that can be resolved once and for all, much less through a constitutional design. These legal instruments open a whole range of possibilities, the realisation of which will necessarily depend on the processes of political confrontation and on the capacity to appropriate and deepen the instruments generated in this struggle – see Denis (2001) and Izarra (2004).

The most important development in Venezuela in recent years has not been the implementation of the new institutional mechanisms of participation, but rather the evident transformations in the political culture and in the processes of inclusion, as subjects of political and organisational action, of the poor majority, which historically, and especially in the last 20 years, had been increasingly excluded. This active presence of the 'dangerous classes' on the political scene (increasingly informed, mobilised and organised, and unwilling to return to their previous passivity) largely explains the rejection of *chavismo* by those who see this presence of the 'others' – characterised in a racist way as the *chavista* mobs and hordes – as a threat to their privileges, and by those who view the deep current divisions in Venezuelan society as the product of Chávez's discourse.

Without Chávez's pedagogical and communication skills, the mobilisation and growing incorporation of large excluded sectors of the country would have been difficult. However, this very style of leadership could become an obstacle to a process of democratisation if many of the key and small decisions of the process remain in his hands, thereby closing the door to the urgent necessities of the institutionalisation of public administration and of the organisation and autonomy of the popular movement. The great dependency of the transformative process on one person makes the process itself very vulnerable. In addition, the continued substitution of institutionalised public administration capabilities and autonomous social organisation by the actions of the armed forces – with its inevitable logic of vertical non-deliberative authority – can likewise place obstacles on the road to building a more democratic society.

The world of popular social organisation has expanded in an extraordinary way, both through the revitalisation of previously existing experiences as well as through the creation of many others (health committees, cultural groups, Bolivarian circles, water committees and community water councils, committees and groups of participation and support for the *misiones*, electoral battle units, urban land committees and organisation around the local public planning councils, etcetera). Since the start of 2006, thousands of urban neighbourhoods and rural communities have been organising *Consejos Comunales* (communal councils). The relationships between these social organisations and the state and *chavismo's* political organisations have varied over the years, and have at times been tense. Given that a large proportion of the tensions have arisen in the context of the political-institutional changes and the implementation of public policies, the state is an inevitable point of reference. These social organisations have had a broad and varied range of experiences as regards their degree of autonomy vis-a-vis the state.

Given the boundaries that define the present polarisation of Venezuelan society, it is difficult to imagine that the collision of government and opposition forces will lead to the definitive political defeat of one or the other side. The continuation of a significant division of the society is foreseeable for the medium term. Consequently, the consolidation of the process of change must meet the challenge of constructing a new *hegemony*. It requires policies and discourses that go beyond the social sectors that constitute the current base of support for the government.

This possibility for a new hegemony encounters severe obstacles in the feedback dynamic of confrontation and total negation of the *other*, that characterises both the discourse of the government and that of the opposition, and in the consequent absence of opportunities for encounters or dialogue between the two sides.

Polarisation reaches extreme points when it comes to fundamental *cognitive ruptures* between both sectors of society. Under such conditions, a discussion around *the interpretation of the meaning of events* is no longer possible, since agreement on the very events themselves is impossible. The more sectarian *chavista* tendencies are apparently unable to accept the fact that as long as they close the door to the participation of important professional groups, and in general middle-class sectors who feel excluded politically, culturally and economically from the project underway in the country, the more likely it is that these sectors will opt to rupture relations, thereby making consolidation of the process of change much more difficult.

Here the role of the media is critical. Most of the private sector media outlets have abandoned their role as information providers in order to become instruments of systematic denunciation of the government, taking on the functions of opposition political parties. In addition, they have helped to create a climate of permanent anxiety among a significant sector of the population. In response, the public media act more as government than as state media. The most genuine experience in the direction of the democratisation of mass communications is that of the community television and radio stations, which have expanded considerably over these years. Their potential was illustrated when they became the main source of information in the days following the coup d'état of April 2002. At the time the state media were closed down and all the private media decided to carry out an information blackout in order conceal the broad popular mobilisation that led to Chávez's return to the presidency and to the restitution of constitutional order.

ALTERNATIVES TO NEO-LIBERALISM:
THE ECONOMIC MODEL

In Chávez's speeches as a presidential candidate and at the beginning of his presidency, he repeatedly stressed the importance of the popular, the national, issues of sovereignty, equality and participatory democracy, the critique of savage capitalism and neo-liberalism, as well as the rejection of a uni-polar world and an insistence on the priority of relations with the countries of the Global South, particularly those of Latin America. Nevertheless, a basic question remains unanswered: what would a viable alternative project consist of in the current context of global militarised neo-liberalism? Is it the search for greater national autonomy? Is it a return to developmentalism and import substitution? Is it a model of endogenous development? Is it a welfare state? Is it an anti-neo-liberal project within capitalism, a *humanist capitalism*? Is it an anti-capitalist project? (see Camejo, 2002).

The initial, most systematic proposal of an alternative productive model was the so-called *Alternative Bolivarian Agenda* of 1996. This document outlined five production sectors that define the mixed nature (public/private) of the proposed economic model. This mixed economy orientation between the state and private enterprise was reaffirmed in the definition of the socioeconomic regime established in the 1999 Constitution.

The constitution guarantees economic freedom (Article 112) and private property (Article 115), while defining a clear and central role for the state in trade policy and in the defence of national industries (Article 301). It reserves to the state control over the oil industry and other strategic industries (Article 302), and assigns it a leading role in the development of sustainable agriculture and food security (Article 305).

With the notable exception of oil policy, during the first years of government there was neither an integral proposal for a model of development nor an economic policy that was consistent with the radicalism of the government's political discourse. In the oil industry, basic reorientations were undertaken from the very beginning. The policy of increasing production, which by basing itself on the priority of increasing market participation had significantly contributed to the collapse of global oil prices, was radically reversed. International initiatives involving oil-exporting countries, including both those belonging to the Organization of Petroleum Exporting Countries (OPEC) and other important oil-exporting non-members of OPEC, were undertaken. These initiatives led to an immediate and effective strengthening of OPEC, which made the policy of restricting supply possible and contributed to the recovery of oil prices. Concomitantly, the process of liberalisation of the oil sector that formed part of the strategy of privatising the management of Petroleos de Venezuela (PDVSA, Venezuela's state-owned oil company) was suspended. At the same time, the executive branch undertook the initial steps to regain control over oil policy and over the basic orientations of

PDVSA, a nominally state-run company which in the preceding years had acquired increasing autonomy (Lander, 2003; Mommer, 2003).

As a result of the almost exclusive priority given to political and institutional change during the first year and a half of government, there was no coherent global direction in the other areas of economic policy. Monetary and fiscal policy was orthodox, as priority was given to controlling inflation and to balancing the other macroeconomic variables. The external debt was paid in a timely manner and incurring any new debt that would require negotiations with the IMF was avoided. Some measures such as the full opening of the telecommunications sector (Organic Telecommunications Law of 2004 and the Investment Promotion and Protection Law of 1999) were celebrated by 'market' spokespersons. Their reaction to the body of 49 laws – especially the Fishing and Aquaculture Law of 2004, the Land Reform and Agrarian Development Law of 2001 and the Organic Hydrocarbons Law of 1999 – was the opposite. President Chávez passed these laws by decree under the authorisation of the National Assembly, through the so-called 'enabling law' passed in 2001. Business people, opposition parties and most of the private media viewed these laws as an attack on private property and as proof of the authoritarian and communist nature of the government. Demanding their revision, these groups organised the first national business strike in December 2001.

In order to explore the potential of the Venezuelan process as an alternative to neo-liberalism, it is clearly not enough to review the main programmatic texts of the government's project for change or to analyse the new constitutional design. There is a wide margin for interpretation and possible action within these broad ideological guidelines. It is by confronting the problems and experiences accumulated by the government in the execution of its programme, in the internal divisions among the forces promoting change, in the struggles against the opposition, and in the way that obstacles are addressed that its policies will acquire greater definition and substance and generate more precise proposals for the future. As the confrontation with sectors of the opposition sharpened, polarisation became consolidated in Venezuelan society and the window for political opportunities rapidly closed, and so solutions were sought that pointed towards a more consistent break with the neo-liberal model.

Two basic conditions appear to have been assumed implicitly in the design of the government project, but these turned out to have an extremely precarious base: the existence of a solid national business sector with which it would be possible to advance policies of national development, and an administrative state apparatus with the capacity to respond to the growing demands assigned to the public administration by the government's project for change.

The government's policies of protection, financing and other forms of support for national industry found little resonance among the principal productive sectors, as a result both of their weak internal productive capacity and of the political climate of conflict that was generated in the country. The participation of the vast majority of the business sector in the coup d'état of April 2002 and in the lockout of December 2002 to February 2003 led the government to re-examine its relationship with business, especially the leadership of FEDECAMARAS, and the big conglomerates such as the Cisneros and Polar groups, which played a leading role in the efforts to overthrow the government. From the moment Chávez assumed the presidency, practically speaking, Venezuelan business has been engaged in an investment strike, with a rate of capital flight that is unprecedented in Venezuelan history.

The lockout not only confirmed the extent of the country's dependence on imported food, but also the extreme concentration of the processing and distribution of these and other basic products, exposing the extreme vulnerability of the Venezuelan economy – and of the current political process – to the manipulations of international trade (price and access) and to the will of oligopolistic business sectors.

How does one respond under these conditions, when neither socialism nor the nationalisation of the economy formed part of the original constitutional design, nor were they foreseen in the political project? In addition to the government's broad popular support and the armed forces' endorsement of the democratic institutional framework, resistance to the oil and business strike was made possible by the exceptional characteristics that oil revenues play in the Venezuelan economy. Due to the existence of international reserves, it was possible to arrange emergency imports (of food and fuel) that contributed to the defeat of the strike. The oil revenue, in the hands of the state, also allowed for the creation of new measures to confront the political and economic changes brought about by this conjuncture. Viewed not only as a short-term measure (the immediate political impact of employment generation), but also as a strategic option, the government adopted a development model that was defined as *endogenous* and that prioritised the 'social economy' (see Vila Planes, 2003). In addition, the government initiated a policy of exchange controls with the aim of restoring the level of international reserves.

Through the various forms of micro and small credits granted by state financial entities, new productive organisations of the social economy are being fomented: small and medium-sized companies, co-operatives and other forms of associative production. The government promoted an extraordinary drive to purchase and contract public sector services in order to generate productive capacity. *Business rounds* were organised to announce future purchases and contracts to potential bidders in order to identify technological, financial or managerial deficiencies that needed resolving in order to be able to respond to the demands of the public sector. PDVSA and other state companies, such as the water and electricity companies and the basic industrial enterprises of the Venezuelan Corporation of Guayana, promoted training programmes and funding for the creation of co-operatives with which to establish purchasing contracts, maintenance and outsourcing of various services. Given the particular weakness of the agricultural and livestock sector – the country imported around 70 per cent of the food it consumed – special emphasis was given to these areas.

Recognising the precariousness of state management structures in implementing public policies – particularly the new social policies – the government came to the conclusion that the political conjuncture of the Venezuelan conflict could not wait for administrative reforms to improve management capacity in view of the new and urgent tasks ahead. For this reason, the executive chose to create the *misiones* (missions), a range of extraordinary programmes that, by bypassing state bureaucracy, sought to respond to the main social problems that had been identified as critical and in need of urgent solutions.

Misión Robinson is a civil-military programme that aims to achieve literacy for the estimated 2 million citizens who are unable to read and write. In the latter stages of the programme, it is anticipated that those who complete the literacy programme will enter a programme of primary education. *Misión* Rivas aims to incorporate into secondary education people of any age who, having completed their primary education, are unable to complete their secondary schooling. *Misión* Sucre's objective is to incorporate those who have completed their secondary education into university education, giving priority to students from poor and lower-middle-class backgrounds. *Misión* Mercal aims to market foodstuffs and other essential products in order to guarantee the supply of high-quality affordable goods to low-income sectors. The process of creating alternative channels of production and commercialisation is intended to encourage co-operatives and small businesses. *Misión* Barrio Adentro, with the massive participation of Cuban doctors, aims to take primary and family medical care to popular sectors throughout the country. *Misión* Zamora aims to distribute land titles to *campesinos*, along with the provision of technical and marketing assistance, infrastructure, services and funding. *Misión* Vuelvan Caras aims to generate permanent employment by means of skills training, socio-cultural education, and the creation of nuclei of endogenous development in the areas of tourism, agriculture, infrastructure, services and industry.

In contrast with the focused social policies that predominated throughout the continent in recent years, these policies are directed towards achieving social equity and overcoming political inequality and cultural exclusion. In order to achieve this, participation and the building of citizenship have been emphasised (Parra and Lacruz, 2003). They were not conceived as compensatory policies to counteract the negative social consequences of economic policies, but rather as an integral part of the latter. The announced goal is that the *misiones* will eventually achieve a rising level of co-ordination in order to build the productive and social fabric of the new Venezuela, as well as a new public institutional framework.

These programmes are heavily dependent on oil revenues, to the point that a significant decrease in the latter could endanger their continuity. On the other hand, the improvisation and the lack of institutionalisation that has characterised these programmes, due to the conditions in which they were established, make them a breeding ground for corruption. The classic institutions of the comptroller general, including the judiciary, are less and less effective and their legitimacy is increasingly being questioned. The new forms of social management that constitute a vital aspect of participation are only in an incipient stage of development and are encountering strong resistance in different areas of public administration, on the part of both *chavistas* and the opposition.

Analysis of the principal public policies makes it possible to identify, in a preliminary way, those orientations that are relatively clear and those in which the major voids reside. The managing role of the state in the oil, petrochemical and other basic industries is clear, as defined in the constitution. Does the state play a central role in the creation of infrastructure? Are there at the present time enough investments in roads, trains, rapid urban transport, systems of water collection and treatment, and the generation and transmission of electricity? In addition, the model of endogenous development to some extent limits the role of small and medium-sized producers and suppliers of services, and in general, the role attributed to the *social economy*.

However, this set of policies does not yet constitute something that can be called an *alternative development model* or a clear alternative to neo-liberalism. These policies occur in the context of the urgent need to respond to political conjunctures in permanent motion. Implementation frequently precedes theoretical formulation. Given the state of political confrontation and the absence of strong business groups willing to support a more endogenous model of development, the character of the future articulation between the set of policies promoted by the state and the activities of the private business sector is not very clear. The complementary role between public and private activities set out in the constitution has encountered greater difficulties than initially anticipated. In the short term, the main Venezuelan business groups counted on the fall of the government and postponed their investment decisions during the first years of the Chávez government. It was only after the strong economic recovery of 2005 and 2006 that an increase in the use of idle industrial capacity occurred and new investments were undertaken. Meanwhile, there was a growth in the participation of international capital in important sectors of the economy, such as finance, gas, telecommunications, electricity and food products.

The business sector that has been most favoured by this conjuncture has been finance. The extraordinary increase in fiscal income and public expenditure as a result of the large increase in oil prices, together with the policy of exchange controls, has resulted in an accelerated increase in the circulation of money. The banking sector has benefited both from the deposits made by public entities and from the interest on the purchase of government bonds issued as part of a Central Bank policy to remove money circulating in the economy in order to contain inflation.

The initial impetus given by the government to endogenous development and the social economy was financed by using oil revenue. This raises difficult and extraordinary challenges for the viability of this proposal. Its success will be determined by the extent to which the social economy and the activities associated with endogenous development in general become an increasingly autonomous process of accumulation, which requires the creation of a self-sustaining process for generating employment and demand for goods and services, as well as a new capacity for investment that does not depend on the transfer of state resources. This proposal will fail, however, if there is a continued dependence on massive public subsidies and the creation of a clientelistic culture, in which political contacts are more important than autonomous productive capacities.

THE VENEZUELAN PROCESS IN THE REGIONAL
AND INTERNATIONAL CONTEXT

Clearly, the search for alternatives to neo-liberalism will occur via the exploration of options in the present uni-polar world. The rejection of the unilateralism of the United States and the central role played by the IMF and the World Bank in the current savage capitalist order are recurrent themes in Chávez's discourse. He has also defended the need to democratise and strengthen the United Nations system. As a foreign policy priority, the Venezuelan government has sought to deepen trade and political relationships with the countries of the Global South and has defended the need for the economic, political, cultural and even military integration of Latin America.

Given the influence of the United States in the world and its role as Venezuela's main trade partner, the Chávez government has, in general, been cautious in its handling of some critical issues in its economic relations with the Unites States. Venezuela has repeatedly assured the United States of long-term oil supplies, guaranteed the legal security of foreign investments and paid its foreign debt on time.

Nevertheless, each of Venezuela's principal international initiatives and many of its domestic policies have been regarded by the US government as contrary to its interests. Among these, the following stand out:

- the decision to halt the policy of liberalisation of the oil industry and production expansion plans initiated during the last Caldera government
- the contribution to re-launching OPEC and the reduction of the global supply of oil, and the consequent recovery of oil prices
- the denunciation of the *Plan Colombia* as a plan of war
- the refusal to authorise military flights of the so-called 'war on drugs' over Venezuelan territory
- diplomatic relations with and presidential visits to OPEC countries regarded by the US as members of the 'axis of evil', in particular Iran, Libya and Iraq
- the refusal to support unconditionally the 'war against terror', expressed in Chávez's assertions that it is not possible to fight terrorism with more terrorism
- fraternal relations with the Cuban government, especially the provision of oil in contravention of the US blockade of the island

- Venezuela's independent voting decisions in various international forums and organisations
- condemnation of the overthrow of Haiti's president Jean Bertrand Aristide by US armed forces
- the active role assumed in the ministerial meetings of the World Trade Organization (WTO) in Cancún and Hong Kong
- the systematic questioning of the Free Trade Area of the Americas (FTAA) as a project that favours large US multinational companies to the detriment of the development of Latin American countries and the living conditions of the majority of the continent's population
- the purchase by the Venezuelan government of armaments from Spain and Russia
- the denunciation of the Israeli government's criminal attacks against the peoples of Gaza and Lebanon, and of the US government's full political and military support for these attacks
- Venezuela's candidacy for a seat on the UN Security Council to represent Latin America.

US policies toward the Venezuelan government have been increasingly aggressive. In addition to President Bush himself, the main spokespersons of US foreign policy, Condoleezza Rice and Colin Powell, as well as those responsible for Latin America in the State Department (Otto Reich and Roger Noriega), have issued repeated public 'warnings' to the Venezuelan government. There is also no longer any doubt that the Bush administration supported the coup d'état carried out by sectors of the opposition in April 2002 (Lander, 2002). In addition to meeting repeatedly with those responsible for the coup, the State Department (through the National Endowment for Democracy) provided funding to the main party-based, trade union, business and self-proclaimed 'civil society' organisations that participated in the attempt to overthrow Chávez – see Valero (2004) and Golinger (2006). Moreover, the US Agency for International Development (USAID) has been executing a vast programme titled 'Venezuela: Confidence-building Initiatives', which provides funding of \$10 million (2002–04) aimed at influencing the Venezuelan political process, with support once again going to organisations that played a leading role in the 2002 coup. In March 2004, General James T. Hill, Commander of the US Southern Command, characterised the Venezuelan government as part of a 'radical populism' that represents 'a growing threat to the interests of the United States' (Hill, 2004).

Upon assuming the presidency in 1999, Chávez found himself deeply isolated in a Latin American context in which nearly all the governments could be characterised as neo-liberal and submissive to US government policies. If that context had remained unaltered, there would have been few possibilities for this experiment in change. Nevertheless, much has happened in the continent and in the world since the struggles against the WTO in Seattle in 1999. The progress and strengthening of movements of resistance to neo-liberal globalisation can clearly be seen in the development of the World Social Forum, which first took place in Porto Alegre in 2001 and most recently in Bamako, Karachi and Caracas in 2006. Moreover, the movements opposed to structural adjustment policies, and to privatisations in particular, have achieved important successes in the continent, as is the case of the 'water war' in Cochabamba.

In addition, in recent years, neo-liberal governments have been overthrown by popular mobilisations in Ecuador, Argentina and Bolivia. As explained in other chapters of this volume, starting with the election of Luiz Inácio Lula da Silva in Brazil, and Nestor Kirchner in Argentina, a reshaping of the continent's political map has been taking place. This shift towards the left in the Latin American political spectrum was confirmed with the victory of the Broad Front in the Uruguayan elections at the end of 2004, the election of Evo Morales a year later, and the victory of Andrés Manuel López Obrador in Mexico in July 2006 (whether or not this was recognised by Mexico's fraudulent electoral apparatus). Despite the inevitable difficulties resulting from distinct political processes, with their very different rhythms and possibilities, for the first time in decades, the conditions exist for the creation of economic and geopolitical proposals contemplated from and for Latin America.

Whether this represents the end of neo-liberal hegemony on the continent is another matter. Neo-liberalism is much more than a set of policies or economic doctrines. Three decades of neo-liberalism have generated deep productive transformations in the relations of power between social and class sectors, in the role of the state and its degree of autonomy in formulating and implementing public policies, as well as in the aspirations and attitudes of these societies. The coming to power of presidents or parties from a leftist, and even a socialist, tradition is no guarantee that there exists the capacity (or even the will) to produce substantive changes in this model of organisation of society. This is particularly problematic in the cases of Chile, Brazil and Uruguay.

In the politics of opposition to the FTAA, there has been a rich experience of dialogue and coordination between the networks of social organisations, which have taken part in this struggle all over the continent, and some sectors of the governments of Argentina, Brazil and Bolivia. Given the radical criticisms that the Venezuelan government has formulated against this imperial project, its relations with these organisations of continental resistance have been particularly fruitful, which illustrates the rich possibilities that are emerging for greater confluence and collaboration between these organisations and governments with different degrees of commitment to opposing neo-liberalism.

The present Venezuelan political process is part of the worldwide and continental struggle against the destructive dynamic of neo-liberal militarised globalisation. The deepening and even the survival of this process are at stake within this global confrontation. The course taken by these processes of Latin American integration – which are not just economic but also political and cultural – will, in this sense, be decisive. It is an open process that is generating many expectations. The FTAA appears to have suffered a definitive death at the Fourth Summit of the Americas, which took place in Mar del Plata in November 2005. Venezuela became a full member of MERCOSUR, and has signed a multiplicity of political, economic and energy agreements with CARICOM (PetroCaribe) and with South American countries. The project of the Televisora del Sur (Telesur, Television of the South) seeks to respond to a critical issue: the almost total monopoly of the North American corporate media as the source of information in the continent. The ALBA (Alternativa Bolivariana para las Américas, Bolivarian Alternative for the Americas) has been proposed as an option for integration of the peoples set against the logic of the FTAA and the free trade agreements. One of the first decisions of the new Bolivian government was to propose another alternative, the TCP or Tratado de Comercio de los Pueblos (The Peoples' Trade Agreement).

ELECTORAL PROCESSES AND THE FUTURE
OF THE BOLIVARIAN REVOLUTION

In accordance with Article 72 of the constitution, and after much conflict over the quantity and validity of the signatures presented, it was confirmed that the opposition had collected signatures equal to more than 20 per cent of the national electoral register. Thus, the National Electoral Council called for a presidential recall referendum to be held – for the first time in the history of the continent – on 15 August 2004. At stake was not only Chávez's presidency, but also the extraordinary dilemma between continuing along the conflictive path of change or reverting to a neo-liberal political and economic model and to a geopolitical realignment of Venezuela with the United States. Chávez's mandate was reconfirmed with the support of 59 per cent of the voters, with an abstention rate of 30 per cent. These results confirmed three basic characteristics of Venezuelan politics:

- First, the government maintained solid electoral support in spite of all the difficulties and obstacles that it has faced in recent years (the coup d'état, the oil-business strike, the systematic campaign of radical opposition by virtually all the privately owned media, and recurrent threats by the United States government).
- Second, Venezuela is a deeply divided society, and this division has a clear class content. In the higher income sectors, the 'Yes' vote (for the recall of Chávez) fluctuated between 80 and 90 per cent, while in the popular sectors, the 'No' vote oscillated between 70 and 80 per cent. The problem for the opposition is that the poor sectors make up a clear majority of the population.
- Third, the leadership of the Venezuelan opposition once more demonstrated its limited disposition to accept the rules of the democratic game when these rules do not favour them. The results of the referendum were consistent with all the main opinion polls, and were recognised as valid and legitimate by the OAS (Organization of American States) and the Carter Center – the organisations that the opposition leadership itself had indicated were the only ones whose verdict they would accept. Nevertheless, they refused to recognise the results. Not knowing the reality of the *other*, and expressing their racist disdain for the popular sectors, they could not accept the possibility that the poor, the majority in the country, could voluntarily opt for a political project that they themselves rejected. Under these circumstances, they could find only two possible explanations: either the votes of the poor were bought by the government;[4] or an extraordinary and sophisticated act of fraud was carried out, whose mechanisms even their international advisors, experts of the highest level, were unable to detect.

Consistent with this policy of refusing to recognise the legitimacy of the electoral arbiter, and also clearly as a result of public opinion polls that indicated that they were certain to receive many fewer votes than they had obtained in the recall election, at the last minute, all the opposition parties withdrew from the congressional elections of December 2005. With an abstention rate that reached 75 per cent, the coalition of parties supporting the government won every seat in the National Assembly.

The most recent presidential election took place in December 2006. The Bolivarian Constitution allows candidates to run in consecutive elections, and therefore Chávez was running again. And once again, the results gave him a large majority: 62.8 per cent of the vote. Immediately before the election the opposition organisations were severely weakened. The mistakes and successive defeats in previous years (the coup d'état, the oil-industry strike and the recall election) had left them demoralised and divided. Their leaders had lost credibility and had a limited capacity to motivate and mobilise their potential followers. Part of the opposition, led by what remains of AD, defended the policy of abstention, arguing that the conditions for a fair election did not exist. Finally, the opposition agreed to take part in the elections and rallied around a strong candidate, Manuel Rosales (governor of the oil-producing state of Zulia), who, despite having little chance of defeating Chávez, contributed to unifying the opposition around a longer-term project.

Thus, 2007 will be the start of a new and complex period in the history of the Bolivarian project. Tackling many of the problems and tensions within the process has been postponed time and again until after the December 2006 elections. These include relations between competing pro-Chávez currents, the demands for achieving greater levels of political institutionalisation, the need to deal with the notorious inefficiency of the public administration, and the growing corruption that threatens to corrode the legitimacy of the process of transformation.

In January 2007, the National Assembly passed a new 'enabling law', which will allow President Chávez to legislate by decree in eleven different areas for a period of 18 months. Chávez argued that such powers were needed to accelerate the process of transforming Venezuela's state and economy into *socialismo del siglo XXI* ('twenty-first century socialism'). He also announced the nationalisation of the country's electricity and telecommunications sectors, confirmed plans to strip foreign companies of majority stakes in oil projects, and threatened to seize control of supermarkets and other retail outlets.

Some weeks before, the president had announced another major political initiative: the establishment of a unified party of the forces supporting the Bolivarian process. On 15 December 2006, ten days after his crushing election victory, he simply announced that he had decided it was necessary to create a new party. He suggested calling it Partido Socialista Unido de Venezuela (United Socialist Party of Venezuela). He told a rally of political followers: 'I invite whoever wants to join me to come with me. Those parties that want to stay [as parties], go ahead, but they will be out of the government. I only want one party to govern with me.'

Following the electoral victory in December 2006, conditions were optimal for initiating a wide-ranging debate about the next steps in the transformation of the country. Chávez's electoral support was not only maintained but, in percentage terms, slightly increased. The electoral results were recognised as legitimate by the opposition candidate, international observers and even the State Department. The opposition was fragmented and lacking in political initiative. The US government was increasingly bogged down in Iraq and Afghanistan, which had severely compromised its ability to open up new fronts of confrontation. The Venezuelan economy maintained its trend of sustained growth whilst consumption grew markedly in all sectors of the population. The communal councils, despite their improvisational character and multiple problems, had given a new impetus to participation of the poorest sectors. In that context, Chávez launched in early 2007 a process of constitutional reform towards a 'socialist democracy'. However, neither in the manner in which it has been elaborated and presented to the public, nor in its content, does the constitutional reform contribute adequately to the necessary debate over the future of the Bolivarian process.

The issue of socialism had been repeatedly brought up by Chávez throughout his presidential election campaign, but beyond the term 'twenty-first century socialism' there had not been any progress in characterising the model of socialism which was sought. Given that it was called socialism for a new century it was clear that we were not dealing with the socialism of the past; in particular, not the Soviet version of socialism. Nevertheless, Chávez did not explain what the difference would be and in what respect twenty-first century socialism should differ from the Soviet experience of the twentieth century. In the negation of the single-party model? In other modalities of relations between the state and political parties? In the rejection of an official ideology of the state? In generating alternatives to the monocultural model that negates any differences? In forms of political organisation and participation orientated towards avoiding a repetition of the so-called 'popular' or 'proletarian democracies' that ended up negating the very idea of democracy? In an economic model that is not based on centralised bureaucratic planning? In a radical questioning of industrial productivism based on limitless growth, as represented by the Soviet Union, and today by China – a systematic war against the rest of nature, against life on the planet itself, similar to what capitalism has historically done and continues to do today? Are we talking of a socialism with political pluralism that is compatible with what is established as one of the fundamental principles of the present constitution?

None of these issues can be assumed to be implicit. Each of them requires investigation, debate, and theoretical and political confrontations over the characteristics of the model of socialism in the last century, over the processes which culminated in the implantation of a bureaucratic and authoritarian statism, and its failure as a historical option to capitalism. Learning about what happened in the past opens up the possibility of not repeating it. Today we have the obligation to think about the future that we want to build, incorporating a critical reflexive analysis about the past as well as the new political, cultural, economic, technological and environmental conditions that we are living under today.

NOTES

1. Some of the founders of MAS (Teodoro Petkoff and Pompeyo Márquez) withdrew from the party in disagreement with the decision to support Chávez's candidacy. The only exceptions to the left's support for Chávez were *Causa R*, which, following the split that led to the creation of the PPT, had begun its journey towards ever more right-wing positions, and *Bandera Roja* (Red Flag), which, continuing with its traditional policy of abstention, did not participate in the elections. *Bandera Roja* took part for the first time in the presidential elections of 2000 in support of the main candidate opposing Chávez, Francisco Arias Cárdenas, and obtained 16,582 votes.

2. The book *Habla el Comandante* is a compilation of interviews conducted by the historian Agustín Blanco Muñoz with Hugo Chávez between 1995, following Chávez's release from jail, and 1998, prior to his election to the presidency. The more than 600 pages represent the most detailed account of Chávez's ideas prior to becoming president.

3. As David Raby (2003) argues, much is said – and in a pejorative sense – about Chávez's 'populism', but without recognising what the populism of Perón, Vargas and Cárdenas represented for the imagination of the peoples – and for the real development of – Argentina, Brazil and Mexico.

4. We can find a clear expression of this racist scorn for the poor in the Venezuelan Cardinal Rosalio José Castillo Lara, who declared on Radio Vatican that these results were due to 'the poor being given 50 or 60 dollars if they voted "No"'.

4 URUGUAY
The Left in Government:
Between Continuity and Change
Daniel Chavez

The path followed by the Uruguayan left from opposition to national government illustrates the central dilemmas confronting any progressive political force with real possibilities of gaining power. Like other progressive Latin American governments of the past and present, the Uruguayan left was expected to confront multiple political, social and economic pressures. On the one hand, it would face the pressures of the country's political and economic elites, international financial institutions, the US government and other conservative forces that would seek to minimise the emancipatory nature of the new administration. On the other hand, it would be pressured to undertake the left's historic programme, attempting to respond to the demands and expectations of the most vulnerable social sectors – in the context of an extremely severe crisis inherited from more than three decades of authoritarian, inefficient and exclusionary rule. Just about two years after ascending to national office, the accumulated tensions within the Uruguayan left have already demonstrated the difficult transition from an electoral project to a government capable of devising viable solutions to the concrete problems of the present without betraying its political banners and roots.

The most recent parliamentary and presidential elections took place in October 2004. The left achieved victory in the first round, obtaining 1,124,761 votes, equivalent to 50.5 per cent of the total nationwide. Tabaré Vázquez, a socialist medical doctor and a charismatic leader of the coalition *Encuentro Progresista-Frente Amplio/Nueva Mayoría* (Progressive Encounter-Broad Front/New Majority, EP-FA/NM), began his five-year presidential term on March 2005. The coalition also succeeded in obtaining an absolute majority in parliament, electing 16 senators and 53 representatives.

[99]

THE UNIFICATION AND RISE OF THE LEFT

Political dynamics in Uruguay have historically been more open and inclusive than in other Latin American countries, since President José Batlle y Ordóñez established the basis of the modern state at the beginning of the twentieth century. Throughout most of the past century, Uruguay was considered a model for other countries in the region, given its advanced political structure and the scope of its social policies. Comparative studies have highlighted the strength and consolidation of its party system, in contrast to the weakness and dispersion observed in neighbouring countries (Mainwaring and Scully, 1995). However, after the Second World War, and particularly since the late 1950s, the country moved steadily towards social polarisation and political authoritarianism. The military coup of June 1973 was a long-expected response to the growth, unification and radicalisation of left parties and social movements.

In Uruguay, the political parties and the most influential social movements evolved from early waves of European immigrant workers, from which emerged a large urban middle class that has constituted the core of the hegemonic political culture in the country. Two major parties, the Partido Colorado (Crimson Party, PC) and the Partido Nacional or Blanco (National or White Party, PN), hegemonised politics almost without interruption and without competition from the 1830s until the early 1970s.[1] Both parties managed to articulate diverse forms of co-government in all spheres of the state.

In this context, the foundation of the Frente Amplio (Broad Front, FA) in 1971 was greatly influenced by the profound structural crisis of the political system, which ran parallel to the social and economic crisis. The Broad Front coalition constituted the organic space for the confluence of diverse political and social forces concerned about the rapid deterioration of the country's democratic institutions, economic foundations and living standards. The principal novelty of the FA was its peculiar identity as a political coalition that included elements as diverse as the populist reformism of breakaway sectors of the two traditional parties, the sexagenarian Marxist left and the various expressions of the new radical left.

The FA was conceived as a permanent front that would unite all the competing 'families' of the left under a common programmatic agenda for radical social and political changes. The founding document of March 1971 was signed by the two major Marxist parties, the Partido Comunista del Uruguay (Communist Party of Uruguay, PCU) and the Partido Socialista (Socialist Party, PS); several revolutionary groups, including the legal arms of guerrilla organisations; the Partido Demócrata Cristiano (Christian Democratic Party, PDC), founded by progressive Christian groups; dissident fractions of the two traditional parties; intellectuals; trade unionists; and nationalist military officers.

The organisational structure of the FA was originally conceived as a decentralised network of *Comités de Base* (Grassroots Committees) dispersed throughout the country. Regardless of its internally very hetero-geneous identity, the FA was able to keep itself united and survive a decade of severe repression (1973–84), with its principal leaders impris-oned, exiled or murdered by the dictatorship. In 1985, the return to liberal democracy meant the restoration of the political structure that had existed in Uruguay prior to the military coup: in the first post-authoritarian elec-tions of 1984, the Broad Front and the two traditional parties occupied almost the same ideological niches as in 1971.

The left's contribution to democratisation took many forms. First, before the electoral victory of 2004, the FA had succeeded in capitalising on popular discontent, offering an alternative space for participation in politi-cal institutions. Consequently, electoral politics prompted internal changes in both the 'social' and the 'political' left, which in turn promoted the partic-ipation of social leaders first as candidates and then as policy-makers within the framework of institutional politics. Second, the united left exposed the deficiencies of liberal democracy and proposed concrete policies for the broadening and deepening of democratic institutions. From the mid 1980s until the electoral victory of 2004, the FA was at the forefront of national campaigns centred on issues such as the full establishment of human rights and overcoming the authoritarian legacy of the dictatorship, resistance to the privatisation of state-owned enterprises, denunciation of corruption by public officials, and defence of public services and social standards under the pressure of neo-liberal restructuring.

It has been argued that the strength of the FA and of Uruguayan soci-ety as a whole is their 'old-fashioned resistance' and their obstinate oppo-sition to privatisation and the decline of the welfare state (Rankin, 1995). In a referendum called by popular initiative in December 1992, 72 per cent of the electorate voted against a law that would have permitted the privati-sation of practically all the state-owned enterprises and the consolidation of the neo-liberal project. This has been the only case in the world of a nation that has been consulted on full-scale privatisation and has rejected that possibility by way of referendum.

During the last three decades, the FA has dramatically increased its electoral support. It went from gaining 18 per cent of the vote in 1971 to more than 50 per cent in the first round of the 2004 elections. In the late 1990s, the two traditional parties, foreseeing the inexorable triumph of the left, joined forces to approve (with the support of some leftist parliamentarians) a constitutional reform that instituted a run-off between the top two presidential candidates. Anchored in an implacable political rivalry for more than 160 years, in 1999 the two traditional parties united in the second round of the elections to prevent the triumph of the left. The results were 44 per cent for Tabaré Vázquez – the candidate of the unified left – and 52 per cent for Jorge Batlle – the conservative bipartisan candidate. A similar strategy had been arranged by the two traditional parties for the 2004 elections, but was aborted by the left's victory in the first round.

The EP-FA was a broader political coalition in which the FA was the fundamental partner. It included centre-left movements that broke off from the traditional parties and some of the founding members of the FA that had left the coalition at the end of the 1980s (in particular the PDC) and that rejoined the left in 1994 as part of the Encuentro Progresista (Progressive Encounter, EP). For the 2004 elections, the breadth of the coalition of parties, groups and political movements that supported Vázquez's candidacy and the FA expanded further. The addition of 'NM' to the acronym identifying the left coalition referred to the formation of the Nueva Mayoría (New Majority, NM), the electoral and programmatic platform that brought together the EP-FA, the Nuevo Espacio (New Space, a social-democratic party formed by legislators that had split off from the FA at the end of the 1980s) and progressive leaders from the two traditional parties. The final phase of the process of reunification concluded in November 2005, when the left was already in government, with the reintegration of all the *progresista* parties and movements into an expanded Broad Front.

The process of amalgamation of the Uruguayan left is the most original and ambitious of all such attempts in Latin America. Since 1971, the FA has experienced a constant broadening of the number of parties and movements that comprise it. In 2004, when the left won the national elections, the FA was made up of 16 coalition members (the number increases to almost 30 if we consider all the groups that constituted the EP and the NM). In practice, considering electoral and programmatic agreements between the different fractions, the left platform was comprised of eight politically relevant sectors. According to the latest national election results, the largest sector (29 per cent of the total votes for the EP-FA/NM) was the Espacio 609/Movimiento de Participación Popular (MPP), a sub-coalition dominated by the former guerrillas of the Movimiento de

Liberación Nacional-Tupamaros (MLN-T), but also including centre-left sectors that broke away from the two traditional parties. Second place (18 per cent) was occupied by Asamblea Uruguay, a heterogeneous combination of independent left activists and ex-communists. The third force was the Espacio 90, a sub-coalition dominated by the Socialist Party. Fourth place (9 per cent) went to Vertiente Artiguista, a party whose name refers to the democratic and libertarian ideas of José Artigas, the national hero and leader of the nineteenth-century struggle for independence. Fifth place (9 per cent) was taken by the Alianza Progresista, the sub-coalition led by the vice-presidential candidate, comprised of breakaway sectors of the traditional parties and ex-communists. Sixth place (8 per cent) was taken by the Nuevo Espacio. In seventh place (6 per cent) was the Espacio Democrático Avanzado, the sub-coalition led by the Communist Party, which for several decades had been the main political force of the Uruguayan left, until the collapse of the Soviet bloc in the 1980s. And lastly, there were several groups aligned with the radical left, marginal in terms of electoral weight but with political influence in the unions, co-operatives and other organisations of the 'social' left.

For more than a decade, the undisputed leader of the 'acronyms soup' of the left has been Tabaré Vázquez, a renowned oncologist. An element that distinguishes *Tabaré*, as he is popularly known, from the majority of Uruguayan and Latin American politicians is the fact that he comes from a working class background. In the mid 1990s, political analysts had already anticipated the future influence that Vázquez would have on the electoral growth of the left, referring to his 'sympathetic bedside manner in politics, a warm empathy combined with a laid-back style that plays well on television and translates into an understated charisma in person', concluding that 'Vázquez is a post-modern caudillo, a leader for the 1990s, an era in which traditional politicians are viewed with disdain in Uruguay – as elsewhere' (Winn and Ferro Clerico, 1997:450–51).

In Montevideo, where half of the slightly more than 3 million Uruguayans live, the political hegemony of the left has grown stronger with each election. In 1989, the left won the capital city with 35 per cent of the local vote; in 1994, the electorate confirmed its confidence in the FA local government by granting it 45 per cent of the vote; and in May 2000, the EP-FA coalition obtained an overwhelming third victory with more than 58 per cent of the vote. In the local elections of May 2005 – the first after the national triumph of October 2004 – the left won eight of the 19 'provincial' governments of Uruguay, including the five most influential in political and economic terms.[2] The left won in Montevideo (with 59 per cent of the vote), Canelones, Paysandú, Salto, Florida, Maldonado, Rocha and Treinta y Tres.

Uruguayan researchers have offered various hypotheses to explain the consolidation of the left as the dominant political force in Montevideo and its continued growth throughout the length and breadth of the country. Some argued that the expansion of the left must be understood as a simple translation of demographic changes into politics, suggesting a 'natural' correlation between young voters and a left-wing identity, in opposition to the more conservative profile of older voters (González, 2000). Others pointed to more general socioeconomic factors, such as the growing popular discontent with the economic situation prevailing in the country (Canzani, 2000). Still others suggested more profound changes in the national political culture (Moreira, 2000). A final and clearly influential factor has been the solid record of good governance established by the left in Montevideo for more than a decade before winning the national government.

THE LEFT IN GOVERNMENT:
THE EXPERIENCE OF MONTEVIDEO

In March 1990, the FA took office in Montevideo with a programme that went far beyond that traditionally expected of a Uruguayan provincial government (see Chavez, 2004). One of Tabaré Vázquez's first measures was a decree that established the creation of 18 districts, with the opening of a *Centro Comunal Zonal* (district communal centre, CCZ) in each of the new local jurisdictions. The CCZs were conceived as politically and administratively decentralised units, responsible for a more efficient provision of public services and support for the local government. The process was strengthened by the organisation of *Asambleas Deliberativas* (deliberative assemblies) as the new space for citizen participation in local governance.

The initial design of decentralisation offered a participatory structure in which the institutional authority of each actor was unclear, but which was much more open and socially inclusive than the structure finally institutionalised in 1993. Toward the end of the first year, Vázquez had already inaugurated 16 CCZs and conducted public assemblies in the entire city, which discussed the priorities of each zone in matters of investment towards the five-year provincial budget. At that point, the level of participation was equivalent to that achieved a decade later in the much more famous participatory experience developed by Brazil's Partido de los Trabajadores (Workers' Party, PT) in Porto Alegre. Figures published by local researchers indicate that approximately 25,000 people participated in the deliberative assemblies (Portillo, 1991; González, 1995; Harnecker, 1995).

The definitive institutional structure of decentralisation was established in December 1993. The *Juntas Locales* (local boards) became the political and administrative authority in each of the city's 18 districts. Each *Junta* has five members, two nominated by the opposition and three by the ruling party, who serve for a period of five years. The *Consejos Vecinales* (Neighbourhood Councils) were institutionalised as advisory bodies, composed of between 25 and 40 elected members. The CCZs became de-concentrated structures for local administration and provision of public services in each district.

Shortly after the installation of the local boards and neighbourhood councils, bureaucratised participation and institutional formality replaced the enthusiastic and horizontal participation of the previous stage. Two new structures (one political and one social) mediated the interaction between city residents and the local government, and two parallel authorities filtered social demands, with little communication between the two. The limited power granted to the neighbourhood councils, in contrast to the broad political responsibilities reserved for the local boards, discouraged social participation, as indicated by the growing rate of desertion among the councils, which in 1997 averaged 45 per cent (Calvetti et al., 1998).

The various proposals for the design of decentralised institutional structures promoted by the leftist coalition before taking office shared the conviction that the opening of new channels of participation would be sufficient to catalyse the active and enthusiastic commitment of 'the neighbours'. That premise was flawed. In Uruguay, and in Montevideo in particular, there was no tradition of neighbourhood or territorially based social organisations comparable to that found in other countries. Uruguayan civil society has been historically strong and well structured by Latin American standards – with a noticeable development of trade unions, student unions, co-operatives and mutual aid societies, sporting clubs and human rights organisations, among other associations that make up the social capital of the country. But it has evolved in accord with sectoral rather than territorial interests. The leadership of the left failed to recognise that the principal identity of the majority of Montevideo residents was not that of *neighbour*, but rather that of *citizen* – or in many

[105]

cases simply that of *voter*. Many activists with a personal history of activism in left parties, unions, student organisations or housing co-operatives soon realised that the experience of civic engagement in local government at the neighbourhood level was a new and completely different challenge; one for which they were not prepared.

In addition to the fall in citizen participation, the evolution of the decentralisation process was marked by the permanent hostility of the two traditional parties, and the resulting need for negotiations between the left and the rest of the political system. Until 2005, the government of Montevideo also had to confront the political and financial obstruction carried out by the national government. Although Uruguayan legislation guarantees the governing party at the local level an automatic majority in the *Junta Departamental* (departmental council), the law also permits interference by the national parliament around any local issue. The left was thus forced to negotiate with the traditional parties the scope of decentralisation agreed to in 1993, which greatly restricted the radical, social and participatory character of the left's original project. From the very beginning in the early 1990s, as Veneziano Esperón (2003) has emphasised, decentralisation was one of the policies most obstructed by the central government, because it carries implicit new forms of articulation between state and civil society and between social and political actors. In addition, the traditional parties perceived decentralisation as a 'dangerous alternative' to the clientelistic political networks that they historically used for the recruitment of votes.

The right-wing opposition was made evident by the constant discrimination in the allocation of public resources. From 1990 onwards, while the government of the National Party continued with the traditional transfer of substantial public resources to the country's other 18 local governments, all of them run by the two traditional parties, Montevideo became the only local government excluded from such benefits. During its first term of government in Montevideo (1990–95), the left also attempted to reform the local property tax system, in order to make the collection of taxes more efficient and socially just. After a long institutional battle in parliament, which declared the project 'unconstitutional,' the FA was forced to negotiate a new proposal that erased the most progressive aspects of the original initiative. Nevertheless, despite all the external obstacles, and the decline in citizen participation, the government of Montevideo was able to introduce substantial improvements in practically all services and policies under its control.

Until the late 1970s, Montevideo was clearly ahead of the majority of other Latin American capitals. However, the economic and administrative crisis that began during the military dictatorship and continued during the post-dictatorship government of the Colorado Party (1985–89) culminated in a clear decline in the quantity and quality of services and a sharp deterioration of the quality of life of popular sectors. More than a decade of neo-liberal policies had produced a growth in poverty, social and spatial segregation, and the informalisation of the work force, resulting in a process characterised by Uruguayan analysts as the *latin-americanisation* of Montevideo (Veiga, 1989). When the left took office, Montevideo had become a dual city: on the one hand, a coastal area of high per capita income, with social indicators and services at European standards; and, on the other hand, a growing peripheral belt of squatter settlements (the so-called *cantegriles*) lacking urban infrastructure and basic social services. Toward the end of 1995, official statistics from the Ministry of Housing registered 111 irregular settlements in Montevideo, inhabited by 10,531 families and 53,800 individuals. The 'new face' of poverty in Montevideo involved 'growing levels of marginality, establishing new social problems linked as much to an increase in the level of violence between individuals as to the permanence and deepening of the structural effects of marginalization' (Gómez, 1999:364).

Besides growing poverty, when the left won the government of Montevideo, the city was 'full of puddles and potholes, dirty and dark, with problems of transportation, sanitation, the environment and housing' (Rubino, 1991a:6). Opinion polls from the period immediately preceding the rise of the left showed a very negative perception of the local administration: in 1988, 52 per cent of Montevideo residents regarded the Colorado local government as 'bad', 35 per cent considered it 'fair', and only 10 per cent described it as 'good' (Aguirre et al., 1992). Another poll from 1990 showed that 48 per cent of the local population perceived the Colorado local government as 'similar' to the local administration of the military dictatorship; 42 per cent considered it 'worse', and only 9 per cent saw it as 'better' (Rubino, 1991b). A decade later, similar surveys showed very different opinions. After seven years in local government, the left could boast of polls reporting that 73 per cent of Montevideo residents stated they were living in a 'better' or 'much better' city (Doyenart,1998). Other polls confirmed the highly positive image of basic services under the leftist government (Bergamino et al., 2001; Goldfrank, 2002). The positive evaluation of the left's performance was also supported by extensive data that demonstrated objective improvements in the quantity and quality of urban services (Chavez, 2004).

[107]

In addition to traditional services, since 1990 the government of Montevideo assumed responsibility for a broad range of social policies that were not part of the institutional agenda of local governments in Uruguay. Toward the end of 2001, the local government was investing approximately 45 per cent of its budget in social policies. While participation within the framework of territorial decentralisation tended to stagnate, many of the new social policies included a significant degree of citizen engagement. For example, from its first days in government, the FA decided to play an active role in support of local civic organisations. Among other initiatives, Montevideo established a 'land portfolio' to distribute real estate among housing co-operatives and other community-based organisations, resulting in a programme that benefited more than 5,000 low-income families. It also promoted a pilot housing programme aimed at the participatory rehabilitation of depressed areas in the city's central core. These initiatives implied close co-operation with the country's strongest urban social movement: the Uruguayan Federation of Mutual-Aid Housing Co-operatives, FUCVAM (Chavez and Carballal, 1997).

Other social policies included the creation of a network of primary healthcare centres in the poorest neighbourhoods of the city, support for a network of community daycare centres and NGOs providing services for youth and children, and the *ComunaMujer* programme, which seeks to create participatory spaces for interaction, dialogue and promotion of proposals for social change led by women.

At the same time, despite the serious economic crisis that plagued Uruguay from the late 1990s onwards, in the context of harsh reforms implemented by the national government, the salaries of workers also improved. In a decade of progressive local administration, between February 1990 and June 2000, the growth of the average salary for all Uruguayan workers (in both the public and private sectors) was 2.8 per cent in real terms, while the equivalent for the local government's workers was 101.5 per cent (Rodríguez, 2001). Still, the severe impact of the neo-liberal economic restructuring promoted by the national government directly challenged the sustainability of the new model of governance implemented by the left since 1990, in which the extension of social policies has been one of its strongest elements. In December 2002, the Montevideo Director of Decentralisation published an article warning of the 'test of fire' posed by the profound recession of the national economy, which resulted in an abrupt fall in revenues, caused by a massive default on the payment of local taxes (de los Campos, 2001). Years later, the city's finances are still in the red, but the investment in social policies has not been substantially diminished. Moreover, the prospects of co-operation with the current national government are quite auspicious.

In summary, between 1990 and 2004 the government of Montevideo showcased the capacities of the Uruguayan left to govern in a responsible and efficient manner, but it also showed the clear differences that can exist between initial political ambitions and the concrete results of a progressive government. The original objective of the left was not only to provide 'good local governance' but to expand and radicalise citizen participation as well. There is ample empirical evidence of improvements in services and policies in the city from 1990 to the present, but there are also clear indications that the process of participatory decentralisation launched in the early 1990s did not fulfil its potential. Benjamin Goldfrank has asserted that the design of the programme was crucial to the outcome; that the decentralisation programme 'aided the advance in city services by providing the government with better information about the citizens' needs and preferences' and that the process of decentralisation 'failed to boost civic engagement because the channels of participation offered did not convince average citizens that their input in public forums would have a significant impact on governmental decisions' (Goldfrank, 2002:52). In general, on the basis on my own research, I agree with this interpretation. However, it is important to highlight the fact that the implementation of the programme has been subject to relations of power that clearly transcend the limits of local government.

The correlation of political forces at the national level did not allow the left to develop its initial proposal for participatory decentralisation. The right used all its legal and institutional weapons – including the attempt to financially suffocate the local government – to prevent radical political transformations. On the other hand, the limited and declining popular participation in decentralised government has its roots in a political culture that tends to favour representative democracy over participatory democracy, consistent with the statist and party-centric evolution of the Uruguayan political system and the historic weakness of territorially based social organisations. This factor also explains the relatively 'non-participatory' profile of the current national government.

Several trends indicate that a new phase was initiated in March 2005, with the left also governing the country and several other provinces, leaving behind many years of confrontation with the central government. A promising development has been the re-launch of participatory budgeting, including the real transfer of decision-making power over public investment to the citizens. Since 2006, the local government allocates a fixed amount of resources to each of the 18 districts, to be invested in public works and social services at the neighbourhood level. The citizens deliberate in thematic or general assemblies, elaborate local development plans, and finally vote on a portfolio of projects to be funded by the city's budget. The example of Montevideo – including learning from the capital city's mistakes – has been followed by the other seven provincial governments run by the Broad Front. The departments of the hinterland, in particular Paysandú, have been experimenting since 2005 with innovative and so far much more ambitious forms of participatory budgeting and democratic decentralisation, providing significant space for citizens' engagement in local politics and policies.

FROM THE *ELECTORAL* PROJECT
TO THE *POLITICAL* PROJECT

When the left took office, it had to face the profound crisis of the country's social welfare structure. During the previous two decades, Uruguay had suffered a growing gap between the quality and reach of social policies and the magnitude of the social emergency. This was the result of the failure or unwillingness of previous governments to adapt the welfare structure to two main social transformations: changes in the labour market and changes in the composition of the family. In March 2005, the social profile of Uruguay was characterised by the rise of structural unemployment and the precariousness of labour relations, plus the emergence of new forms of family arrangements. The particular form of welfare state developed in the past century, built upon the assumptions of formal employment and a nuclear bi-parental family, was no longer appropriate in a society where almost half of the population was unemployed or in the informal sector, and where a growing portion of children were born in single-parent or re-arranged households.

The socioeconomic reality that the new left government inherited, despite the relative and very fragile recovery of macroeconomic indicators in 2004, constituted a daunting challenge. The National Household Survey (INE, 2004) revealed an exponential growth of social exclusion during the last coalition government of the two traditional parties. In 2003, 21 per cent of households, 31 per cent of the population and 57 per cent of children under the age of 6 were recorded as poor.

In addition to responding to the social and economic crisis, the new government was also expected to address the issue of human rights violations during the dictatorship of 1973–85. With the acquiescence of all four previous civilian governments, for more than two decades the military had enjoyed a level of impunity unchallenged either by the executive or by the judiciary.

The programmatic horizon of the left in government does not envision either the building of socialism or the introduction of radical changes in the power structure of Uruguayan society. The proposed transformations are much more modest and oriented toward 'consolidating a national project' (the title of the final declaration of the IV Congress of the Broad Front, passed in December 2003). The changes that the left committed itself to pursue for the five-year period, according to the policy synthesis presented by the FA immediately before the last national election, would be focused on five thematic programmes:

- *El Uruguay Social.* The social policies of the progressive government should be fundamentally oriented toward the sectors most affected by neo-liberalism, with precedence given to children and youth, women, people with disabilities and the elderly.
- *El Uruguay Productivo.* The restructuring of the national economy should imply an active and directive role for the state in order to ensure employment as a fundamental right. A profound reform of the financial and tax system should be implemented in an effort to redirect investment toward priority productive sectors.
- *El Uruguay Inteligente.* The progressive government should support scientific and technological development through greater investment of public resources, and should promote the return of Uruguayan researchers currently dispersed around the world. Additional resources should also be reassigned to public education.
- *El Uruguay Integrado.* The Uruguayan state should integrate itself into the Common Market of the South (MERCOSUR), Latin America and the world, promoting a truly national foreign policy with broad support from all political forces.
- *El Uruguay Democrático.* The new government should promote the construction of a new model of a transparent and responsible state, based on absolute respect for human rights, an all-out campaign against corruption, and the extension and deepening of decentralisation and broad citizen participation in decision-making.

Although the level of detail found in the left's manifesto visibly exceeded that of the traditional parties, the concrete measures that the government would implement to achieve the proposed transformations were never precisely defined by the Broad Front during the electoral campaign. For fear of losing votes with statements that could be interpreted as very radical, the left's programme was deliberately ambiguous. In the words of a radical activist (quoted by Peralta, 2004), before the elections of October 2004:

> Perhaps it is a growing pain that the left is confronting at a particular historical juncture. The risk is that the electoral project may grow to dominate the political one. The electoral project seeks to avoid disrupting the growth in support, from whatever sector, and to compose its ideological message in such a way that it appeals to everyone.

The moderation of the discourse of the majority of the parties and movements that supported Vázquez's candidacy included even sectors that not long ago had identified themselves as the most extreme component of the Uruguayan left, as is the case of the Popular Participation Movement. The MPP argued that the 're-founding of the country' and economic growth should be accomplished through the development of an 'authentic capitalism, which increases the amount of available resources before initiating the distribution of wealth'. The ex-guerrilla leader José Mujica, a former Tupamaro senator currently serving as minister of agriculture – and the most popular figure of the current government, according to many opinion polls – acknowledged and justified this moderation shortly before the election of 2004 (interviewed by Pereira, 2004):

> I do not believe that we would come to power, precisely now, on the crest of a revolutionary wave. We are almost asking permission from the bourgeoisie to let ourselves in, and we have to play the role of stabilising the government if we get there, because we are operating under the rule of law. A government of our own will have to manoeuvre. And furthermore, I sincerely believe that we have many things to do before socialism. And we have to send the right signals, from an electoral point of view. What do you want me to do, scare the bourgeoisie?

The left's social policy

The main policy response of the left to the social emergency from previous neo-liberal governments was the creation of a new ministry, the Mides (Ministry for Social Development) and the launching of an ambitious anti-poverty programme (Panes – National Action Programme Against Social Emergency), which includes the sub-programme Infamilia, centred on the implementation of an integrated strategy for the welfare of children, adoles-cents and families at 'social risk'. The implementation of the new institutional framework was not easy and it took several months before the novel ministry began to operate. The minister, a former communist senator, was repeatedly accused of inefficiency by the right, and had to face an initially cold reaction from the non-governmental sector (after dismissing in public the possibility of joint work with NGOs). Basically, the Panes consists of a monthly allowance – a so-called 'citizen income' – for indigent families. The programme is supplemented by two other initiatives aimed at facilitating people's re-entry into the labour market. The Mides distributes an electronic debit card to beneficiaries that allows basic expenditure in food and other essential products in local shops. The Rutas de Salida (The Way Out) sub-programme consists basically of training workshops and community work, whilst the Trabajo por Uruguay (Working for Uruguay) initiative is structured around the provision of subsidised jobs.

When the Panes was launched, the Mides expected to cover approx-imately 45,000 households, or roughly 190,000 individuals. Sixteen months later, in July 2006, the programme had reached 83,000 house-holds – around 350,000 individuals (Mides, 2006) – covering most of the country's deprived population. In general, despite early criticisms, the Panes has merited a positive evaluation, but with serious doubts about its prospects and long-term impact. It has been argued (Filgueira and Lijtenstein, 2006:64) that:

> Panes and Infamilia are clear attempts to overcome the real frac-tures of the Uruguayan welfare system. In this sense, both programmes should be acclaimed as good news, since they fill the voids that the system was not covering. The Panes was conceived as an emergency remedy, and Infamilia as a time-limited and highly focused model. The problem is that the current social voids are not conjunctural, not focused, and not just an emergency. They are structural problems, universal and long-term for Uruguayan society as a whole.

So far, the combined result of the anti-poverty programme is in general positive. However, a report published by two local researchers (Vigorito and Amarante, 2006) demonstrated with sound statistical data that poverty has indeed been reduced – although it still affects between 25 and 30 per cent of the population – but the worrisome parallel trend highlighted in the study was the sustained concentration of wealth.

The left also promoted changes in the field of education and health. The new government sought to strengthen the traditional centralised matrix of the Uruguayan educational system, which has historically assigned a major role to the state in decision-making, service delivery and financing (following a pattern advanced in the country as early as the nineteenth century). It also sought to reinforce the budgetary allocation and engage civil society in a truly deliberative process. The process began with the establishment of a multi-stakeholder committee, involving representatives of the government, the universities, the trade unions, and other social and political actors, which published a document for discussion focused on five topics: 'education for all', 'education and citizenship', 'education and development', 'education in the framework of the knowledge society', and the formation of a 'national educational system'. Throughout 2006 the committee promoted a long series of workshops and seminars across the country, making this process the most participatory example of the *Uruguay Democrático* undertaken by the left during the electoral campaign (in fact, it has been one of the few truly participatory processes promoted by the new government). The process concluded in December 2006 with the installation of the National Congress of Education, with 1,900 delegates from educational institutions and civil society organisations. Despite multiple criticisms from the two traditional parties – which criticised the process for being ideologically biased – and its non-binding status, the congress formulated long-term guidelines for a thorough restructuring of educational policies.

With regard to public health, the left had committed itself to promote a 'radical reform', aimed at the creation of a national health system. The new directives would be focused on the promotion of primary care and the guarantee of universal access to health services through the implementation of a national insurance system (*Seguro Nacional de Salud*). The new financial structure would be based on contributions from the state, employers and workers, and on fees (according to an income-based sliding scale). The system would also enhance co-ordination between public and private (the so-called *mutualistas*) health institutions. As in the field of education, the government promoted a deliberative process through the creation of the Health Advisory Council, composed of representatives of professional associations (medical doctors, dentists and psychologists), *mutualistas*, trade unions and consumers. During the past two years, several proposals have been elaborated and some improvements have already been implemented, but the bulk of the ambitious new national health system is expected to begin to be implemented in 2008.

In another crucial social area, gender and equality policy, the personal judgement of the president has prevailed over the programme of the left and progress has consequently been limited. A legislative proposal that would decriminalise abortion was initially discussed in Parliament in 2004, but never passed. Vázquez declares himself a socialist, but where women's rights are concerned he is a very conservative politician, who even threatened to veto the law were parliament to legislate on reproductive rights (Uruguay and Chile remain the only two countries in the region without progressive legislation on this matter).

Labour policy

Some analysts had predicted that the new government would clash with the union movement, despite their ideological empathy. Notwithstanding the generalised decline in unionisation – from 236,640 members in 1987 to 122,057 in 2001 – the relative political power of the different components of the workers' movement was quite varied when the left came to power. The drop in unionisation had been much more acute in the private sector, giving public-sector unions a dominant role in leading the workers' movement (Superville and Quiñónez, 2003).

The real change in labour policy began in March 2005, immediately after the left took office. After 14 years of not applying the national legislation, the government re-established the *consejos de salarios* (salary negotiation councils). The reintroduction of tripartite bargaining between employers, workers and the state was a response to the main demand of the labour movement since the early 1990s. This measure was followed by the sanction of a new law on the *fuero sindical* (full recognition of trade union rights) and the derogation of norms that allowed the police to intervene in case of occupation of the workplace during strikes. As expected, these moves provoked a quick and angry reaction from the business associations and right-wing parties, which accused the government of not being impartial and even promoting 'revolutionary' upheaval. In general, however, most Uruguayan entrepreneurs seem to have accepted the idea of a leftist government. Soon after the inauguration of Vázquez's presidency a survey published by the business media showed that 80 per cent of the entrepreneurs felt that the new government had responded to their expectations (*Búsqueda*, 9 June 2006). The government is praised for 'its moderation, its gradualism and the balance between the objectives and the limitations that the country must face, assessing as positive the agreement reached with the International Monetary Fund' (ICP, 2006:104).

Nevertheless, not everyone is happy; the antagonism of nonconformist business groups became evident at the end of October 2006, when the association of lorry owners – backed by the rural landowners' associations – decreed an industrial lockout, with a major impact on the availability of petrol, agricultural produce and other essential goods. The alleged reason was the government's intention to increase the price of diesel fuel to subsidise public transport. The labour movement responded with an immediate strike 'in defence of democracy'. The lockout was called off after three days, but it showed that, despite the current government's market-friendly approach, part of the national business elite still has no confidence in it. For its part, the labour movement – which overreacted to the action of the lorry owners, since democracy was never at risk – seems to be satisfied with the new policies towards unionised workers, but at the same time demands deeper and faster changes, as well as a turn to the left in economic policy.

Human rights and the military

In 1986, the Uruguayan parliament passed the so-called 'Law of Expiration of the Punitive Aims of the State', popularly known as the 'law of impunity', which was later ratified by referendum in 1989. Before taking office, Vázquez and all the principal leaders of the left had declared that the law of impunity would not be nullified, but highlighted the fact that the very same law – which the left had strongly opposed when it was approved in the 1980s – offered the possibility of allowing the investigation and eventual prosecution of human rights violations during the dictatorial period.

Almost two years after taking office, the actions promoted by the left in the field of human rights had the clearest impact. For the first time since the recovery of democratic institutions in 1985, Uruguayan society moved closer to the satisfaction of the long overdue claims for *verdad y justicia* (truth and justice). Within a few months, the country witnessed a series of events that had seemed impossible during the previous two decades. The leftist government followed three main lines of action. The first was the

search for *desaparecidos*, demanding a detailed report from the command-
ers of the army, the air force and the navy, and then promoting the work
of forensic anthropologists in places presumed to contain clandestine
graves from the time of the dictatorship (1973–85), including digging in
army barracks. Second, the government put an end to the arbitrary interpretation of the official pardon approved in 1986 – which granted the president full control over the judiciary – enabling the magistrates to
investigate and eventually prosecute military personnel and civilians
engaged in human rights violations. These actions led to the prosecution
of top leaders of the authoritarian regime (including the imprisonment of
Juan María Bordaberry, a former president). Third, the government authorised all foreign requests for extradition approved by Uruguayan judges.
The investigation of the fate of the *desaparecidos* produced only limited
results – only two bodies were recovered – but practically all the human
rights organisations recognised that the government had done its best to
advance as far as possible in the inquiry.

The resolution of the human rights debate was expected to have a
bearing on the relationship between the left government and the armed
forces, considering the track record of other progressive governments in
Latin America. In the case of the Broad Front, awareness of the need to
establish a specific policy toward the armed forces was also the result of
the historic presence of progressive military officials within the leadership of the left, including in particular the first presidential candidate
and historic leader of the coalition, General Líber Seregni (imprisoned
during the entire dictatorial period). The resolute attitude of the government over the investigation of the fate of the *desaparecidos* and the
prosecution of military officers initially caused noticeable apprehension
among right-wing hardliners, but in general the three branches of the
armed forces accepted the democratic chain of command and isolated
the dissidents. The process included the dramatic escape and subsequent
suicide of an indicted retired colonel, but this incident did not cause any
stir in the military establishment.

Reform of the state and public services

Another contentious issue that the new left government had promised to
tackle was the modernisation of public administration and the fight against
corruption. One of the recurring elements in the discourse of recent right-
wing governments in Uruguay, in tune with similar processes in other countries of the region, has been the constant call for 'reforming the state'.

Beyond rhetoric, between 1985 and 2005 few advances were achieved in this area in terms of greater efficiency, effectiveness, or transparency of the public administration. From the neo-liberal perspective, reforming the state was synonymous with privatisation and deregulation, rather than the promotion of real transformations in the state apparatus. Throughout the country's history the national government and the majority of local governments had been in the hands of the two traditional parties, which led to a symbiotic relationship between the state structure and the party structure, evident in the traditional allocation of positions within the public administrations on the basis of strictly political criteria, without consideration of the experience or technical aptitude of the functionaries. Nepotism, clientelism and the old-boy network permeated all levels of the state apparatus and the ensemble of political groups tied to the two traditional parties. Although the dimensions of the bureaucratic apparatus and the peculiar characteristics of Uruguayan society have prevented corruption from reaching the spectacular levels observed in other Latin American countries, the left had repeatedly claimed that positions of trust throughout the public administration have been used by the right as channels for personal enrichment or party benefit (see Caetano et al., 2002).

During the electoral campaign, Vázquez had argued that the eradication of clientelism, nepotism and corruption would generate enough savings to finance a substantial part of the social transformations proposed by the left, leading him to announce that as president he would order an audit of all state agencies and the eventual trial of those suspected of corruption. Other initiatives included the introduction of a more just and efficient tax system – including most importantly the establishment of personal income taxation – the de-bureaucratisation of the state, the modernisation of administrative practices and the elimination of superfluous expenses, in order to generate additional resources for investment in social policies and productive development.

According to Vázquez, the main aim of the left's first national government would be to *poner la casa en orden* (literally, 'put the house in order'), meaning a thorough appraisal of the public administration, including the search for proper information about financial accounts and irregularities committed under previous governments. Moreover, the broader proposal of *Reforma del Estado* is expected to be led by the Planning and Budget Office (OPP), a governmental unit with ministerial rank. The OPP, which until now has been an auxiliary unit, would assume new functions in the fields of long-term planning of public investment, local development and international co-operation. Another essential component of the reform is expected to be decentralisation, using the legal possibilities for the transfer of authority to departamental governments enabled by the constitutional reform of 1996.

In the area of public services, the most important transformation of this period has been in the field of water and sanitation. In 2003, faced with the negative results of the partial privatisation of the water network implemented by the government of the Colorado Party, a broad coalition of environmental, social and labour organisations created the National Commission in Defence of Water and Life (CNDAV). The name clearly alludes to the experience of Cochabamba, Bolivia (see Luis Tapia's chapter in this volume). In October 2003 the CNDAV presented 300,000 signatures to the Electoral Court demanding a plebiscite, which took place on 31 October 2004, parallel to the national elections. The result was indisputable: 64.7 per cent of the voters supported a constitutional reform that forbids privatisation of water and sanitation services. The change in the constitution established that: 'the public services of water and sanitation which delivers water for human consumption, will be a direct and exclusive responsibility of state institutions.' The reform also ruled that access to water and sanitation are 'fundamental human rights', and stated that the provision of such services should be done 'prioritising social reasons above economic reasons'.

Reversing the support previously given by the left to social mobilisation around the constitutional reform, the government issued a very particular interpretation of the legal change, stating that the reform would only affect *future* concession of services. The CNDAV demanded a literal reading of the reform, which would affect *all* concessions, including those that had motivated the original campaign. Referring to the existence of a bilateral investment protection agreement between Uruguay and Spain, the company Aguas de Bilbao took the Uruguayan government to court, claiming the violation of a legal treaty. The other affected company, Aguas de la Costa – a Suez subsidiary – also threatened to take the case to the International Centre for Settling of Investment Disputes (CSID) at the World Bank. Fearing a potentially long and costly legal process, Vázquez's government decided to allow the foreign companies to continue their operations in Uruguay, but Suez finally opted to abandon its investment in the country, after the government offered to buy all the shares controlled by private corporations – with the payment of more than $3 million in mid 2006.

From the viewpoint of the civic organisations and movements integrated in the CNDAV, the results of the negotiations with the European corporations – together with repeated declarations by high-ranking public officials about the possibility of eventual 'de-monopolising' reforms (and even partial privatisations) in other public services – are cause for serious concern. The solution achieved in the dispute about private corporate involvement in water delivery, though it implied the exit of a very powerful transnational such as Suez, clearly contradicts the letter of the constitutional reform passed in October 2004 (see Santos et al., 2006).

ECONOMIC POLICY: THE ONGOING DEBATE

In an interview published by the daily *La República* on 10 October 2006, the Minister of Economy and Finances declared his personal satisfaction with the government's performance, which he mainly attributed to the application of a very orthodox policy:

> If there is any better model, I am willing to study it, but I do not know any alternative. The results of the Uruguayan economy – from a productive, labour and social perspective – are quite good. The country is growing as never before, unemployment is the lowest in ten years, the rate of employment is the highest in 20 years, real salaries are growing in both the private and the public sector, poverty is falling and the distribution of wealth has improved. Because of all that we are satisfied.

The characteristics of the economic policy to be applied by the incoming government had been kept deliberately unclear throughout the electoral campaign. Vázquez and other leftist leaders had referred ambiguously to 'the need to promote productive specialisation and increase the quality of national products', 'changing the economic model', 'the fight against financial speculation', 'state support for technological innovation' and other proposals in the same vein – all of them 'progressive', but whose concrete implementation was not clarified in advance in any detailed manner. In presentations directed to business circles, Vázquez's economic advisors had indicated that the programme of the Uruguayan left would be affiliated with the Latin American neo-structuralist vision, which advocates international competitiveness, macroeconomic stability and outward-oriented development. Meanwhile, the left wing of the coalition argued for significant and urgent improvements in the value of workers' salaries and the primacy of the 'domestic social debt' over the foreign debt, with references to the measures implemented by Néstor Kirchner in neighbouring Argentina.

During its first two years in office the Uruguayan left had to overcome multiple challenges, but the end results have been fairly positive in macroeconomic terms. The variables that market analysts had expected to react negatively to a left government were not affected by the political transition. On the contrary, the economy grew significantly in 2005 (6.6 per cent) and 2006 (7 per cent), and macroeconomic stability has been secured (the inflation rate reached 4.9 per cent in 2005 and 6.4 per cent in 2006). The country achieved record figures in exports and imports, and the overall economic policy has been praised by global media outlets such as *The Economist* and *The Financial Times*. The rather austere five-year government budget was approved without any significant social opposition and the workers' demands were contained and negotiated with the PIT-CNT, the national union federation.

The positive indicators exhibited by the Uruguayan economy are not necessarily the result of a coherent and well-articulated policy. The right, while praising the 'responsibility' of the Uruguayan left in recognising the validity of 'their' orthodox policies, has criticised the government for not having pushed even further towards market-friendly reforms. From the left, analysts concerned about the 'neo-liberal digression' of the government have argued that the social costs of the current economic policies will be very negative in the coming years, and that the current good macroeconomic performance is simply the product of the favourable evolution of the international prices of commodities traditionally exported by Uruguay, and the economic recovery of its two principal neighbours: Argentina and Brazil.

Months before the election, in February 2004, the leadership of the Broad Front received a delegation of World Bank economists, who declared that they had been assured that the FA would 'honour all the international commitments inherited from the previous government in the event that they win the elections'. The FA, for its part, announced that 'honouring commitments' would involve some type of renegotiation of the foreign debt, and that the government would give priority to 'productive reactivation, the democratisation of the state, job creation and attention to social policies', without giving a proper account of the concrete measures to be implemented.

Economic policy is clearly the area in which the left has innovated the least. The government inaugurated in 2005 has maintained practically the same monetary policy, liberalisation of trade and rigorous payment of foreign debt instituted by previous neo-liberal governments. All of the government's plans for the long term are conditioned on sustained economic growth as a way to reduce the burden of foreign debt and free up resources for social policies. Top government figures even argue that the focus on stability and growth is indeed 'a left policy'. Supporting this claim, local political scientists (see IPC, 2006) have identified a package of four policy developments that would mark the difference between the leftist government and its predecessors:

- a renewed concern for improving the revenue-generating capacity of the state
- a progressive reform of the taxation system, which includes the introduction of personal income tax and the reduction of indirect taxes
- the implementation of the 'emergency plan' for the poorest segment of the population
- the modification of the institutional framework that regulates labour–capital relations.

A common argument used to question the viability of progressive transformations in a country so economically dependent on fluctuations in the regional and global economy is that which refers to the left's 'limited room for manoeuvre'. As we already have emphasised in the introductory chapter to this volume, this dilemma is faced by leftist governments throughout the region. In this respect, the following statement by the main regional advisor of the United Nations Economic Commission for Latin America and the Caribbean (ECLAC), Ricardo Ffrench-Davis (cited by Papa, 2003), is particularly relevant when one looks at the current prospects of the Uruguayan government:

> The problem in Latin America is that many people have become more neo-liberal than the IMF and do not defend the interests of the people. ... In some cases, our governments have been [stronger adherents of IMF doctrine] than the Fund itself and address fiscal deficits by attacking the nerve centres of equity and sustainable development.

In Uruguay, the debate over the left's economic orientation began immediately after Vázquez named Danilo Astori as the Minister of Economy and Finances of an eventual progressive government in July 2004. The announcement was made in Washington, during a dinner with businessmen at the headquarters of the Inter-American Development Bank (IADB). The nomination, and the messages the minister was to communicate in meetings with US corporations and directors of the international financial institutions, simultaneously drew the enthusiastic approval of the national and international right and criticism from the most radical sectors of the left. Despite his political and professional past as a radical leftist academic, since the early 1990s Astori has been moving closer to economic orthodoxy. He has publicly stated that neo-liberals are correct when they argue for macroeconomic stability or liberalisation of trade and investment.

The economic cabinet's main declared concern has been to guarantee stability and reduce financial vulnerability. Six weeks after taking office, at the annual meeting of the Board of Governors of the IADB, the new minister praised the policies of preceding governments and committed himself 'to the strict fulfilment of our previous commitments [meaning full and regular payment of the debt], productive investment and growth, which demands stability and therefore very prudent fiscal behaviour'.[3]

Such a stand is consistent with the government's sustained efforts to attract foreign investment and its sending of 'positive signs' to the global markets. With the same passion that in the early 1970s the Uruguayan left celebrated the 'Chilean democratic path to socialism' under the leadership of Salvador Allende, a significant segment of the contemporary Uruguayan left proposes to emulate Chile in the liberalisation of trade and the negotiation of bilateral agreements with Northern countries. The most significant move in this direction has been the proposal of a free trade agreement (FTA) with the United States.

The original communication of the government's intentions took place in December 2005, in parallel with the launching of a series of criticisms against MERCOSUR, of which Uruguay is a full member (together with Brazil, Argentina, Paraguay, and eventually Venezuela). For more than a year, the government demanded greater flexibility of rules of integration from the regional bloc, requesting a special authorisation to sign a bilateral deal with the United States – something that the current rules of MERCOSUR, which has a common external tariff, does not allow. Uruguay even threatened to leave the bloc altogether or become an 'associate member' (as Chile currently is), while arguing almost daily that the 'malfunctioning' of MERCOSUR caused the country heavy losses in terms of lack of access to international markets, stagnant employment and reduced access to foreign investment.

The discussion around the FTA highlighted the resilience of ideological differences within the Uruguayan left. Since the FA took office in March 2005, two factions have been competing inside the government. On one side, there is a faction led by Danilo Astori, backed by three political groups: Asamblea Uruguay, the Progressive Alliance and the New Space. This faction looks to Chile as the model to follow and supports the pursuit of bilateral agreements with Northern countries instead of regional integration. The second faction, without denying the shortcomings of MERCOSUR, argues that Uruguay should rely on a regional platform and strengthen its influence within the existing bloc. Such a view is represented by the socialist and communist parties, the MPP, the Vertiente Artiguista and the radical extra-parliamentary left. Vázquez's discourse oscillated between both views throughout 2006, giving mixed signals to both poles. Finally, facing a strong leftist opposition, Vázquez announced in December 2006 that his government had discarded the idea of an FTA, announcing instead the signing in January 2007 of a non-binding deal in the form of a 'trade and investment framework agreement' (TIFA).

The discussion around the TIFA is, despite Vázquez's announcement, not yet fully settled. Several officials have taken various opportunities to declare that the TIFA should be read as the first step towards a full-fledged FTA.[4] From the left of the Broad Front, those parties originally opposed to the start of negotiations outside MERCOSUR are once again raising the flag of anti-imperialism and have declared themselves on the alert against any move towards closer interaction with the powerful neighbour to the north.

Moreover, in parallel with the discussions about the pros and cons of liberalisation of trade, the government had to face a problem inconceivable at the time of Vázquez's inauguration. Soon after taking office, Uruguay engaged in a severe conflict with Argentina, caused by the construction of two cellulose mills near the Uruguayan river – the waterway that separates the two countries. The projects led by Ence – a Spanish corporation – and Botnia – a Finish corporation – are said to represent the largest foreign investment projects in the history of Uruguay: above $2 billion. Despite all the assurances of environmental safety and respect for technical regulations, the initiation of construction works generated massive demonstrations on the Argentine side of the river, including the constant blockage of the bridges linking the two countries. The conflict led to the presentation of claims to MERCOSUR – which finally opted not to intervene – and the International Court of Justice in The Hague. The World Bank – which will provide credit to the corporations – declared that the projects met its environmental standards and that emissions would be 'well below' accepted levels', but such statements have been contested by independent researchers.

Ence and Botnia will take advantage of cheap land and labour, plentiful direct and indirect subsidies for the establishment of eucalyptus plantations, economic benefits ensured with the concession of a free trade zone – exempted from taxation – and the unlimited and free use of water required to grow the trees and process the pulp for paper production. In addition, the Uruguayan state will improve roads and other facilities at no expense to the private corporations. The European companies will make use of a mechanism set up in the framework of the Kyoto Protocol, known as the 'clean development mechanism' (CDM), which authorises Northern polluters to 'offset' their carbon emissions by investing in the South. Faced with this reality, the left government has been accused of betraying its public stance on sustainable development. In exchange for unproven economic growth, it would allow the deterioration of environmental standards. In the words of the well-known Uruguayan writer Eduardo Galeano, these kinds of projects are inscribed 'in the purest colonial tradition: vast artificial plantations that they call forests, converted into pulp in an industrial process that dumps chemical waste into rivers and makes the air impossible to breath' (cited by WRM, 2006:3).

REVIVING UTOPIA?

Less than a year after becoming President of Brazil, Lula da Silva declared in December 2003 that the experience of governing the country had made him abandon some of the early dreams of his militant past. Around the same time, and facing the very real possibility of a similar electoral victory, Tabaré Vázquez declared to the Fourth Congress of the Frente Amplio that 'we have to revive utopia. We have to recreate the illusion. We have to build the future from the uncomfortable reality of our own times.' Such an idealistic proposal was, nevertheless, immediately followed by a much more realistic warning: 'aspiring to the impossible is as irresponsible and reactionary as resigning oneself to the status quo' (cited by Waksman, 2003).

Based on his personal and political experience as the first mayor elected by the Uruguayan left, Tabaré Vázquez was conscious of the gulf that exists between the values and political expectations that may exist *prior to* winning an election, and the options available to the left *after* taking office. This would appear to be illustrated by the experience of governing in Montevideo, where the original authentically participatory character of the first leftist local government in the early 1990s had to face the determined opposition of conservative forces, later evolving into a highly efficient model of 'good government' but without any radical dose of citizen participation.

Since the return to democracy in 1985, the FA had served as an 'escape valve' for the Uruguayan political system. On the one hand, the existence of an institutionalised and united left contributed to moderating the most extreme aspects of the neo-liberal project advanced by the two traditional parties – in particular, through its persistent resistance to the privatisation of public enterprises. On the other hand, it 'regulated' social discontent and thereby avoided explosive situations. It is no coincidence that, despite the rapid and generalised deterioration in the living conditions of popular sectors after the financial collapse of 2002, Uruguay did not suffer political crises like those experienced by neighbouring Argentina. Demands such as *'que se vayan todos'* ('throw them all out'), which catalysed the popular mobilisations on the opposite bank of the Rio de la Plata, were not echoed in Uruguay owing to the existence of an alternative political force to the discredited traditional parties.

Between 1971 and 2005, the Uruguayan left, which had always advocated strong state intervention in society and the economy, helped to strengthen the *Batllista* political culture that had made Uruguay a very peculiar society in the Latin American context. However, the current insertion of the country into a globalised economy puts into serious question the viability of reconstructing the 'Uruguayan-style welfare state' that the left had traditionally defended. In the context of limited financial resources, the current progressive government must respond to very diverse and contradictory demands from the different social sectors that make up the left's heterogeneous social base. The experience of Lula's government (see the chapter on Brazil in this volume), however, has already shown the virtual impossibility of a balanced response to the demands of social and economic sectors with distinct and even antagonistic interests.

Just two years after the left took national office in Uruguay there are already clear breaks and continuities vis-à-vis previous governments. The most obvious connections with the recent past are observed in the area of economic policy, where policies implemented by the Broad Front's administration are noticeably in line with those favoured by the right. At the same time, the left has achieved real transformations in other areas, such as labour policy, social welfare and human rights. In general, the current profile of the Uruguayan administration is more similar to the governments of Chile and Brazil than to the governments of Venezuela, Bolivia and Argentina. Moreover, the path followed by Tabaré Vázquez's administration seems full of contradictions and uncertainties, not having been able to develop a clear vision or long-term project.

If the Uruguayan left manages to maintain its current ties to civil society (which although weaker than a decade ago, are still quite active) without resigning itself to being an appendage of the government or a vehicle for silencing or marginalising internal political or ideological dissent, Uruguay would prove that the existence of a democratic left that does not renounce its founding principles is still possible in Latin America.

Toward that end, the Broad Front, as the backbone of the very pluralist and heterogeneous Uruguayan left, would have to assume the role of active intermediary between the government and the social movements, with the aim of contributing to the construction of political proposals that challenge the *TINA* mantra.[5] With this objective in mind, the FA would have to remain very much aware of its own history: a history of resistance to authoritarianism, resistance to privatisation, defence of the state patrimony, promotion of citizen participation, and convergence of practically all the 'families' of the left under a common programme and a structure for political action based on open debate and internal democracy.

It would be sad if, after so many struggles and so much sacrifice – including sustained resistance to over a decade of military dictatorship and two decades of the Washington Consensus – the Uruguayan left concludes its first experiment in national government fulfilling the programme of neo-liberal 'structural reforms' that the traditional parties had not being able to complete.

NOTES

1.   The names of the parties, *Blanco* (white) and *Colorado* (crimson), refer to the banners used during the bloody battles of the period between the 1830s and the 1900s. Both parties were born of the civil wars that followed the struggle for independence. At first, they reflected the conflict between the rural interior (the *Blancos*) and the city (the *Colorados*). Today, both parties share a very ambiguous and flexible centre-right ideology and are coalitions more than parties, with internal tendencies that range from the centre to the extreme right.

2. Despite the promotion of decentralisation in the constitutional reform of 1996, Uruguay remains a highly centralised country. There are 19 *departamentos*, including the capital city, Montevideo – which contains roughly half of the population. Therefore, the country lacks a specific 'municipal' level of government, as the departmental governments have jurisdictions over vast territories that cover both urban centres and rural areas.

3. Danilo Astori's full speech is available at <www.mef.gub.uy/noticias/noticia_200504_02.php>.

4. Before the left took office, the outgoing government had negotiated an 'investment protection agreement' (IPA) between Uruguay and the United States. The left, while in opposition, criticised such an agreement, but its formal signature took place in December 2005, when the Broad Front was in government. The signature of the IPA occurred in Mar de Plata, in the context of the failed FTAA summit. Paradoxically (or not?), Uruguay signed the IPA at the same time that the five presidents of the MERCOSUR (including Vázquez) led the Latin American opposition to the US-driven FTAA initiative.

5. *TINA*: an acronym of UK Prime Minister Thatcher's declaration that 'There is no alternative' to neo-liberal policies.

5 COLOMBIA

The New Left: Origins, Trajectory and Prospects

César Rodríguez-Garavito

The emergence of new parties and electoral coalitions of the left and right has reconfigured Colombian politics in the last decade. With this, it appears that the centrist inertia of Colombia's long-term two-party political discourse has been broken – a centrism that, discrediting open ideological debate in democratic arenas, has created incentives for violent political expressions. In the short term, this shift has made it possible for the labels 'left' and 'right' – common in other countries of the region – to become part of the lexicon of political discussion and analysis in Colombia for the first time in several decades. In the medium to long term, as we shall see below, the emergence of solid political blocks of the left and right may signify the transformation of the political system as a whole and force the traditional political parties (Liberal and Conservative) to reinvent themselves accordingly.

This chapter focuses on one of these new poles: the *new Colombian left*.[1] Specifically, it is concerned with the parties and electoral coalitions of the left that, since the founding of the Frente Social y Político (FSP, Social and Political Front) in 1999, have made unprecedented electoral advances, including the election of congressional candidates with some of the highest vote totals in the 2002 elections, the election of the first leftist mayor of Bogotá in 2003, and the highest vote ever for a leftist presidential candidate in 2006. The chapter also examines the articulation between these parties and social movements and other political forces that constitute a nascent leftist block, in opposition to the new rightist block that has formed around the figure of President Álvaro Uribe.

Given that the resurgence of the left is a regional phenomenon, as the other chapters in this volume demonstrate, this chapter places the study of the Colombian case in the context of the new Latin American leftist parties and movements. Consequently, it attempts to achieve a balance between: (1) an analysis of how the peculiarities of the Colombian situation have conferred certain particular features on the recent evolution of the left in the country; and (2) an analysis of the similarities and influences between the Colombian left and the new left currents that have emerged throughout Latin America.

In relation to the central themes of this book, laid out in Chapter 1, several theses inform the description and analysis presented in the pages that follow. First, I argue that the origins and characteristics of the new left should be understood as part and parcel of a 'thawing process' of the bipartisan political system dating from the nineteenth century (Gutiérrez, 2007). I further argue that an equally central component of this process is the consolidation of a 'new right' in the country. For this reason, throughout the chapter I underline both the parallel origins of and the contrasts between the two blocks, and the changes these have produced in Colombia's political system.

Second, with respect to the links between political parties and social movements, I argue that their articulation is still incipient and that, in this context, the parties have tended to be the most visible actors of the new left. This contrasts with the Bolivian and Ecuadorian cases – and even the Argentine and Mexican cases – in which social movements have been the original engines of the left's resurgence. It also contrasts with the Brazilian case, in which the articulation between social movements and the party was fundamental from the very beginning of the Workers' Party (PT).

Third, I attempt to demonstrate that the considerable electoral gains since 2002 by leftist parties in municipal, congressional and presidential elections occurred before those parties had consolidated themselves – that is, the political juncture has been such that the new left has had to attempt to organise viable parties *after* having reached Congress, the Bogotá Mayor's office and other democratically elected offices. In this sense, the Colombian experience contrasts with those of Brazil and Uruguay, in which the PT and the Frente Amplio (Broad Front) respectively went through processes of organisation and consolidation for several years before rising to positions of political importance.

Fourth, with respect to the proposals of the new left, I contend that its nucleus consists of a combination of, on the one hand, political negotiation and protection for democratic rights as a solution to the armed conflict and, on the other hand, its opposition – formulated in very general terms – to economic neo-liberalism. In view of the rights-centred and redistributive character of the 1991 Colombian Constitution and the repeated efforts of the Uribe government to reform it, the new left has tended to condense its platform in defence of the constitution. The Colombian context creates a situation – paradoxical in historical and comparative perspective – in which the left tends to take the lead in defending existing institutions and offer more detailed alternatives with respect to public order (a topic in principle more favourable to positions of the right) than with respect to the management of the economy (a topic in principle more favourable to the left in situations of deepening inequality and persistent poverty such as the one obtaining in Colombia).

ANTECEDENTS AND FACTORS BEHIND THE EMERGENCE OF THE NEW LEFT

Antecedents: the Colombian left in the twentieth century

Throughout the twentieth century, the magnetic force of Colombia's two-party system compelled the left to oscillate constantly between becoming part of the Liberal Party and establishing independent movements and parties. For example, the existence within the Liberal Party of political figures who sympathised with socialism, and the difficulty of creating a successful third party, made it possible for the Liberals to absorb the first Socialist Party and co-opt the vibrant popular protest movements of the 1920s (Sarmiento Anzola, 2001). The Communist Party, founded in 1930, also participated in various alliances with the Liberals throughout its history.

The same destiny awaited the Unión Nacional de Izquierda Revolucionaria (UNIR, National Union of the Revolutionary Left), founded by Jorge Eliécer Gaitán, who joined the Liberals in order to lead the most powerful populist movement in Colombian history. The assassination of Gaitán in 1948, when he seemed likely to win the forthcoming presidential elections, marked the beginning of the period of *La Violencia* (The Violence), and established the basis of the armed conflict that continues to this day. In fact, the Fuerzas Armadas Revolucionarias de Colombia (FARC, Revolutionary Armed Forces of Colombia) have their remote origin in the peasant self-defence squads promoted by the Communist Party in order to respond to the brutal state repression of *La Violencia* (Ferro and Uribe, 2002). In 1961, the

[131]

Communist Party adopted the strategy of the 'combination of all forms of struggle', the armed component of which evolved into mobile guerrilla warfare in 1964 following the state bombing of the peasant self-defence camps in Marquetalia (Tolima) and neighbouring zones. It adopted the name FARC in 1966 (Pizarro, 2004a).

The installation of an official bipartisan regime, the *Frente Nacional* (National Front), through which the traditional political parties agreed to alternate power between 1958 and 1974, closed off the electoral road for alternatives of the left (Chernick and Jiménez, 1990). As in other parts of the region, the blockage of the political system, the influence of the Cuban revolution and the ideological effervescence of the 1960s paved the way for the creation of guerrilla movements of distinct types. In addition to the agrarian-Communist guerrillas of the FARC, these included several *foquista* groups such as the Ejército de Liberación Nacional (ELN, Army of National Liberation, founded in 1964) and the M-19 (Movimiento 19 de Abril, founded in 1970), as well as groups that combined agrarian-communist and *foquista* elements, such as the Ejército Popular de Liberación (EPL, People's Army of Liberation, founded in 1967) (Palacios and Safford, 2002).

The strategy of 'combination of all forms of struggle' continued to leave its mark on the Colombian left during the 1980s, the scars of which are visible in the internal debates of the new left today. As a result of peace talks between the government and the FARC, the M-19 and the EPL, in 1984 the FARC created its own political party, the Unión Patriótica (UP, Patriotic Union). It consisted of demilitarised members of the FARC, militants of the Communist Party and other sectors of the left. The FARC's military opponents – including sectors of the Army and paramilitary groups – persecuted the UP to the point of bringing about its extinction. Although precise figures do not exist, it is estimated that close to 3,000 UP militants were assassinated, among them two presidential candidates (Sarmiento Anzola, 2001).

During the 1990s, the ranks of the unarmed political left were enlarged by members of guerrilla groups that signed peace accords with the government and demobilised: the M-19, the EPL, a sector of the ELN (the Socialist Renovation Current), the Partido Revolucionario de los Trabajadores (PRT, Revolutionary Workers' Party) and the Quintín Lame. From the demobilisation of the M-19 emerged the Alianza Democrática M-19 (M-19 Democratic Alliance, AD–M-19) which, despite a promising electoral start that included a high vote in the National Constituent Assembly in 1991, rapidly lost its political capital and fell apart.

The political and economic conditions
for the emergence of the new left

The historical trajectory of the left, briefly summarised in the preceding section, appeared to lead it into a political dead-end by the mid 1990s. The extermination of the UP marked the failure of the combination of political and armed struggles, as well as the abandonment of politics by the FARC in favour of a concentration on its military strategy (Valencia, 2002). Further, the short life of the AD–M-19 served as proof of the difficulties of creating democratic left alternatives in a context marked by the dominance of the traditional parties and the military and the dramatic decline in popularity of the armed left.

How does one explain, then, the emergence of the new left at the end of the 1990s? Before examining in detail the composition and evolution of the new left, it is worth considering four political and economic factors that, to my mind, created the 'political opportunity structure' (Tarrow, 1998) for the emergence of the new left:

- the atomisation and decline of the traditional political parties
- the resurgence of social movements
- the intensification of the armed conflict involving leftist guerrillas
- the economic crisis that began in 1999 and came to an end in 2002.

The following sections briefly examine each of these factors, as well as their impact on the political landscape.

The weakening of the traditional parties

The 1990s brought important changes to the party system, eroding the hegemony of the Liberal and Conservative parties that had its origins in the middle of the nineteenth century. On the one hand, while the political rules of the game embodied in the 1991 Constitution opened the way for the rise of new political forces, they simultaneously accentuated the tendency towards atomisation of the parties that had begun during the 1980s. In particular, the electoral rules stimulated the creation of small movements of short duration, based on individual political figures and linked to the parties only through vague ties of formal support and little or no party discipline.

These 'electoral micro-enterprises' were the mechanisms through which both the members of traditional parties and those of new independent forces accommodated themselves to rules that made it easier to get elected to Congress and other electoral bodies with a small number of votes based on atomised strategies, rather than by means of many votes for a unified party (Pizarro, 2001). By the late 1990s, this trend resulted in a situation in which, although the candidates supported by the traditional parties continued to receive the greatest number of votes in elections, such parties were in practice a collection of factions with little ideological cohesion or political discipline (Gutiérrez, 2001, 2003; Mainwaring, 2001; Ungar, 2003).

In addition, a growing number of citizens have distanced themselves from the traditional political parties, swelling the ranks either of independent voters or of abstainers. For example, the most recent comprehensive surveys indicate that while support for the Liberal Party fell from 44 per cent of the population in 1993 to 31 per cent in 2002, and Conservative Party supporters fell from 17 per cent to 12 per cent during the same period, the proportion of those surveyed that claimed to sympathise with another party or no party at all rose from 39 per cent to 55 per cent (Hoskin et al., 2003). Similarly, political parties received the lowest rating in surveys on the degree of citizen confidence in public institutions during the 1990s (Masías and Ceballos, 2001).

This erosion of the parties has facilitated the success of dissident or independent political strategies, both on the right and on the left. Based on an anti-political discourse that highlights honesty and moral leadership rather than adherence to any ideology or party, these strategies have put the traditional parties on the defensive (Gutiérrez, 2003). The most vivid example of this phenomenon on the right of the political spectrum is the electoral triumph and popularity of President Álvaro Uribe. Despite building his political career within the Liberal Party, Uribe presented himself as an independent candidate in the 2002 elections, and since then has cultivated an anti-party discourse and a government centred on his personal leadership and authority (Duzán, 2004a).

As we shall see below, an *uribista* movement has emerged around the President that includes both Liberals and Conservatives, and is discernible as a parallel rightist force to the traditional parties. In fact, this new rightist formation has become hegemonic in Colombian politics, to the point of garnering the steady support of 70 per cent of the electorate and public opinion, and managing to amend the constitution to allow for Uribe's re-election in 2006. On the left, the most important instances of this tendency have been the successful candidacy for Mayor of Bogotá of Luis Eduardo (*Lucho*) Garzón in 2003, and the unexpected second place finish of leftist candidate Carlos Gaviria in the presidential elections of 2006, overtaking the candidate from the traditional party that had thus far been the hege-monic political force in the country. As will be explained briefly below, the achievements of both the Garzón and the Gaviria candidacies were partially based on the support of independent voters who were receptive to a message opposed to traditional politics that, with different ideological tones, Uribe has also transmitted. This explains the intriguing fact that many of the Bogotá residents who voted for Uribe in the 2002 presiden-tial elections also voted for Garzón as Mayor in 2003, and then voted for Uribe again in 2006.

The weakening of the two traditional parties opened the way to the electoral gains of 'third' forces, following the establishment of popular elections for mayors in 1988 and governors in 1991. In effect, an analysis of municipal election results between 1988 and 1997 shows that third parties won in approximately half the Colombian municipalities, although they won more than one election in only 22 per cent of those municipali-ties during this period (García, 2000). Third parties have been especially successful in medium-sized or large cities, where independent voters have tended to shun candidates from the traditional parties. As we shall see below, this tendency became stronger in the 2002 municipal elections, in which third parties – the majority with left-leaning platforms – won six of the most important mayoral races in the country.

In addition to the rise of truly independent third-party candidates and forces, these trends have entailed the ascent of 'transitional' politi-cians who, having started their careers within the traditional parties, have reinvented themselves as 'independents' by creating or joining loose political coalitions. Uribe is the quintessential transitional figure in Colombian politics, having made his name in the Liberal Party and then splitting from it to launch a successful dissident presidential campaign in 2002. All in all, these processes have finally brought about the long-expected unravelling of the bipartisan system, in parallel to similar processes in other Latin American countries, from Venezuela to Ecuador to Uruguay (Gutiérrez, 2007).

The key short-term effect of the collapse of the traditional party system is the consolidation of three political blocks. The right pole of the political spectrum is occupied by *Uribismo* and the Conservative Party. The unconditional support of the Conservative party for the constitutional amendment that cleared the way for Uribe's re-election in 2006 is illustra-tive of this alliance. The partnership is also cemented by ideological convictions. As Conservative Senator Enrique Gómez put it, 'Uribe has made conservatism fashionable and conservatives have never felt as well represented as with Álvaro Uribe' (Duzán, 2004a:60). On the left side of the party system the main force is the Polo Democrático Alternativo (PDA, Democratic Alternative Pole), possibly in alliance with some left-leaning sectors or figures among third parties and within the Liberal Party. The panorama is completed by the Liberal Party, located in the centre, subjected simultaneously to the pull of both the left and the right, and consequently finding it difficult to maintain a minimum degree of organisational and programmatic cohesion.

The strengthening of social movements

A consensus exists among analysts of Colombian social movements regarding the relative organisational weakness and fragility of grassroots political mobilisation during the second half of the twentieth century – from the proletarian vanguard movements of the 1960s to the popular movements of the 1970s and 1980s – due in large part to the violent repression of popular organisations and leaders (see Archila, 2001). However, as in other countries of the region, Colombian social movements gained visibility and strength during the 1990s. Although on a smaller scale and with more limited influence than the indigenous movements of Ecuador and Bolivia, the *piquetero* movements of Argentina, or the landless movement in Brazil (discussed in other chapters of this volume), social protest in Colombia has gradually passed from the terrain of particular material demands – land, wages, public services – to more general political demands, such as civil and social rights, multiculturalism and opposition to neo-liberalism (Archila, 2003, 2004). As is demonstrated by the fact that the pioneering party of the new left (the FSP) emerged from the heart of the Central Unitaria de Trabajadores (CUT, Unitary Workers' Confederation), the shift by the union movement and social movements in general towards more universal political agendas helps to explain the resurgence of the left in Colombia.

The space opened by the weakening of the traditional parties has been occupied not only by new parties, but also by social movements. In the case of the indigenous movement, one of the central new political actors, the two tendencies have converged. In fact, as Van Cott (2003) has shown, the indigenous have combined protests and direct actions with electoral participation via ethnic political parties to advance demands for rights to territory, self-government and cultural autonomy. For example, the Movimiento Indígena Colombiano (MIC, Colombian Indigenous Movement) emerged from the heart of the Organización

Indígena de Colombia (ONIC, Indigenous Organisation of Colombia) in 1994. Similarly, the Alianza Social Indígena (ASI, Indigenous Social Alliance) – one of the most successful indigenous parties – has broadened its political agenda via alliances with independent, afro-Colombian and leftist sectors. It won the Medellín mayor's office in 2003, having emerged in 1991 from an initiative of the Consejo Regional Indígena del Cauca (CRIC, Indigenous Regional Counsel of Cauca), the pioneering organisation of the indigenous movement. Together with Autoridades Indígenas de Colombia (AIC, Indigenous Authorities of Colombia), these parties have not only put forward candidates for the seats reserved for indigenous peoples in Congress, but have also competed with growing success in the general elections for Congress and city and state governments (see Van Cott, 2003).

Although not as swiftly or as successfully as the indigenous movement, other social movements (among them the labour movement) have also intensified their protests, gradually converging towards a movement of opposition to President Uribe. Successful grassroots opposition to the 2003 government-promoted referendum to introduce unpopular political and economic reforms, as well as a mobilisation against the negotiation of a Free Trade Agreement (FTA) with the United States that lasted several years, are the most visible signs of the ascendance of social movements within Colombian politics in general.

The deepening of armed conflict

The intensification of armed conflict during the 1990s influenced the restructuring of the political spectrum and the emergence of the new left in two distinct ways. First, it marked the abandonment of the doctrine of combination of all forms of struggle, and the rupture between the armed left and the legal left. In view of the genocide of the UP and the adverse international scenario at the beginning of the decade – which saw the decline of Latin America's 'second revolutionary wave' with the signing of peace accords in Guatemala and El Salvador, as well as the electoral defeat of the Sandinistas in Nicaragua (Sader, 2001) – the FARC decided at its Seventh Conference in 1993 to 'devote itself fully to the war, cancel all legal political expressions, and commit itself to armed struggle... [Thus], the FARC was saying goodbye to politics' (Valencia, 2002:107). The result was a distancing between the FARC and the Communist Party and an escalation of the armed conflict, which included an increase in attacks against the civilian population by illegal armed groups of the left and right, and the deepening involvement of both in the 'war economies' of extortion, appropriation of land and natural resources, and drug trafficking (Pizarro, 2004a).

Although this shift toward war by the armed left increased the risk that the legal left might be stigmatised and discredited – with the consequent danger this posed to the lives of the latter's social and political leaders – abandoning the doctrine of the combination of all forms of struggle also created a space for the emergence of a left dedicated to the institutional and electoral path, and explicitly opposed to the armed path. This was the opportunity seized by the new left that emerged at the end of the decade, which constructed its political identity to a considerable extent precisely in terms of its opposition to violence from both left and right.

Second, the worsening of the armed conflict and the failure of the peace talks during the government of Andrés Pastrana (1998–2002) moved Colombians to the right. As Gutiérrez (2003) has shown, studies of voter preferences in the 2002 presidential elections reveal that Colombians from all social classes have moved to the right in their views on public order (military repression instead of dialogue with illegal armed agents) and the economy (economic opening rather than economic nationalism), and thus have abandoned the centrism that has traditionally characterised them.

This tendency is more favourable to the emergence of a new right than to that of a new left, insofar as the hard-line discourse toward armed political agents (especially guerrillas) naturally corresponds to the right. However, it has also opened space for the emergence of a new left, for two distinct reasons. First, the polarisation of the electorate and public opinion and the migration of traditional politicians toward the ascendant rightist coalition have created a political vacuum that has been filled by new parties and coalitions of the left. These coalitions have gained visibility as leaders of the opposition to the Uribe government, a visibility that they would not have had in the centrist political scenario of years past. Second, the ascendance and consolidation of *Uribismo* in power following Uribe's re-election in 2006 functioned as a potent incentive for leftist forces to overcome their secular factionalism in order to undertake joint political initiatives and present united electoral alternatives to their right-wing counterpart. Indeed, as the current secretary of the unified party of the left (Polo Democrático Alternativo) put it, 'the great unifier of the left has been Alvaro Uribe Vélez'.

The economic crisis and the resurgence of 'the social'

In light of the turn to the right in matters of security, Garzón's ascendance to the office of Mayor of Bogotá and the prominence of the left in the national political debate cannot be understood without taking account of the socioeconomic situation. As in other countries of the region, the economic and social crisis induced by neo-liberal programmes has created a political opportunity for the resurgence of proposals based on attending to basic needs, job creation and the redistribution of wealth.

Due to the tradition of gradualism and stability of economic policy, and the consequent absence of cycles of 'economic populism' and crisis typical to most Latin American countries (Urrutia, 1991), the adoption of neo-liberal policies in Colombia was less sudden than in countries like Argentina, Peru, Bolivia or Chile (Huber and Solt, 2004). Gradualism, however, slowed but did not avoid the economic crisis and the regressive social effects generated by the policies of structural adjustment.

When the crisis arrived in 1999, for the first time in a generation the middle classes saw their jobs disappear and a considerable part of the lower class plunged below the poverty line. According to figures of the Comptroller General of the Republic (Garay, 2002), 66 per cent of the population is below the poverty line, while 31 per cent live in extreme poverty. Unemployment oscillates between 15 and 20 per cent, and 60 per cent of the urban population works in the informal sector. Inequality is also dramatic: Colombia has the second highest concentration of wealth in Latin America, a region characterised by stark inequalities (Garay, 2002:xxiv–xxv).

Under these conditions, and in view of the focus of the traditional parties and the new right on public order, the left has taken the initiative in advancing a critique of this situation and offering proposals on social policy. It has managed to channel the generalised discontent with the deterioration of material conditions of life and has influenced political discourse and citizens' perceptions to the point that in Bogotá, following Garzón's campaign for mayor, the principal concern expressed by the population was no longer public order, but rather unemployment. In ideological and political marketing terms, Garzón's victory was based in large part on having detected and exploited this vacuum in the political discussion, and having consistently insisted on making social issues the core of his electoral message and his government policy. This strategy was replicated in Carlos Gaviria's presidential bid in 2006, which, as will be explained below, made social policy the central element of its platform.

EVOLUTION AND COMPOSITION OF THE NEW LEFT

The foundational stage

The political, economic and social factors examined in the previous section converged to create an auspicious opportunity structure for the rise of the new left, which emerged in 1999 with the proposal of the CUT, then led by Lucho Garzón, to create a Frente Social y Político (FSP, Social and Political Front) that would unite the different expressions of the democratic left that until then had been dispersed in innumerable movements and micro-parties. The Frente also emerged as an effort to unite the aforementioned social movements (including the union movement from which it emerged) and the political parties.

Given its goals, when the FSP was formally launched in 2002, it brought together a very mixed bag of leftist movements and organisations, among them the CUT, the Communist Party (from which Garzón had withdrawn after being one of its leaders between 1988 and 1991), Presentes por el Socialismo (Present for Socialism), the Partido Socialismo Democrático (Democratic Socialism Party) and Unidad Democrática (Democratic Unity). To these and other organisations were allied academics, members of NGOs, artists and independent politicians seeking to promote a left alternative to the traditional parties.

The Frente's electoral calculus was based on the auspicious results of the municipal and state elections of October 2000, in which it is estimated that 2 million voters backed independent candidates, among them six candidates for governor sympathetic to leftist ideas. With this background, which confirmed the rise of third parties, the Frente launched its first Congressional electoral campaign in March 2002. The success of the campaign led to the election of the former Constitutional Court Justice Carlos Gaviria to the Senate, with the fifth highest vote in the country, as well as the election of two Deputies, Wilson Borja in Bogotá and Alexander López in el Valle.[2]

To the electoral success of the FSP was added that of other leftist candidates who received some of the highest total votes for Congress, among them Antonio Navarro (ex-militant of the M-19), Jaime Dussán (a representative from the teacher's union) and Samuel Moreno of the Alianza Nacional Popular (National Popular Alliance, ANAPO), a popular party that has existed for four decades. These successes fostered the idea that the left could do well in the presidential elections in October that same year. Toward that end, an electoral coalition was founded, the

Polo Democrático (PD, Democratic Pole), made up of seven movements with very diverse trajectories: the FSP, Democratic Union, Vía Alterna (Alternative Path), the Partido Socialdemócrata Colombiano (Colombian Social Democratic Party), ANAPO, the Indigenous Social Alliance, and the Democratic Socialism Party. The PD backed the presidential candidacy of Garzón, who at the time was the head of the FSP. His political charisma and his consistent message of reconciliation and negotiated settlement of the war (which contrasted to the military solution proposed by Uribe) made Garzón a well-known figure to the electorate. He received 6.16 per cent of the vote, a percentage that, although lower than initially hoped for, was unprecedented for the left and placed Garzón ahead of all the other third-party candidates. For the FSP, however, the cost of electoral success and the formation of the PD was a premature emphasis on short-term political strategy and a consequent indefinite postponement of programmatic and ideological debate.

Following the presidential elections, the PD continued to operate as a political coalition. The senators and representatives from its various parties formed a caucus that intervened in legislative debates. Out of this collaborative work emerged a set of critical positions vis-à-vis the Uribe government that became the most visible and consistent expression of the opposition. Similarly, the caucus undertook new political initiatives, such as the elaboration of an alternative development plan in March 2003. The emphasis of this plan on social policy as a means of achieving 'human security' contrasted sharply with the National Development Plan proposed by the government. The latter, which was eventually approved, placed a higher priority on security policy than on social policy.

Despite these advances, the caucus was far from acting in a disciplined manner and its internal differences were a portent of the debate and divisions that would later arise. For example, regarding Uribe, divergences emerged between those who opted for outright opposition to the government's policies, such as Senator Gaviria, and those who opted for a position of selective critique and dialogue, such as Senator Navarro (see Navarro, 2004). With respect to the National Development Plan, political differences also divided the caucus when members of Congress from the teacher's unions (Jaime Dussán and Luis Carlos Avellaneda) decided to support the government's proposal. These two cases illustrate how, during its short existence as a parliamentary caucus in the first half of 2003, the PD did not manage to unite the multiple parties and personal leaderships existing within it. As Senator Gaviria explained, reflecting on the PD caucus: 'we existed more in people's minds than as a political reality, because we never made an effort to [identify] which projects we agreed on and which ones we did not' (2004a:38).

Under the pressure of the electoral calendar, differences over the pace of creating a new unified party were added to divergences over ideology and political strategy already evident within the PD congressional caucus (FSP, 2003a). The result was that only three of the seven parties within the PD decided to dissolve in July and unite under a new party, the Polo Democrático Independiente (PDI, Independent Democratic Pole), in conformity with the new electoral rules that sought to strengthen the parties. The three parties that dissolved were the Alternative Path, headed by Congressman Antonio Navarro and Gustavo Petro; the Colombian Social Democratic Party, headed by Senator Dussán; and the Democratic Socialism Party, led by the ex-union leader Angelino Garzón.

In practice, two more parties from the PD coalition – ANAPO and the Indigenous Social Alliance – supported the founding of the PDI. Although these parties did not dissolve in order to conserve their historical and social roots, their leaders (Samuel Moreno and Francisco Rojas Birri, respectively) joined the PDI as individuals. The most notable absence in this new party was that of the FSP, the original nucleus of the PD, which decided to remain an autonomous organisation, while simultaneously reiterating its affinity with the PDI in its official communiqués (FSP, 2003b). At its September party congress, the FSP ratified this decision and elected Senator Gaviria as its president. Democratic Union, the seventh member of the PD, followed the same path. As will be seen in the following sections, this separation between the PDI and the FSP would become one of the principal sources of internal debate within the left.

The PDI fielded several candidates for election as mayors and governors, and supported candidates that, without belonging to the party, were close to their ideological platform. Attention was focused on the campaign for Mayor of Bogotá, which Garzón entered barely three months before the election. Garzón's campaign was founded on the continuity of the message he had communicated during the presidential election and on the same political virtues that had given him national prominence (García-Peña, 2003). To counteract the fear aroused by economic elites and influential sectors of the media, who supported his main rival from the centre-right and warned of the dangers of a populist leftist government in Bogotá, Garzón communicated a centrist message of reconciliation at the same time as he effectively insisted on the need to prioritise social policy. The spontaneous tone of his speeches and his use of calming images (such as using the colour yellow instead of red in his political propaganda) fitted well with his centre-left ideology, which saw him criticise the old 'stale and propagandist' left and offer a social pact between classes based on a policy of job creation and social assistance (Becassino, 2003). Through a constant invitation to reflect on the social problems of the city, the PDI candidate merged his views on the war and on the economy into a single message of reconciliation which developed into a centre-left platform based on a 'social pact' similar to that proposed by Lula's PT in Brazil.

The message was credible, in addition, because Garzón came from modest origins (his mother was a domestic and he was never able to finish his university education) and his political biography, despite including a stint as leader of the Communist Party and the Unión Patriótica, demonstrated a consistent rejection of violence by both the right and the left (Garzón, 2004). The result was a dramatic rise in the polls, in which the number of voters who favoured Garzón doubled (from 23 per cent to 46 per cent) between August and October. With this latter figure, which amounted to almost 800,000 votes, Lucho Garzón became the first leftist Mayor of Bogotá, the most important electoral achievement by the left in Colombian history. The PDI, furthermore, obtained the highest number of seats on the city council (eight, the same as the Liberal Party), which reinforced its electoral success in the capital.

The political importance of Bogotá gave the PDI national visibility that surpassed that which it would gain from electoral results in the rest of the country, where the Polo won only one mayoralty (in Barrancabermeja, an oil city in the eye of the hurricane of the armed conflict).[3] The results were less auspicious for the FSP and Democratic Union: each won two mayoralties, but did not receive sufficient votes to elect representatives to the Bogotá City Council.

The separation between the PDI, on the one hand, and the FSP and other leftist forces, on the other, intensified at the end of 2003. In November, five Senators and four representatives belonging to leftist movements – FSP, Democratic Union, Movimiento Ciudadano (Citizens' Movement), Movimiento Obrero Independiente y Revolucionario (Independent and Revolutionary Workers Movement, MOIR), Partido Comunitario Opción Siete (Comunitarian Party Option Seven) and the Indigenous Authorities of Colombia Movement – formed the Alternativa Democrática (AD, Democratic Alternative), a congressional caucus distinct from the PDI with six senators and two deputies.

Between the left and the centre: the political currents of the new left

With the consolidation of the PDI and the foundation of the AD, the land-scape of the new left was consolidated, with two distinct currents visible within it. While the PDI explicitly sought to locate itself at the centre-left, AD identified itself as a leftist political formation. In this sense, at this stage the Colombian debate closely followed – and in fact was directly influenced by – the internal lines of division within the Brazilian PT during the Lula government.[4] On one side was a sector in which various prominent members of the PDI took an explicitly social-democratic, centrist tone. In the words of Garzón (2003a), 'it is a centre-left proposal and the centre has to affirm it.' In a similar way, when asked whether the elections of October 2002 had been a victory for the left, Navarro objected: 'I would say [it was a victory] for the centre-left' (2003a).

For Navarro, this was 'the left that seeks power; that is not content with being oppositional and symbolic. We want to govern and one cannot govern if one is not centre-left' (Navarro, 2003b). The prevailing mode in this sector was one of pragmatism, which implied a disposition to negoti-ate with different political sectors (including the right) and a rupture with the confrontational left, the left of the 'propagandist' critique, in the terms used by Garzón (2003b). This earned it a favourable reception from Colombia's principal media outlets, who saw in this position the possible modernisation of a left 'that fits with the contemporary realities of democ-racy and the market' (*El Tiempo*, 2003) and 'the globalised pragmatism of the 1990s' (*Semana*, 2003).

The explicit comparison with other Latin American leftist experiences has been essential in this task of differentiating between the centre-left and the left to this day. In fact, the creation of the identity and political message of the centre-left has been based as much on its explicit location within the spectrum of other Colombian and Latin American leftist parties and movements as on its concrete political proposals. In this sense, the central point of reference for the Colombian centre-left has been the Brazilian experience of Lula's PT. Garzón shares with Lula not only a militant unionist past, but also a gradual turn toward a vision of political and social reconciliation based on a belief in a grand pact among social classes and different sectors of civil society (Garzón, 2003a).

The political message of reconciliation that Garzón consistently defended during his campaigns for president and mayor implied, as in the case of Lula, a distancing from union sectors and an attempt to build bridges with the business class. For Garzón, the PT represented the left that is 'capable of governing', at the same time as it is distant from populism and capable of accommodating different ideological tendencies (Garzón, 2004). Therefore, within the Latin American spectrum, as Navarro (2003a) has maintained, this sector seeks to locate itself close to Lula's Brazilian model and the Mexican model of López Obrador, and distance itself from the Venezuelan experience of Chávez and that of the Bolivian social movements.

Another important sector explicitly positions itself to the left and attempts to differentiate itself from the centrist tendency. This was the predominant position, for example, in the FSP and the other members of the AD caucus. The process of constructing the identity of this position was intimately tied to the formation of an all-encompassing opposition to Uribe's government. For Carlos Gaviria, given that 'it is necessary that there is a clear opposition' to the right-wing government – with respect to both its security and its economic policies – the FSP sought to fulfil that function and, in so doing, differentiate itself from the centre-left position (Gaviria, 2003b). In interviews conducted at the time with leaders of the FSP–AD, this contrast was formulated by appealing to the distinction between a principled position represented by the left and a pragmatic negotiating position adopted by the centre-left.

As in this last case, those who prefer to call themselves simply leftists have had to distinguish themselves as much from the positions of the right as from the historical positions of the left, for example, through the rejection of guerrilla violence. This sector's goal of becoming the opposition – combined with the fact that it included groups with historical roots in the old left (especially the Communist Party) – made it such that the emphasis in its discourse lay more on criticising and offering alternatives to the proposals of the right than on distancing itself from the old left.

The distinction between the left and the centre-left embodied by the AD and the PDI, respectively, captures the main ideological and organisational split keeping the new left from cohering into a unified party during this period. However, it is important to note the existence of two additional currents that would come to figure prominently later on. An influential grouping within the PDI challenged Lucho Garzón's centrist approach – a 'pinkish, Lula-like project', in the words of one of his critics – and insisted on a rapprochement with the AD in order to create a unified party. Led by Gustavo Petro, the most visible congressperson from the new left, this current eventually gained the upper hand within the PDI. This was shown by the results of the May 2005 PDI presidential primary, in which Antonio Navarro, with Petro's backing, prevailed over the centre-left's candidate. Since this time, this grouping has become the main electoral force within the new left, as well as its main connecting node with social movements.

A fourth grouping of minority currents includes 'transitional' politicians from the progressive sectors of the Liberal Party and independent political forces. Although many within the PDI sought to attract this sector into an inclusive leftist coalition – among them Congressman Petro, for whom this fourth pillar was the 'leg missing from the table of the left' – it has thus far remained largely outside the leftist parties. It has only forged alliances with the parties on the occasion of specific campaigns, such as the failed opposition to the 2005 constitutional amendment allowing Uribe to run for re-election in 2006.

The unification of the left

As the division between the PDI and AD took root, the left seemed to return to its long-standing factionalism. Thus, it is not surprising that the process leading to the unification of the left took nearly two years, and that it was based on conviction as much as on necessity. The catalysts were the 2003 reform of the electoral law and the prospect of the 2006 legislative and presidential elections. While the former raised the entry barriers for small parties, the latter created a formidable electoral challenge in light of the new right president's skyrocketing popularity. Both, therefore, created a structure of opportunities that tilted the balance in favour of currents within the PDI and AD, urging their merger into a strong, unified party.

On the PDI side, the turning point came with the May 2005 national conference. In addition to adopting democratic and participatory rules for decision-making (see below), the internal vote was won by those proposing unification. Reflecting the predominance of this tendency, Senator Navarro was elected as its presidential candidate. Among the decisions made at the conference was the instruction to Navarro and the party's national directorate to push forward negotiations with the AD with a view to the organisational consolidation of the left and the election of a unity presidential candidate.

A similar, simultaneous process took place within the AD, leading to the formation of a Committee of Unity composed of seven delegates from the PDI and seven from the AD. The committee, which operated during the second half of 2005, effectively replaced the two parties' directorates and produced the Unity Agreement that sealed the unification of the left on 10 December 2005. This agreement, which to this day remains the most developed ideological statement of the new Colombian left, incorporates three consensus points that would come to constitute the core of its political platform:

- the broadening of welfare programmes
- the deepening of democracy
- the rejection of armed struggle.

This common ground allowed the transformation of the four above-mentioned political leftist sectors into currents within a single party.

Importantly, the new unified party – the Polo Democrático Alternativo (PDA, Democratic Alternative Pole) – imported the PDI democratic decision-making and operational rules, ranging from open affiliation to grassroots participation in the selection of candidates for municipal and national offices. As one member of the PDA national directorate put it, the new party was endowed from its inception with modern, participatory procedures that contrast with the heavy-handed, top-down modus operandi that had characterised the old Colombian left.

In line with such procedures, the Unity Agreement established that the PDA candidate to the 2006 presidential elections would be chosen by popular vote between the PDI and AD candidates (Navarro and Gaviria, respectively). The Navarro–Gaviria confrontation illustrated vividly the diversity of the new left. While Navarro was a former guerrilla member with a 15-year political and government career, Gaviria was an intellectual and former judge with no political experience beyond his recent stint in Congress. In March 2006, Gaviria surprisingly won the election and became the PDA's unity candidate. Running on a platform centred on redistributive social policies and all-out opposition to Uribe's law and order policies, Gaviria became Uribe's main rival for the May presidential elections, thus eclipsing the candidate from the traditionally hegemonic Liberal Party. While Uribe won by a landslide (62 per cent of the vote), Gaviria's 22 per cent was an unprecedented vote for the left and more than tripled the number of votes obtained by the Garzón presidential candidacy in 2002. With this result, the unified left gained national electoral prominence and came officially to occupy the visible space of the opposition within the Colombian political spectrum.

Thereafter, the unified party consolidated itself at its December 2006 national conference, which entailed two key developments. First, the PDA's membership skyrocketed beyond insiders' and outsiders' expectations. While party cadres and analysts expected 150,000 citizens to become card-carrying PDA members and participate in the election of delegates to the 2006 conference, a record number of over 550,000 citizens turned out at the polls. Second, the correlation of forces among the four above-mentioned sectors within the left translated itself into a new distribution of seats in the PDA executive organs. Senator Petro's current (which, as we saw, originally stood to the left of the social-democratic current led by Garzón within the extinct PDI) became the largest sector within the new party, with approximately 45 per cent of the vote. Garzón's centre-left group won nearly 25 per cent of the vote, as did the leftist group originally affiliated with the extinct AD. Other sectors represent the remaining, small fraction of the party's membership. Importantly, the fact that no sector has a majority has meant that alliances and consensus building have become the norm within the unified party.

THE PROPOSALS OF THE LEFT

For the contextual features mentioned at the beginning of this chapter, the two central issues in Colombian politics are the armed conflict and the economy. The rise of *Uribismo* is due, in part, to its capacity to articulate a coherent programme with a clearly conservative orientation on both fronts: a military solution to the armed conflict and a continuation of economic neo-liberalism. In this sense, the proposals of the Colombian new right are similar to the neo-conservative combination dominant in the Republican Party of the United States during the George W. Bush administration.

As Loïc Wacquant (2001, 2004) has shown in analysing these programmes, the combination consists, on the one hand, of the deepening of market liberalisation and, on the other, of marginal social policies and increased social control (use of the military and police force, increase in the prison population, etc.) aimed at limiting the destabilising effects of that process. In addition, in the Colombian case, the intensity of the armed conflict and the demand for security on the part of the public make it possible to postpone social policies, on the basis of the argument – popularised by influential economists – that violence is not linked to poverty and inequality, and that without public order social investment is wasted. The imposition of authority and public order, from this point of view, is the best social investment in the short term.

In this scenario, the viability of the left depends to a large degree on its capacity to articulate a political programme that offers an alternative combination of security, economic and social policies. In what follows, I briefly examine the content of this alternative and maintain that this analysis reveals an interesting paradox. The current conditions of the rightward shift by Colombians in matters of public order, on the one hand, and their growing concern for persistent poverty and growing inequality, on the other, would be more favourable to the development of an alternative economic programme by the left than to security policies different from those of the rightist government. What is occurring, however, is the contrary. As we shall see, the left has more comprehensive and concrete proposals with respect to security than it does with respect to managing the economy.

While, with respect to the first issue, the left has offered detailed ideas and proposals *for* 'human security' that are clearly different from those of the right, with respect to the second issue the ideas tend to gravitate toward a position *against* neo-liberalism, but without a detailed agenda of alternative policies. In addition, given the orientation of the 1991 Colombian Constitution in favour of the effective protection of civil and social rights – and the attempts of the Uribe government to limit both – in practice the positions of the left on public order and economic policy have been combined in a defence of the institutional order existing under such a constitution (see Gaviria, 2003a; Petro, 2004). Let us examine each of these elements in turn.

Security and armed conflict

In contrast to the military emphasis of the government's security policy, the left insists on a negotiated political solution to the armed conflict. Despite recognising the state's duty to combat all illegal armed groups, the left views military pressure as a component of a comprehensive strategy in which political pressure predominates. The proposal has four central elements. First, it promotes dialogue with the parties to the conflict, both paramilitaries and guerillas.[5] Second, with respect to ongoing peace negotiations such as those between the government and paramilitary groups, it highlights the need to compensate the victims of violence while stripping the paramilitaries of their economic, political and military power. Third, it includes the strategy of exercising political pressure on armed groups, through programmes that attend to the political and socioeconomic causes of the violence. With respect to the guerrillas, the proposal consists of the democratic development of the social agenda (agrarian reform, state reform, redistribution of wealth, etc.), which until now has been colonised by the discourse of the guerrillas, in such a way that the latter can be 'politically cornered'. For this reason, the left has opposed Plan Colombia, financed by the United States and designed to increase the military component of the battle against illegal armed groups and the 'war on drugs'. Finally, while the armed conflict persists, the left insists on respect for the rule of law, human rights and international humanitarian law. This implies, therefore, an opposition to the government's multiple initiatives that seek to suspend civil guarantees in order to broaden the repressive power of the state. Political polarisation and the shift to a military approach to the armed conflict have thus given rise to the historical paradox that, as presidential candidate Gaviria (2004a) has put it, 'the left has become the bulwark of liberal rights in Colombia'.

The synthetic formula that has frequently been used to describe this set of policies is 'human security', which implies 'economic, food, health, personal, environmental ... and political security' (PDI, 2003). This concept corresponds, therefore, to the reverse of the order–equality equation offered by the right, that is, to the affirmation that equitable social policies are the first step in restoring public security. During his term as mayor between 2004 and 2007, for example, Garzón insisted that his programme for fighting hunger in the poor neighbourhoods of Bogotá was a security plan, insofar as it was there that the urban cells of armed groups grow. The experience of the left in Bogotá also allowed for experimentation with alternative citizen collaboration and policing policies (more dissuasive than repressive).

Economic policy

The level of detail of the proposals and policies related to the armed conflict contrasts with the generality and ambiguity of the current debate on the left with respect to economic alternatives to neo-liberalism. As explained in Chapter 1, the difficulties of offering an alternative economic programme to neo-liberalism, given the international constraints and inherited national institutions of structural adjustment of the 1990s, are a common problem for parties of the left in the entire region, and have been particularly evident in the experience of leftist governments such as those in Brazil and Uruguay.

In Colombia, these restrictions are intensified by the tradition of gradualism and economic orthodoxy that make experimentation difficult, even with economic policies that are compatible with the postulates of neo-liberalism, such as the social and redistributive policies initiated by the PT in Brazil at the local and national level. In part because of the combined effect of these restrictions, and in part because of the lack of debate and of solid government experience, the Colombian left appears to oscillate between an opposition to neo-liberalism without offering concrete alternatives and a position favourable to economic liberalisation, 'but with conditions' that are generally not made explicit.

Despite the vagueness of the debate, it is possible to detect some general lines that characterise these two positions, as evident in the debates within the PDA that led to the economic policy proposals of the Gaviria presidential campaign in 2006. With respect to globalisation, the electorally dominant sectors of the PDA (i.e., those originating in the PDI and associated with Senator Petro and Mayor Garzón) tend to distance themselves from a protectionist position and favour cross-border trade subject to national and international regulations. This explains their defence of 'fair trade' based on Latin American integration as a platform for insertion into the global economy (PDI, 2003). A sector with less electoral strength, but supported by the mobilisation of teachers' unions, peasants and indigenous peoples against the negotiations of the free trade agreement with the United States between 2003 and 2007, is radically opposed to economic liberalisation. Spearheaded by MOIR, this current continues its historical defence of import substitution and a national class alliance similar to that which underpinned developmentalist policies between the 1930s and 1970s in various countries of the region (Robledo, 2004).

With respect to financial markets and the public debt, the predominant position remains within the orbit of long-standing Colombian centrism, and advocates a 'sensible and responsible' modification of the policy of debt and fiscal deficit management, without specifying the mechanisms for carrying it out (PDI, 2003). Moderate trade, monetary and fiscal policies imply the acceptance of what has been called the 'first generation' of Washington Consensus reforms (Naím, 2000). In this sense, the dominant currents within the PDA tend to follow the path of the Brazilian PT by accepting the monetary stability measures of that Consensus as a requirement for economic and social reforms. Other sectors such as MOIR appear less convinced of the virtue of this strategy (FSP, 2003a; Robledo, 2004).

Beyond macroeconomic stability, it is difficult to find a comprehensive inventory of economic proposals that the new left has discussed and promoted. In fact, this is a matter of ongoing debate, in which multiple objectives figure importantly, from agrarian reform to the democratisation of credit to food security (PDI, 2003; FSP, 2003a). More than detailed economic platforms, therefore, it is the practice of elected governments that make it possible to determine clearly the content and reach of leftist social policies. I will return to this issue in the concluding section in assessing Garzón's record as Mayor of Bogotá, which shows interesting developments with regards to economic and social policy.

The social base and electorate of the left

To whom are such proposals and political message aimed? The study of the internal discussion about the social bases of the leftist parties and recent voting for candidates of this political affiliation produces interesting results that contradict the traditional image of the electorate of the left.

Who votes for the left in Colombia? The most detailed and reliable figures on this question come from polls taken for the 2002 presidential election, in which Garzón was a candidate (Hoskin et al., 2003; Gutiérrez, 2003). The classification of those polled who voted for Garzón produces a demographic and socioeconomic profile of the leftist voter that is distinct from the working class voter. In fact, the typical left voter in those elections was undertaking or had completed university studies, was under 45 years of age, did not profess any religion, had a job or was independently employed, lived in Bogotá or in the eastern region of the country, did not have any attachment to the traditional political parties, and was 'politically sophisticated', insofar as he/she based his/her voting decision on an analysis of the campaigns and platforms of the candidates (Hoskin et al., 2003). Gender was not a determining variable in the vote for the left.

To these traits, two more may be added that are especially interesting. The first is that voting by social class – understood as a combination of occupation and income – demonstrates that support for Garzón came fundamentally from the middle and upper-middle classes, rather than from popular sectors. In fact, close to 50 per cent of those polled that voted for Garzón had incomes between four and eight times the minimum wage, and close to 25 per cent had incomes between two and four times the minimum wage. By occupation, approximately 50 per cent of Garzón voters were students, while the other half was divided roughly equally between employees and independent workers. On the basis of this result, analysts have concluded that social class was not a relevant factor in the vote for the left (Hoskin et al., 2003).

Although the preceding figures support this thesis in general, there are a couple of important pieces of data that suggest that in relation to a specific sector of the population – the wealthiest – the class factor determines its position vis-à-vis the left. In fact, a significant – though not altogether surprising – figure in the poll is that *not one* entrepreneur or voter with an income higher than eight times the minimum wage supported Garzón. This means, as Gutiérrez (2003) has emphasised, that for the upper class the only serious option was to vote for Uribe's new right. More surprising are the figures concerning another social class, which should constitute an electoral group favourable to the left: the unemployed and those who earn the lowest incomes. In the aforementioned poll, none of the unemployed voted for Garzón, and only 4.2 per cent of those earning less than the monthly minimum wage did so. Although it is possible that a similar study on voting for the mayoralty of Bogotá in 2003 would show some variation in voting among the popular sectors as a response to Garzón's social message, these figures suggest a considerable gap between the left and the electoral preferences of the popular sectors (who in the 2002 and 2006 presidential elections voted in massive numbers for Uribe), confirming the tendency observed in several countries in Latin America during the neo-liberal era (Roberts, 2002).

The second notable trait is the positions of leftist voters with respect to the armed conflict and the economy. Based on a right–left political index composed of the answers of those polled to questions about their views on the war (e.g., a political versus a military solution) and economic policy (e.g., liberalisation versus protectionism), electoral analyses have shown that Garzón voters were located primarily between the centre and the right of the political spectrum. In particular, it was surprising that, despite the left's insistence on a negotiated political solution, the majority of Garzón voters came from sectors that supported strengthening military repression (Hoskin et al., 2003). The paradox of this conclusion, and the fact that it contradicts the observation regarding the political sophistication of left voters, suggests that these figures should be viewed with caution. If valid, they reinforce the conclusion about the growing importance of personal image and moral and anti-party messages – at the expense of ideological positions – as dominant factors in the electoral preferences of Colombians. It is possible that a large proportion of the electorate, independent of its ideological preferences for the left or the right, is prepared to vote for a charismatic candidate who has an image of honesty and an effective political message. This would explain, for example, the fact that a map of the distribution of Bogotá voters who preferred Uribe in 2002 is very similar to that of those who backed Garzón for mayor in 2003. The same middle or upper-middle class student who welcomed the right's anti-corruption and pro-authority message was similarly receptive a year later to the left's conciliatory message with a strong social emphasis.

CONCLUSION: THE PROSPECTS OF THE NEW LEFT

The left's advance on the Colombian electoral scene is an open-ended history whose outcome will be determined in the coming years. For this reason, any conclusion about the new left must be equally open-ended and concentrate on an analysis of the prospects of the parties and movements within the political setting in which they must operate. Looking to the short and medium term, I outline in this section the central tasks and dilemmas of the consolidation of the democratic left in Colombia.

The strengthening of the party and the broadening of its social base

As I have shown throughout this chapter, the left's electoral triumphs predated its organisation. In this respect, the process of political construction of the Colombian left has been the reverse of that experienced by leftist parties in other countries of the region (e.g., the Uruguayan Broad Front or the Brazilian PT), which underwent a long process of incubation and experimentation before gaining control of the highest levels of governmental power. For example, Garzón was elected Mayor of Bogotá before the PDI was consolidated as a party. According to the PDI's former Secretary of Culture, the writer Laura Restrepo, 'Its weakness is not having a party' (Restrepo, 2004:1–10). In the words of the then president of the PDI, Gustavo Petro, the party has multiple weaknesses: 'lack of resources, lack of experience in government, [the co-existence of] multiple organisations that thus far have been crushing each other' (Petro, 2004:6A).

In this context, the future of the unified party will depend on three fundamental factors. First, the degree of internal democratisation will determine both its organisational strength and its political cohesion. In this regard, the developments and modus operandi of the PDA since early 2006 bode favourably for the consolidation of the new left. Indeed, the broadening of its social base and membership via registration efforts have proved highly successful, while participatory decision-making mechanisms – such as the use of primaries for the selection of party candidates – have taken root and helped solve otherwise intractable leadership battles.

Second, the construction of ideas and proposals through open debate may provide the indispensable 'ideological cement' for organisational cohesion (Fals Borda, 2004). Since, as a PDA leader put it, 'the left has spent all its time searching for votes high and low', there is still a glaring absence of ideological, programmatic discussion and elaboration. The continuation of this vacuum would probably dilute the positions and message of the sectors located at the centre-left and confuse them with those of the centre or even the centre-right (Duzán, 2004b), particularly in view of the opportunistic migration of members of traditional parties who, lacking any other option, attempt to position themselves in an amorphous 'centre-left' (Caballero, 2004). As for the currents that situate themselves more to the left, the lack of ideological proposals and positions attractive to the electorate may diminish their possibilities for influencing both the centre-left as well as the political debate more generally.

Third, the future of the electoral left depends crucially on the precise contours of its articulation with social movements. Given that the PDA does not have the kind of anchor in popular movements that other Latin American left parties have – for example, the Brazilian PT or the Bolivian Movimiento al Socialismo (MAS, Movement Toward Socialism) – and that popular mobilisation has been historically weak in Colombia, the link between the new parties and emerging social movements will depend on a deliberate strategy of building ties between them. This task remains largely incomplete, despite initial progress made in 2007 through the incorporation of selected social movement leaders – from unionists to afro-Colombians and gay rights activists – as members of the PDA's national executive committee.

The strategy of scales and the importance of local governments

As shown throughout this book, the left's credibility as an alternative for national government depends in large part on the performance of local administrations. This has been the case, for instance, with the rise of the PT after its initial government experience in the mayoralty of Porto Alegre, as well as that of the Broad Front in Uruguay after its experience in the government of Montevideo.

This highlights the importance of the 2003–07 Garzón administration in Bogotá for the prospects of the new left in the rest of the country. Starting with Garzón's government, the Colombian left has pursued the same strategy of scales – proceeding from the local to the regional and national – that characterised the ascent of the PT and the Broad Front. It is no coincidence, therefore, that upon winning the election, Garzón announced that he would implement three policies that closely follow the successful experiences of the PT in Porto Alegre: participatory democracy, the battle against hunger, and the creation of an Economic and Social Council (Garzón, 2003b).

On both of the key policy fronts outlined above (economic and social policy, and security), Garzón's mayoral administration put in place policies that, albeit avoiding leftist language and shying away from the more progressive approaches advocated by most PDA leaders, clearly delineated the contours of an alternative approach to the new right's policies implemented at the national level. With respect to the poorest sectors, the government launched social assistance programmes inspired by Lula's *Fome Zero* (Zero Hunger) initiative and has emphasised the expansion of access to public education. Crucially, Garzón's administration dramatically increased the budget devoted to the expansion and improvement of schools, and reversed the trend toward the privatisation of the educational system. Similarly, as mentioned previously, the Garzón administration experimented with a 'human security' model that included community policing and social services in the areas of the city with the highest poverty levels and insecurity.

The results of these programmes are widely regarded as a success story that helped make the left a credible government alternative. As shown by a comprehensive private-sector assessment of Garzón's administration, unprecedented progress was made with regards to access to education, poverty reduction and hunger elimination in the city. Toward the end of Garzón's term, 93 per cent of children of school age had access to the public education system. Further, the proportion of the population below the poverty line decreased from 46.3 to 28.5, while those facing extreme poverty reduced from 14 per cent to 4.5 per cent.[6] Such gains – which are substantially better than those made at the national level over the same period – help explain the fact that Garzón's popularity ratings remained at between 60 and 70 per cent throughout his term.

In sum, Garzón's administration was an auspicious beginning for the left's strategy of scales. However, in light of both the volatility of Colombian politics and Garzón's own efforts to distance himself from the PDA base and cadres, it remains to be seen whether it will translate itself into the consolidation of the left as a durable alternative in both Bogotá and other major cities of the country. A key step in this direction has been the PDA's decision publicly and unequivocally to condemn the armed left – in particular, the atrocities committed by the FARC, which have been widely repudiated by Colombians from all classes and regions. This has also led the PDA to distance itself from national and international political forces and governments that continue to have an ambiguous stance vis-à-vis the FARC. Together with the pending work of ideological consolidation, participatory decision-making and the forging of links with social movements, the strategy of scales will define the future trajectory of the unprecedented rise of the democratic left in Colombia.

NOTES

1. The qualification 'new' is used here in a descriptive – rather than a normative – sense. Consequently, the leftist currents that I examine are new insofar as they are recent, not in the sense of being superior or inferior to left alternatives of the past. As will be explained below, these and other labels – for example, centre-left versus extreme left, democratic versus anti-democratic left – are in themselves objects of debate both within and outside the contemporary Colombian left. Thus, in order to analyse these tendencies, it is necessary to make use of a descriptive typology that does not adopt a priori the language in which the political actors themselves express their agreements and disagreements. In Colombia, given the presence of the longest active armed left on the continent, a substantive contrast is superimposed on the temporal contrast between this old left and the new left: the new parties and movements reject armed struggle and make electoral competition and peaceful social mobilization the focus of their strategies. It is to this latter sector that I am referring when, for the purposes of style, I speak simply of *the left* in this chapter.

2. The electoral success of the FSP, however, was not accompanied by a similar advance in the unification of the left. The Movimiento Obrero Independiente y Revolucionario (MOIR, Independent and Revolutionary Workers Movement), a party of Maoist inspiration, did not join the FSP. At the same time, the Democratic Union, a party based in the teacher's unions, withdrew over differences with the Communist Party, while the Democratic Socialism Party withdrew over differences with the other members of the FSP concerning the participation of one of its leaders in the Pastrana administration.

3. In addition, the PDI backed 15 other Mayoral candidates who were elected (Santana, 2003:11).

4. On the divisions within the PT, see, among others, Sader (2004).

5. In fact, the dialogue with the paramilitaries was initiated from Congress by then Senator Carlos Gaviria, who was the author of the law that paved the way for negotiation with those groups (see Gaviria, 2003a).

6. See report of the *Bogotá Cómo Vamos Commission,* March 2007 (www.camara.ccb.org.co).

6 ARGENTINA
The Left, Parties and Movements: Strategies and Prospects
Federico L. Schuster

A BRIEF HISTORY OF THE ARGENTINE LEFT

An archaeology of the left in Argentina would take us perhaps to the nation's very origins. In 1810, the first national government was formed and within it there were already political and strategic debates that may have marked a distinction between the left and the right. Clearly, this distinction is closer to that of the then recent French Revolution – whose diverse positions were reflected intellectually and politically in the nascent republic – than to what we would today call the *left*. While these days such a label requires some definition with respect to Marxism, socialism and the like, in those days the *leftists* were Creole Jacobins – Mariano Moreno, Juan José Castelli or Bernardo de Monteagudo, for example. It was not until the end of the nineteenth century, with the influx of an enormous wave of foreign immigrants, that the modern Argentine left emerged. This occurred as a result of the first labour struggles, led primarily by foreign workers of European origin and anarchist and socialist inspiration.

The anarchist-led labour struggles resulted in the creation of important trade union organisations such as the Federación Obrera Regional Argentina (Regional Workers Federation of Argentina, FORA). The socialists, meanwhile, also had their origins in worker and trade union struggles. In 1894 the newspaper *La Vanguardia* hit the streets, and two years later Juan B. Justo founded the Partido Socialista (Socialist Party, PS). Much of the rest of the history of the left consists of the developments, internal conflicts, crises or divisions of these forces, particularly of the PS. In 1918, the *Partido Comunista* (Communist Party, PC) was created from a split by a left-wing socialist current, whose origins date to 1912. While the PS assumed a distant and critical position toward central figures of international revolutionary Marxism, the PC was Leninist and adhered fervently to the Russian Revolution. This enthusiasm was later transferred to the entire future development of that revolution, including Stalinism and subsequent processes. Only recently, around 1980, did the first internal criticisms of those positions emerge. The remainder of the traditional Argentine left – represented by Marxist-Leninist groups, Trotskyists and Maoists – was born out of the ideological and political critiques of the Socialist and Communist parties. These critiques were directed as much toward questions of theory and ideology as toward interpretations of historical events, both in the world at large and in Argentina in particular. With respect to the latter, there is no doubt that the left has always had great difficulty forging a unified position vis-à-vis the country's most significant mass political movements – *radicalism*, and especially, *Peronism*.

'Radicalism' refers to the Unión Cívica Radical (Radical Civic Union, UCR), a party that emerged from the radical factions of the Civic Union, which itself was a political movement that had fought for universal suffrage at the end of the nineteenth century. Founded in 1891 by Leandro N. Alem and Aristóbolo del Valle, the UCR quickly became the principal challenger to the conservative parties, which had long maintained the political hegemony of Argentina's landowning oligarchy by means of electoral fraud. Following the passage of an important electoral reform law in 1912 (the so-called Sáenz–Peña Law), UCR candidate Hipólito Yrigoyen won the presidency in 1916. The Yrigoyen government marked a breakthrough in the struggle for the political rights of Argentina's nascent middle class (specifically, small urban and rural producers, merchants and some sectors of labour). Later, the UCR came under the control of liberal groups, and even a degree of conservative influence.

Peronism came to power in 1946 with the strong support of workers in the nascent industrial sector who had recently migrated to large urban centres and undergone a process of proletarianisation in the wake of Argentina's rapidly evolving Second World War economy. Colonel Juan Domingo Perón, Minister of Labour in the de facto government created by the 1943 coup d'état, had won strong popular support after enacting a series of pro-labour measures. His support was such that in October 1945, after he had been expelled from the government and incarcerated, a large social movement with a labour and popular base demanded his freedom and gave birth to a new political movement that would leave a profound mark on Argentina's subsequent political development. Its political structure was built from a small party with union roots, the Labour Party, and once in government following the 1946 elections, it consolidated itself through the creation of the Partido Justicialista (Justice Party, PJ). There is no doubt, however, that it was through union support, with its nucleus in the Confederación General del Trabajo (General Workers' Confederation, CGT), that the party built its large power base.

Peronism divided the Argentine left time and again, and as we shall see, it continues to do so. While the majority opposed Peronism and saw in it an ideology directly tied to fascism, some sectors joined the new movement and considered it authentically revolutionary. Perón was re-elected in 1952 and overthrown three years later by a military coalition with civilian support from the dominant class and broad sectors of the middle class, as well as the principal political structures of the left. Resistance to the coup, especially to the proscription of Peronism and to subsequent military dictatorships, led many middle-class and leftist youths to embrace the Peronism that their parents rejected. In this way, a Peronist left emerged, which Perón himself encouraged from his exile in Spain (as he also did with the right, it should be noted). In the 1960s and 1970s, some of these sectors opted for armed struggle as a form of resistance and founded movements such as the Montoneros, the Fuerzas Armadas Revolucionarias (Armed Revolutionary Forces, FAR) and others. These and other left Peronist groups sought to promote a kind of leftist nationalism that coincided with that of certain elements of the left opposed to the traditional Socialist and Communist parties. Other elements of the non-Peronist revolutionary Marxist left, such as the Ejército Revolucionario del Pueblo (People's Revolutionary Army, ERP), also chose to take up the armed struggle at this time.

The 1955 coup led to elections in 1958, in which the Peronists were banned from participating. Arturo Frondizi, a dissident radical who benefited from some Peronist support, was elected president. In 1962, however, under heavy pressure from the military, Frondizi was forced to cede the presidency to Vice-president José M. Guido. The following year, new elections – this time with the clear abstention of the Peronists – brought the radical Arturo Illia to the presidency, only to be overthrown in another coup d'état in 1966. A new military dictatorship was installed, which endured internal conflicts within the armed forces under three presidents until 1973. In 1969, an event of great historical significance occurred. A large social movement led by militant trade unionists (Peronist as well as non-Peronist) and supported by university students confronted the military dictatorship in Córdoba, one of the three most important cities in the country. The event, which came to be known as the *Cordobazo*, not only dealt a strong blow to the authoritarian government, but also demonstrated the relevance acquired by a new social and political movement that linked sectors of the traditional left to the Peronist resistance.

In 1973, the Peronists were able to participate again in elections, although without Perón as their candidate. As a result, a Perón confidant, Alberto J. Cámpora, was elected president. Cámpora received strong support from the Peronist left, which provoked a deep crisis with other Peronist factions. Shortly thereafter, Perón returned from exile and attempted to restore some balance to the competing Peronist factions, but in poor health and overwhelmed by the variety of expectations he himself had encouraged, was unable to do so. His death in 1974 brought to power his wife and vice-president-elect, María Estela Martínez, who quickly fell under the control of right-wing Peronist elements. Argentina began to suffer the effects of the international oil crisis, armed groups renewed the violence they had suspended with the return of democracy, the crisis of Peronism deepened, and hard-line elements of the bourgeoisie took advantage of the situation to bring about a major reorientation of Argentine politics. In 1975, the latter won from the government a series of anti-popular measures that initiated the cycle of neo-liberalism in Argentina. The following year, they encouraged a military coup and assumed direct control of the economy, which enabled them to deepen the neo-liberal model.

The ensuing bloody dictatorship capitalised on middle-class discontent with armed groups to eliminate not only the guerrillas, but also any trace of popular resistance. Trade unionists, activists, students and intellectuals all fell victim to a new and terrifying form of repression – forced disappearance. Approximately 30,000 people disappeared in Argentine in those years, according to Argentine human rights organisations. The victims were tortured and assassinated, and their bodies were thrown into the river or the sea, or into unmarked communal graves. By 1982, however, the military government was facing a growing crisis, and in a surprise move, then President Leopoldo F. Galtieri decided to retake the Falklands/Malvinas Islands, territory claimed by Argentina that had been occupied by the United Kingdom since the nineteenth century. The military defeat in this brief war was the *coup de grâce* for the government, and initiated its retreat from power. In 1983, open general elections were held and, to the surprise of many, the UCR won, bringing to power President Raúl Alfonsín.

In the years that followed, the traditional left continued to fragment. In the 1980s, the Partido Intransigente (Intransigent Party, PI), which emerged from the more progressive elements within radicalism and enjoyed the support of other sectors of the left, became the third largest electoral force in the country. Shortly afterwards, it was a Trotskyist party, the Movimiento al Socialismo (Movement towards Socialism, MAS), that was in the political ascendancy. Nevertheless, the left continued to divide, and whatever electoral and political advances these parties had achieved were subsequently lost. Today, the political stage of the Marxist left presents the old Socialist Party united once again, the Communist Party weakened, the Partido Comunista Revolucionario (Revolutionary Communist Party, PCR) with some growth among unemployed workers, and the Troskyist parties severely divided. An attempt at forming a united front, the Izquierda Unida (United Left, IU) alliance, only managed to bring together the Communist Party, the Socialist Workers' Movement (a Trotskyist party) and several other minor parties, but with very little electoral success, and with at least as many leftist sectors outside the alliance as within it. The Argentine left has never succeeded in constituting anything similar to the Brazilian Workers' Party or the Uruguayan Broad Front, for example.

SOCIETY AND POLITICS DURING THE CRISIS

On 19–20 December 2001, Argentina entered a new and critical stage of the political, economic and social crisis that had engulfed it for years. On December 20, in response to popular pressure, President Fernando de la Rúa resigned and the country was left leaderless. Since there was no vice-president,[1] the presidency was temporarily assumed by Ramón Puerta, the provisional President of the Senate, who convened the Legislative Assembly to elect a new president to complete de la Rúa's term of office. The Assembly proclaimed Adolfo Rodríguez Saá, the former governor of San Luís province, as president. Rodríguez Saá, however, remained in office for only one week, during which he declared the country in default on its immense external debt. Meanwhile, in an attempt to generate a new base of popular legitimacy for the government, he initiated an open door policy of holding interviews with anyone interested in doing so. He succeeded in generating a strong populist image, but was nonetheless unable to restore calm to the country. The proximity to power of certain figures suspected of corruption during the early 1990s gave rise to a new wave of popular protests. The resulting social and political instability, along with the lack of support from his own political party (the Peronists), led Rodríguez Saá to resign the following week.

The procedure was repeated once more. Puerta resigned, ceding his position to Eduardo Caamaño, the President of the Chamber of Deputies. Caamaño reconvened the Legislative Assembly, which in turn elected Eduardo Duhalde (an important Peronist leader, ex-Governor of Buenos Aires province, and 1999 presidential candidate) as the new president. Duhalde assumed office in conditions of obvious weakness and his term was characterised by a climate of social mobilisation. As soon as he assumed office, he put an end to the programme of parity between the peso and the dollar (the so-called law of convertibility) which had been in place since 1991, thereby re-establishing the peso as the basis of the economy. The peso rapidly lost value, eventually reaching a stable equilibrium of three to the dollar. The transition to a peso-based economy created new conflicts with banks, debtors and creditors in dollars, holders of government bonds, and savers who had deposited dollars in banks and financial institutions.

In addition, during the Duhalde presidency, two young activists from the *piquetero* (unemployed workers) movement were brutally killed by the police in July 2002 during a protest demonstration. This event left an indelible mark on the government and Duhalde called for early elections for 2003. In the elections, which took place on 23 April 2003, the vote was split between various candidates, but the top three – who cumulatively won 60 per cent of the popular vote – were Peronists (Carlos Menem, Néstor Kirchner, Rodríguez Saá). According to the 1994 Constitution, with no candidate gaining an outright majority, there was to be a second round between the top two candidates (Menem and Kirchner). However, with polls indicating that he was headed for a major defeat, Menem decided to withdraw from the race a few days before the second round was scheduled to take place. Néstor Kirchner was thus proclaimed President of Argentina. With this, the country slowly began to return to a condition of relative politico-institutional normalcy. Nevertheless, many dimensions of the crisis remain latent within a reality whose basic hard facts – both objective and subjective – have not disappeared.

December 2001 thus marked the end of an historic period in Argentina. The crisis that expressed itself so vividly at that moment is the crisis of a regime of accumulation, one which has little historic precedence in modern capitalism because it is at once economic, political, social and cultural. Of course, as stated above, it was not new or spontaneous, but rather the extreme form of a process of structural deterioration that had been underway for three to five years. When the regime of accumulation that had been initiated in the mid 1970s was consolidated in the early 1990s, the processes of wealth concentration, privatisation of state assets and heavy indebtedness accelerated rapidly. The negative consequences of this regime were already apparent, especially in the high rate of unemployment and in the deterioration of labour conditions in general. The lack of investment in social development programmes (such as education and health), which had endured for more than a quarter century and only began to be reversed in 2002, were hallmarks of a model that has brought Argentine society to its present critical situation. In the political arena, the crisis has its origins in a democracy that from its restoration in 1983 was held hostage to economic and financial powers, a fact which severely weakened the capacity to construct any project that did not follow the latter's dictates. The over-ambitious promise that 'democracy delivers food, health and education' thus turned out to be impracticable.[2] At the same time, the period was characterised by a decline in the public image of politicians, due not only to their inability to transform the general conditions of the regime, but also to the growing suspicion of generalised corruption within the system. In this context, social protest constituted an increasingly important political resource in Argentina, to the point of becoming in a certain sense a normal part of the country's political activity. With time, however, social protest fostered a redefinition of the actors themselves and generated conditions of political accumulation that ultimately led to moments of rupture, the most important of which was undoubtedly that of December 2001.

It is noteworthy that the politicians failed to hear the message of social protest, or heard it so weakly that they continued to believe that the mechanisms of representation would function beyond the contents of real politics. It is striking that the message had not been heard, given that it was at its loudest between 1997 and 2000.

In 2001, the cards were already dealt. The Alliance – which consisted of the UCR and the Frente País Solidario (Front for a Country of Solidarity, FREPASO) and was the governing coalition from 1999 until its abrupt fall in December 2001 – advocated political reforms aimed at eliminating corruption and partisan patronage. This was a clear demand of the majority of Argentine society. However, from the moment President De la Rúa assumed power, it was clear that there was no clear will to act. The cost, in the end, was high.

In any event, as stated above, this crisis has a long history. It is interesting to note that the presidency of Raúl Alfonsín (1983–89) became a prisoner of its own inability to control economic variables and the aforementioned foreign and domestic economic and financial powers. Carlos Menem had two presidential terms, owing to a constitutional amendment that permitted his re-election. During his first term (1989–95), he engineered an enormous economic transformation (consolidating the privatisation of state-owned enterprises, transforming the pension system, introducing greater flexibility in labour relations, establishing a free market economy and controlling Argentina's chronic inflation). As a result of these measures, as well as his own political capacity, he was able to attain a hegemonic position. But the result of this deepening of the neo-liberal model and the alliance with sectors of the upper bourgeoisie and the finance industry was a profoundly unequal and exclusive society, with high unemployment, a loss of national productive capacity and an immense transfer of resources, not only from the working and middle classes to the upper classes but also from national to international interests, with constant capital volatility.

In this sense, the crisis could not have come as a surprise; on the contrary, its unfolding was an open secret. From an economic perspective, it was known that reduced productivity, capital volatility, a fixed exchange rate and high state debt were leading to disaster. From a social perspective, beginning in the early 1990s, every study predicted that the model would produce a highly exclusionary society. From a political point of view, expectations for the Alliance were heightened by the disillusionment of vast sectors of the citizenry due to Alfonsín's inability to resolve the country's economic and political problems, the distrust arising from charges of corruption against the Menem government, and the resulting social outcomes. Perhaps few realised that this was the final chance, that the crisis of the Alliance would mean the crisis of the entire political model. And, as mentioned above, the Alliance did indeed fail.

One might debate why this occurred, but there is no doubt that the Alliance was not able to manage the complex economic situation, nor could it produce the promised political change, or even govern within the existing parameters. It was therefore not surprising that in the social protests that followed, an idea developed that came to be expressed in one great mass slogan: *que se vayan todos, que no quede ni uno solo* ('the lot of them must go, not a single one must remain'). The cumulative social disillusionment with the UCR of Alfonsín, the PJ of Menem and the Alliance of de la Rúa gave rise to the idea that there was no place within the structure of the Argentine political system for the representation of broad and diverse social demands. Today this has changed substantially, although still only partially and without full consolidation, as a result of the institutional restoration produced by the presidential election of April 2003 and, in particular, the performance of the Kirchner government.

From the point of view of the social forces involved in the protests, the events that followed December 2001, as well as the explosion of the situation described above, were also not extreme or unexpected. My own work, as well as that of my colleagues,[3] reveals a growth of protests in Argentina (at first in quantity, then in strength, and most recently in organisation) for more than half a decade. Indeed, since mid 2001, the combination of social, economic and political conditions (unemployment, unprecedented inequality, extreme poverty, recession, fiscal deficits, external debt, lack of economic productivity, weak governments, crisis of representation, growth in social protest forces, social conflict, etcetera) has been such that events like those that occurred at the end of that year have come to be expected. However, those of us who dedicate ourselves to the social sciences know that it is one thing to be able to anticipate future conditions and something very different to know exactly how the future will unfold. Indeed, the concrete form the future takes often surprises us, even when we are aware of the conditions that bring it about. That concrete form is what occurred in Argentina and is characterised by the social protests that in December 2001 dealt the *coup de grâce* to an already weak president and since then have given rise to an unending state of social turmoil and mobilisation. In fact, existing narratives from the days that followed tell the story of multiple changes in the meaning of the conflict, and finally its precarious stabilisation (Schuster et al., 2002).

At that time, the *cacerolazo* was progressively transformed into the expression of at least two fragments of the middle classes.[4] One of these engaged in an all-out battle to regain its confiscated savings, which had been lost in the collapse of the financial system. The other was the *asambleas* (assemblies), which permitted the continuation of the conflict and thus avoided their closure as a consequence of a process of deliberation that infinitely broadened the multiple meanings of the *cacerolazo*. The *asambleas* nevertheless progressively closed in on themselves as they attempted to find the central nucleus and objectives of these new forms of political participation.

Both phenomena nonetheless represented a substantial change in recent Argentine politics. On the one hand, the capacity for protest by furious savers could constitute the beginning of a political movement of consumers who are responsible, disillusioned, and willing to rein in unbridled capitalism, with the peculiarities that this represents in Argentina. On the other hand, the assemblies may have constituted themselves as poles of political participation that once again provide content to urban neighbourhood politics. Both things occurred only partially, although with greater success in the latter case than in the former. The assemblies, although diminished in size by the inexorable wear that takes place in the absence of a stable organisation capable of guaranteeing the continuity of this type of social and political practices, survived in larger numbers than one might have expected at the time. In that sense, the few remaining at the moment of writing continue to be an original form of territorial participatory collective action and of broadening of the public debate – that is, of political spaces in the strict sense (Arendt, 1993). The mobilisation of the savers exhausted itself, especially when a few of their complaints received some response, even if this response did not seem entirely satisfactory to all those involved. In this case, then, collective action dissolved into a more straightforward individualism.

In a 1985 article, the historian Charles Tilly (1990) suggestively analysed the fallacies that theoretical explanations of collective action offer to explain situations of intense political instability, such as revolts, uprisings, crises or cycles of mobilisation. Much like the spring of 1906 in France, the Argentine crisis of December 2001 gave the impression of uncontrolled disorder. To a large degree, these accounts of the facts – among which the uprising represents the paradigm in the recent history of protests in Argentina – are constructed on the basis of prejudices and stigmatising definitions that governing authorities and elites often have with respect to social mobilisations. However, they also rely on visions that homogenise all forms of popular struggle based on mobilisation and protest, ignoring the 'details' that Tilly seeks to recover and thus precluding a denser version of the facts that contains, at a minimum, the perspective of the actors themselves.

The expectations that lower and middle classes had first of *Alfonsinismo* and then of *Menemismo* ended with resounding disappointment for the majority of their voters. The Alliance, as a political novelty, appeared as the last hope of the existing political system, even if many of its own members did not see it. Its failure exhausted the possibilities for a system that from then on was unable to regain legitimacy in the eyes of the citizenry. Only the left was spared from the shipwreck, but the inability of the majority of the parties of the left to generate a broad-based political option for building popular power (in the fashion of the PT in Brazil or the Broad Front in Uruguay) represented a lost historical opportunity. In the meantime, new forms of political construction, built from within society rather than the political system, emerged on the Argentine scene with unusual force. *Piqueteros*, *caceroleros* and *asambleístas*, arising from the popular organisation of workers and the middle classes, are the result of the crisis of political parties on the one hand, and the crisis of the traditional unions, on the other. In particular, the *piquetero* movement is a product of a form of accumulation of social and political experience that dates back to the mid 1990s and reached its full development in 2001.

THE POLITICAL LEGACY OF THE CRISIS

The power of protest has been perhaps one of the most important lessons derived from the events of December 2001. The protests appeared with unprecedented strength and ended by hastening the resignation of an already weakened president. But the power of protest is nothing new. Protests have produced similar effects in other parts of the world and, to a certain degree, in Argentina as well. It is worth recalling the impact of the labour strikes of the early twentieth century, or of the mass movement of 17 October 1945, or of the *Cordobazo* of 1969. It is enough to refer to the fact that, as already noted, during the 1990s three provincial governors fell under a wave of diverse protests.

On the other hand, the scene for December 2001 had been set several months earlier. It had been set in economic, political and social terms by the inability of the government to confront a recession that had been sharpening for three years, by the rising levels of unemployment and by a heavy transfer of financial resources abroad. With respect to the structure of the protests, one could say that toward August, with the organisation of the *piquetero* bloc, the situation was set for an outcome like the one that occurred. In any case, it is true that the December events involved a group of actors (sectors of the middle class) and types of actions (*cacerolazos* and popular assemblies) that resulted in a political and social novelty (Schuster and Pereyra, 2001).

Social protest has been undergoing a process of transformation since the return to democracy in 1983 and has included moments of growing intensity and others of decline. This corresponds to what specialists have referred to as *cycles of protest* (Tarrow, 1998). Of course, public opinion is influenced by the moments of growth, despite the fact that studies of social protest in democratic Argentina (1983–99) demonstrate the continuous existence of protests throughout the entire period.[5] Those studies make it possible to construct the following pattern in the concentration of protests.

Between 1983 and 1988, 75 per cent of the protests were led by unions, especially industrial unions. Beyond those, only the protests linked to human rights attained significant numbers during this period. It was a time when the public was hoping for punishment for the crimes of the dictatorship and knowledge of the fate of the disappeared, and the great majority was alarmed by any attempt to destabilise the system. There are two axes along which protests can be categorised: the *social-economic-labour* and the *political-citizen* axes. The first includes labour mobilisation, which is linked to the world of work, to the transformations of the Argentine economy, and in large measure to the expectations generated by the democratic transition (in terms of an improvement of salaries and general living conditions). In general, the protests were tied to the salary conditions of workers and, secondly, to the confrontations between the unions (generally Peronist) and the overall policy of the government (radical). The second axis concerns the demands for justice deriving from the crimes committed by the dictatorship, the defence of human rights more generally, and the defence of democracy.

Between 1989 and 1994, 60 per cent of protests still occurred within a union matrix, but the vast majority of these were linked to the service unions (state employees, teachers, utility employees, etcetera).[6] There were protests by the retired, some concerned with human rights, and several that brought together entire towns to demand regional economic reactivation, the defence of some industry in crisis, or justice for a crime in which they believed a powerful person was implicated. During this second period, coinciding with Menem's first term of office, protests focused in particular on the issue of institutional reform of the state. In general, they were oriented toward defending the sources or conditions of work that were believed to be threatened by the privatisation of state-owned enterprises, by the 'rationalisation' (downsizing) of the state bureaucracy or by the disappearance of industries with a regional impact.

Finally, beginning in 1995, a large diffusion of protests occurred. Protests within a citizen matrix flourished: for justice, against police violence, for equal opportunity or rights, against environmental destruction, for employment. Some new forms of protest also emerged: protests by the unemployed and, in general, outside any form of union organising; there was the surprising occurrence of roadblocks throughout the country.

The roadblocks originated in particular in two regions in the interior of the country, both with a history of oil development: Neuquén (in the south) and Salta y Jujuy (in the north). It started in Neuquén, when the provincial governor decided to impose a substantial cut in the salaries of state workers.[7] In response, the provincial teachers' union resolved to cut off an important access bridge to the province. The harsh police repression undertaken by the government garnered the support of other residents of the province, especially public employees, and led to new revolts. Expelled by force, many of the demonstrators headed for Cutral-Có, a town in the interior of the province. The residents, the majority of whom had been left unemployed following the privatisation of the state oil company (YPF) some years earlier, had already organised a protest of the their own the year before against the state of poverty and abandonment in which they had been left by the national government. That initial protest action was taken up by the unemployed, who cut the roads crossing the region and thus initiated a form of protest that would spread rapidly, first to the north and then to the entire country.

The roadblocks established by the unemployed received wide coverage in the national press and put an end to the obscurity of the actors themselves. The unemployed existed publicly once again due to their capacity for action. In this way, they converted themselves into politically relevant actors, as well as defining an issue that would have a lasting impact on the country's political agenda in the years to come. It was an authentically novel and largely unprecedented social and political development. The unemployed built a capacity for action out of their own need for material and symbolic survival, with little or no previous organisation or collective history. They became known as the *piqueteros*, a title that did not derive from their social condition (as unemployed) or from their demands, but rather from their actions. As in the classic factory picket lines, human barriers that strikers often place at the entrances of factories to impede the entry of strike-breakers, the roadblocks amounted to pickets that impeded vehicle traffic. In this way, they came to be known as *piqueteros* (picketers), a name which they themselves adopted.

The analysis presented here makes it possible to interpret the transformation of social protests in Argentina on the basis of two principal assertions: first, during the 1990s, there was a disarticulation of the union matrix of protests, progressively giving way to the emergence of protests of a citizen or human rights matrix; second, the protests underwent a progressive fragmentation, with the social and political identities of those involved multiplying and growing increasingly complex, the demands becoming more particular, and the forms of protest broadening.

This characterisation experienced a partial reversal in 2001, which makes it possible to understand the relative political aggregation that led to the events of December of that year, as well as to present circumstances. The cycle of protests that has occurred in Argentina since then is the most important of all the developments since 1983, owing to the number of protests, their geographic breadth, and the quantity and variety of the subjects involved. At the same time, it is interesting to note that this cycle may have marked a new stage of protests in the country. In effect, for the first time, three factors appeared that support this hypothesis:

- The sectors of the population affected by unemployment, underemployment and precarious employment, who emerged as actors in protests toward the mid 1990s, demonstrated for the first time the forms of systematic organisation and consolidation of a social movement.
- Trade union sectors (fragmented, to be sure) regained their role as protagonists in the protests. This applies in particular to two union organisations that are dissidents of the traditional CGT: the Central de Trabajadores Argentinos (Confederation of Argentine Workers, CTA), a breakaway faction of the CGT; and the Corriente Clasista y Combativa (Militant and Class-based Current, CCC), a non-Peronist leftist organisation made up of grassroots union formations and the unemployed in the north of the country, which would later become national in scope. The CGT, meanwhile, was never able to establish a genuine articulation with the unemployed.
- The incorporation of middle class sectors – harmed by the freezing of their savings (in the so-called *corralito financiero*) or simply overwhelmed by the disillusionment over an uncertain future, the material collapse of work and the moral collapse of their system of expectations – constituted a very important additional factor for the final result.

These factors signalled the opening of a phase whose unfolding characterises the present social and political landscape in Argentina. This does not mean that a single homogenous actor has emerged. However, diversity is a normal feature of all protests and is even evident in great revolutionary movements of world history. Indeed, diversity does not necessarily pose an obstacle to the formation of a movement. As already noted, the question that must be addressed is the degree of articulation that protest networks achieve.

THE POLITICAL LEFT, SOCIAL MOVEMENTS AND INSTITUTIONAL REORGANISATION

Contemporary Argentine politics are undergoing a moment of redefinition, almost of re-foundation. The government of Néstor Kirchner adopted a centre-left orientation, with special emphasis on issues of human rights and the recovery of the historic memory of the popular movements of the 1970s. Indicators of public confidence in the government have remained relatively high since the president took office. Social movements, for their part, have been confronted with the challenge of defining their position in this new context.

While it cannot be said that the crisis has come to an end, there is no doubt that a significant economic and political recovery has occurred. With an annual growth rate of over 9 per cent for four consecutive years, and the recuperation of political and institutional authority, Argentina has experienced a significant change under the Kirchner presidency. Nonetheless, the structure of inequality has changed little with the new government. Rates of poverty, indigence and unemployment have diminished, but remain at very high levels. Wages suffered a serious blow with the major devaluation of 2002, although there has been a relative recovery during the last year and a half, the result of both union struggles and of government policy decisions. The unequal distribution of income remains unaltered. With respect to the economy, the so-called Argentine boom has been sustained by the surge of agro-exports following the devaluation of the Argentine peso and especially the rise in the international price for soy beans. The government has undertaken significant and controversial initiatives in the area of foreign debt, with major consequences for the economy and the independence of the country. It renegotiated debts with the majority of individual holders of Argentine bonds overseas (in general, small and medium-sized savers), under conditions favourable to the Argentine state and, surprisingly, followed the Brazilian strategy of paying off its entire debt with the International Monetary Fund (IMF). In the political arena, the reconciliation of sectors of society with institutional politics should not lead one to conclude that the conditions that produced the slogan 'throw them all out' have completely disappeared; more accurately, they remain latent and are likely to reappear, although perhaps not with the same intensity. Distrust and scepticism have not disappeared from Argentine society.

Meanwhile, the protests, though weakened, continue, and diverse groups of citizens are searching for alternative political formations. The *cacerolazos*, the popular assemblies and the road blocks already constitute an experience of popular empowerment that, come what may, have left an indelible mark on Argentines. However, the new formations should include the existence of a new movement of Argentine society, one which is heterogeneous, diverse and fragmented (although less so than some years ago), but has the capacity to define political limits and take the construction of the social future into its own hands.

The unfolding of the crisis of December 2001 confronted broad sectors of Argentine society with the breakdown of the pillars of civic life in three concurrent spheres: in the sphere of civil rights, as a consequence of the flouting of republican controls by successive governments in their eagerness to enhance their prerogatives and their discretionary management of the public administration; in the sphere of political rights, as a result of the crisis of representation of a political system that is fragmented, overrun by sectoral interests without programmatic proposals or defined ideological positions, and incapable of incorporating and processing the growing demands of numerous social sectors affected by the transformations of the social regime of accumulation; and finally, in the sphere of social rights, as a result of the dismantling of labour protections and the destruction of the labour market (Pérez, 2004).

Within this framework, the problem put forth by the assemblies, the *piqueteros*, the savers and other groups can be formulated in the following manner: how can the relationships among broadened political participation, assembly deliberation, political representation and decision-making processes be redefined in the face of the collapse of the traditional political system, the deepest manifestation of which was the crisis of December 2001? With different modulations and in accordance with the set of opportunities, possibilities, and interests specific to each of these groups, they all expressed a *crisis of legitimacy* – that is, in the strict Weberian sense, the loss of inter-subjective validity of the dispositions that orient action toward obedience in the face of a certain type of political domination.

On this stage of intense socio-political conflict, there is no doubt that of all the movements mentioned in previous pages, the *piquetero* movement is the most systematic and consolidated. That this is the case can be easily explained if we recall the historical formation of the different popular movements described earlier in this chapter. It is thus evident that the *piquetero* movement emerged before 2001 and became consolidated over time, whereas the assemblies and the *cacerolazos* have been more closely tied to the specific process of the unfolding of the crisis. However, it should be emphasised that even today there are assemblies functioning in different cities of the country and that, as stated earlier, the historical experience of the social and political process that these movements signify or signified remains ingrained in the active memory of Argentines.

With respect to the *piquetero* organisations, an important question is the degree to which they have succeeded, in this context of crisis in which they are protagonists, in becoming new political actors capable of redefining central aspects of the political order, such as modes of representation, processes of legitimisation and the function of the state as an agent of social integration.

Thus, one must recognise the open conflict among the *piqueteros* as a consequence of their distinct positions vis-à-vis the political opportunities generated by the crisis. The manner in which the organisations resolve each of the challenges facing them makes for distinct modes of internal organisation and varying degrees of importance in decision-making processes. The same occurs with the distinct projects and strategies that each organisation defines in relation to the state, the political system and civil society, as well as to the transformations of the cultural and ideological frameworks produced within the organisations in the face of the crisis.

With respect to these issues, it is possible to advance some working hypotheses for the social and political analysis of the processes in question:

- The crisis of 2001 opened up a context of political opportunities for the actors in question, favouring the move from defensive and oppositional positions to the development of projects and strategies directed at redefining processes of legitimisation and the configuration of the social order.
- In this context of increasing political opportunities, the strategies put forward by different organisations produced high levels of conflict within the *piquetero* universe.
- The methods by which the identities and projects of different organisations are defined should be analysed according to three axes of conflict:
  - the models of internal organisation and decision-making processes that each organisation employs
  - the type of relationships among democracy, the state, the political system and civil society that they propose
  - the transformations with respect to traditional frameworks and ideological questions that they experience.

The complexity of the collective actors that have emerged during this process requires the utmost care in the use of theoretical and methodological tools of analysis. Therefore, it is necessary to consider the organisations we are studying as collective actors, understood as the contingent result of conflicting processes of subject formation organised according to a triple order of relations (Foucault, 2001): those that the collective establishes with processes of legitimisation of the political order (relations of domination); those that link it to the prevailing regime of accumulation (relations of production); and, finally, those that turn their own self-representation into a unity of interests, objectives and strategies (relations of identification). Thus, it is a question of analysing the degree to which the *piquetero* organisations can consider themselves new political actors in accordance with their ability (or inability) to intervene and restructure one of these three orders of relations.

Following the historical analyses of the *piquetero* movement (Oviedo, 2001; Kohan, 2002; Svampa and Pereyra, 2003), it is possible to identify the existence of three principal political aspects: the union aspect, the party aspect and the autonomist aspect. This categorisation is the result of the integration of the aforementioned variables, making it possible to consider not only the models of internal organisation and decision-making processes that each of these organisations employs, but also the type of relations among democracy, the state, the political system and civil society that they propose, as well as the transformations with respect to traditional frameworks and ideological questions that they experience.

Following this distinction, in the first group one can place those organisations that are linked to trade unions, but which at the same time engage in their own union organising activities, such as the Federación por la Tierra, la Vivienda y el Hábitat (Land, Housing and Habitat Federation, FTV), linked to the CTA or the CCC. In the second group are those organisations tied more or less closely to pre-existing political parties or to some partisan project, such as the Polo Obrero (linked to the Worker's Party), the Movimiento sin Trabajo (to the Socialist Worker's Movement), the Movimiento Territorial de Liberación (to the Communist Party),[8] or Barrios de Pie (to the Free Homeland Party), among others. The last group includes those organisations that are perhaps the most novel, those that define a horizontal, grassroots and assembly-based model of organisation, with an autonomous political project that not only does not recognise but tends to reject any trade union or partisan alignment. The Movimiento de Trabajadores Desocupados (Unemployed Worker's Movements, MTD) from different neighbourhoods or regions in the country constitutes the best example of this type of organisation.

While, as noted, the growth of these organisations has a history of more than five years from the time of their emergence through December 2001, their political development took off thanks to the political opportunities opened up by the crisis, increasing the level of mobilisation and favouring the strategic position of subaltern actors. In this sense, we can focus special attention on the existence of three political moments relevant to the topic under discussion: one, the very process of disintegration of the political system, which got underway in December 2001; another, the repression of the *piquetero* organisations that were demonstrating on 26 June 2002; and lastly, the distinct positions taken up by the organisations with respect to the presidential elections of May 2003.

An important point for understanding the current situation is the relationship of these organisations to the national government, whose policies have provoked different positions among *piqueteros*. It has become clear that the government made a reversal in its relationship with the *piqueteros* and, avoiding repression, sought to isolate the most militant sectors while simultaneously negotiating with those more open to dialogue. This gave rise to a demobilising strategy. On the one hand, the president affirmed that reducing debt payments was a national cause and that it is society that must defend its own interests. However, he did not create spaces for participation such that this national cause could be expressed by society. The call, then, constructed a closed hegemony on the part of the government, and in the long run could weaken the government vis-à-vis the large bourgeoisie which maintains control over the axis of economic power in Argentina.

The idea of isolating *piquetero* groups considered most hard-line is a strategy of wearing them out, which in general has produced good results for the government. The experience of the two fatalities in July 2002 remains very present in the public consciousness and marks a limit to the government's repressive will. Kirchner knows that any minimal repression can lead to a similar result. Faced with this prospect, he has preferred a strategy of wearing out the resistance. It has become clear that any organisation of popular resistance is difficult to sustain indefinitely in these times, at least at a level of constant effective action. This is even more the case in organisations one might regard as relatively young and with limited structure and consolidation.

It is possible, of course, to engage in a political evaluation of this government strategy. Such an evaluation would need to be laid out in two senses: strategically (or instrumentally) and normatively. From the instrumental point of view, it is evident that this strategy is well thought out and that it is proving effective. From the normative point of view, however, there is a serious problem. Despite his statements on the debt, on the defence of national interests, Kirchner is not undertaking a mobilising strategy, an inadvisable course of action given that he will need support from some source in order confront the interests of the dominant bourgeoisie. The president seems to have gained some understanding of this in the past year, although there have been no systematic proposals for political institutional reforms oriented toward generating spaces of systematic popular participation.

Along with this, there is also a set of pressures coming from the urban middle class who, after the institutional normalisation, isolated the *piqueteros* as well as the *asambleístas*. It is evident that there is a change in mood that has to do with a relative return to order. The economic variables have been adjusting upward, and this has generated expectations among the middle classes of a progressive return to a situation of normalcy and improving prospects. The idea that things need time has been revived among these groups. It is an attempt to return to normalcy, by sectors that have in many cases suffered serious harm and that are still suffering the impacts of the crisis, as against those who have not been able to come out of the terrible crisis, not even minimally.

The middle class thinks it is better off than it really is, and over-values its objective conditions. There is an expectation of improvement that, although it has some support, appears exaggerated with respect to the reality of the 1990s. The country, from a structural point of view, remains the same as in 2001.

The objective of the government appears to be that the *piquetes* (roadblocks) will gradually disappear as general conditions in the country improve, but this is not likely to happen. It is comparable to attempting to eliminate strikes. As long as there are workers and labour conflicts, and therefore also organisations that represent them, the only form in which the worker and the union can protest is by stopping production. What course of action is available to unemployed workers whose only space is the neighbourhood, the territory or province where they live, when the organisation that includes them and represents them is set up for those who are in the same situation (unemployed, in precarious employment, on social assistance)? They cannot stop production. Instead, it is their capacity to erect roadblocks on the public highways that has given them a temporary solution in their struggle for subsistence. This option might suffer a relative decline, but if they disappear from public space, they run the risk of extinction, because no one will remember them.

Finally, let us pose a crucial question for a central debate of this book. What effect have the parties of the left had on the *piquetero* movement? In this regard, two things are noteworthy. One, of a positive nature, is the decision by the left to pay attention to these social actors who in another time would have been considered members of the *lumpenproletariat*, inappropriate subjects for the development of a revolutionary consciousness. That they are no longer regarded as such and that the left works with them in building political movements is appropriate. But it is necessary to be somewhat critical of the role played by the parties of the left in this process. Instead of encouraging the development of these movements, the majority of the leftist parties that have begun working with the unemployed have only ended up contributing to division, attempting to bring as many people as possible into their ranks, rather than building an authentic movement, a broad space that respects the movement's self-determination. This has contributed to one of the greatest problems of the *piquetero* movement, which has ended up exacerbating its weakness – namely, dispersal. Today there are some 20-odd different groups, with distinct strategies. At times it is difficult to know who is who. And the other element is that dispersal increases the likelihood of infiltration and provocation. Some organisations have a more moderate strategy, others are more violent or more radical, and the coordination between them is limited or non-existent. Perhaps it is a good thing that there is no united front, but at least there is a need for a space for coordination. In this, regrettably, the parties of the left once again have contributed to weakening the movement, just as happened with the popular and neighbourhood assemblies.

What will happen in Argentina in the future? Kirchner's demobilisation strategy may be effective in the short term, but in the medium term it will be counterproductive, even for his own government; that is, if, as he has repeatedly asserted, he is committed to transforming the economic order in the country. Thus far, the issues the president has confronted have not been insignificant, but he has great difficulties ahead of him. The government must restore employment, reverse the process of wealth transfer, stand up to business demands for increased fees for public services (which have a direct impact on wages), as well as resist pressures from multilateral lending institutions on national sovereignty and in favour of capital. There is a need for a space for mobilisation, for debate by society that resumes the capacity for mobilisation and participation that has come from December 2001.

POSSIBLE STRATEGIES AND FUTURE PROSPECTS

On the basis of the analysis offered above, we are now in a position to draw certain conclusions and suggest some possible future developments. In the first place, it should be noted that the term *left*, used here without any discussion thus far, could perhaps be fruitfully replaced by the plural term *lefts*. This is the case, because in Argentina (and surely many other countries of the world) there is no single way of being a left-ist. The same may be said, as noted in the introductory chapter, for leftist formations in Latin America in general. In Argentina, we might even imagine the following typology of lefts, as these present themselves to the contemporary analyst:

- The political left:
  - socialist parties
  - communist parties
  - Trotskyist parties
  - Maoist parties
  - revolutionary nationalist parties
  - non-Marxist progressive parties
  - sectors of the left or centre-left of the traditional political parties.
- The social left:
  - movements of the unemployed (*piqueteros*)
  - popular assemblies
  - movement of occupied factories
  - militant unions
  - human rights organisations
  - anti-capitalist globalisation movements[9]
  - progressive or leftist intellectuals

It has become clear that in addition to the diversity that the simple list-ing of these varied types of political and social leftist organisations seems to demonstrate, almost by definition, the concrete history of their mutual relations only emphasises, deepens or aggravates their irreconcilable differences, and the recurring and multiple fractures between them. The Argentine left is far from building a united front like those of its Uruguayan and Brazilian neighbours. The effort of the United Left (IU) has not succeeded in bringing together important sectors of the left, including the Marxist left. The unity of the Social-ist Party has not ended the isolation of the forces under its banner, nor has it permitted the reclaiming of a political option that formerly carried weight in the country's history. The efforts of the progressive non-Marxist sectors (and even some Marxist ones) to build centre-left fronts have tended to fail spectacularly. The most dramatic case in recent history was surely the Frente Grande (Big Front), a party launched by dissident Peronist sectors during the Menem administration that aimed to unite activists and leaders from other political stripes and offered a centre-left electoral option (FREPASO) that momentarily experienced rapid electoral growth.

As already mentioned, in 1997 FREPASO formed the Alliance with the UCR (Radical Civic Union) and in the subsequent presidential elections succeeded in defeating the Peronist candidate (the former governor of Buenos Aires province and Menem's vice-president, Eduardo Duhalde). Fernando de la Rúa, a traditional UCR leader and former congressman and senator, thereby became President of the Republic. His failure has already been extensively analysed above. After only a brief tenure as vice-president, FREPASO leader Carlos Chacho Álvarez resigned out of disgust over de la Rúa's policy decisions. This action provoked a significant institutional crisis and left FREPASO completely orphaned. It was a key defeat for the broad front strategies of the national progressive forces – the most serious of all, but not the only one. As stated earlier, in the 1980s the PI and later the MAS had experienced more or less notable growth, only to end up bleeding themselves to death in internal disputes, losing all that they had built. Is it that the left, in any of its forms, is incapable of becoming an option for the masses? The question requires no answer. The Argentine left has not always aspired to offering such an option – nor does it now – and it has always been faced with the great challenge of Peronism.

There is no doubt that if any political force has demonstrated the capacity to govern in contemporary Argentina, whether for good or for ill, it is Peronism. In addition, the large union structures continue to be associated with it. Indeed, whether aligned or not with the PJ, whether more bureaucratic or more militant, Argentine workers' organisations have always been Peronist in some way. More leftist or more rightist, critical or devoted, their ideological roots and their social and political conceptions refer, in some way or another, to the model of country promoted by Perón in the 1940s and 1950s. These so-called national and popular ideas continue to dominate the heart of the Argentine workers' movement. It is very difficult to conceive of a mass leftist party if it cannot count on a sufficient social base and, above all, the indispensable working class base. It is because of this that the recent growth of hard-line Marxist sectors, as a result of their insertion into organisations of the unemployed or the *piqueteros*, is on the one hand a new doorway into political movement building. But on the other hand, it has challenged these political forces, insofar as it has obliged them to redefine their connections to the reserve army of capitalism, traditionally rejected because of their limited revolutionary consciousness.

Increasingly organised social protests and the social movements that potentially result from them have brought many leftist dogmas into question, but they have also obliged the traditional parties to rethink their political strategies of representation, leadership and construction of political hegemony. The same is true of Peronism, for example. In the same way that with Menem, Peronism governed from the right in clear alliance with the most hard-line sectors of the neo-liberal bourgeoisie and transnational capital, with Kirchner, it has repositioned itself on the political scene as a force with progressive aspirations.

However, a question remains with respect to this issue. Is Kirchner a leftist president? That is, can it be said that he is advancing left policies? In this regard, we can offer two observations that go some way toward providing a possible answer. In the first place, we have already analysed aspects that speak to the progressive stance of the government, for example in the areas of human rights, justice, institutional order, foreign debt, education, social policies and foreign policy. Nevertheless, Kirchner has not yet confronted the important question of the distribution of wealth in Argentina (which has become more intensely unequal in recent decades), while his critical attitude toward the IMF and big business has been more rhetoric than reality.

In the second place, the president has demonstrated a strong tendency toward governing from above, with very little democratisation of decision-making. This is partly justified, given the situation of institutional chaos that the country has recently experienced. But it is progressively becoming a more permanent form of governing which, in the medium term, does not favour the construction of a popular pluralist movement capable of challenging from below the established clientelistic and paternalistic modes of building political power in Argentina. Kirchner's attempt to build a new pluralist political force has thus far consisted of what has been called *transversality* – that is, the articulation of political spaces with figures coming from diverse partisan or political sectors, beyond Peronism itself. Nonetheless, it is clear that the president has accumulated a significant degree of political power and has given a new direction to the Argentine political scene. He has competed in the electoral arena supported by a political apparatus distinct from the PJ, namely, the Frente para la Victoria (Front for Victory, FV). His political capacity is the most significant political force in the country today; radicals, socialists, independents and old recycled Peronists form a heterogeneous base of leaders that comprise the structure of the FV throughout the country. In 2007 there will be a presidential election – with Cristina Fernández de Kirchner, the FV candidate, as the frontrunner in the polls at the moment of writing – and for that very reason 2007 is key to the country's future.

In opposition to the government, another political party is competing for leadership of the centre-left: Afirmación para una Republica Igualitaria (Affirmation for an Egalitarian Republic, ARI), led by Elisa Carrió, a former leader of the left-wing of the UCR. If Kirchner today represents the Peronist left (or the centre-left or progressivism) with transversal pretensions, Carrió is the equivalent from the radical side. The situation approximates a repeat of the classic political confrontation in Argentina during the second half of the twentieth century, albeit in a centre-left version and with its own nuances. The struggle to appropriate the political discourse of the centre-left has led the two political leaders into a sharp confrontation. In fact, it may well be that Carrió has come to represent Kirchner's strongest opposition, at least with respect to political discourse.

With respect to Kirchner, then, it can be said that he represents the current version of left Peronism, modernised for the times. His approach to politics is strongly nationalistic and popular rather than class-based and, in that sense, represents a populist expression. In any case, it must be said that the concept of populism applies in this case in more of a theoretical, as opposed to a pejorative, sense. As some writers have noted, populism – as a practical definition of an open subject and as the construction of an alternative to a given situation at a social crossroads – in some manner or other becomes a constitutive element of politics, at least insofar as the latter aspires to achieve hegemony (Laclau, 2004). Thus, any kind of politics aimed at attaining power would include a populist dimension as a last resort. Nevertheless, at least to date, the most reactionary expressions of populism (such as the use of a demagogic discourse aimed at popular sectors, without the inclusion of a project of social transformation) are relatively weak in Kirchnerism.

Obviously, this nationalist, popular and non-class-based outlook, as well as the lack of a revolutionary conception of politics, strongly separates Kirchner from the traditional left and makes dialogue between the two practically impossible. Nevertheless, some decidedly leftist (though popular-nationalist) forces, like the Movimiento Libres del Sur (Southern Freedom Movement), formerly the Partido Patria Libre (Free Homeland Party), some *piquetero* currents and other sectors with revolutionary Peronist origins, are attempting to form an internal current within Kirchnerism that is more clearly oriented in this direction.

In any case, what is clear is the government's opposition to the neo-liberal model: the recuperation of the state as an active agent in the economy and in society, the restoration of public policies and the reorientation of foreign policy towards Latin America. This last point is especially important and is perhaps one of the greatest opportunities that current government policy is creating in Argentina. The strategic alliance with Brazil, the rebirth of the Mercado Común del Sur (Common Market of the South, MERCOSUR) as a political and not just a trade project (despite the bloc's frequent institutional crisis and a long-standing dispute with Uruguay about the construction of a paper mill on the river that separates the two countries), the co-operative relationship with Venezuela, the restoration of a positive dialogue with Cuba, and the concerted effort to resist the pressures exerted by the G8 and international financial institutions all mark a clear and decisive course on the only path in today's world capable of achieving relative autonomy and defending the interests of nation-states and weak and dependent peoples. In this sense, all left politics, in whatever use of the term outlined here, will have to follow, with varying potential, a path of this sort.

One particular foreign policy issue concerns the hegemonic interests of the United States, which if today they pose a grave threat to the entire planet, they easily do to the American continent. In this sense, the position of the traditional left (both Marxist and nationalist) has been clear and explicit – they have strongly rejected any US military intervention in the world (Iraq, Colombia, Haiti and elsewhere) and have actively participated in organised protests to that end. They have done the same against the great North American continental commercial project, the Free Trade Area of the Americas (FTAA). Less clear is the position of the national government, which rejected any form of support for the war against Iraq but sent troops to Haiti.

As for the FTAA, the Argentine government has adopted a prudent position, but with a clear course of action. That course of action emerged from what has already been highlighted with respect to the strategic alliance with Brazil and the so-called Group of Twenty (headed by Brazil, South Africa and India). Thus, Argentina is a crucial component of the decision-making process of MERCOSUR (together with Brazil), and participates in global arenas offering alternatives to the hegemonic model. This limits Argentina's margin of autonomy in political decisions, but it gives it consistency. If pressure from left parties is sustained, especially with the strength currently given to it by the country's social movements, this will force or will help – depending on one's point of view – the government to maintain a strong position vis-à-vis US interests. Obviously, by virtue of the above analysis, this will also depend on the positions taken by allied countries, especially Brazil.

In sum, Argentina today has a strong leftist presence, but one which is highly fragmented, with little capacity to articulate a single political electoral option, in the style of the Brazilian PT or the Uruguayan Broad Front. The country's own political culture, together with the actual annihilation of an entire generation during the dictatorship of 1976–83 and the historic challenges of political interpretation that popular movements, and especially Peronism, have posed for the Argentine left, explain today's remarkable incapacity for collective and pluralistic construction, which in turn has an enormous effect on the possibilities for an anti-capitalist alternative. The Peronist government, meanwhile, offers shades of black and white, but there is no doubt that many of its actions can be regarded positively from a left perspective, providing support for some strategies – like the international or human rights strategy or the rejection of neo-liberalism – while assuming a critical attitude toward others.

To conclude, the great new political development in present-day Argentina is the movements that arose in the context of the neo-liberal social destruction of the 1990s and the crisis of 2001. It is a matter, as noted previously, of a social left that constitutes the potential and existing social force for founding an authentically transformative political movement in Argentina. Who will participate in that eventual space is something that remains open to the contingencies of history and will depend as much on objective conditions as on contemporary actors' subjective capacities for action. The potential spectrum of that space extends from Kirchnerism and its progressive opposition on the one hand, to the most radicalised parties on the left and the union and autonomist movements on the other. The coming years will write the historic text. Today, meanwhile, the scene is that which has been described.

NOTES

1. Álvarez, who had been elected as de la Rúa's running mate in 1999, had resigned shortly after assuming office.
2. Statement quoted from Raúl Alfonsín, during his electoral campaign.
3. See for example Scribano (1999), Scribano and Schuster (2001), Schuster (1997), Schuster and Pereyra (2001).
4. *Cacerolazo* refers to the form of protest, generalised in Argentina in those days, that consists of collective mobilisation accompanied by the banging of pots.

5. Extensive data was gathered by a research group that is part of the Gino Germani Institute at the University of Buenos Aires' Science and Technology Unit. More detailed versions of this material can be viewed in Schuster (1997, 1998). The information gathered here was complemented with data from Scribano (1997, 1998, 1999), and journalistic research from newspapers (*Clarín, La Nación, El Cronista, Página 12*) and the web pages of television networks (especially TN).

6. The concept of the *matrix* comes from a complex compilation (*integration*) of five categories of analysis that were proposed for the study of social protest: *identity, structure, demands, format* and *political impact.* Under specific conditions of analysis, protests can be constructed around the first three. Ideal types result, which thus permit a conceptual organisation of the empirical analysis. See Schuster (2004).

7. For more details on this case, see Favaro et al. (1997), Klachko (1999) and Svampa and Pereyra (2003).

8. In this case, there is a combination with the trade union model.

9. See Seoane and Taddei (2001) and Boron (2004).

7 MEXICO
Yearnings and Utopias:
The Left in the Third Millennium
Armando Bartra

GENEALOGY

The 'philanthropic ogre'

Mexico entered the twentieth century with a triumphant *campesino* revolution that in the end benefited the common people but made life difficult for the doctrinal left. The 1910 uprising was a democratic insurrection that demanded social justice and whose leadership-turned-government launched an agrarian reform but also rebuilt the state and re-organised society. Thus, for over 70 years, successive governments proclaimed themselves of the left, because they considered themselves heirs of the revolution: a historical heritage that gave identity to state institutions, the 'nearly' one-party state, the large trade unions and the political discourse of the so-called 'revolutionary family'; but also to public art, civic rituals, textbooks, nationalist paraphernalia and the political culture of ordinary Mexicans. In Mexico, presidents wrapped themselves in red flags (Plutarco Elías Calles, 1923–27), were anointed 'First worker of the nation' by the trade unions (Miguel Alemán Valdés, 1946–52), defined themselves as of the 'extreme left within the constitution' (Adolfo López Mateos, 1958–64) or proclaimed themselves champions of anti-imperialism (Luis Echeverría, 1970–76). Our country was a left-wing country by decree, where for nearly the entire twentieth century the governing party was called the Partido Revolucionario Institucional (Institutional Revolutionary Party, PRI).

If during the twentieth century the left identified itself with socialism, which in turn meant state ownership of the means of production, then Mexico was extremely leftist. At the beginning of the 1980s, the public sector of the economy was made up of more than 1,300 companies, comprising trust funds, decentralised bodies and state-owned enterprises, which gave the government total or partial control over a vast array of industries and basic services. Development banks were also traditionally state owned, and in 1982 the entire financial system was nationalised. Consequently, at the beginning of the penultimate decade of the last century, the public sector comprised approximately 50 per cent of total investment (González Casanova, 1981).

But the 'philanthropic ogre' of which Octavio Paz spoke did not just govern a large part of the economy and manage the state as if it were the property of the so-called revolutionary family. Paz's maxim that 'Patrimonialism is private life embedded in public life' (Paz, 1979:85) also reigned over social organisation; workers' confederations and large industrial trade unions, *campesino* leagues and confederations, and so-called popular-sector organisations were disciplined members of the PRI. In the same way, the business associations, confederations and chambers were corporately linked to the state, which, by means of concessions, advertising, sponsorship and corruption, also ran almost all the mass media and a large part of the artistic and cultural sector (González Casanova, 1965).

In such a country, being right-wing was simple: it sufficed to be in opposition to the regime. By contrast, in the realm of the institutionalised revolution, the left always had problems of position and identity, especially the left that did not align itself with revolutionary nationalism, the political current of the reformist project deriving from the 1910 insurrection.

A 'proletariat without a head'

From precursors such as the Catholic Association of Mexican Youth (1911) and the National Parents' Union (1917), to the National League for the Defence of Religious Liberty (1925), which organised the *Cristero* insurrection against the government of Calles; the National Synarchist Union (1937), which fought the 'communist' policies of President Cárdenas; and the Partido Acción Nacional (National Action Party, PAN), founded in 1940 to disassociate itself from the governing group, the Mexican right (whether democratic or authoritarian) has always defined itself by its opposition to the 'revolution-turned-government' (Campbell, 1976; Jarquín Gálvez and Romero Vadillo, 1985; Meyer, 1973).

In contrast, the trajectory of the left has been winding and faltering. After the death of their leader, the intransigent *campesino* Zapatismo of

Morelos allied themselves with President Álvaro Obregón, a member of the current that had opposed them. The 'red' agrarians and the anarcho-syndicalists, who in the immediate post-revolution seized land, led strikes and were angry opponents, ended up in the 1930s in one way or another united with the clientele of the state. And the Partido Comunista Mexicano (Mexican Communist Party, PCM) in 1939 decided that in Mexico the Popular Front (then known as the Party of the Mexican Revolution) was the party in power and squandered its political capital in a suicidal tactic of 'unity at all costs' (Martínez Verdugo, 1971).

With the political left absent, from the middle of the century the democratic and social-justice-oriented opposition expressed itself in social movements such as those led by teachers and rail workers in the late 1950s, and *campesinos* from different states in the early 1960s. It is worth noting that at the forefront of this era's popular struggles there were nearly always prominent members of the Communist left, such as the teachers' organiser Othón Salazar, the railroad workers' leader Valentín Campa and the *campesino* leader Ramón Danzós, all of whom were members of the PCM. Paradoxically, the political reform of 1977 – which led to the legal-isation of left parties such as the PCM and the Partido Socialista de los Trabajadores (Socialist Workers' Party, PST) and their participation in the 1979 federal elections – far from bridging the gap between the political and social left, instead fuelled a growing disagreement which endured throughout the 1980s.

The incoherent behaviour of the non-governmental left stemmed less from their mistakes than from the undoubted hegemony exerted by revo-lutionary nationalism for over half a century. In the words of the novelist and PCM member José Revueltas, who lamented the historical alienation that rendered the Mexican proletariat 'headless':

> The Mexican revolution ends up rounding off its ideological myth and can claim to be ... not bourgeois-democratic but an *agrarian, national* and *workers'* revolution ... a unique, 'essentially Mexican' movement and 'the most advanced and revolutionary' of our times.
>
> (Revueltas, 1962:109)

Still, the hegemony of the PRI regime was not simple ideological manip-ulation. It was based on the unmistakable achievements of a system which, while clearly authoritarian, distributed land, provided basic services to the majority of the population and, until the 1980s, achieved sustained growth that, though uneven in regional and class terms, generated a rising and generalised improvement in social welfare. This condensed into a not necessarily negative ideological myth and, in the end, the inspiration for modern millenarian movements. In the collective imagination of Mexicans of the twentieth century, *Cardenismo* – which began with the radical reformism of President Lázaro Cárdenas (1934–40) and remained a more or less institutional political current until the mid 1980s – symbolised the social justice face of the post-revolutionary regime. After leaving office, General Cárdenas maintained a low profile, and although he encouraged *soto voce* some questioning of the regime, he chose 'critical support' and 'loyal opposition' as institutional formulas to avoid major 'deviations' and to 'defend the revolutionary conquests'.

With the exception of his public support for the National Liberation Movement (a broad civil anti-imperialist front) in 1961, and his support for the formation of the Independent Peasant's Confederation in 1963, Cárdenas was not directly involved with the political or social left. Even so – and perhaps because of this – for Mexican workers and *campesinos* of the second half of the twentieth century, *Cardenismo* represented the only available left with any chance of winning: the only social-justice-oriented political trend which, precisely because it was 'institutional', appeared to be endowed with a presumed efficiency.

In a country where one questions and struggles against the government, but with the conviction that the outcome is ultimately in the hands of the all-powerful Leviathan, the anti-system left could not appear as anything but a purely utopian current, an ideological luxury, an anti-establishment or symbolic minority, always self-sacrificing and sometimes heroic, but not very effective in the here and now.

The fact is that the Communists did not manage to further popular causes: either through winning elections, legislating and governing, or by leading social protest struggles to victory, or, of course, through revolution. With respect to elections, the saga of the left is discouraging. In 1979, the PCM inaugurated political reform by taking part in federal elections, and at the head of a left-wing coalition obtained 4.8 per cent of the vote and its first 18 deputies. But its debut was its best moment. In 1980, the coalition participated in municipal elections and 15 governors' races, and obtained only 1.6 per cent of the vote, when a year before it had obtained 2.9 per cent in the same federal races. In 1982, the Partido Socialista Unificado de México (Unified Socialist Party of Mexico, PSUM) – which brought together the PCM, the Socialist Revolutionary Party, the Party of the Mexican People, the Movement of Socialist Action and Unity, and the Movement of Popular Action – obtained 3.8 per cent of the vote in the presidential elections. Finally, in 1985 the PSUM saw its electoral support decline further, obtaining only 3.2 per cent, which also represented an absolute decline in votes (Moguel, 1987). In contrast, however, with the electoral decline experienced by the parties of the left from the late 1960s until the mid 1980s, social movements were on the rise.

Popular insurgencies

Representing the culmination of a long period of post-war material prosperity, the student movement of 1968 was a negation of the supposed Mexican 'miracle', since without putting in doubt the macroeconomic virtues of 'stabilising development', it rebelled against the growing and oppressive lack of political freedoms. The liberationist explosion was followed by 15 years of sectoral insurgencies in which the struggle for freedom of association was combined with social and economic protests, given that in the early 1970s the post-war growth model had begun to falter: first came the agrarian crisis that triggered the impetuous *campesino* movement, and then, the general debacle that sent successive waves of workers, inhabitants of marginal suburbs, teachers and, once again students in the early 1980s, onto the streets.

The rural insurgency was launched at the beginning of the decade, and was centred on the struggle for land, expressing itself through countless occupations of *latifundios*, both large-scale livestock land-holdings in the central and north-central part of the country, and intensive irrigated farming operations in the northeast. In 1979, dozens of associations and regional fronts, as well as some national organisations, converged around the Coordinadora Nacional del Plan Ayala (National Co-ordinator of the Ayala Plan, CNPA), which embodied the first national and programmatic neo-zapatismo of the post-revolutionary period. The CNPA reached its peak on 10 April 1984, when it mobilised more than 50,000 *campesinos* in Mexico City on the anniversary of Emiliano Zapata's death to protest against the government's attempts to put an end to the agrarian reform (Bartra, 1985).

The labour movement fought for higher salaries, better working conditions and against job cuts, but also for democracy and trade union independence and, as stated in the Guadalajara Declaration (SUTERM-Tendencia Democrática, 1975), for 'taking the Mexican Revolution forward'. A wide array of trade union organisations staged a decade of strikes and demonstrations, which in 1976 converged in the First National Conference of the Popular Worker and Campesino Insurgency and gave rise to the Frente

Nacional de Acción Popular (National Front for Popular Action, FNAP) (Ortega and Solís de Alba, 1999). At the end of the decade, the powerful teachers' sector joined the worker protests through the Coordinadora Nacional de Trabajadores de la Educación (National Co-ordinator of Education Workers, CNTE) (Pérez Arce, 1982).

The urban movement, almost extinct following the tenant battles of the 1920s, re-emerged at the beginning of the 1970s with struggles for housing and services, which took place mainly in the big cities of Mexico City, Chihuahua and Nuevo León and later extended to the urban centres of Durango, Nayarit, Guerrero, Guanajuato and other states. Beginning in 1979, organised settler movements began to merge, formally uniting in 1981 in the Coordinadora Nacional del Movimiento Urbano Popular (National Coordinator of Popular Urban Movements, Conamup) (Ramírez Sáiz, 1986).

After 1968, student unrest persisted in some state universities, but it was not until the mid 1980s that it took on a new militancy, when students, teachers and administrative staff of the National Autonomous University of Mexico (UNAM) mobilised in opposition to the neo-liberal reforms being promoted by the rector. In 1986, the newly formed University Student Council organised two big marches in Mexico City, and a three-week strike the following year, leading to the suspension of the rector's plans and an agreement to hold a Democratic Congress for university reform (Cazés, 1990).

From 1982 to 1984, in the context of the economic and political crisis that afflicted the latter part of the José López Portillo administration (1976–82), the popular 'protests', which had lasted just over a decade, demonstrated both their potential and their limitations. Early 1983 witnessed the unleashing of a cycle of street demonstrations, strikes and work stoppages, in which teachers from the CNTE, the National Union of University Lecturers (SUNTU), and the Amalgamated Trade Union of Nuclear Industry Workers (SUTIN) played a leading role. These actions converged with hundreds of demands or eruptions of strikes by unions linked to the PRI-ist Confederación de Trabajadores de México (Confederation of Mexican Workers, CTM), which was seeking to renegotiate its deal with the government. The outcome was a major political defeat, as President López Portillo and pro-government forces reached an agreement on a National Solidarity Pact that rejected the demands advanced by the state-dependent organisations and left the independent organisations on their own to face repression.

The ultimately unsuccessful mobilisation severely hindered 'the capacity of the trade union leadership, whether state co-opted or independent, to represent with even minimal efficiency the most basic interests of the workers' (Garza Toledo and Rhi Sausi, 1985:224). And although there were popular mobilisations in 1986 and 1987, the events of 1983–84 signalled the beginning of the end, both for traditional corporatism and for the 'insurgencies': forms of articulation of the popular movement which, though sectoral and focused on specific demands, also advanced a left politics emerging from combined interest group mobilisation.

Neo-Cardenismo or nostalgia

By the 1980s, the possibilities of the inward-oriented development model launched 40 years earlier had been exhausted, such that President López Portillo's irresponsible spending and debt accumulation only gave the *coup de grâce* to the model. By the middle of the decade, it was already evident that the country needed a change of course. And it was also clear that that change would not be the one advocated by the political and social left in the 1983 days of protest, but rather the recipes of macroeconomic adjustment, deregulation, privatisation and trade liberalisation promoted by the International Monetary Fund (IMF).

The outcome of this policy, which culminated in the signing of the North American Free Trade Agreement (NAFTA) in 1993, was an increase in exports to the United States, a country on which Mexico now depends for approximately 90 per cent of its foreign trade, and from which the level of direct foreign investment has tripled in ten years. The problem resides in the fact that the main export drive is concentrated in the *maquiladoras*, which buy only 3 per cent of their components in the domestic market, and in a handful of large industries, nearly all of which are foreign-owned. Whereas in the past these industries obtained 90 per cent of their components from domestic sources, they now import 73 per cent. These enclave economies do not produce multiplier effects in other sectors and their expansion has been accompanied by a brutal death rate among small and medium-sized domestic industries. Thus, in the decade since NAFTA was implemented, the per capita GDP grew at less than 1 per cent per year and employment in the manufacturing sector declined by 10 per cent.

The unilateral economic disarmament that was necessary for Mexico to be admitted into the northern trade club finished off our national economy; that is, our *campesino* agriculture and our small and medium-sized industries, which were the sectors that generated employment. The outcome is one of the biggest exoduses in the history of humanity: in ten years, nearly 5 million Mexicans have fled over the northern border. Today, 23 million compatriots live in the United States, of whom nearly half were born in Mexico, and just under half of those crossed over without documents. Each year, they send more than $20 billion in remittances back to Mexico, an amount exceeded only by India, with a population ten times bigger.

It is no coincidence that the so-called Corriente Democrática (Democratic Current) which emerged within the PRI in 1986, and which left the party the following year, promptly identified itself as neo-cardenista. Neither is the fact that its candidate in the 1988 presidential election was Cuahutémoc Cárdenas, the son of the former president. As noted above, in the collective imagination of ordinary Mexicans, *Cardenismo* represents the greatest contributions of the revolution-turned-government. So much so that when city and rural workers feel assaulted by the neo-liberal reforms, their political reflexes lead them to those who symbolically represent anti-imperialism and social justice.

Cárdenas' candidacy, promoted by the Democratic Current, took shelter in the membership lists of three phantom parties (the Authentic Party of the Mexican Revolution, the Cardenista Front for National Reconstruction, and the Popular Socialist Party), which in January 1988 formed the Frente Democrático Nacional (National Democratic Front, FDN). Meanwhile, the PSUM, which had become the Partido Mexicano Socialista (Mexican Socialist Party, PMS) following its merger with the Mexican Workers' Party, promoted the candidacy of the latter's founder, Herberto Castillo, thus risking the same low share of the vote (4 per cent) that it had received in the two previous elections. In the end, this failure was averted, as Castillo stepped down in favour of Cárdenas a month before the elections. Thus, the socialist left, historically anti-system, and the Mexican revolutionary left, which had only just broken with the system, converged around the candidacy of the general's son.

With no clear organisational structure or programme, no money and the mass media against him, Cárdenas travelled the country amid spontaneous demonstrations of hundreds of thousands of sympathisers, and on 6 July, won the election. I say won, because a week later – after 54 per cent of polling stations had reported – the FDN had 39 per cent of the vote, while the PRI accounted for 35 per cent and the PAN 21 per cent, which was seen as an irreversible trend. It was a statistical certainty, however, that was reversed when in the rest of the polling stations the percentage of votes for the PAN held at 21 per cent, but mysteriously the FDN dropped to 12 per cent and the PRI rose to 67 per cent, enough for the PRI candidate to make off with the victory. It goes without saying that the votes from the last 25,000 polling stations could never be verified because, by agreement between the PRI and the PAN, they were burned (Barberán et al., 1988).

Instead of kicking up a fuss, with predictably fatal consequences, the cheated forces decided to go along with the popular perception created in 1988 that the PRI could be defeated through the electoral path, in order to create a political organisation capable not only of winning elections but also of defending victories. Thus, in May 1989, the Partido de la Revolución Democrática (Party of the Democratic Revolution, PRD) was founded, inheriting the membership lists of the PMS. Below we will examine the implications of this convergence of *Cardenistas* and Communists that for some signified the dissolution of the doctrinal left into neo-populism, and for others, the founding of the first electorally viable centre-left party in a country in which the left had heretofore been purely symbolic.

Neo-zapatismo or delusion

The student movement of 1968 culminated on 2 October in a massacre that some on the left regarded as closing down all open forms of liberation politics. Thus, in the 1970s, numerous armed urban groups, often of student origin, such as the Comando Lacandones, the Revolutionary Action Movement, the Union of the People, and the September 23rd League (a merger of Communists and Christians) were added to the post-revolutionary *campesino* guerrilla experiences of Morelos, Chihuahua and Guerrero. Nevertheless, while armed struggle and political action may have coexisted within the movement, in reality the image of these groups was primarily one of kidnappings and expropriations. And the dirty war unleashed by the government soon cornered and annihilated them, such that by 1982 the September 23rd League was practically dismantled (Bellingeri, 2003).

A couple of years later, out of step with the rising mass movement (the trade unions were unleashing waves of strikes and tens of thousands of *campesinos* were marching on the country's capital), some activists of the Forces of National Liberation, a group formed in 1969 by students from Monterrey, began to organise an anachronistic *foco* guerrilla force in the mountainous communities of Chiapas. A decade later, thanks to a transfusion of indigenous blood, the guerrillas re-emerged as the Ejército Zapatista de Liberación Nacional (Zapatista National Liberation Army,

EZLN) accompanied by hundreds of Tzeltales, Tzotziles, Choles and Tojolabales, in what was the latest indigenous insurrection of the saga begun in the nineteenth century and the first anti-capitalist uprising of the third millennium.

If in 1994 few well-informed Mexicans acting in good faith would have denied the right of rebellion to the afflicted indigenous communities of the southern state of Chiapas, very few of them would have believed that resorting to arms was the way to resolve matters. Thus, as the EZLN began to identify itself as a truly indigenous organisation, support for its cause triumphed over rejection of its method, so that first the political-social left and then many ordinary citizens have come out against a repressive solution and in support of the reasonable and at the same time 'excessive' demands of the rebels: work, land, housing, food, health, education, independence, freedom, democracy, justice and peace.

It is not too surprising that with the imminence of the 1994 presidential elections, the government preferred to gain time by negotiating with the rebels rather than get mired down in an unpleasant and difficult war. It is surprising, however, that on the eleventh day of fighting, those who for ten years had been preparing for insurrection accepted a ceasefire and five weeks later initiated a dialogue with the government. But this was just the first pleasant surprise. Although the negotiations did not lead to an agreement, the EZLN decided to maintain the suspension of hostilities without laying down its weapons (with the aim of 'allowing civil society to organise itself in the ways it considers pertinent in order to achieve the transition to democracy'), and in its Second Declaration of the Lacandon Forest (EZLN, 1994), called for a Convención Nacional Democrática (National Democratic Convention, CND).

The EZLN strategy consists of promoting the transformation of the country through a 'transitional government', a 'new constituent assembly' and a 'new constitution'. If there was any doubt that five months after its armed uprising the EZLN was energetically promoting participation in the elections, Sub-comandante Marcos clarified the matter: 'the proposal of the Convention is to try to force a change via the electoral path. ... We are making an effort to convince our people to place their bets on the election, that it's worth it' (Morquecho, 1994:173). In that context, the convention that took place in early August in Aguascalientes de Guadalupe Tepeyac, Chiapas, with approximately 6,000 people in attendance, and which spread from there to all the states of the Republic, was an unusual political 'happening' and the EZLN's first direct experiment with so-called 'civil society'. But above all, it was a pact with *Cardenismo* and the PRD, which for the second time was trying to win the presidency with Cuahutémoc Cárdenas as its standard bearer.

The left failed in the 1994 elections because the vote was rigged (as usual), but more importantly because the civilian insurgency of 1988 had run out of steam and the electorate's nostalgia for the past had faded. It also failed because progressives were obviously going to vote for Cárdenas – with or without the EZLN – so victory depended on the undecided, who were possibly frightened by the perceived ties between the candidate and the rebels, and faced by uncertainty, opted for 'peace' (that is, for the system). The electoral defeat served to weaken the alliance between neo-cardenismo and neo-zapatismo and led to the failure of the Convention. Despite its efforts, this alliance could not transform itself into an autonomous social front with a strategic project and sustained from below by organised popular sectors, and right up to the moment of its demise, it depended too much on the directives and initiatives of the EZLN (CND, 1995).

The new government took office with a treacherous military incursion into insurgent territory and a failed attempt to annihilate or capture the Zapatista leadership. But thanks to persistent popular support, and in another demonstration of strategic resolve mixed with tactical flexibility, in March the EZLN reinitiated negotiations with the national government and in August carried out a successful national consultation. In the latter, more than a million people manifested their support for the demands of the Zapatistas and for the formation of a 'political force'.

The formal negotiations between the EZLN and the government began in late 1995 with a broad agenda that embraced all of the country's economic, social and political problems. The negotiations assembled a very wide range of intellectuals, experts and representatives of progressive associations, especially from the Zapatista side, who turned them into a hitherto unheard-of national dialogue about the future of Mexico and the Mexican people. Out of this ambitious agenda, only those issues relating to indigenous rights and cultures were fully examined, resulting in agreements that were summarised in a project of constitutional reform. With respect to the second issue (democracy and justice), the forces convened by the EZLN proposed a reform of the state centred on participatory democracy. But the government decided to undermine the process by capturing two alleged Zapatistas and putting them on trial for terrorism. It was an obvious provocation, to which the Zapatistas responded by suspending negotiations until the prisoners were set free, the army vacated EZLN territory, and the agreements about indigenous rights and culture were incorporated into the constitution. In December 1996, President Ernesto Zedillo disowned what had been negotiated.

The EZLN meanwhile demonstrated its ability to attract young people disaffected with the old-fashioned left and multiply its global ties with the implementation of the First Intercontinental Conference For Humanity and Against Neo-liberalism. But above all, neo-zapatismo strengthened its ties with the new *indianismo*. On the rise since the 1970s, this current found expression in numerous movements and local organisations, until the late 1980s when, catapulted forward by the commemoration of 500 years of resistance, it came together nationally, established ties with other indigenous organisations in the region, and developed a political platform centred on the recognition of indigenous autonomy (Bartra, 2001). Despite its communitarian base and the fact that the concept of indigenous autonomy has been a part of its discourse since 1994 (Sánchez, 1999), the EZLN had not drawn up an *indianista* agenda. Its position was that the national ethnic movement had been built (Díaz-Polanco, 1988, 1990; Díaz-Polanco and López y Rivas, 1994), and that it had been part of the PRD programme and legislative agenda since 1990 (Ruiz Hernández, 1999). But in 1996, in the context of the San Andrés talks, the EZLN convened the First National Indigenous Forum, which was followed by numerous meetings in the states. The process culminated in October with the formation of the Congreso Nacional Indígena (National Indigenous Congress, CNI), sponsored by the liberation army that transformed a supposedly 'vulnerable' sector into a symbol of dignity and resistance.

Considering the fact that the EZLN is not a sectoral force, but rather one with a universalistic vocation, it is paradoxical that such broadly based alliances as the CND, the Movimiento de Liberación Nacional (National Liberation Movement), or the Frente Zapatista de Liberación Nacional (Zapatista National Liberation Front, FZLN), have been short-lived or have had a limited following, while the link between the insurgents of Chiapas and the indigenous movement has been deep and long-lasting. In fact, *indianismo*, *otromundismo* (the struggle to build an alternative world), and the sympathies encountered in countercultural youth circles have defined the Zapatista mind-set since 1996, whereas its ties to other large sectors and movements, such as the *campesino*, worker, teacher, student and civic-electoral movements – all of which have been militant during the last decade – have been scarce, distant, sporadic or outright hostile.

The CNI held its Second Congress in March 1997, when 1,111 Zapatistas from Chiapas toured the country, and its third in 2001, which coincided with the March for Indigenous Dignity, headed by the EZLN leadership and Sub-comandante Marcos. This march 'of the colour of the earth', which constituted the peak of the 1990s indigenous movement, focused on constitutional recognition of their autonomous regions (Vera Herrera, 2001).

Unfortunately, it did not turn out as hoped: in 2001, the National Congress received the bill drafted by the Comision de Concordia y Pacificación (Commission of Concordance and Peace, Cocopa) from the executive, but weakened it to such an extent that the resulting constitutional monstrosity was loudly rejected by the Indians and the Zapatistas. Since then, towns and communities have focused on exercising 'de facto autonomies', while for four years the EZLN took refuge in its support bases organised in municipal self-governments and reinforced from 2003 on with regional structures called *Juntas de Buen Gobierno* (good government committees). Entrenched in this way, at the end of 2003 and beginning of 2004, Zapatismo celebrated its tenth anniversary.

The EZLN maintained this introspective posture until late 2005, when it issued the Sixth Declaration of the Lacandon Forrest and Sub-comandante Marcos, re-named *delegado cero* (delegate zero), travelled across the country with the aim of organising the 'real anti-capitalist left'. His long trip coincided with the 2006 presidential campaign, and significantly was called *La otra campaña* (the other campaign). One of its main tasks was to discredit the presidential candidate Andrés López Obrador, as Marcos did not consider him left-wing but rather a 'mirror' of ex-president Carlos Salinas – the author of the neo-liberal turn in Mexico – and a politician who, if he were to come to power, 'would screw us all' (Bartra, 2006:12). However, the campaign rallies that López Obrador held throughout the country significantly overwhelmed the structures of the PRD and galvanised over 3 million enthusiastic followers who saw in him the opportunity for a 'real change'. As a result, 'the other campaign' ended up going against the tide, becoming a marginal initiative confined to a few local radicalised movements and backed by splinter groups of the old left, among them some Stalinists.

CARTOGRAPHIES

From the crisis of authoritarianism to the crisis of democracy

The new Mexican left is the product of the progressive exhaustion of the post-revolutionary order: the crisis of authoritarianism, which from 1968 left the political legitimacy of the system in doubt; the crisis of clientelism, gradually deserted by its interest group base during the 1970s and 1980s, which brought its social legitimacy into question; and, finally, the crisis of the model of reproduction of federal power, unleashed in 1988 on the occasion of the presidential succession, which threatened the viability of the 'nearly one-party' state.

By the end of the 1980s, the debacle of the system had condensed into revolutionary nationalism, when a decade and a half of social insurgency had been transformed into civil insurgency, culminating in the rare – and stolen – electoral victory of the FDN. In the mid 1990s, the crisis focused on the diverse neo-zapatista left, which went from preventing war to promoting the causes of the EZLN from the grassroots. In the late 1990s, the crisis came together around the promises of the new right, which turned the 2000 elections into a plebiscite, and aided by the 'useful vote' of the left (Velasco, 2000), succeeded in removing the PRI from the Presidential Mansion in Los Pinos. The progressive aspirations of neo-cardenismo, the reformist revolution of neo-zapatismo, and the changes promised by President Vicente Fox (2000–06) are all expressions of the country's disgust with the system: an exasperation that with Cárdenas became nostalgia, with Marcos became delusion, and with Fox became banana skins.

I say banana skins because, with the first PAN government, the incipient Mexican democracy stumbled seriously. As the illusion that the right-wing government would promote real socioeconomic change faded and President Fox's ratings plummeted, popular support for the Mexico City government of Andrés Manuel López Obrador grew, transforming the charismatic native of Tabasco into the Mexican politician with the highest approval ratings in recent years and the natural PRD candidate for the 2006 presidential elections. It was then that the ostensibly democratic right showed its true colours: faced with an imminent electoral victory by the left, which appeared unstoppable by lawful means, the first post-revolutionary government to emerge from real, pluralist elections showed its authoritarian reflexes by unleashing a fierce, illegal campaign to disqualify López Obrador, and later to impose its own right-wing candidate on the presidency.

The country has changed. At the beginning of the 1990s, our anti-democratic political system was in its terminal phase. An unlawful president, elected through electoral fraud, was in power. The PAN was negotiating behind the scenes with the PRI for support of Carlos Salinas's legislative initiatives and for electoral posts. And the members of the PRD were being decimated in a scattered, silent and as yet unsolved massacre (Hernández, 2000). At the start of the millennium, the PAN had replaced the PRI in the presidency, the PRD held the reins in the capital city, and there was pluralism in Congress, the states and the municipalities.

But our incipient democracy is ailing: people are increasingly sceptical of politics, they are deserting parties, and the abstention rate has sky-rocketed. While 58 per cent of registered voters participated in the 1997 elections and 65 per cent in the 2000 elections, only 41 per cent took part in the 2003 congressional elections (Tello Díaz, 2003). In 2001, we had 'alternation' but not the anticipated 'change', and if previously it was the anti-democratic system that was in crisis, today it is a democracy which, contrary to the deluded expectations of ordinary Mexicans and part of the intelligentsia, was not enough to change the system.

Undoubtedly, the political class showed its true colours and corruption sprouted daily. But that is not the reason that democracy has cheated us. The fact of the matter is that we Mexicans, formed in the absence of the rule of law and always disapproving of civic-mindedness, have a magical idea of electoral democracy and a concept of participatory democracy that is more anti-establishment than mutually responsible. In a country where for centuries we expected to get everything from the Virgin of Tepeyac and *papá gobierno* (daddy government), we still think that changing the president changes Mexico and that with the election of the new *tlatoanis* (Aztec king), all we have to do is sit back and wait for the new rulers to fulfil their promises.

By riding on the deservedly bad reputation of what in Mexico is pejoratively known as *polaca* (politics), the mass media systematically demonise the institutional spheres and rites of the public sector, claiming that elections cost us too much money, that all politicians are corrupt, that parties only defend their own interests, and that overpaid members of Congress only serve to obstruct the president. Television, in particular, turns public affairs into an embarrassing reality show directed by the media's authoritative 'big brothers'. In this way, 'to politicise' has become synonymous with 'to pervert', since it is assumed that to follow the lead of parties is to sacrifice the common good.

And there is no need to invent anything, as the negative discourse about public institutions and mechanisms is based on verifiable facts, as overwhelming as the images of a poisonous video. Without a doubt, there are corrupt politicians, and in the last two years it has been discovered that not only the PRI but also the PAN and the PRD have received illegal campaign contributions. There are also shady legislative lawsuits, such as the one in late 2003 in which two PRI factions fought for control of the party's congressional delegation. And there is certainly excessive campaign spending – for instance, in the 2003 elections, the parties spent approximately $800 million, more than double the figure spent in equivalent elections in Japan (Cervantes and Gil Olmos, 2003).

And if we cannot trust politicians, or parties, or deputies, or senators, or public employees, whom can we trust? The answer of the omnipresent electronic media is clear: faced with the general crisis of political values, only television 'commentators' are left. Upright, incorruptible, untainted men and women like *Brozo the gloomy clown* who in 2004, on the order of the federal government and Televisa, Mexico's largest media company, launched the first on-screen offensive against the PRD, and in particular against the capital's mayor. The media lynching continued during 2005, when President Fox attempted to prosecute López Obrador on a minor issue in order to disqualify him as a presidential candidate, a sinister venture in which the Prosecutor General, PAN and PRI deputies, the President of the Supreme Court, the business elite, the church hierarchy and, naturally, the mainstream media were all complicit. When more than a million people marched in Mexico City to protest against the move to strip their mayor of parliamentary immunity, Fox was forced to back down. However, the following year, during the presidential campaign, the official and de facto powers closed ranks against López Obrador, unleashing a hate campaign in which anti-populism replaced the anti-communism of the 'cold war' and in which television electoral advertising resembled the Nazi propaganda of Joseph Goebbels.

It should come as no surprise that, according to polls, three out of every four Mexicans do not trust parties and only 47 per cent prefer democracy as a form of government. Even more disturbing was the response to a survey conducted by the magazine *Este País*, in which 33 per cent answered that it was 'preferable to sacrifice some freedoms of expression, assembly and self-organisation in exchange for a life without economic pressures' (Sánchez Rebolledo, 2004:21). Thus, during the 2006 election campaign, the conservative, but initially not repressive, government of Vicente Fox escalated the violence against mining–metallurgical workers, *campesinos* and teachers, leaving four people dead, countless others injured, hundreds detained and many others physically abused. All of this in the context of a rightist campaign that cast López Obrador as another Hugo Chávez and as 'a danger to Mexico', and sought the 'fear vote' at all costs with the help of images of street violence.

However, there were also anti-political voices coming from the progressive, sunny side of the street, which rejected elections as a means of change and agreed with the right on the disqualification of López Obrador. Neo-zapatismo and its followers hold that the parliamentary left has no agenda and that when it governs it behaves the same as the right; that the once-progressive parties only want to win elections in order to obtain public sinecures; that the political left rides on the backs of popular movements and recruits their leaders; that certain social leaders have sold out their movements for a seat in the Chamber of Deputies; or that if occasionally left-wing leaders such as López Obrador are popular, it is undoubtedly because they are populists. Nor could we do without the old cannibalistic and paranoid syndrome of the left, according to which we have in every leftist politician, either potentially or in their actions, a traitor to the social movements (in other times, they would have been called reformists, agents of imperialism or revisionists). There is a lot of truth in this: we suffer from a crisis of utopias, vote-chasing parties and corrupt leaders. However, once again the problem is in the tone.

And in the anti-systemic left, the melody behind the precise critique of institutional politics is not fascism (which to be sure exists), but rather the apocalyptic hypothesis that national states are totally devoid of content, that representative democracy as a political system is no longer useful, and that there is no alternative other than the globalisation of resistance and local self-governance. These generous and visionary ideas call our attention to relatively new phenomena, but by exaggerating their conclusions, they confuse certain tendencies with all-encompassing realities. Even more serious is that when the arena of institutional politics is deserted, the terrain is ceded not to traditional party bureaucrats and their ancient rituals, but to the Thermidoreans of the PRI and the neo-authoritarians of the PAN. Because in the current Mexican conjuncture, the discrediting of representative democracy, institutions and formal public procedures does not help to overcome the alienation from bureaucratic apparatuses, but rather to restore submission; it does not foment post-politics, but rather pre-politics.

Sectors of both the right and the left coincide in their anti-politics, but with very different starting-points and conceptual foundations. From the fundamentalist right, the exhaustion of politics – and the end of history – originates in the acknowledgement of the market as the automatic provider of all available happiness. From the radical left, the exhaustion of national states and institutions – and the beginning of real history – is accompanied by a wager on society as the self-managing, solidaristic provider of all possible happiness. With symmetrical extremisms – from the fundamentalism of the automatic market or of social autarky – neo-liberalism and progressive anti-politics reject the national state as a sphere in which the course of history is also defined.

I totally agree with the wager on the social and the rejection, on principle, of both the market that subordinates use value to exchange value, and the state that subjects its citizens to institutions. In an earlier work (Bartra, 2003a: 126–38), I explained my agreements and differences with the anti-politics advocated by John Holloway (Holloway, 2002). But this is a theoretical digression and in Mexico the dilemma is above all of a practical nature. In 2001, after the National Congress refused to recognise indigenous rights under the terms of the Cocopa Law, the president accepted the failure of the legislation and the Supreme Court refused to intervene in the matter, the EZLN concluded that the three branches of government had turned their backs on the people and that all institutional doors were closed.

Marcos himself stated in the Thirteenth *Estela* (declaration): 'If the state is seen as a private company, it is best that is managed by managers and not politicians. And in the neo-enterprise "nation-state.com", the art of politics is no longer useful' (Sub-comandante insurgente Marcos, 2003:3). These same ideas were reproduced in the Sixth Declaration of the Lacandon Forrest, and they inspired the organisational project behind 'the other campaign' national tour. These conclusions are understandable, since the EZLN's principal demand for renewing political negotiations with the government – namely, to make the Cocopa Law constitutional – had been frustrated on two occasions, in 1996 and 2001. But this assessment, whether true or biased, could hardly authorise them to discredit the work of party or social forces that have decided to continue pursuing 'institutional politics', much less to label them as accomplices of repression and counter-insurgents: 'the "nice" forms of dialogue [with the government] help to delegitimise radical protests and criticisms, and open the door to stigmatising and repressing whoever does not submit to the rules of the game imposed by the authorities' (López Monjardín and Sandoval Álvarez, 2003:38). These positions, published in January 2003, at the very moment when the mass rural movement was in full deployment (and had itself negotiated with the government at various moments), served to demonise the *campesino* leadership, particularly those who moved in Zapatista circles (Bartra, 2003b).

Thus, an armed force that favoured the electoral road in 1994, that pushed for negotiations with the government as a way to achieve reforms between 1995 and 1996, and that demanded constitutional changes favourable to the indigenous population in 2001; a paradoxical army that chose peace, that does not want power, and that gave rise to some of the most original and significant social mobilisations of the 1990s; rebels who for almost eight years dedicated themselves to pushing for reforms in a revolutionary manner, finally decided that the terrain of institutional politics is a minefield. Apparently, some of them first arrived at this conclusion in 1984, when the Fuerzas de Liberación Nacional (National Liberation Forces, FLN) entered the jungle to organise an army, and again in 1994, when the EZLN declared war on bad government. Maybe at the time they were right, since Mexico was living under an institutional dictatorship, anti-establishment militants were dropping like flies, and the indigenous peoples were suffering a slow agony. But in the last decade, for better or worse, we have inaugurated democracy, not as an infallible cure for all evils, but as a battleground.

In mid 2006, the left had 15 million voters. It governed around 20 million Mexicans, including those living in the capital city. It regularly mobilised 3 or 4 million people on the streets. It was capable of unifying the majority of organised rural and urban workers, including significant numbers of the old state trade unionism, behind its national project. It assembled the cream of the intelligentsia, both in the sciences and the arts, and it brought together the best of civil society organised into networks and NGOs. Because of all of this, but also due to its percentage of votes and its power in the national Congress, as well as in state legislative and executive bodies, the left was already the second most important political force in the country.

The liberationist programme that Mexico has been following over the last decade has been reinforced by practices in intensive direct democracy, while innovative, representative democracy is not a settled matter, but rather unfinished business involving many people. Despite the disappointment that its effects have not been magical, the majority of citizens continue to believe that it is worth having elections and that the parties have to reform, because they are necessary. As for the social movements that have been very active in recent years, it is clear that the broadest and most representative of them are seeking (and finding) opportunities for negotiating power, with both the executive and legislative branches of government. For citizens and interest associations, the 'doors' that the EZLN speaks of are neither completely open, nor totally closed.

This willingness to pursue the institutional path was illustrated by the increased voter turnout in the 2006 presidential elections, which was more than 10 per cent higher than that of 2003. Moreover, the viability of this path for popular sectors seeking a progressive alternative is demonstrated by the 15 million votes that went to the centre-left candidate, in spite of the dirty and malicious electoral campaign that he confronted and the subsequent manipulation of the results.

Neo-populism?

In Mexico, the debate about populism does not only refer to its dubious validity as an alternative programme or to the necessary settling of accounts with certain periods in our history; above all, it has to do with the profile and structure of the new left that has emerged in the last decade and a half. This is a central concern of a book on the Mexican left (Semo, 2003) in which the author reports on, among other things, the difficult incorporation of local socialists into the world of elections. This has been a difficult transition for those who are used to thinking of revolution as a definitive rupture, but all the more so because in Mexico's perfect dictatorship, elections were in fact a farce. Therefore, the electoral experiments of 1979, 1982 and 1985 were very modest experiences, which became election prehistory when the civic insurgency of 1988 put the system in a predicament. Out of the crisis and the electoral fraud, the PRD emerged as a fusion of the communist and socialist left grouped together in the PMS, along with the Democratic Current that split off from the PRI.

'The new party was born in the midst of the ideological wreckage of the old left. The PMS abandoned socialism without explanation' (Semo, 2003:113), writes the communist historian and activist, who laments that the historical left went astray at that critical moment, diluting itself in neo-populism, revolutionary nationalism and *caudillismo*. Perhaps the doctrinaire left did not in fact fully reclaim its heritage in the merger, but even so the mixture seems basically fruitful, since the contribution of neo-cardenismo is not limited to favouring electoral insurrection and goes beyond the undesirable baggage of narrow statism and nationalism. The convergence of the PMS with the Democratic Current is not an ill-fated accident that interrupted the supposed modernising course of Mexican socialism, but rather a fortunate encounter of two currents of our historical left ('possibilist' Cardenismo and utopian communism, pro-system and anti-system progressives), against the backdrop of a powerful and generalised social mobilisation.

Although it saddens those of us who are cultivating another genealogical tree, the truth is that in 1988 the capacity to convince large sectors that the left's agenda was viable came mainly from the Democratic Current identified with revolutionary nationalism. And with this template, the initial phase of the new left had to be nostalgic, whether for twilight or dawn is unknown. But that is what the historical Zapatismo was as well: a gesture by some *campesinos* who rose up because 'they did not want to change' (Womack, 1969:xi), and ready for anything, decided to change everything, because when it comes to social movements, the new is always born looking back. The idealised past is a powerful lever. The only problem is that the retro trend is an ephemeral political resource, and if the new Mexican left does not want to become conservative and backward-looking, it will have to build alternative projects by looking to the future.

The new Mexican left, like that of the entire world, is united in its opposition to neo-liberalism, not so much for doctrinaire reasons as for the fact that every day we are having to collect the dead. But to go from there to an alternative project that diverges as much from savage capitalism as from real-existing socialism and the 'third way', is a long stretch. Above all because it is not about applying make-up to the most repulsive features of the existing order, nor is it about drawing up plans for a perfect utopia, which at the indicated hour is to be built everywhere by means of social engineering. Rather than either dull pragmatism or vacuous hallucinations, let us instead seek an alliance between 'possibilism' and utopia.

Apart from that, we have accumulated some experiences in the task of giving positive content to the project of making another world possible. And these contributions – in the fields of economy, society, culture, technology and politics – come from below (from the activism of the communities, networks, collectives and professional civic associations), but also from above (from the parties of the left, reformist governments and progressive legislators). A substantial part of these contributions comes from the extraordinary social ferment that is neo-zapatismo, particularly because of its convergence with the indigenous movement, whose struggle for constitutional recognition and for the practical exercise of autonomy connects with the long-term struggle of ordinary Mexicans to rid themselves of the interfering post-revolutionary Leviathan. In the 1940s and 1950s, it was the struggles against corporatism and for the independence of interest group organisations; in the 1980s, it was battles for self-management in the areas of the economy and services; and since the 1990s, it has been the indigenous struggle for autonomy, the symbol of everyone's aspirations – indigenous and *mestizo* – to develop effective self-government. Successive phases and coexistent spaces of the people's anti-authoritarian zeal, independence and self-management are not enough to shake off the cobwebs of power. Political self-determination is what is needed. And in this, the indigenous are inescapable, since the radical nature of their autonomies derives from their being founded on a prior right, in a certain sense outside the hegemonic order. They were already there when the Spanish arrived and founded the colony from which the nation-state that we call Mexico emerged. The indigenous are not a crack in the system because of some ontological virtue or because they have remained outside it – in fact, they have not.

In contrast to Enrique Semo, for whom the main ideological confrontation in contemporary Mexico is between neo-populism and neo-liberalism (Semo, 2003), I argue that the historical tension that we are experiencing today is that between neo-liberalism and its various critics. And the range of these critics is the spectrum of what we can call the left: a broad and diverse left that includes those who are content with moderating the excesses of the system as well as those who advocate its total overthrow. Undoubtedly, among the opponents of neo-liberalism there exists outdated populism, regressive statism and coarse nationalism; just as one can also find old-fashioned socialist yearnings, naïve voluntarism, millenarianism and all sorts of narrow particularisms of which so-called civil society is so fond. But this is what plurality is made of; especially when we are only just beginning to recover from our recent disfigurements and from the debacle that the twentieth century represented for the left.

Movements and parties: the left on the streets

While the mass media delight in the intrigues of palace politics, progressive parties suffer recurrent internal crises, social Zapatistas resist and political Zapatistas conspire with the old left, there is a country where millions of irate citizens protest in the plazas; a country where organised workers and *campesinos* have founded numerous popular fronts; a country where neo-liberal policies are defeated time and time again, in the streets and in parliament, thanks to the concerted action of the social and the political left; a country where the civic left mobilised nearly 3 million people in protest against the electoral fraud of 2006.

Certainly it is not the Mexico depicted hysterically on television, nor the Mexico desired by the forces of restoration and fascism. The country that calls for optimism is the Mexico of the common people that in 2003 and early 2004 filled the Plaza de la Constitución a dozen times (demanding salvation for the countryside and an end to privatisation, opposing taxes on food and medicine, rejecting the anti-worker reform of the Federal Labour Law, defending the pensions of retirees, and showing support for the left-wing government of Mexico City). We also filled the Plaza Mayor on 12 April 2003, protesting against the war in Iraq, and on 21 June claiming the right to be gay, lesbian, bisexual or transsexual without dying in the attempt.

On 27 March 2003, at the height of the demonstrations of the movement for the salvation of the countryside, a mass convergence of trade unions and rural organisations founded the Labour, Campesino and Social Front to push for food self-sufficiency, employment, a dignified life and sustainable development. The Front represents something very similar to the providential worker–peasant alliance, on which we leftists had pinned our hopes. In times of non-traditional and post-class movements, this convergence of workers does not exhaust the available cast of social actors, but the fact is that since its formation, it has been engaged in continuous activity.

The majority of Mexicans chose to push the democratic transition from the right. We are paying dearly for it. We have spent half a decade struggling bravely to stop the regressive changes driven by the 'government of change'. And we have not done a bad job: the surrender of energy utilities to multinational capital, the privatisation of education and health, the tax reform that would have the rich pay less and the poor pay more, and the new Federal Labour Law forged by phoney leaders and businessmen – none of these passed. What the left needs to do now is to put forward its own alternatives, first looking for broad popular consensus and then negotiating pragmatically in order to form the necessary parliamentary majorities, since purely symbolic logic no longer satisfies anyone.

During the days of protest in the winter of 2003, the rural organisations did this by reaching an agreement on a *Campesino* Plan for the third millennium, which helped them in their negotiations with the government. Through it, the *campesinos* placed themselves at the vanguard as a sector, but also demonstrated that to resist is not the same as to build; that *no* sometimes wins in one fell swoop, as when the ominous projects of the 'enemy' get 'derailed', whereas *yes* requires gradual building of viable collective proposals, dialogues with the same 'enemy' in perpetually difficult negotiations, broad alliances with very diverse and sometimes dubious organisations, slow and sinuous accumulation of strength; and everything through prolonged processes with brief spectacular moments and long grey periods, as well as with encouraging advances but also setbacks that discourage, confront and disperse. That is the life of grassroots organisations, and anyone who thinks that it is about resisting and protesting does so because they do not have to work for a living.

But it is not only the *campesinos* who have proposals. The indigenous peoples constructed a solid position on autonomy some time ago and have translated it into legal terms (EZLN and Gobierno Federal, 2003). The workers know how to modernise the electric industry without privatising it. There are those in the independent union movement who not only reject Fox's labour reforms but are also proposing an alternative. The parliamentary opposition has put forward progressive tax proposals. The municipal movement is demanding the strengthening of local government and putting forward very precise ideas for this. Environmentalists are advancing solutions to the problems of sustainability. And the women's movement has a clear idea of what it means to incorporate gender into the legal framework and public policies.

Thus, the most promising left is in the streets. And it is in the streets, plazas, factories, schools, maize fields and orchards where the social left is developing actors and weaving plans. The social left, however, is not the entire left. Plural as they are, the movements have the wealth of their diversity and the weakness of their particularities. Without a doubt, horizontal agreements make it possible to assemble mergers and draw up common platforms. But universality is not merely the sum of different parts. The consensual construction of the common good with preferential treatment for those at the bottom of the heap (like the challenge of steering the boat we are all in with distinction, justice and seafaring skill) is a political task that calls for political subjects in the strict sense of the word. Understanding that all of us are always and everywhere involved in the making of politics, there are actors, moments and spaces in which politics is condensed.

It is there that the 'rubber meets the road', as our political left stumbles on and its largest party, the PRD, has yet to emerge from its crises. To transform the inorganic civic insurgency of the late 1980s into a structured political institution was in the end a good choice. However, it was not a good idea to try to repeat the magic of 1988 in the federal elections of 1994 and 2000, or to go from electoral maximalism (winning the national presidency at all costs) to electoral minimalism (concentrating on winning seats in Congress and the Senate, electing mayors and state governors). Above all, because in the rat race for electoral positions the PRD had the experience of dogs that run after cars and old men who chase young girls: once they got them, they forgot why they wanted them. However, there are exceptions: since 1997, similar to what has occurred with progressive governments in Porto Alegre, Montevideo and Bogotá, the successive PRD Mayors of Mexico City became the bastion of the left and a showcase of the progressive approach to public administration.

After four years of governing Mexico City, Mayor Andrés Manuel López Obrador enjoyed the highest popular approval rating of any national politician and became a candidate for the 2006 presidential elections. For the first time in the history of Mexico – a country in which leftism has always been anti-establishment and marginal – a progressive opposition party had the opportunity to attain national power, due not so much to the bad government of the right as to the good government of the left. López Obrador's election campaign, moreover, was a true accomplishment, given that in these times of media-driven politics, he toured the country three times, most often by land, bringing nearly 3 million supporters into the streets. The result was a doubling of votes for the PRD and, according to followers, a victory at the polls that the official authorities and de facto powers sought to deny him.

DIRECTIONS

Revolutionising democracy, democratising revolution

Distancing oneself from both neo-liberalism and Mexican-style populism implies defining a path distinct from savage capitalism as well as revolutionary nationalism, a model which makes economic growth, social justice and environmental health compatible, and which harmonises globalisation and national sovereignty. But this is only part of the package, because populism is equally a political order in which the state–society relationship is based on loyalties, patronage and compensations rather than democratic mechanisms. The political alternative to populism must therefore be a new democratic model. Hence, when representative democracy is in crisis, such that authoritarian temptations are revived from both above and below, the option is a different democracy, a renewed democracy.

In these times of unbridled globalisation – aptly called neo-liberal – we are told that the state has withered away, leaving to the market the task of allocating resources and putting everyone in his or her place. Such is not the case. Rather than stepping aside, the state allies itself with the cause of the market and its sharks. Under savage capitalism, politics is perverted and exacerbated, becoming the continuation of the economy by other means. For its part, colonial war, which daily splatters us with blood, is the condensation of politics.

The dilemma of the twentieth century (state versus market) has been left behind. Today we know that under the absolute mercantilist order, the political Leviathan ends up doing the bidding of the economic Leviathan. In the casino economy, the state is the croupier who deals marked cards to the big betters; likewise, in a world of bourgeois thieves in which the corporations practise organised crime, the state is the corrupt police force and the venal judge. Thus, the wager of the third millennium must be society, as we have no other choice.

To make revolution, to toss the tortilla on the griddle, is to put things on their feet; it is to enable workers and citizens to assume power over the economy and over politics, which at present is usurped by the market and the state. This is the new democracy: a broadened, radical, 'high intensity' democracy, like that envisioned by Boaventura de Sousa Santos (2003a), who has called for 'democratising democracy'. To bring the market under control and bring the state down a peg or two, it is necessary to strengthen society, and this presupposes demystifying politics. We need a secular politics, one that is also practised outside party institutions: in factories and the fields, in the suburbs, communities and schools, as well as in professional associations and social movements.

But reclaiming the value of informal or non-professional politics is not to disparage public institutions (such as parliaments and political parties), where there is a bit of everything, both good and bad, or the arena, norms and practices of formal democracy. The state is not a dead dog, especially if is a question of *maintaining* the existing order (with its colonial wars, counterinsurgencies and repressive campaigns). But it is also not completely inadequate when it is a question of *changing* the existing order. In order to maintain things as they are, power from above is sufficient. But in order to bring about fundamental change, it is essential to have power from above and below, from outside and inside. We are in need of both the positive force of the stone and the negative force of the flame: structures that stabilise and processes that counteract their inertia. At times of crisis of the political system, to reject the institutional sphere as a strategic terrain and to bet on reactive 'rebellions' or to entrench oneself in autarchic 'resistance' (with the logic of someone seated at the entrance to a house waiting for the system's corpse to pass by) is to cede half the terrain to authoritarianism.

Representative democracy spurns direct democracy, but as Santos reminds us, the latter also has its delegated representatives. Thus, we need a basically participatory democracy that also employs the mechanisms of representative democracy. Formal democracy (trustworthy elections, pluralist competition, freedom of association and expression, transparency, accountability, the possibility of removing officials from their posts and the right to information) is essential; but without broadened democracy (referenda, informed deliberation, participation in consensus administration and creation), formal democracy is empty of content. And without participation, representative democracy becomes discredited and gives way. But it is not self-management itself that is validated, but rather authoritarian procedures.

For self-management to flourish, we need a democratic, active, energetic and strong state. Low-intensity democracies are fragile and cannot support pluralist participation and thus tend towards authoritarianism. In contrast, high-intensity democracies, with robust and legitimate institutions, welcome and favour the broadest and most diverse self-management, which allows them to become consolidated, because there is in fact not a single democracy, but several; that is, diverse but articulated ways of sharing authority, which coexist, overlap, compete, confront and succeed each other.

In reality, there is no one democratic system or even many democratic systems; rather, there are transitional democracies or processes of democratisation. And at a time when the struggle against the culture of 'power over' and the shared exercise of 'power for' is not yet over, but rather is in the process of being destroyed and rebuilt, norms and institutions must be fluid, flexible and provisional.

Slow revolutions

The twentieth century has demonstrated that capitalism was not, after all, in its terminal phase, and that in the face of long-standing global structures, national anti-capitalist revolutions, understood as sharp political turns, were insufficient, since the employers they sought to overthrow returned in different guise. Today we have also lost faith in reforms, understood as precise, isolated corrections that in general the system reabsorbs without undergoing change. We are experiencing a crisis with respect to both the idea of revolution as a privileged, all-embracing event, as well as the idea of reforms as a series of partial touch-ups; just as we are seeing the disappearance of the paradigms of premeditated historical change, whether of the intensive or the extensive variety. Nevertheless, there is no doubt that we need another world, and that we need it urgently, even desperately. Thus, in order for another world to be possible, it occurs to me to think about reformist revolutions or revolutionary reforms, as well as long-term incremental subversions, or successive and articulated touch-ups in strategic plans for radical change.

I distrust instantaneous justice and speedy utopias, just as I do instant coffee, fast food and the promises of politicians. I believe in slow, but stubborn and persistent, revolutions; in reformist revolutions that favour a smooth, diverse mode of production; in just revolutions against the exploitation of those who are within the system and the genocide of those who are outside it; in gradual revolutions that procure markets that, if they are not just, are at least docile; and in progressive revolutions that favour social interactions based on solidarity with diversity and states penetrated by the people. On the other hand, we do not want 'the revolution', but rather many revolutions: parallel, consecutive, alternating and interlocking (for we are wary of unanimous paradises and fatal utopias).

Slow revolutions do not end with the 'seizure of power'. In our times, those who take winter palaces will be disappointed, as it is not the same to overthrow czars as it is to build new societies. Fettered by iniquitous trade pacts, subjected economically by corporations and multilateral organisations and politically by the crudeness of great imperial powers, the governments of second-rank countries have lost dignity and legal authority. Thus, in the view of the marginalised, getting into government – by whatever means – is not 'taking power', since it is not enough to make any real change in direction. But neither do large societies change course through resistance and self-management alone. Neither the state nor society has the power needed to improve the market and its corporate and imperial sharks – at least, not separately. If at all, it would be through their virtuous interaction, their combined action. The fact is that the power that we need so urgently is not at the local, the national, or the global level. It might possibly be in the interconnection of all three spheres. It is better that it were so.

Toward utopian realism and an ecumenical left

The new left is utopia mixed with possibility, it is dreaming and wakefulness, it is revolution and reform, it is to demand (of ourselves) the impossible while doing what can be done, because without inspiration, technique is worth little, and without the dreams of *campesinos*, 'realistic' politics is devoid of content. Progressive pragmatism inclines to the moderate and conservative centre left, because that is where majorities can be formed; but in order for democracy not to exhaust itself in parties that alternate in power, we also need to engage in a form of politics that is eccentric, extremist, representative of minorities, with a vocation for opposition, and of utopian inspiration, as only in that way will we achieve the political changes that will move the centre towards the progressive end of the spectrum.

In Mexico we have a pragmatic parliamentary left embodied in the PRD, which co-governs and legislates; an anti-system and utopian left inspired by neo-zapatismo, which sustains inspiring self-management experiences; and a social left in the form of associations and civic organisations, which promotes popular fronts, convergences, networks and campaigns. But while each focuses on its own interests, there will be no way forward.

Thus, it would be good to reclaim the old formula that spoke of a plurality of *lefts*, since what we need most is the fruitful encounter of diverse communities and groupings: a politics that transcends particularities without negating them. However, in these difficult global times, when domination and genocide are being universalised by the insatiable appetite of a single aggressive power, counter-politics must also become globalised. Not in the old logic of the 'Internationals', in the hermeneutic of the 'founding fathers', or in orthodoxy and vanguards (socialist countries lead humanity, the proletariat leads the peasantry, and the party leads the soviets), but rather in the multi-centric perspective of virtuous diversity.

Thus, I bet on the lefts, or if you prefer, on an ecumenical left, in the Greek sense of the totality of the inhabited world and in the Christian sense of the point of encounter of multiple denominations. And this polyphonic left will be global, national and local; militant in its diversity, but fraternal and convergent when it comes to larger causes; and utopian, so that it is not living for some postponed happiness and yearning for the future. For every day, it goes against the current in building forms of solidarity in the interstices of the system, and is unanimous in the hope that another world is possible, but plural in its horizons, because one does not dream the same dream in a hammock as on a carpet, or on a mat as on a mattress.

8 BOLIVIA
The Left and the Social Movements
Luis Tapia

What we call *left*, or left-wing, positions tend to be a combination of various forms of political entities. For the purpose of this analysis we can identify four of these: political parties, trade unions, political-ideological groups and social movements. In different times and countries, the left has been a variable combination of these and other forms of political action. This chapter summarises the principal historical tendencies that explain the current state and prospects of the left in Bolivia today.

Given that the trade unions and the workers' movement have predominated within the spectrum of the Bolivian left, any historical analysis hinges on the relationship between unions and parties. The study of the contemporary left, however, will be centred on the existing link between social movements and the *campesino* party of the left over the last few decades.

The chapter begins with a historical introduction to the main characteristics and events of the Bolivian left in the twentieth century. The second part describes and analyses the composition of the present-day Bolivian left, maintaining as a historical reference point the account given in the first part. Finally, the future prospects for the left, in particular the possibilities for links between social movements and parties, will be examined.

A BRIEF HISTORY OF THE BOLIVIAN
LEFT IN THE TWENTIETH CENTURY

For much of the last century the make-up of the left revolved around two axes: class and nation. At the end of the century a third axis was incorporated: democracy. This means that the left had organised to condemn exploitation by local and international elites, and dedicated itself to organising the working class. There is a workerist-socialist element which runs throughout this period, and an anarchist element which developed primarily in the first three decades of the century.

The first socialist party was established in 1914. During the 1920s various regional socialist parties were founded, which in their discourse, programmes and composition combined ideas and militants of anarchist and socialist origin. The Trotskyites organised the Partido Obrero Revolucionario (Revolutionary Workers' Party, POR) in 1934. About the same time, local workers' federations were established and newspapers with considerable anarchist involvement and influence were published.

As already mentioned, a central characteristic of the Bolivian left is the relationship between the parties and trade unions of this political orientation. From the beginning of the last century, there was actually a parallel growth of the parties of the left on the one hand, and the trade unions and workers' federations, on the other. Thus, in the first years of the century, nuclei of working-class organisation emerged which evolved into the country's main parties and trade union centres between the 1920s and 1940s. What is unique to the Bolivian case is that historically the parties of the left have been intrinsically connected to the trade unions. And so, in the 1950s – and particularly after the national revolution of 1952 – the unions were at the heart of the Bolivian left.[1]

As far as ideology is concerned, it was Gustavo Navarro – a socialist better known as Tristán Marof – who in his book *La justicia del Inca* (The Inca Legal System, 1926) set out the programme of the left for the twentieth century: the land for the people and the mines in the hands of the state – in other words, agrarian reform and nationalisation. What is noteworthy about this text is that whilst setting out what would go on to be the programme of revolutionary nationalism and, more broadly, that of the nationalist revolution of 1952, it makes a positive assessment of the way the Incas were organised and of their principles of justice. Therefore, from its inception, the left was made up of three components: the socialist tradition, the national question and the recovery of ethnic roots and local pre-hispanic history. The last component was to disappear from the Bolivian left in subsequent decades and only reappeared at the end of the last century. As I will demonstrate further on, the programmatic integration of the three elements which Marof set out in *La justicia del inca* and in *La tragedia del altiplano* (The Tragedy of the Highlands, 1934) still constitutes the core of the Bolivian left at the end of the twentieth century and the beginning of the twenty-first century, to which a new component (democracy) has been added, stemming from the struggles of the 1970s.

The second great historical project of the left was set out in a document published by the *Federación Sindical de Trabajadores Mineros* (Trade Union Federation of Mineworkers), founded in 1938, which is known as the *Tesis de Pulacayo (The Pulacayo Thesis*, 1946). It is a workerist, socialist and anti-imperialist manifesto. From then on, the trade unions and their nationwide voice from 1952 onwards – the Central Obrera Boliviana (Bolivian Workers' Confederation, COB) – were where the political programmes and projects of the Bolivian left were set out. The Communist Party and the Socialist Party drew up their programmes and political projects, and presented them to the trade unions and the COB for their approval as the official position of the workers' movement.

This tendency continued and became more widespread, as can be seen by the COB's *Tesis política (Political Thesis)*, passed in 1970. A common feature of the two documents, drawn up 24 years apart, is that the working class and its political activity should be united around a workers' confederation, which in the 1970s took the form of the COB at a national level. This means that, in the main political strategy documents recognised by the left, the specific form class unity and political organisation would take was not through a party or parties, but through the workers' confederation, which indicates the clear predominance of trade unions over parties.

Given the characteristics of the Bolivian economy, with its traditional dependency on extraction of natural resources (from silver to copper and gas), two of the central features of the left's discourse and programmes in the twentieth century were nationalism and anti-imperialism. Therefore, for the three decades following the revolution of 1952, the nationalisation of natural resources and of the companies that exploited them invariably figured among the proposals of the Bolivian left. In these proposals, the combination of nationalism and statism took the form of a developmentalist state which would encourage the industrialisation of the country and the economic sovereignty of the nation.

The co-government of 1952, which reappeared in the popular assembly of 1970, was a result of failures in organisation of the working class which took on the responsibility of representing the rest of the workers and governed first alongside another part of Bolivian society which was organised as a nationalist party, and then later with the parties of the left. The existence of a working-class, nationalist and statist project continued until the end of the 1970s, when the Partido Socialista (Socialist Party, PS), led by Marcelo Quiroga Santa Cruz, became the core of a multi-class project. So the Socialist Party presented its project both to the COB and to the general public in the hope of mass electoral support. As a result, the party received 7.65 per cent of the popular vote in 1980, which led to the election of eleven parliamentarians.

As already mentioned, in the 1960s and 1970s, the left took on the defence of democracy to add to its nationalist, statist and workerist platform. In the context of the right-wing dictatorships of René Barrientos in the 1960s and Hugo Banzer in the 1970s, the left put the emphasis on demanding political rights and freedoms for the working class and the Bolivian population in general.[2] The left's leading role in this movement symbolised a shift in its traditional position in relation to democracy. In the past, democracy was in fact seen either as a means of organising the dominant class's political power (for example, within organisations such as the POR), or else as a step towards socialism (for example, within groups such as the Socialist Party's PS-1). With the left's shift towards the demand for democracy and civil liberties, manifested in the mass trade union mobilisation against the dictatorship and the crucial pressure of the parties and coalitions of the left such as the Unidad Democrática Popular (Popular and Democratic Union, UDP) and the Socialist Party, the government was forced to call elections in 1978.

The transition to democracy, therefore, led to the electoral strengthening of the left, mainly of the UDP, a coalition of over 20 organisations including the majority of the parties of the left and non-party organisations. At its core were the Movimiento Nacionalista Revolucionario de Izquierda (Nationalist Revolutionary Movement of the Left, MNR-I), the Partido Comunista de Bolivia (Bolivian Communist Party, PCB) and the Movimiento de Izquierda Revolucionario (Revolutionary Left Movement, MIR). That is, the nationalist revolutionary left, the communist left and the left of Christian-democratic origin. The coalition's programme consisted mainly of recovering and continuing the nationalist project of 1952.

The UDP won three consecutive elections. In 1979, it won with 31.22 per cent of the vote, in 1980, with 34.05 per cent, and probably with a larger margin in 1978, but there are no official figures since the armed forces again staged a coup d'etat, thus cancelling the election results. When the UDP returned to the corridors of power in 1982 during the transitional government, it obtained 57 of the 150 parliamentary seats, a figure which, although high, was not enough to form a majority and left it subject to blockade by the parliamentary right.

In the 1980s, however, the limits of the left's trade union–party class-based project became evident. On the one hand, the link between trade unions and parties continued to be too weak to promote lasting electoral victories. On the other hand, the workers' movement showed remarkable power of resistance, capable even of causing a continuous crisis in both government and state, but still incapable of reforming one or the other. In conclusion, the workers' movement and the left had not yet resolved the classic dilemma of the inclusion of the rest of the country's social sectors in its political programme. It was a political platform of class democracy, and in this lay the strengths and weaknesses of the left in the last century.

THE CONTEMPORARY LEFT IN BOLIVIA

The political programmes of contemporary movements and parties revolve around two fundamental axes. The first is national sovereignty, which entails autonomy with respect to the country's macroeconomic policy decisions and, above all, the recovery of legal, economic and political control over property, exploitation and commercialisation of natural resources, in particular of hydrocarbon reserves. In this sense, there is a point of continuity between the *old* left and the *new* left, which presupposes the nationalisation of resources and economic sovereignty as a prerequisite for the political democratisation of the country (see Zavaleta, 1983, 1986).

The second programmatic axis of the left is democracy, based on two propositions: to extend the presence of workers in parliament and government through new party organisations, and to call for a constituent assembly in order to carry out structural reform of Bolivia's political institutions.

The rise of new movements and parties

Confronted by the decline of the left during the 1980s and 1990s, the organisations which composed it followed different paths. Those parties with a middle-class social base and nationalist ideology gradually adopted neo-liberal programmes. Others have continued their electoral work on a left-wing platform. Among the latter, the case of the Izquierda Unida (United Left), whose parliamentary representation declined from ten parliamentarians at the beginning of the 1990s to four by the end of the decade, stands out.

The decline of the left was counteracted by a process of reorganisation of the popular sectors, initiated around 1985. The main impulse for the growth of the contemporary left is *campesino* trade unionism, represented mainly by the Confederación Sindical Única de Trabajadores Campesinos de Bolivia (Confederation of Peasant Workers' Unions of Bolivia, CSUTCB). Founded in 1979, this organisation is the result of a process of political consolidation of *Katarismo*, an Aymara Indian political movement which emerged in the Aroma province of La Paz (Hurtado, 1986), and which towards the end of the 1970s achieved *campesino* trade unionism autonomy through the foundation of the Movimiento Revolucionario Tupak Katari (Tupak Katari Revolutionary Movement, MRTK) and the Movimiento Indio Tupak Katari (Tupak Katari Indian Movement, MITKA) in 1978.

Katarismo has had a profound influence on the culture and politics of the country, both inside and outside the left. Its emergence was not only an indication of the country's ethnic and cultural diversity, but also of the fact that this diversity entailed different concepts of the world and history, which could be organised politically in an autonomous manner in order to challenge political power and promote reform of the Bolivian state. In turn, *Katarismo* resulted in class-based political autonomy together with the reorganisation of *campesino* trade unionism and the introduction of political and intellectual Aymara autonomy – that is, what *Kataristas* have called the two-sided expression of class and nation.

Trade union federations of the *cocaleros* (coca leaf growers) from the regions of Yungas and Chapare, led by Evo Morales, were organised within the CSUTCB. Morales joined the *cocalero* trade union movement in 1981 and, since 1994, has presided over the five federations of the tropic of Cochabamba (Oporto Ordoñez, 2002), which in 1995 gave way to the political organisation of the Asamblea por la Soberanía de los Pueblos (Assembly for Peoples' Sovereignty). The Asamblea would later be called Movimiento al Socialismo (Movement Towards Socialism, MAS). The 2002 elections marked the move towards the independence and predominance of the *cocaleros* – organised inside the MAS – within the Bolivian left. The MAS obtained 20.94 per cent of the national vote, which secured it 34 out of the 157 congressional seats. Although the novel political movement won in four of the country's nine departments, by virtue of the electoral rules it obtained only around a fifth of parliamentary representation.

The most recent Bolivian presidential election was held on 18 December 2005. The two frontrunners were Evo Morales and Jorge Quiroga, the candidate of the Poder Democrático y Social party (Democratic and Social Power, PODEMOS) and former leader of the Acción Democrática Nacionalista party (Nationalist Democratic Action, ADN) respectively. Morales won the election with 54 per cent of the vote, an absolute majority.

The MAS is explicitly organised from within the *cocalero* trade unions, that is, as a result of a class decision to organise a party from its own midst. Its nucleus is in the assemblies and the *cocalero* trade union federations. In this sense, the history of the MAS is similar to that of European social democracy, insofar as it represents a trade union initiative to organise parties in order to seek power in parliament and in the executive through the electoral route. That is where MAS's novelty lies, in contrast to the already mentioned secular tendency of the Bolivian trade unions and parties to act as parallel structures, coming together for specific joint actions.

The second group of *campesino* trade unions, which constitutes the backbone of the contemporary left's social mobilisation, revolves around the CSUTCB. Under the leadership of Felipe Quispe, principal organiser of the MITKA, this centre of *campesino* trade unionism mobilised on a mass scale, particularly in the highlands, in order to oppose neo-liberal policies and to demand a change in the country's legal and economic structures. In the case of both the MAS and the MITKA, the change in the composition of the left's leadership can be seen by the fact that its leaders, Evo Morales and Felipe Quispe respectively, are Aymara.[3] The leadership of the left has gone from being middle class to being of *campesino* and worker origin. In this sense, Bolivian politics, in particular the trajectory of the MAS, which – unlike the MITKA – explicitly calls itself left wing, has tuned into a tendency previously observed in the Brazilian Workers' Party (PT), which has been led by a former trade union leader since its foundation.

Therefore, the substantial change in the new left in relation to what we looked at in the previous section is that while its axis continues to be the trade unions, these are no longer worker, manufacturing or miners' unions, but mainly *campesino* unions. Therefore, the transformation of the party system is being led from the periphery, from the countryside to the city. The growth in the left's influence, both in parliament and in politics in general, is rooted in the resurgence of class organisation (specifically the case of the *cocaleros* from Chapare) and its links with *campesino* community organisations based on the Aymara Indian cultural identity.

The change in the composition of the social forces which are at the heart of the renovation and political essence of the left is reflected in changes in its ideology and discourse. The most noteworthy shift is the replacement of a workerist discourse with one centred on the indigenous nations and the *campesinos* as political subjects (see Albó, 2002). This transformation has its roots in the *Katarista* movement of the 1970s and in the process of political organisation of the indigenous peoples of the Bolivian east, the Amazon and Chaco regions, who are descendants of the Chiriguano-Guaraní peoples. The original name of the MAS (Asamblea por la Soberanía de los Pueblos, Assembly for Peoples' Sovereignty) already took on board the *cocaleros'* criticism of the sovereignty of one single Bolivian nation and its demand for sovereignty over all Bolivia's peoples.

In the ideology of the new left, therefore, Bolivia is seen as a country which contains various peoples who have developed their own systems of traditional authority throughout history. The indigenous element in Bolivia is something plural and heterogeneous, which is reflected in the east and in the *altiplano* (highlands plateau) in its own forms of organisation and government that were not eliminated during the Spanish domination or the post-colonial republic, and which today are the organisational support for agrarian trade union mobilisations. In addition to this mobilisation of traditional and community grassroots movements, there exist modern trade union practices on the land where the 1952 agrarian reform resulted in an increase in small properties and their modernisation, as in the valleys of Cochabamba.

The political strengthening of movements and parties has led to the re-emergence of an old project of the Bolivian left, focused on direct popular participation in government. This project was put forward during the co-government of the nationalist or left-wing parties following the 1952 revolution and the Popular Assembly experience of 1970. The contemporary embodiment of the co-government project was the proposal to hold a National Constituent Assembly to re-found Bolivia's institutional framework with the participation of representatives of all the country's peoples and of all the organisations of the working class, *campesinos* and indigenous communities. Thus, the left's idea of co-government has broadened considerably, from being a proposal for participation of trade unions, nationalist parties and the left in the executive power, to being a proposal for radical democratisation that involves the incorporation of political participation by all communities, workers' organisations and peoples of the country in a permanent and structured manner.

The experience of the Co-ordinator
for the Defence of Water and Life

The decline and lack of organisation of the working class, as a result of neo-liberal reforms, has been offset by new democratic forms of popular organisation which emerged in the movement against the privatisation of the municipal water utility in Cochabamba, in 2000. Known worldwide as the *water war,* it has become one of the icons of the international left and of the resistance to neo-liberalism. For the purposes of this chapter, what is most relevant about the water war is the type of political organisation that was behind it, insofar as the Coordinadora de Defensa del Agua y de la Vida (Co-ordinator for the Defence of Water and Life, hereafter known as the Co-ordinator) represents the convergence of new democratic forms of social mobilisation, which are central to the new left.

The coalition of forces represented by the Co-ordinator which made it possible to reverse the contract to privatise the water system that the Bolivian government had signed with Bechtel – a US-based transnational corporation – arose from mass engagement in the organisation and revival of local organisations, trade unions and peasants committees (around irrigation rights), leading to the opening of windows of opportunity for political participation and the resurgence of local democracy. As a reaction against the subjugation of national democracy to obscure deals signed by political parties and the economic elites, alternative opportunities emerged or re-emerged for participation and mobilisation against the country's privatisation policies. Thus, at the end of the 1990s, grassroots democratisation and local democracy had already taken the form of links between diverse social and political groups and consultative and decision-making assemblies which were linked to forums of larger-scale participation to which they elected representatives (see Olivera, 2004).

The Co-ordinator was conceived as a way of connecting these local direct-democracy groups through mechanisms such as popular consultation, open discussions and assemblies for decision-making and consultation about strategies in the struggle for water. At the same time, the Co-ordinator is a representative form of democracy, since in its co-ordination efforts it includes the participation of representatives from all the organisations that form part of it, which in turn are founded on territorial or sectoral consultative assemblies and the election of representatives.

It is important to highlight the difference between the functions of the Co-ordinator and that of *campesino* and worker union confederations. Whilst the union confederations link together networks of trade unions from one particular sector of workers, the Co-ordinator organises different sectors and types of organisations – not all of them class-based or sectoral in origin – interested in participating in a reorganisation of politics and society that would allow more sovereignty and enable local self-governance to be restored. What is special about the Co-ordinator is that whilst it is an organisational body for direct democracy in the Cochabamba region, it is also a representative structure for the organised sectors and for those who do not have a sectoral organisational referent, but who identify themselves with this general form of representation. Given the success of the water war, an attempt has been made to reproduce or incorporate this form of co-ordination to further the organisation and broader impact of processes and struggles initiated by other sectors.

The direct democracy project represented by the Co-ordinator has become part of the agenda of popular and worker organisations, as shown by the proposals made by these organisations to hold a National Constituent Assembly and the commitment to grassroots democracy in a new constitutional charter. According to this proposal, the new institutions would combine means of direct democracy – in consultative assemblies, local decision-making assemblies (neighbourhood, communal, trade union and others) – and the election of representatives of these local forums to other large-scale consultative bodies. Thus, direct democracy would be combined with representative democracy, the latter subordinate to the former.

In this sense, the Constitutional Assembly project, which was launched by the Co-ordinator in 2000 shortly after the water war, symbolises the attempt to turn direct democracy and its linkage with representative democracy into a permanent system. Equally, it shows the Co-ordinator's attempt to move from the local (Cochabamba) and sectoral level (the struggle for access to water) to politics at the national level.

THE PROPOSALS OF THE CONTEMPORARY LEFT

In relation to the first programmatic axis of the contemporary left, the MAS has stressed the issue of national sovereignty right from the start, initially in relation to the US-led 'war on drugs'. Its main demand has been to nationalise coca policy and therefore move towards multilateral industrialisation and commercialisation of the leaf and its processed products. After MAS took national office in 2006, the centre of its political platform has moved towards the nationalisation of hydrocarbon reserves and the industrialisation of Bolivian gas.

As far as the second axis is concerned, the MAS has become one of the pillars of democracy in Bolivia, and of its renewal through the inclusion of workers' representatives. This position has helped to counteract the erosion of the credibility of the institutions of electoral democracy, which in the 1990s had lost their legitimacy due to being controlled by discredited parties. That is, despite the polarisation it generated in parliament (or because of it), the MAS has strengthened the system of political party representation by turning parliament into a substantive and diverse debating body.

The combination of the left's two basic propositions – national resistance to neo-liberalism and defence of democracy – has resulted in a third, which emerged from the water war in 2000. It is a case of going from a simple critique of privatisation to building an alternative to it through the democratic management of the state and of state-owned companies, as has been attempted with the public water service in Cochabamba. After the water war and the repeal of the law that extended privatisation to the whole country, the groups participating in the Co-ordinator initiated a debate around the management of this service through the participation of neighbourhood organisations and the citizens of Cochabamba. If extended to the national level, this proposition by the social movements would involve collective self-management of the public services, which the central government of Bolivia had fiercely opposed. In this field, the ideas of the left continue in the direction of strengthening state companies and nationalisation of mineral resources taken from the 1952 revolution model.

The nationalisation of hydrocarbon reserves was announced by Evo Morales on 1 May 2006. The social mobilisation of October 2003 and May–June 2005 – popularly known as the *guerra del gas* (the gas war) – had provoked the forced resignation of two neo-liberal presidents: Gonzalo Sánchez de Lozada and Carlos Mesa. Although the left parties and the social movements agreed in demanding nationalisation, there was no agreement around the form and scope of such a measure. While the most radical positions demanded an immediate takeover by the Bolivian state without financial compensation to foreign companies, other sectors – including the MAS – proposed a 'procedural nationalisation' without confiscation and with proper compensation. Once the left took office, Evo Morales opted for the second alternative, taking control of hydrocarbon reserves but without a complete rupture with foreign corporations.

The decree of May 2006 substantially increased the Bolivian state's share of profits from two major gas fields, from roughly 50 per cent to 82 per cent. Under the new legal framework for the hydrocarbons sector, the government is able to renegotiate contracts and set the base price of gas according to changes in the global market, thus increasing the taxes and royalties the state receives. Before nationalisation, approximately 18 per cent of Bolivian energy revenues went to the state and 82 per cent to foreign companies; the new legal scheme reverses these percentages.

THE LINKAGE OF SOCIAL
MOVEMENTS AND PARTIES

Before closing this survey of the contemporary Bolivian left, we must think about the relationships between its two components: that is, the parties and the social movements. The milestone of the water war, which marked the reversal of the defeats of recent left movements, illustrates the most developed forms of links between movements and parties. The *cocaleros* and their organisations were actively involved in the water war and in the Co-ordinator's struggles. At the same time, the Co-ordinator has constantly supported and linked with the mobilisations that the *cocaleros* have deployed in recent years in Chapare. It is this link that has facilitated the co-ordination of the trade unionism of the *cocaleros* in Chapare with the trade unionism of the *campesinos* from the *altiplano*.

The Co-ordinator – and in particular its leader, Oscar Olivera – has played a central role in building links between movements and parties on a local and national scale. As a result of these efforts a project came about to create a co-ordinator of social movements – the so-called Estado Mayor del Pueblo (People's Joint Command), which was made up of trade unions, social movements and the political left of the MAS. However, the project of a national co-ordinator not linked to specific issues suffered a blow with the return to mobilisation around a specific cause – opposition to the export of natural gas – in 2003 and 2004. The success of the Co-ordinator for Gas, which halted the government's project to commercialise gas and contributed to the fall of the then president Gonzalo Sánchez de Losada in October 2003, suggests that it is easier to co-ordinate efforts around specific and immediate objectives than around a project of overall linkage between all the mobilisations, demands and projects of the organisations of the country.

Before taking control of the national government, the MAS was the main instrument for political articulation between trade unions and other movements. However, the MAS is not the party of the social movements, although electorally speaking it does feed off their mobilisation. It continues to be a party that represents the *cocaleros* and their trade unions, although gradually it has become the party of the workers of Bolivia, in the sense that various working-class sectors which do not have direct organic trade union links with the MAS feel they are represented by it within national politics.

CONCLUSION: PROSPECTS AND
STRATEGIES OF THE NEW LEFT

In view of the historical course of development of the Bolivian left, what are the prospects for the movements and parties described in the previous section? Given the plurality of the new Bolivian left and the fact that its strength is based on the linkage between different movements and parties, it is clear that its prospects depend largely on what happens to the process of co-ordination between these. The main driving force of the left is the social mobilisation of trade unions, communities, and the peoples' assemblies of the east and the highlands. Therefore, the electoral victory of the left in the national elections of December 2005 and the prospects of the government that took office in 2006 must be related to its ability to take on the demands and the fragments of political projects that were already developing in various social spheres across Bolivia.

Likewise, the future course of development of the left will depend on the strengthening of local democracy and the co-government of the trade unions, communities and other forms of popular and consultative representation. In this sense, the future of the left depends largely on state reforms that establish institutional frameworks favourable to direct democracy. Discussion of this issue in the constituent assembly comes up against different concepts of democracy represented by propositions that range from the administrative and political decentralisation of the country and minor adjustments to the existing liberal framework (for example, the election of prefects and departmental councils) to the federalisation of the country and autonomy for indigenous regions.

The left's political prospects are therefore fundamentally dependent on the future of democracy and local self-government processes which currently exist in three different forms. First, there are indigenous government community structures, which predate the Spanish conquest and in which the state has had little involvement. Recognition of these community structures as forms of self-government would require state reforms to incorporate them within the national political system.

Second, the trade union tradition brings with it nuclei of consultative assemblies, which on various occasions have become forms of local authority, as occurred in the mining centres in 1952 and as occurs today; and also in the experience of local democracy in the municipalities governed by the MAS in Chapare. In the latter, the mould of liberal representative democracy has become infused with direct-democracy content through the trade union assemblies. The trade union monitors the performance of the municipal authorities and of the party, and at the same time is the main nucleus of deliberation.

Third, the neighbourhood councils, above all in the popular neighbourhoods (particularly in the city of El Alto), are a form of direct democracy and self-government. Although their original purpose was to campaign for access to public services and to access 'city rights', these organisations have gradually developed public management competence and have become public arenas for consultation and social mobilisation.

The future of the left in Bolivia therefore depends largely on the conservation and promotion of these forms of local and sectoral democracy and self-government, and on their linkage with democratic structures of representation and consultation throughout the country. At the national level, the MAS's political strength has become evident in five of the country's nine departments: La Paz, Oruro, Cochabamba, Sucre and Potosi. These departments have a relatively diversified economy and strong civil society. In the other half of the country, the MAS and the left in general have been relatively weak, due to the persistence of patrimonial and clientelist structures, in which the elite of a monoproductive economy has traditionally controlled the politics and civil society of the region.

In the last elections for the Constituent Assembly, on 2 July 2006, the MAS broadened its influence in all the country's departments, since it also won in Santa Cruz and Tarija. The new legislative body will be based in the city of Sucre (the country's legal capital) and is expected to draft a new constitution for the Bolivian state within a year. The MAS won the largest number of seats in the assembly, but not the two-thirds majority needed to pass its proposals. The Morales government proposed to invest the assembly with powers of 'origination', meaning that it would be above the existing legal framework, with powers to modify the structure of the Bolivian state.[4]

The MAS was also successful in the simultaneous referendum held in July 2006 around the issue of decentralisation, which revealed a key conflict underlying the Bolivian state. The majority of the population rejected the proposal of creating 'autonomous departments', but in four departments – Santa Cruz, Pando, Beni and Tarija – the majority vote was in favour of decentralisation. The MAS was defeated in precisely those departments where an influential white and mestizo population residing in areas rich in mineral resources seeks a high level of self-government or even independence.

The MAS's most influential model has been the Brazilian Workers'

Party, which built its national power on the back of local government experiences. This demonstrates the common characteristics of these two parties, in spite of the considerable differences between the political histories of Bolivia and Brazil, since they are both new parties of the left which have developed around worker leadership, and they come from trade unions linked to a variety of organisations. Although the MAS's initial image was that it was a party of the *cocaleros*, right from the start it sought to establish itself as a comprehensive national party. Today, it is a party of the workers in general. The votes in 2002 and 2005 should be interpreted as follows: workers who voted for workers, and a class vote as well as a vote for the principle of national sovereignty.

The long and medium-term tendencies can be summarised in the following way. The growth and electoral victory of the party-based left has been possible thanks to relatively long processes of organisation of the peoples of the lowlands and highlands, of the mobilisation of the agrarian trade unions which have organised parties of their own and of the links with social anti-privatisation movements, of water and gas in particular. The strength of civil society and social movements has resulted in the growth of the party-based left, which is of *campesino* origin but has far-reaching national and pluri-national projects due to the need to integrate the different cultures and peoples in the country's government.

The project of the era was generated collectively, from different processes and centres of organisation and mobilisation, and it is likely that it will continue to be so. The slogan of the constituent assembly emerged in 1990 in the great march for land and the dignity of the peoples of the lowlands, was then re-launched by the Co-ordinator at the end of the water war and later became part of the overall political programme of the left. Once the MAS attained national office it fulfilled its pledge to convene a constituent assembly, which began functioning in 2006. It is likely that the process of designing and enacting reforms to Bolivia's government structures will not end with the constituent assembly and will be a central element of the political life of the country for a long time to come.

With the MAS's victory in the national elections of 2005 there appears to have been a shift to a new phase of the historic accumulation of popular and community forces in Bolivia. This phase began with the change in leadership of the Bolivian state, through the advent of Evo Morales and the MAS, but is likely to continue as a process with a growing political presence of *campesinos* and indigenous peoples in the leadership of the Bolivian state, which will be a defining characteristic of Bolivia's political future.

In the same way, it seems that other long-term issues will be the processes of nationalising natural resources and the setting up of a new network of public companies for the exploitation and transformation of these resources on the one hand, and the process of land redistribution on the other. The process of the privatisation of natural resources took place over the last two decades. Now, another process of re-nationalisation is commencing, which began by regaining ownership over and majority control of hydrocarbon reserves, and water in some regions, and which will probably move into mining and then to forests and other natural resources over the next decade. In this sense, the policy of the left in Bolivia essentially signifies nationalisation and a growing presence of workers in the political processes of leadership.

From the time of Hugo Banzer's dictatorship, in the 1970s, the land was privatised and handed over to the military, politicians and oligarchic sectors, shaping an ample sector of *latifundio* (extensive uncultivated areas controlled by a few landlords) in Bolivia's rural sector. The state was used in order to expand this private land owner-ship on behalf of the bourgeoisie and political elites. Now a new period has begun in which *campesinos* and indigenous peoples will use their political presence in public arenas and state institutions, in particular the executive, legislative and constituent assembly, to reverse this process of *latifundista* concentration of the land and the hereditary structures which reproduce it, so as to redistribute the land according to modern and communitarian criteria. This process of agrarian reform, which is also a process of long-term transformation of the relationships of power, is and will be the object of the country's main social and political struggles over the next decade. In this sense, the policy of the left in Bolivia will continue to revolve around agrarian reform which, due to the sort of politicisation and political presence of indigenous peoples already deployed and about to be deployed, will also be a process with aspects of decolonisation.

In short, it could be said that the programme of the left in Bolivia at present comprises nationalisation, agrarian reform, multicultural democ-racy and decolonisation. The left that has shaped it and that will have to support it in this period is made up of a set of anti-privatisation social movements, agrarian trade unions and a party of *cocaleros* that has become a national workers' party. The latter now also operates as an axis of political alliances with the organisations of the indigenous peoples of the *altiplano* and the lowlands, which do not think of themselves as left wing but as indigenous and pro-decolonisation.

NOTES

1. In April 1952 a political revolution took place, which displaced the mining oligarchy based on an alliance between a nationalist party (the *Movimiento Nacionalista Revolucionario,* Nationalist Revolutionary Movement, MNR) and the mining and manufacturing proletariat who constituted the foundations of the new political regime and the reform of the state and the economy. Mines were nationalised, universal suffrage was established, agrarian reform was launched and state capitalism was inaugurated in Bolivia.

2. In August 1971, Hugo Banzer led a military coup against the government of Juan José Torrez. The dictatorship lasted until 1978. In 1977, mobilisations achieved an amnesty and convening of elections for 1978. In 1978 a new military coup led by the candidate backed by Banzer, Pereda Asbún, took place to prevent the left-wing coalition (UDP), which had won the elections, from assuming power.

3. Felipe Quispe later became the leader of a new organisation called *Movimiento Indígena Pachakuti* (Pachakuti Indigenous Movement, MIP), which adopted a highly exclusionary rhetoric against the *qa'aras* (whites). Quispe's discourse, centred on the interests of the Aymara nation, alienated non-indigenous as well as many indigenous voters, including the Quechua population. As a result, his party never managed to obtain a significant share of the vote outside Aymara-speaking areas.

4. The MAS proposed to change the requirement of a two-thirds majority stipulated by the original legislation as the condition to approve the new constitution, requiring instead a simple majority to be followed by two-thirds of the vote in a national referendum. The referendum should approve or reject the entire constitutional project. The right-wing opposition – led by PODEMOS – contested the MAS' proposal, as their 33 per cent minority in the Constituent Assembly was enough to block any progressive initiative. After several months of constant clashes over procedural regulations, a multiparty agreement was about to be reached as this chapter is being written (January 2007), allowing two dozen thematic commissions to begin complex deliberations about the content of the new constitutional chart.

9 PROMISES AND CHALLENGES
The Latin American Left at the the Start of the Twenty-first Century
Atilio A. Boron

CHALLENGING *LA PENSÉE UNIQUE*

The aim of this chapter is to examine some aspects of the renewed presence of the left in Latin American political life. This presence can be seen not so much in the traditional arenas – the party system, parliamentary representation and so on – as in the emergence of a series of governments that, albeit vaguely, identify themselves as 'centre-left' or 'progressive' and, in a very special way, in the tumultuous appearance of new social movements that, in some countries, have acquired enormous influence. This was expressed in various ways, from the 'taking of streets and squares' in resistance to neo-liberal policies, to the irruptions that in recent years have brought about the collapse of successive governments in Peru, Ecuador, Argentina and Bolivia.

In his day, Edward H. Carr (1946) observed that to the nostrils of the bourgeoisie and their allies in the mid nineteenth century, democracy gave off a very disagreeable stench. The smell of the expressions 'left', 'leftist' and 'populist' is proving to be just as disagreeable to their senses today. These names are usually used to refer to political positions or proposals that the mandarins of conventional wisdom strike down as being 'foolish', 'at odds with the times' or simply 'demagogic'. In the ideological context in which we live, 'good sense' means obedience to the policies (not only economic) dictated by the International Monetary Fund (IMF) and, more generally, by the exponents of the Washington Consensus. Reconciliation with the ineluctable demands of the era means that political actors have realised we live under the empire of globalisation and that, as President Fernando H. Cardoso once commented, with a resignation that does not cease to surprise us, 'inside globalisation there are no alternatives; outside globalisation there is no salvation.' Thus, in order not to be at odds with the times, governments must silently comply with the orders of the Washington Consensus, and act accordingly. In this way, the undisputed reign of *la pensée unique* and its correlate, *la politique unique*, is established. The root of such nonsense is not difficult to ascertain: the final and definitive triumph of the markets will translate, according to the neo-liberals, into the existence of a single policy type. This is none other than that which takes us down the narrow paths of fiscal discipline, the fight against inflation, the absurd 'independence' of the central banks (an independence that, of course, does not exist in relation to financial capital and its allies), and the eternal and Sisyphean task of attracting the confidence of investors with renewed concessions that threaten humanity's very survival.

Neo-liberal theorists repeatedly complain about the 'noise' democracy introduces into the supposed serenity of the markets. To summarise, republican good sense and accountability to both society and history are incompatible with the 'demagogy' that characterised the dark times of populism and socialism in Latin America. Times in which political leaders, in an unbridled display of irresponsibility, proposed – and attempted to implement – aggressive redistribution of income and property, nationalised and/or took state control of foreign monopolies, redistributed land among *campesinos* and rural labourers, and established irritating regulations in the fields of labour, commerce and finance. The regulations shackled what Joseph Schumpeter cynically described as the capitalist process of 'creative destruction'. This era of demagogy was, if we accept the dominant neo-liberal discourse, the principal cause of the wave of dictatorships that swept through the region's fragile democracies. Leaders such as Salvador Allende in Chile and Juan José Torres in Bolivia paid with their lives for their fascination with these out-dated and utopian discourses. Others were forced into exile, and the peoples of the region suffered for many years under some of the bloodiest tyrannies in the region's history.

THE PARADOXICAL CRISIS OF NEO-LIBERALISM

The situation has changed. Large social movements blossomed during the closing decade of the last century, starting with the pioneering Zapatista revolts in 1994, the appearance of the Argentinean *piqueteros*, the massive citizens' and workers' strikes in France and South Korea shortly afterwards and, towards the end of the century, the ripening and international consolidation of the protests and alternative summits in Seattle and Porto Alegre. The massive popular mobilisations in Argentina, Ecuador, Bolivia and Peru, which brought down unpopular governments, form part of the same tendency. Consequently, new political forces, loosely defined as 'progressive', have come to control governments (in countries such as Venezuela, Brazil, Argentina, Uruguay and, more recently, Bolivia, Ecuador and Nicaragua). These governments are considering the need to abandon policies that have, as everyone is all too well aware, wreaked havoc in the past. This was demonstrated with rare didactic force by the catastrophic collapse brought about by neo-liberal policies in Argentina. Nonetheless, we must be clear that, in general, the most significant changes have been produced in the blandest terrain of discourse and rhetoric (the cases of Lula da Silva, Néstor Kirchner and Tabaré Vázquez) and not in the tough and harsh terrain of economic policies (with the exception of the cases of Hugo Chávez and Evo Morales). However, even with all these limitations, the change in the Latin American ideological climate is very significant, and it would be a mistake to underestimate its scope.

In a previous work (Boron, 2003a), I reviewed some of the most important transformations that have taken place in Latin American countries, all of which strongly influenced the emergence of new forms of social protest and political organisation. Briefly, I draw attention there to the extraordinary complexity that has come to characterise the slow but progressive exhaustion of neo-liberalism in this region. Without a doubt, the decline of neo-liberalism since the mid 1990s has reversed the overwhelming influence it had acquired since the 1970s at the hands of the two bloodiest dictatorships in memory, Chile and Argentina. It may be absurd to argue that neo-liberalism is, today, in retreat. It is, however, no less absurd to state that its influence over Latin American societies, cultures, politics and economies has remained unscathed with the passing of time (see Gentili and Sader, 2003). In this sense, the spectacular collapse of the neo-liberal experiment in Argentina – for many years the 'model country' of the IMF and the World Bank – has played an immensely important educational role. Crises teach, and crises like the one suffered in Argentina have revealed with exemplary efficiency the consequences produced by the strict application of neo-liberal policies.

What we are seeing now is somewhat peculiar. There is a striking disjunction between the consolidation of neo-liberalism, particularly in the crucial areas of the economy and policy-making (that is to say, in the minds of civil servants, treasury and economy ministers, central bank presidents, political leaders and others) and its manifest weakening in the fields of culture, public consciousness and politics. Neo-liberal economic policies follow their course. However, in contrast to what happened in the 1980s and early 1990s, they can no longer count on the support – manipulated, to be sure – that in past years was guaranteed by a civil society striving to leave behind the horrors of dictatorship and therefore willing to accept, at times reluctantly, the recipe promoted by the imperial masters and their local representatives.

In any case, this disjunction between the economic and the politico-ideological components of hegemony is far from unprecedented in Latin America. In the work mentioned above, I suggest a certain analogy between the prolonged crisis of the oligarchic hegemony in our region and the current decline of neo-liberalism. If the former reached its apogee in the period immediately before the Great Depression of the 1930s, its slow decay was to extend over several decades. As Agustín Cueva (1976) demonstrated in a text that is a classic of Latin American social sciences, the irreversible deterioration of the material bedrock of the oligarchic hegemony did not lead to its immediate collapse. Instead, it meandered down a number of routes that influenced, and in some cases postponed, its final decline for decades, precisely until the irruption of the populist regimes. While it is not possible to draw linear conclusions from historical experience, perhaps it would be reasonable to consider a hypothesis – dishearteningly pessimistic, to be sure – that predicts that the unquestionable bankruptcy of the basic economic conditions that made the rise of neo-liberalism possible will neither necessarily nor immediately lead to its disappearance from the public stage. The ideological and political components amalgamated in its economic primacy can guarantee it an unexpected survival, even in the midst of extremely unfavourable conditions. To paraphrase Gramsci, it could be said that the slow agony of neo-liberalism is one of those situations in which 'the old is dying and the new cannot be born'. As the great Italian theorist reminds us, at such moments, all manner of aberrant phenomena often appear. Examples of political aberrations include: the clamorous breach of electoral contract perpetrated by governments which upon reaching power immediately break their campaign promises; the shameless betrayal of principles by certain 'left wing' parties and organisations; the prolonged political survival of characters such as Augusto Pinochet in Chile, Carlos Menem in Argentina, Alberto Fujimori in Peru and others of their ilk; or the outrageous social situation in Argentina, Brazil and Uruguay, where large majorities of the populations needlessly go hungry in countries that could be the granaries of the world.

[235]

WHY NOW?

A question that arises is why these new rebellious political and social forces have appeared at this moment. The reasons are, of course, many and complex, and their impact varies from country to country. Nevertheless, there are some basic underlying causes. First, there is the exhaustion of neo-liberalism mentioned above. This process heightened the contradictions generated by the painful economic and social restructuring that took place in the preceding years, creating new social actors (such as the *piqueteros* in Argentina), and increasing the influence of others that already existed but were not mobilised or organised (such as the *campesinos* in Brazil and Mexico, or the indigenous peoples of Ecuador, Bolivia and parts of Mexico, to name only a few). The increasing poverty and social exclusion generated by the policies of the Washington Consensus also attracted intermediate social groups and sectors (the so-called 'middle classes') to the ranks of those opposed to neo-liberalism.

Second, it is necessary to mention that the emergence of these new expressions of the political left is closely tied to the failed models of democratic capitalism in the region. I have explored this theme extensively elsewhere, and therefore will not repeat all those arguments here (Boron, 2000). Suffice to note that the frustration generated by the actions of the so-called democratic regimes in this part of the world has been intense, profound and prolonged. It was under these peculiar 'democracies' that bloomed in the region beginning in the 1980s that social conditions worsened dramatically. This took place, moreover, in a context of intensifying globalisation, which among other things, has magnified the unsettling impact of the so-called 'demonstration effect'.

While in European countries, democratic capitalism appears to be the generator of material well-being and social justice – and I say 'appears to' because these things are in fact the product of the social struggles of subordinate classes against capitalists, rather than some kind of natural by-product of democratic capitalism – in Latin America, democracy has brought structural adjustment and stabilisation policies, increasingly precarious labour conditions, high levels of unemployment, a dizzying increase in poverty, external vulnerability, unbridled debt and the foreign takeover of our economies. Democracies, in other words, that are empty of all content, reduced – as Fernando H. Cardoso recalled before becoming President of Brazil – to an unemotional facial gesture incapable of 'eliminating the stench of farce from democratic politics'. A stench that was produced – as he assured us – by the inability of this political regime to introduce fundamental reforms in the system of production and in the forms of distribution and appropriation of wealth (Cardoso, 1985, 1982).

Our region has barely attained the lowest level on the limited scale of democratic development permitted by the structure of capitalist society. We have merely electoral democracies; that is, political regimes that are essentially oligarchic in character, controlled by big capital – which enjoys complete independence from the governing parties who assume the tasks of managing the country in its name. The people, meanwhile, manipulated at will thanks to the control exercised by dominant groups over the mass media, are called upon every few years to elect those who will be charged with the task of subjugating them. In democracies of this sort, it is no accident that, following repeated frustrations, rebellious social forces begin to emerge (see Boron, 2006).

Third, it must be said that this process has also been fed by the crisis that has brought down traditional forms of political representation. There is little doubt that the new morphology of social protest in our region is a symptom of the decadence of the great mass political parties of the past, and of the traditional models of trade union organisation. This decadence can, without question, be explained by the transformations that have taken place in the 'social base' of these forms of organisation as a result of the policies of neo-liberal restructuring characteristic of contemporary peripheral capitalism: the growing heterogeneity of labouring classes, tied to their declining relative position among subordinate classes as a whole; the appearance of a massive 'sub-proletariat' (or what Frei Betto has called the *pobretariado*), which reflects the increasing economic and social exclusion of contemporary capitalism that discards growing segments of the popular classes as un-exploitable; the significant rise in the ranks of the unemployed and those working in conditions of extreme precariousness, with very weak ties to the formal economy; and finally, the explosion of multiple identities (ethnic, linguistic, gender, sexual orientation and others) that have significantly reduced the relevance of traditional class-based variables. If we add to this the inability of political parties and trade unions to 'read' the new realities of our time correctly, the sclerosis of their organisational structures and practices, and their outdated discourses, it is very easy to understand why they have entered into crisis and new social protest movements have emerged.

A fourth and final factor, in what is not intended as an exhaustive list, is the globalisation of the struggles against neo-liberalism. These struggles began and spread rapidly around the globe, based on initiatives that did not emerge from political parties or from trade unions. In the case of Latin America, the star role was played by Zapatismo when it emerged from the Lacandon Jungle on 1 January 1994 and declared war on neo-liberalism. The tireless work of the MST in Brazil, another non-traditional organisation, significantly amplified the impact of the Zapatistas. This was followed, in a veritable avalanche, by large mobil-isations of *campesinos* and indigenous peoples in Bolivia, Ecuador, Peru, and some regions of Colombia and Chile. The struggles of the Argentine *piqueteros* form part of the same general trend. The events of Seattle and similar actions in Washington, New York, Paris, Genoa, Gothenburg and other major cities in the developed world gave the protests against the Washington Consensus a universal stamp, ratified year after year by the impressive progress made at the World Social Forum in Porto Alegre. In this way, a kind of 'domino effect' was produced, which, without a doubt, and contrary to the widely circulated theories expounded by Hardt and Negri (2000) in *Empire*, revealed the intimate connection between social struggles and political processes in play in the most distant corners of the planet.

Given the above, is it possible to say that we are experiencing the emergence of an alternative – or alternatives – to neo-liberalism?

From the outset, I would argue that the problem should be framed differently. Why? Quite simply, because history does not work that way. History is not constructed according to a preconceived plan. This vision of History, with a capital H, which is nothing more than a text written by God, the *Fuehrer*, a central committee or a prophet, and blindly carried out by mankind, is one possible vision, derived from Hegel. The other, which is the one taken by Marx, is that of history as a dialectic process, in which there are no preconceived guidebooks, and the outcomes are undecided. Marx said that revolution was indispensable to the historic overthrow of capitalism. Of course, indispensability is not the same as inevitability. Something may be necessary, but that does not mean that its appearance is inexorable. For this reason, the founder of historical materialism spoke of how the final crisis of capitalism could resolve itself positively, in the direction of socialism, or negatively, plunging humanity into the most terrible barbarism.

It clearly follows that there are alternatives to neo-liberalism and to capitalism. However, they are neither written in a book, nor (thank-fully!) is there a manual to tell us what these alternatives are. This was precisely what Gramsci meant when he wrote his incisive article shortly after the Russian Revolution. He called it 'The Revolution against *Capital*' precisely in order to demonstrate, using Marxism, that revolutionary processes are not born of books, however brilliant these may be. The French Revolution did not flow from the quill of Jean-Jacques Rousseau, nor was the Russian Revolution made in the pages of Marx's *Capital* or Lenin's *The Development of Capitalism in Russia*, nor did the Chinese Revolution emerge from Mao's *On Contradiction*. Leaving aside the raucous character of these revolutions, we can say that the less clamorous re-composition of capitalism following the 1930s was also not the product of John M. Keynes' *General Theory*, nor was the era of post-1970s neo-liberalism the product of Friedrich von Hayek's *The Road to Serfdom*.

That the ideas contained in these books were very important is beyond doubt. However, it is not possible to argue that it was the books that 'made history'. History was made by the people, through their struggles, or it was made by the dominant classes, when the correlation of forces was in their favour. So-called 'Keynesianism' is a phenomenon that transcends Keynes' work, just as neo-liberalism cannot be reduced to Hayek's thesis. In the same way, today, we can say that there is a set of ideas that contradicts the axiological premises and specific policies of neo-liberalism. However, none of this gives rise to any sort of 'model' or set of commandments, such as the famous Washington Consensus popularised by John Williamson. In reality, 'models' and commandments are inevitably *post festum* theoretical constructions, codifications of practices set in motion throughout the historical process.

That said, the starting point is the recognition that alternatives do indeed exist. The dominant *pensée unique,* which has been one of neo-liberalism's basic weapons, incessantly preaches Margaret Thatcher's *TINA*: 'There Is No Alternative'. And this was done so successfully that many left-wing intellectuals and politicians, not to mention that nearly extinct species known as the 'left-wing economist', ended up accepting the neo-liberal mandate to the letter. This is the only way, there are no alternatives, all else is either madness or foolishness. In reality, madness and foolishness more aptly describe those who think that it is possible for things to continue as they are, and that there is no alternative to the depressing panorama of social disintegration and permanent economic crisis prevailing in the region. How can there be no alternative to mass unemployment, the poverty of more than half the population, the absence of social policies, and the unsustainable weight of inequitable and illegal foreign debts? What has been lacking, until now, is a correlation of forces that would make it possible to attempt the existing alternatives, which do not require too much imagination. The problem is not cognitive, but rather political. The good news is that, little by little, this correlation of forces is changing in favour of popular classes and social strata.

Based on the experience of the last quarter of the twentieth century, it has become evident that the alternatives to neo-liberalism (of which there will no doubt be many) will contain, in varying degrees, the following elements. The first is a vigorous reconstruction of the state, which has been destroyed or shrunk by orthodox policies. The state is the foundation on which it is possible to support the democratisation of society, unless one believes that it is possible to establish democracy within the market, or in a civil society divided into classes. Furthermore, without a state there is no force capable of assuming the Promethean task of subjecting markets to a regulatory framework that defends the general interest, preserves public goods, and protects the large majorities whom neo-liberalism has stripped of their most basic rights. Second, the course of economic development should be radically re-oriented towards the internal market, the redistribution of wealth and income, the promotion of development and ecological sustainability. This does not mean a return to the period of import substitution, or to an illusory 'national capitalism', which would be anachronistic in the current context. Instead, it means that the community, through its political expression, the state, should assume control of the processes of production and distribution of wealth. It is essential to revise everything done during the neo-liberal era. For example, privatised companies should be placed under democratic public control; the same applies to the central banks, whose supposed autonomy is a farce. Some firms will remain in the hands of their current owners, while others will become part of the public sector, and still others will become new forms of mixed property under a variety of modalities that involve different degrees of participation from distinct sectors: foreign capital, national capital, the public sector, workers, consumers, the general public and NGOs, among others.

It will be just as necessary to undertake a meticulous revision of all that has been done, with respect to both form and content. It is known that the implementation of neo-liberal policies was an immense source of corruption and that the transfer to private hands of the social wealth accumulated in state enterprises was only in exceptional cases conducted transparently and honestly. It will therefore be necessary to re-nationalise a large part of what was privatised, 're-regulate' what was unscrupulously deregulated, put an end to the reigning liberalisation, and begin to implement active policies in various areas of the

economy and society. In sum, there is a need to stop the inappropriately named 'economic reforms' inspired by the Washington Consensus,
which are really counter-reforms, and begin a genuine programme of
fundamental economic reform that places the economy at the service
of collective welfare and social development. Under the primacy of
neo-liberalism, it is the latter that has been at the service of the
markets, establishing a perverse hierarchy of values whose effects are
obvious.

A priority area of this large, necessary reconstruction is, without a
doubt, taxation policy. This is the Achilles heel of Latin American
economies. The disgrace of being the region of the world with the worst
distribution of wealth and income has, as its corollary, the fact that it
also possesses the world's most inequitable system of taxation. As I have
argued elsewhere, the 'tax veto' of the dominant classes prevails on our
continent. The region's long colonial experience has established a tradition according to which the social groups that inherited the wealth and
privileges of the *conquistadores* enjoy galling prerogatives when it
comes to paying taxes. In practice it is known that the poorest sectors of
the population bear a heavier tax burden, in relation to their very sparse
resources, than that borne by the top 10 per cent of the income distribution. If the new governments do not attack this problem at the roots, and
to date they have shown no sign of having the will to do so, all their
promises and anti-neo-liberal rhetoric will collapse like a house of cards.
Without a fundamental tax reform, there will be neither a reconstruction
of the state, nor active policies for resolving the great challenges of
our time. And without these two things, the status quo will remain
unchanged.

To conclude this section, just as there was no single Keynesian
model in the post-war years, there will also not be a single post-neo-
liberal political model in the years to come. If Keynesianism presented
faces as diverse as those found in Sweden, Japan and the United States,
why should we expect post-neo-liberalism to be a uniform proposal for
all countries? Such uniformity also did not exist in the most recent neo-
liberal experience, in which we can distinguish a variety of sub-types
and specific functional modalities. The alternatives to neo-liberalism
will be as diverse as the political-economic formulas that preceded
them. All of the latter were, in their day, Keynesian or neo-liberal,
because this was the principal tone that coloured them, beyond the
specific features that differentiated them. The same will be true with the
advent of post-neo-liberalisms.

THE CURSE OF CONSERVATIVE 'POSSIBILISM'

Given the above, and granting the existence of alternatives to neo-liberalism, a disturbing question arises: is there room for neo-liberal policies? The answer must be qualified. In some cases it is an unequivocal yes; in others, the response is still positive, but with some reservations. Let us consider the most optimistic case: Brazil. When one asks friends in the Brazilian government why it has not pursued an economic policy that diverges, even slightly, from the rules of the Washington Consensus and that aims to be something other than an intensification of the neo-liberal policies that preceded it, the response from Brasilia is an exact replica of what is taught in US business school textbooks:

> Brazil needs to gain the confidence of international investors, we need foreign capital and we must observe strict fiscal discipline, because if we don't, the country risk rating will go sky high, and no one will invest a single dollar in Brazil.

This was the premise that guided Lula's first term, and nothing suggests that things will be any different following his re-election.

It does not require a great deal of effort to demonstrate the weakness of that argument. If there is a country in the world that has all the necessary conditions to pursue a successful post-neo-liberal policy, it is Brazil. If Brazil cannot do it, who can? Rafael Correa's Ecuador? Tabaré Vázquez's Uruguay? Evo Morales' Bolivia? Perhaps Venezuela, under the leadership of Hugo Chávez, or even Argentina, but only with a strong political will and under extremely favourable international conditions. Brazil, on the other hand, has everything. It covers an immense territory that encompasses every kind of natural resource. It has huge agricultural and livestock resources, enormous mineral wealth, phenomenal sources of renewable energy in some of the largest rivers on the planet, 8,000 kilometres of coastline with extremely rich fish stocks, a population of close to 200 million inhabitants, one of the most important industrial infrastructures in the world, a society weighed down with poverty but with a high level of social and cultural integration, a first-class intellectual and scientific elite, and an exuberant and pluralistic culture. Furthermore, Brazil has sufficient capital, and a potential tax base of extraordinary magnitude, although one which remains unexploited owing to the power of the moneyed classes who have vetoed any initiative in this direction. If, with this super-abundance of conditions, Brazil cannot extricate itself from neo-liberalism, then we are lost, and the best we can do is to prostrate ourselves humbly before the verdict of history that consecrates the final and definitive victory of the markets. Fortunately, that is not the case.

The corollary of 'conservative possibilism', beloved offspring of the *pensée unique*, is that nothing can change, not even in a country with Brazil's exceptional conditions. Going beyond the horizon of the possible and abandoning the dominant economic consensus, certain eminent government officials assure us, would expose Brazil to terrible penalties that would put an end to the Lula government. Nevertheless, a close look at the recent economic history of Argentina may be instructive. 'Possibilism' was intensely cultivated in Argentina, from the early days of Raúl Alfonsín's government to the final catastrophic moments under Fernando de la Rúa's administration. This false realism, ceaselessly promoted by neo-liberal think-tanks throughout the world, drove Argentina to the worst crisis in its history by shackling political will and the administration of the state to the whims and the greed of the markets. What is more, when in the middle of the deepest and most extensive crisis the country had ever known, Buenos Aires defaulted on the foreign debt and began timidly implementing some heterodox policies – the clearest example of which was the cancellation of approximately 70 per cent of foreign debt bonds – the country started on a path of very high rates of economic growth, comparable only to those of China, which have continued uninterrupted for four years now (through early 2007, as the first edition of this book went to press).

As I noted in an analysis written prior to Lula's assumption of office, the 'possibilist' temptation always lies in wait for any government driven by reformist aims (Boron, 2003b). Faced with the objective and subjective impossibility of revolution – a characteristic feature of the current situation not only in Brazil but in the region as a whole – a misunderstood notion of common sense leads to accommodation with one's adversaries, and to a search for some small escape route within the interstices of reality that will avoid total capitulation. The only problem with this strategy is that history teaches us that it is later impossible to avoid the transition from 'possibilism' to immobilism, and then to catastrophic defeat. This was clearly the Argentine experience with the 'centre left' Alianza government, and more generally with social-democratic governments in Spain, Italy and France. In more general terms, this was also Max Weber's theoretical conclusion when he stated, in the final paragraph of his celebrated lecture 'Politics as a Vocation', that 'all historical experience confirms the truth – that man would not have attained the possible unless time and time again he had reached out for the impossible' (Weber, 1982). Weber's words are all the more important in a continent such as ours, in which the lessons of history indisputably demonstrate that real revolutions were needed to institute some reforms in the social structures of the most unjust region of the planet, and that without a bold utopian political vision capable of mobilising people, reformist impulses die out, government leaders capitulate, and their governments end up focusing on the disappointing administration of daily tasks.

The hopes invested in vigorous reformism, while undoubtedly possible, should not mean turning a deaf ear to the warnings of Rosa Luxemburg, who argued that social reforms, however genuine and energetic they may be, do not change the nature of the pre-existing society. What happens is that as revolution is not on the immediate agenda of the great masses of Latin America, social reform becomes the most likely alternative, above all in times of retreat and defeat such as those that have characterised the international system since the implosion of the Soviet Union and the disappearance of the socialist camp. Reform, Luxemburg also reminds us, is not a revolution that advances slowly, or in stages, until, with the imperceptibility of the traveller who crosses the equator – to use Edouard Bernstein's famous metaphor – it arrives at socialism. A century of social-democratic reformism in the West irrefutably demonstrated that reforms are not enough to 'overcome' capitalism. It did, without a doubt, produce significant changes 'within the system', but it failed in its stated goal of 'changing the system'. In the current national and international context, reformism appears to offer the only opportunity for moving forward, until the necessary objective and subjective conditions can be created for the pursuit of more promising alternatives. The mistake of many reformists, however, has been to confuse necessity with virtue. Even if reforms are currently all that can be achieved, this does not make them adequate tools for building socialism. They can, if undertaken in a certain way, constitute an invaluable contribution to advancing in that direction, but they are not the path that will lead us to that destination. In the present circumstances, they are what is possible, but not what is desirable in a barbaric world in need of fundamental transformation, not simply marginal adjustments. If, as the Zapatistas say, it is a question of 'creating a new world', such an undertaking greatly exceeds the cautious limits of reform. However, we cannot wait with our arms folded for the 'decisive day' to arrive. If the reforms are imbued with energy and build popular power, that is to say, if they modify the existing correlation of forces, shifting it in favour of the condemned of the earth, then those reforms contain a transformational potential of extraordinary importance. This is the kind of reformism that, for now and in the absence of a better alternative, we need to see in Latin America.

The case of Argentina demonstrates that in practice even a country that is far weaker and more vulnerable than Brazil can grow despite the very bad (according to Joseph Stiglitz) advice given to Argentina by the IMF for decades and the highly publicised support of the 'international financial community', which today lavishes Lula with the same praise that it previously reserved for the Menem administration. Is it a characteristic of 'realism' to follow the advice of those who, according to Stiglitz, became the principal promoters of crisis throughout the world? Crises that, incidentally, enriched speculators and parasites – those for whom the phlegmatic John M. Keynes recommended euthanasia – while condemning the rest to servility. What serious economist – and we are speaking of economists, not spokespersons for business interests disguised as economists – can believe that a country can grow and develop by fostering economic recession through exorbitant interest rates, reducing public spending, constricting the internal market, increasing unemployment, restricting consumption, facilitating the flow of speculative short-term capital and overwhelming the poorest members of the population with indirect taxation, while subsidising the rich, and consolidating the right of large monopolies to go untaxed? Can this be the path to liberating our countries from the ravages of neo-liberalism?

Successive Argentine presidents opted for governing according to the rules of 'possibilism', calming the markets and punctually satisfying every one of its complaints. The voices of big capital and the IMF resonated deafeningly in Buenos Aires, and the government of the day did not hesitate for a minute in responding to their commands. That same government, however, was deaf to the groans and cries of the condemned. The results are plain to see. The Brazilian experience during Lula's first term painfully proved that neither a respectable leadership nor what was once a great party of the masses like the *Partido dos Trabalhadores* (Workers' Party, PT) was enough to guarantee the correct course of government. Brasilia has gone down the wrong road, at the end of which we will not find a new, more just and democratic society – the goal that gave birth to the PT little more than 20 years go – but rather a capitalist structure more unjust and less democratic than the previous one. A country in which the dictatorship of capital, with a pseudo-democratic veneer, will be even stronger than before, demonstrating that George Soros was right when he advised the Brazilian people not to bother electing Lula, because the markets would govern the country in any case.

THE DIFFICULT TRANSITION TO POST-NEO-LIBERALISM

A brief look at Latin America's recent history helps to illustrate the serious obstacles that seem to affect governments that are, at least in principle and according to their rhetoric, animated by an eagerness to turn the page on the sad history of neo-liberalism in the region. What is certain is that, at times in a grotesque way and at others in a tragic way, the continued supremacy of neo-liberalism in the economic sphere goes unaltered despite the fact that citizens have resoundingly rejected it in the voting booth. In the 2002 presidential elections in Brazil, Lula defeated Fernando H. Cardoso's representatives of neo-liberal continuism, and something similar occurred in 2006. Comparable displays of popular rejection of neo-liberalism have been produced on a variety of stages: the umpteenth ratification of the formidable electoral and social popularity of Hugo Chávez in Venezuela, once again confirmed in December 2006; Daniel Ortega's victory in the 2006 Nicaraguan elections and the election of Rafael Correa in Ecuador in the same year; the massive protests that brought down the Sánchez de Lozada and Mesa governments in Bolivia and culminated in the resounding electoral victory of Evo Morales in late 2005; the unprecedented popularity attained by Néstor Kirchner in Argentina during his first term of office; the stubborn rejection by Uruguayans of the privatisation of state-owned companies in a series of referenda during the past decade and the subsequent triumph of Tabaré Vázquez in the 2004 presidential elections; followed by the triumph of Michele Bachelet in Chile.

Nevertheless, it is necessary to broach a serious question: Why is it that almost all governments who come to power on an impressive wave of popular votes, and with an express mandate to bring an end to the primacy of neo-liberalism, surrender when it comes time to introduce a post-neo-liberal agenda? Various factors explain this situation.

First, it can be explained by the increased power of the markets – in reality, of the monopolies and large corporations that control them – as against the diminished capacities of the state after decades of application of neo-liberal policies aimed at 'shrinking' the state, dismantling its agencies and organisms, and privatising state-owned enterprises. All this confers on the dominant sectors a capacity for blackmail – capital flight, investment strikes, speculative pressures, bribery of officials and the like – over governments that is difficult, if not impossible, for them to resist, and which makes them file away their electoral promises for better times.

A second factor is the persistence of imperialism and its many traps and mechanisms that 'discipline' unruly governments via a range of instruments that assure the continued force of neo-liberal policies. On the one hand, there are the pressures deriving from the need for heavily indebted governments to count on the benevolence of Washington to make their governmental programmes viable, whether by way of a 'preferential treatment' that guarantees their products access to the North American market, the indefinite renegotiation of their foreign debt, or the approval needed to facilitate the flow of capital and investment of various sorts into their economies. All this is expressed in the long list of 'conditionalities' that the guard dogs of imperialism – principally the IMF and World Bank, but also the World Trade Organization (WTO) and the Inter-American Development Bank (IADB) – impose on the governments of the region (see Boron, 2002). On the other hand, the coercion exercised by imperialism also follows other paths, ranging from the direct political demands presented in the context of military aid programmes, the eradication of coca crops, and technical assistance and international co-operation, to the ideological manipulation made possible by big capital's almost exclusive control of the mass media, the creators of the 'common sense' of the times.

Finally, a third factor must be added: the anti-democratic regression that the Latin American states have suffered, which, as I mentioned above, has progressively emptied the democratic project of all content and irreparably weakened, in the current framework of institutional organisation, its capacities for intervention in social life. One of the defining characteristics of this crisis is the progressive displacement of a growing number of issues that affect collective well-being into fields that are supposedly more 'technical' – and therefore distant from the popular will as expressed at election time. This means that, far from being publicly debated, these issues are dealt with in the shadows by 'experts', completely encapsulated and beyond almost any sort of democratic scrutiny. Despite their enormous social impact, these questions are resolved by accords sealed between capitalists and their state representatives. This entire fraudulent operation is accompanied by absurd justifications, such as 'the economy is a technical matter that must be managed in a manner independent of political considerations'. The economy, the science of scarcity and for that very reason the political science *par excellence*, attempts to pass itself off as a mere technical specialisation. The sadly celebrated 'independence of the Central Bank' is an eloquent example of this absurdity: such independence is only in relation to popular sovereignty, as the central banks in our region enjoy no independence vis-à-vis financial capital and imperialism, which they serve unconditionally.

THE LEFT AND DEMOCRACY

Another major issue that I would like to address in this chapter is the problem of the relationship between the left and democracy. The left has always been accused of being anti-democratic, despite the fact that if a radical incompatibility exists between ideology and political regime, it is that presented by the relationship between capitalism and its ideological expression (liberalism in all its variants) and democracy. Though it has been said a thousand times, it bears repeating once again: the central core of liberalism postulates the independence of private interests from the state, and in no way, not even marginally, the democratic organisation of the *polis* and the rule of popular sovereignty.

Nevertheless, independent of that, it is true that democracy, which is an inalienable flag of the socialist tradition, is seen by the great mass of the population as a bourgeois, liberal, capitalist achievement. It is held, not disingenuously, that it was the fusion between a class, its ideology and its mode of production that emancipated society from the chains to which it had been condemned by pre-capitalist social formations. Through this crude manipulation and falsification of historical experience – incessantly reproduced by the mass media under the protection of the 'freedom of the press' – capitalism and democracy were combined in an ideological synthesis that was as false as it was effective. As Milton Friedman contended in his celebrated *Capitalism and Freedom*, democracy is the political face of capitalism, while the free market, quintessence of the same, is nothing more than the economic expression of democracy.

I have examined these ideological schemes more extensively in other works (Boron, 2003a, 2003b, 2000). For the purposes of this chapter, suffice to say that the left unfortunately reacted defensively to these accusations and, to a certain extent and at times in a stupidly defiant way, acquiesced in the right's appropriation of the democratic discourse. The insurmountable contradictions between the latter and the capitalist mode of production were hidden under a clumsy defence of the 'dictatorship of the proletariat', which was understood in Stalinist terms and not, as corresponds to the Marxist tradition, as an unlimited and absolute expansion of democracy, leaping over the hurdles and obstacles that the class-based, hierarchical and discriminatory structures of the capitalist society put in its way.

The capitalist processes of regressive restructuring, underway since the beginning of the 1970s and the disintegration of the Soviet Union and the inappropriately named socialist camp, have forced a reconsideration of the relationship between the left and democracy. The authoritarianism of Eastern European socialism weighed like a gravestone on the imagination of socialist and communist forces throughout the world. However, the brutal political regression exemplified by the dictatorships established in Latin America during the 1970s and 1980s, and the democratic decline experienced in the developed capitalist world under the leadership of Ronald Reagan and Margaret Thatcher conclusively demonstrated that the marriage between democracy and capitalism was hopelessly spurious and superficial, thereby opening the doors to a radical re-discussion of the problem.

In some cases, this welcome reopening of the debate gave rise to 'renovations' that in practice meant a pure and simple capitulation that was as much theoretical as it was political. An extremely illustrative case is the theorising of Ernesto Laclau and Chantal Mouffe (2001), which, motivated by a legitimate enthusiasm for overcoming the limitations of the codification suffered by Marxism at the hands of some of its most dogmatic representatives, ended up embracing a conception of democracy ('radical democracy') that is simply another name for democratic capital-ism, and definitively abandoned all pretence of overcoming the capitalist social order.

In other cases, this revision took more promising paths: a radical re-formulation of the democratic question, as a result of which the traditional understanding of bourgeois democracy – in reality a true contradiction in terms! – was tidily demolished. The extensive work of Boaventura de Sousa Santos (see his chapter in this volume) is one of the most outstanding exam-ples of this attempt at theoretical re-creation. I say contradiction in terms, because under bourgeois democracy the capitalist elements are substantive and fundamental, while the democratic ones are subordinate and dispen-sable in a society constructed on the basis of the buying and selling of labour power, a characteristic that imposes insurmountable limits on any democratic project. However, this revision did not mean that the old prin-ciples of liberal democracy were thrown overboard, converted into insignificant 'formalities' which both the dogmatic left and all shades of the reactionary right competed to disparage. Quite the contrary, those free-doms, rights and individual guarantees that under capitalism are reduced to mere formalities remain necessary conditions for any socialist demo-cratic project. This was recognised, years ago and with singular lucidity, by Rosa Luxemburg, who despite her clear revolutionary position never succumbed to the temptation – which has caused so much ruin on the left – of reviling bourgeois democracy for its exclusively 'formal' character.

The permanent validity of the Marxist critique of the inconsistencies of a regime whose egalitarian and democratic tenets are incongruent with its practical class-based and authoritarian premises, remains irrefutable even today. One only has to look at the desolate panorama of our democracies, maintaining themselves precariously upon structurally unjust societies that condemn millions of men, women and children to exploitation, social exclusion and the rigours of the market, while protecting the rich and powerful. Democracies, in short, that neglect, impoverish and oppress. Do they even deserve this name (Boron, 2006)?

Clearly, following the opening created by Rosa Luxemburg, it is important to understand that the argument about socialist democracy has nothing to do with the reinterpretation the latter suffered at the hands of Stalinism and its acolytes. In the pseudo-Marxist Vulgate, they proceeded, without further ado, to the cancellation of those 'formal' freedoms, citing their irreducibly bourgeois character as a pretext, as though *habeas corpus*, the freedom of expression and association, or *majority rule* are repugnant in both theory and political practice to the popular classes. Or, as Norberto Bobbio correctly asked in the mid 1970s, does a workers' assembly choose its representatives by the legitimate vote of its members, or by appealing to a theocratic principle? Rosa Luxemburg, on the contrary, rightly argued that socialist democracy requires the most emphatic ratification and extension of those freedoms – rendered formal by the prevalent fetishism of bourgeois society – via the 'substantive' democratisation of factories, schools, families – in short, the society as a whole.

Following from this, a couple of problems arise, which should at least be mentioned here. First, to what extent can the full democratisation of the capitalist state close the gap between the 'celestial' equality of the political regime and the 'material' inequality incessantly reproduced by bourgeois relations of production? It is obvious that the programme of democratisation encounters insurmountable pitfalls at this point. It is not a question of ignoring the advances resulting from the democratisation of capitalist states – particularly in Europe – since the First World War. Resolutely driven by popular struggles and instructed by the lessons derived from the Russian Revolution, the First World War and the economic crisis of the 1930s, the capitalist states began to open the floodgates of democracy, introducing a series of reforms that reflected the new national and international correlation of forces. This occurred under a variety of institutional forms and regimes, ranging from the radical Keynesianism of the Scandinavian experience to the

'Progressive Caesarism' (Gramsci) of certain Latin American populisms, and including less well-defined varieties such as Franklin D. Roosevelt's 'New Deal' in the United States. Nevertheless, it is important to remember that all these transformations encountered their limits in the despotism that capital succeeded in maintaining unscathed in the terrain of production. Is it possible, therefore, to resolve the capitalist contradiction between political democracy and the tyranny of the markets? No. To date, there are no historical examples to support any other response. Under capitalism, democracy has been, is and will be an incidental component of social life, never its true foundation.

The second problem is this: is it possible to conceive of the transition from a capitalist to a socialist – or 'post capitalist' – democracy as a gradual and rupture-free slide between two poles on the same axis, as preached in the conventional political science literature? Is the move from one to the other simply an accumulative question, or does it imply a qualitative reformulation? The response in both cases is negative: historical experience teaches us that the possible transition from a capitalist democracy to a socialist one is unimaginable without simultaneously reconsidering the issue of revolution: that is to say, radical changes in the structure of society. Whoever speaks of the deepening of democracy, and of its eventual culmination in some form of 'post-capitalist' democracy, will only be able to do it if she/he is first willing to speak of socialism and revolution. And this is precisely what is not talked about. Few assertions are truer today than that made by Rosa Luxemburg when she argued that 'there is no democracy without socialism, nor socialism without democracy.'

HISTORICAL CHALLENGES OF THE LEFT
AT THE BEGINNING OF THE NEW CENTURY

The forces of the left face formidable challenges, both in government and in opposition. The latter, as opponents to a variety of bourgeois governments, must honour the Gramscian proposal of building genuinely democratic parties, movements and organisations as a way of prefiguring the nature of their future state and of synthesizing the wide variety of economic and other types of demands generated by the contradictions of capitalist society. As though this alone were not an enormous task, the oppositional left must also demonstrate its skill in neutralising the actions of the bourgeois ideological apparatus and in delivering its own message to the entire population, which is certainly not prepared to hear about socialism. On the contrary, the prejudices skilfully cultivated and inculcated by right-wing publicists make them extremely resistant to any discourse that speaks of socialism or communism. In their eyes, this is equivalent to violence and death, and despite the fact that the left has been victim of both of these things in the recent history of Latin America, it is accused of being the representative and bearer of these misfortunes. There is in this attitude a component of resignation and pessimism that cannot be ignored, and which suggests the futility of any attempt to overcome capitalism. Boldness could lead to a bloodbath, and no one wants that. The challenge for the credibility of the left is, therefore, considerable. They have made reasonable progress in this area, but there is still much to be done.

With respect to the 'governing' left, the challenges are different. As already noted, Lula's victory was a milestone, comparable only, in the second half of the twentieth century, to the triumph of the Cuban Revolution in January 1959, that of Salvador Allende in the elections of September 1970 in Chile, the insurrectional victory – unfortunately later squandered – of the Sandinistas in Nicaragua in July 1979, and the eruption of Zapatismo in Mexico in January 1994. Winning the Brazilian elections and taking office was fundamental. However, it was far more important to build sufficient political power to 'govern well', the latter understood as honouring the popular mandate that called for an end to the neo-liberal nightmare. But the results to date have been disappointing. To be sure, the poorest, most marginalised and exploited sectors of society have experienced a certain relief, but this is far from satisfying the ideal of social justice to which the people of Brazil have aspired for so long. On the other hand, the banks and financial capital have enjoyed the highest profits in their history under Lula's first government, making them by far the largest beneficiaries of his policies. In Argentina, always a pioneer in matters of misfortune, the collapse of neo-liberalism was consummated in the major events of 19 and 20 December 2001, but its political alternative is still not clearly defined. The government of Néstor Kirchner declares its good intentions and acts on some particular fronts (such as human rights, the purging of the Supreme Court and a moderate reorientation of foreign policy), but it has an increasingly important unresolved matter in the area of the ecoomy, where it has still not deviated from orthodox policies, except by defaulting on the foreign debt bonds. The bankruptcy of neo-liberal policies is also evident in Peru, Bolivia, Ecuador, Uruguay, Paraguay, and even in Chile – the last 'successful' poster child of the theories of the *pensée unique*. There are ominous storm clouds on the short and medium-term economic horizons.

Will Lula be able to satisfy the popular mandate in his second term? It will not be an easy task, but it is also not impossible. It is no longer a question, as it was in 1989, of saving Brazil from the neo-liberal plague that threatened it under the seductive smile of Collor de Melo; or of rescuing it from its initial ravages, as in 1998. What was accomplished in Lula's first term of office is not very encouraging. Now the mission is much more complex, because the famous 'creative destruction' of capitalism – so exalted by Schumpeter – has already occurred, and it is necessary to undertake the Herculean task of economic and social reconstruction. And this cannot even be imagined without bold social and economic reforms that introduce the hoped-for changes and, at the same time, in an inseparable dialectic, fortify the social bases and the political mobilisation of vast subordinate class sectors, without which the policy initiatives coming out of Brasilia will inexorably succumb to the imperatives of the market.

Hugo Chávez faces similar challenges in Venezuela, having to follow the narrow path of a profound revolution in consciousness and the popular imagination – an issue that has been underestimated in traditional analyses of the left – which, at the same time, runs up against the abyss generated by Venezuela's oil riches and its position as strategic supplier to the empire. After a series of initial vacillations, the 'Bolivarian Revolution' has shown signs of finding its course. The slogan of building 'socialism of the twenty-first century' and the policies undertaken by the Chávez government clearly show that it is beginning to pursue a new and promising path, which is of course not exempt from enormous difficulties.

In any case, in conclusion, it is worth recalling here the lessons derived from the Cuban case. Despite all the obstacles it has faced for nearly half a century, Cuba has been able to make significant advances in the construction of a democratic society – that is to say, a society in which the distribution of goods and services of all types is highly egalitarian, and in which the scandalous gap in wealth that separates the governors from the governed in the rest of Latin America does not exist. Going beyond the peculiarities of the Cuban political regime, imagine what could be achieved by such countries as Argentina, Brazil and Venezuela, which are blessed with many more resources, and are distant from the unhealthy North American obsession with the Caribbean island. When I say that Cuba has made significant advances in the construction of a democratic society, I am saying that, despite such unfavourable conditions – such as the nearly half-century-long blockade and the permanent belligerence of the United States – this country succeeded in guaranteeing standards of health, nutrition, education and general rights (for women, children, the disabled, etc.) that have not been attained even in some developed capitalist countries. If Cuba did it under those conditions, what are the insurmountable obstacles that prevent similar achievements in countries that enjoy much more promising prospects?

The answer will not be found in economic determinisms – which in most cases, are just a convenient pretext – but rather in the weakness of political will. Without a determined will to change the world, the world will go unchanged. But whoever undertakes this task must know two things. First, that by doing so, they will confront the tenacious and absolute opposition of dominant classes and social groups, who will use every possible tool at their disposal, from seduction and persuasion to the most atrocious violence, to frustrate any effort at transformation. It is this reality that is the cause for concern regarding certain Zapatista formulations, such as 'democracy for all', which reflect a political romanticism from which nothing good can be expected (Boron, 2001). Second, that there is no truce in this conflict: if the governors who attempt to change the world are not attacked, it is because their actions have become irrelevant, or, a perverse hypothesis, because they have joined forces with their enemies. It is not that the old masters have become resigned to losing their prerogatives and privileges, but rather that they have realised that their eventual opponents have laid down their arms and can no longer hurt the old order. For this reason, today more than ever, the praise and applause of Washington and its friends are sure signs that the wrong path is being pursued.

10 DEPOLARISED PLURALITIES
A Left with a Future
Boaventura de Sousa Santos

THE PHANTASMAGORICAL RELATION
BETWEEN THEORY AND PRACTICE

The distance between the practices of the Latin American left and the clas-sic theories of the left is greater today than ever. At the present moment, this may be the principal characteristic of the Latin American left. From the Mexican Zapatista National Liberation Army (EZLN) to the Workers' Party (PT) government in Brazil, from the Argentinean *piqueteros* to the Brazilian Landless Rural Workers Movement (MST), from the indigenous movements of Bolivia and Ecuador to the Uruguayan Broad Front, from the World Social Forum (WSF) to Hugo Chávez, we are confronted by political practices that are, in general, recognised as leftist, but which as a whole either were not predicted by the principal theoretical traditions of the Latin American left or may even contradict them.

This reciprocal blindness of practice in relation to theory and theory in relation to practice produces, on the one hand, an under-theorisation of practice and, on the other, an irrelevance of theory. That is to say that the blindness of theory renders practice invisible, while the blindness of practice makes theory irrelevant. This reciprocal lack of co-ordination gives rise to, on the side of practice, an extreme oscillation between revolutionary spontaneity and a self-censored and ultimately innocuous sense of the possible, and on the side of theory, an equally extreme alternation between a post-facto reconstructive zeal and an arrogant indifference to anything unaccounted for by theory. Under these condi-tions, the relation between theory and practice, which still exists, assumes unprecedented characteristics.

On the one hand, theory ceases to be at the service of potential future practices and is instead devoted to ratifying (or not) past practices that were not themselves influenced by theory. Rather than orientation, its purpose becomes legitimation. On the other hand, practice justifies itself by resorting to a theoretical amalgam constructed to serve the needs of the moment, comprised of heterogeneous concepts and language that, from a theoretical point of view, are nothing other than rationalisations or opportunistic rhetorical exercises. From the point of view of theory, a theoretical hodge-podge is never theory. And from the point of view of practice, *a posteriori* theorising is parasitic.

From this phantasmagorical relation between theory and practice follow three decisive political facts that are essential to understanding the current situation of the Latin American left. The first is that the discrepancy between short-term certainties and medium and long-term uncertainties was never as great as it is today. As a result, a strategic behaviour prevails that can be as much revolutionary as it is reformist. This tactical behaviour has also been conditioned by the certainties and transformations of the left's adversary. In the last three decades, neo-liberal capitalism has succeeded in subjugating social relations to those of the market to a degree that was unthinkable not long ago. The brutal aggravation of exploitation and exclusion, and consequently of social inequality, via the dismantling of political and juridical regulatory mechanisms which until recently appeared irreversible, confers on resistance struggles an urgency that permits a broad convergence of short-term goals (from privatisation to the WTO), without having to clarify whether the struggle is against capitalism in general, or on the contrary, against *this* capitalism in the name of another that is substantially different.

This concealed character is not a new problem. On the contrary, it characterised the left throughout the twentieth century. Today, however, it has assumed a new intensity. The devastating force of neo-liberal capitalism is such that collusion can pass for resistance. On the other hand, long-term uncertainty now also has a new dimension to it: one is not even certain that the long term exists. That is, long-term uncertainty is of such an order that it ceases to organise the conflicts within the left. In light of this, the short term is prolonged and it is at times on the basis of the certainties and urgencies of the short term that concrete political divisions occur.

If, on the one hand, the loss of credibility of the long term favours strategic behaviour, on the other hand it prevents divisions over the character of the long term from interfering with short-term divisions. That is, it permits a totally open-ended future on the basis of which consensuses can be built. If until recently the disagreements about the long term were strong, and a convergence existed with respect to the short term, today, with the loss of credibility of the long term, the strong disagreements take place in the short term, where the certainties are. And the certainties, being different for different groups, are the basis for strong disagreements.

The progressive uncertainty and, therefore, the opening up of the long term, is expressed in the transition from the certainty of the socialist future as the scientific result of the development of the forces of production (in Marx), to the dichotomy of socialism or barbarism (as formulated by Rosa Luxemburg), and later to the idea that 'another world is possible' (which presides over the World Social Forum). Among these, many intermediate transitions exist.

The long term was always the horizon of the left. In the past, the greater the difference between this future horizon and the present panorama of capitalism, the more radical was the conception of the way forward. It was from this difference that the fissure between revolution and reform emerged. Today, that fissure has eroded in a manner parallel to that of the long term. It continues to exist, but it no longer has the consistency and the consequences it once had. As a signifier, this distinction is relatively flexible and subject to contradictory appropriations. There are reformist processes that appear to be revolutionary (Hugo Chávez) and revolutionary processes that appear reformist (the Zapatistas) and even reformist processes that do not even appear to be reformist (the PT government in Brazil).

The second decisive political fact resulting from the phantasmagorical relation between theory and practice is the impossibility of a consensual evaluation of the left's performance. If for some the left suffers from the retreat from class struggle since the 1970s, for others this has been a period rich in innovation and creativity during which the left has renovated itself through new struggles, new forms of collective action and new political objectives. There has been a retreat, to be sure, but from the classic forms of political organisation and action, and it was thanks to that decline that new forms of political organisation and action emerged. For those who defend the idea of a general retreat, the assessment is negative and the supposed innovations are the result of the displacement suffered by the struggles for essential goals (the class struggle, in the sphere of production) for the sake of struggles for secondary goals (identity struggles, in the sphere of social reproduction). Retreat would amount to concessions to the adversary, however radical its exponents' talk of rupture. For those who defend the idea of innovation and creativity, the assessment is positive because obstructive dogmatisms would be broken, forms of collective action and the social bases that support them would be expanded, and above all because the struggles, given their form and their sphere, would make it possible to reveal new vulnerabilities of the adversary.

In this dispute over the assessment of the last three decades, both positions resort to the fallacy of hypothetical pasts, whether to demonstrate that had the option for the class struggle been maintained the results would have been better, or on the contrary to demonstrate that without the new struggles the results would have been worse.

The third fact that follows from the phantasmagorical relation between theory and practice is the new theoretical extremism. It has to do with divisions that are simultaneously much more enormous and much more irrelevant than those that characterised the left's theoretical disputes three decades ago. In contrast to the latter, the current divisions are not directly linked to concrete organisational forms and political strategies. Compared with more recent disputes, the distance between the extreme positions of past disputes appears much smaller, even though the option for one or the other position led to much more concrete consequences in the life of the organisations, of the activists and of society. The current theoretical extremism has three dimensions.

With respect to *the subjects of social transformation*, the division is between a well-defined historical subjectivity, the working class and its allies, on the one hand, and indeterminate and unlimited subjectivities, on the other, whether all of the oppressed, the 'common, and therefore, rebellious people', or the *multitude*. Until three decades ago, the division occurred 'only' over the definition of the working class (the industrial vanguard versus retrograde sectors), its allies (peasants or the petit bourgeoisie), or the transition from 'a class-in-itself' to 'a class-for-itself'.

With respect to *the objectives of social struggle*, the division is between the conquest of power and the total rejection of the concept of power, that is, between more radical versions of statism and anti-statism. Until 30 years ago, the division was over the means of taking power (armed struggle versus institutional struggle) and the nature and objectives of the exercise of power once it was taken (popular democracy/dictatorship of the proletariat versus representative democracy).

In *the domain of organisation*, the division is between a centralised party organisation and the total absence of centralism and even of any organisation that does not emerge spontaneously via the initiative of the very agents of collective action as a whole. Until 30 years ago, there was a division between communist and socialist parties, between a single party and the multi-party system, with respect to the relation between the party and the masses, or with respect to the organisational form of the worker's party (democratic centralism versus decentralisation and the right to dissent).

We are thus faced with another type of division, with new and more extreme positions. This does not mean that the divisions of the past have disappeared; they have only lost the exclusivity and centrality that they once had. The new divisions have not failed to have consequences within the heart of the left, but they are certainly more diffuse than past divisions. This is owing to two factors. On the one hand, it is due to the aforementioned phantasmagorical relation between theory and practice, which makes the latter relatively immune to theoretical divisions or to the selective or instrumental use of theory. On the other hand, the actors at extreme ends of the dispute are not fighting over the same social bases, mobilised for the same objectives, or active in the same or even rival organisations, which makes the confrontations within the left appear to be living parallel lives.

These divisions therefore have an important consequence: they hinder the acceptance of pluralism and diversity and make it impossible for them to become the motor of new forms of struggle or of new coalitions and articulations. This is an important consequence, above all given that the extreme positions within the new divisions exceed the universe of leftist culture *tout court*. We are faced with very distant cultural, symbolic and linguistic universes, and without a procedure for translating among them, reciprocal intelligibility is not possible. If on the one hand, we hear of class struggle, correlation of forces, society, the state, reform and revolution, on the other, we hear of love, dignity, solidarity, community, rebellion, emotions, affects, transformation of subjectivity and 'a world that accommodates all worlds'. It is a question, then, of a cultural as well as an epistemological rupture. These ruptures have a sociological base in the appearance of collective actors emanating from subaltern, indigenous, afro-American and feminist cultures that were ignored, if not harassed, by the traditional left throughout the twentieth century.

THE TWENTY-FIRST CENTURY LEFT

Is a synthesis between the extreme positions within the contemporary Latin American left possible? I do not think so, and even if it were possible, it would not be desirable. The search for a synthesis requires a conception of totality that reduces diversity to unity. In my opinion, no totality can contain the limitless diversity of practices and theories within today's Latin American left. Rather than synthesis, I believe it is necessary to search for *depolarised pluralities*. This amounts to inverting a tradition firmly rooted in the left that asserts that politicising differences is equivalent to polarising them. On the contrary, I propose that politicisation occurs by way of depolarisation. It consists of giving *meta-theoretical* priority to the construction of coalitions and articulations around concrete collective *practices*, debating the theoretical differences in the exclusive sphere of that construction. The objective is to transform the recognition of differences into a factor of aggregation and inclusion, eliminating the possibility of rendering collective action impossible as a result of those differences, and thus creating a context of collective political debate in which the recognition of differences occurs on a par with the recognition of similarities. In other words, it is a matter of creating contexts of debate in which the drive toward unity and similarity has the same intensity as the drive toward separation and difference. Collective actions orchestrated via depolarised pluralities give rise to a new conception of 'unity of action', insofar as the unity ceases to be the expression of a monolithic will and instead becomes the more or less broad and enduring point of encounter for a plurality of wills.

The concept of depolarised pluralities would upset all the automatisms of political debate within the heart of the left. It will therefore not be easy to apply. Two important factors are nonetheless working in favour of its application. The first is the current dominance of the short term over the long term (referred to above), with the consequence that the latter has never had such limited influence on the former. In the past, to the extent that the long term was a major polarising factor within the left, the short term – which was always conceived of with some autonomy in relation to the long term – played a depolarising role. In view of this, the tactical behaviour that emerges from the current predominance of the short term may facilitate agreement in order to give meta-theoretical priority to concrete collective actions and thus debate plurality and diversity only in the context of those actions. In the short term, all revolutionary actions are potentially reformist and all reformist actions may come to escape the control of the reformers. Concentration on the certainties and urgencies of the short term does not imply, consequently, only an abandonment of the long term, but also a sufficiently open conception of the long term to include vague agreements and conspiratorial silences. The opening up of the long term may contribute to depolarisation.

The other factor favouring the construction of depolarised pluralities is the recognition, evident today following the rise of the Zapatistas

(EZLN) and the World Social Forum (WSF), that the left is multicultural. This implies that the differences that divide the left go beyond the political terms in which they are normally formulated. These include cultural differences that a 'true' left cannot fail to recognise, since it would not make sense to struggle for the recognition and respect of cultural differences 'out there', in society, and neither recognise nor respect them 'at home'. Thus, we find an already created context for acting on the presupposition that differences are not eliminated by means of political resolutions; rather, we must coexist with them and convert them into a factor of enrichment and collective strength.

In what follows, I will analyse in greater detail the arenas and processes for constructing depolarised pluralities. As it is a question of a project of political renovation, we might begin by identifying the signs of renovation that have been detected in the Latin American left. In fact, the depolarised pluralities project proposes nothing more than to broaden those signs, making them bear fruit in the construction of new and more effective forms of collective action and in a new and more inclusive constellation of leftist political cultures. Without attempting to be exhaustive, I identify four great signs of renovation in the last three or four decades among other such decisive areas for a new left politics. These signs of renovation can be seen in *transformative will*, *ethics*, *epistemology* and *organisation*. The founding moment for the renovation of transformative will can be found in Che Guevara, but its most eloquent manifestations are the government of Salvador Allende, the Sandinista Front, the continent's indigenous movements and the MST. Ethical renovation concerns, above all, the theology of liberation and the manner in which it inserts itself in popular struggles and the imaginary of resistance to oppression. Epistemological renovation began with indigenous and feminist movements and today is most strongly manifested in the EZLN and the WSF. The founding moment for organisational renovation was the creation of the PT and its most significant manifestation the WSF.

All of these are political innovations but they start from different angles and with distinct levels of intensity. On the basis of these innovations, in my opinion, it is possible to think about new paradigms of transformative and progressive action influenced by the operating principle of depolarised pluralities.

The construction of depolarised pluralities is carried out by already constituted collective subjects or those in the process of formation, by those involved in collective actions or available to participate in them. The priority conferred on participation in collective actions, via co-ordination or coalition, allows us to suspend the question of the subject of the action, insofar as if there are actions developing there are subjects evolving. The presence of concrete subjects does not eliminate the question of the abstract subject, but it prevents it from interfering in a decisive manner in the conception or development of the collective action, since the latter is never the product of abstract subjects. In this context, giving priority to participation in concrete collective actions means that:

• Each participating subject avoids assuming that the only important or correct collective actions are those conceived or executed by him or her. In a context in which the mechanisms of exploration, exclusion and oppression multiply and intensify, it becomes particularly important not to miss any social experience of resistance on the part of the exploited, excluded or oppressed.

• Theoretical disputes should take place in the context of actions and always with the objective of making them more visible and strengthening them.

• Whenever a given collective subject questions that objective, the abandonment of the collective action should be done with the least possible debilitating impact on the position of those subjects who remain committed to the action.

• Because resistance never takes place in the abstract, transformative collective actions always begin by occurring on the terrain and on the terms of conflict established by the oppressed. The success of collective actions is measured by the capacity of the collective action to change the terrain and the terms of conflict in the course of the struggle. But at the same time, it is this success that measures the correction of the assumed theoretical positions. The pragmatic conception (on the basis of results) of the theoretical correction creates a readiness for the depolarisation of pluralities as the action takes place.

I move now to a discussion of the most important moments in the construction of depolarised pluralities at the heart of transformative collective actions. I distinguish three principal moments: (1) depolarisation through concentration on productive questions; (2) depolarisation via the search for inclusive organisational forms; and (3) depolarisation through intensification of reciprocal communication and intelligibility. Given that I have discussed points 2 and 3 elsewhere (see Santos, 2003a), in what follows I will concentrate on the distinction between productive questions and unproductive questions, and on how focusing on the former can contribute to the task of promoting depolarised pluralities.

As the point is easily addressed, I will not concern myself with the creation of pluralities in general. I believe that these exist and tend to proliferate and intensify in the interior of the left, leading, as I have already noted, to extremism and polarisation with their familiar negative consequences. I concentrate, therefore, on a new form of plurality, depolarised pluralities, making a distinction between *productive* and *unproductive* questions.

UNPRODUCTIVE QUESTIONS

Productive questions are those whose discussion has direct consequences for the conception and development of collective action and for the conditions in which the latter takes place. All others are unproductive questions and, without necessarily being ignored, should be left at a level of indecision or a state of suspension that opens space for different responses. Many of the questions that fascinated the left in the past and led to the best-known polarisations do not pass this test today and should, therefore, be considered unproductive.

The question of socialism

The question of socialism is a question concerning the model of society that will succeed capitalism. This question suffered a devastating blow with the fall of the Berlin Wall. If it was previously considered a productive question insofar as a socialist future was on the political agenda, at least in some countries, and could therefore have practical consequences for collective action, today this is no longer the case. As an unproductive question, it should be left at a level of indecision, whose most eloquent formulation is the idea that 'another world is possible'. This formulation would make it possible to separate the radical critique of the present and the struggle for a post-capitalist or anti-capitalist future, both of which are promoters of collective action, from a commitment to a specific model of a future society or even to the idea that there is a single model and not several.

Reform versus revolution

The question of reform versus revolution gives rise to several productive questions which I will take up below, but by itself it is unproductive, given that the conditions in which the option of reform versus revolution became a decisive field of political struggle are no longer present. It concerned an option of principle between legal and illegal means of taking power, and consequently between a gradual and peaceful versus an abrupt and violent seizure of power. In either case, taking power contemplated the construction of a socialist society and was, in fact, a precondition for it. The truth is that none of the strategies succeeded in attaining their objectives, and as a result the opposition between them transformed into complicity. When the assumption of power was achieved, it was either to administer capitalism or to construct societies that only with much indulgence could have been considered socialist.

Another manifestation of complicity between the two principles is that historically they have always existed as complements to one another. On the one hand, revolution was always the foundational act in a new cycle of reformism, given that the first acts of revolutionaries, as the Bolsheviks illustrated well, were to impede new revolutions, legislating reformism as the only option. On the other hand, reformism only had credibility as long as the revolutionary alternative existed. And it is for that reason that the fall of the Berlin Wall meant the end not only of revolution but also of reformism, at least in the forms in which we knew it throughout the short twentieth century. It happens that, in light of this and of the transformations of capitalism in the last 30 years, the two terms of the dichotomy suffered such a drastic semantic evolution that it has rendered them unreliable as principles for orienting social struggle. Reformism has become the object of a brutal attack by the forces of capital, an attack that began by resorting to illegal means (the overthrow of the Salvador Allende government in Chile in 1973) before resorting, with its turn toward neoliberalism, to the legal means of structural adjustment, negotiation of foreign debt, privatisation and free trade. In this light, the reformism of today is reduced to a ridiculous miniature of what it once was, as illustrated by the cases of South Africa and Brazil. For its part, revolution, which began by symbolising a maximalist conception of the seizure of power, ended up evolving semantically toward conceptions of the rejection of the seizure of power, if not a radical rejection of the very idea of power, as illustrated by the highly polemical interpretation of Zapatismo by John Holloway (2001). Between these extremes of the seizure of power and its total disappearance, there were, throughout the twentieth century, many intermediate conceptions focused on the idea of the transformation of power, as illustrated early on by the non-Leninist conceptions of revolution of Austro-Marxists.

For all of these reasons, I do not think that the debate between reform and revolution is a productive one. For the past, it is a polarising question. For the present and near future, it is irrelevant. As long as it does not emerge in new terms, I propose that this question be left in a state of suspension that, in this case, means accepting that social struggles are never essentially reformist or revolutionary. They transform into one or the other as a result of the consequences they have (some intentional and others not) for their relation to other struggles of the left and as a function of the resistance of opposing forces. That is, the suspension consists in this case in transforming reform and revolution from principles for orienting future actions into principles for appraising past actions.

The state: principal or irrelevant objective

Related to the previous question, there is another that I consider unproductive, and that consists in disputing whether the state is relevant or irrelevant for a leftist politics, and consequently whether the state should or should not be an object of social struggle. The option is between social struggles that have as their objective the power of the state in its multiple forms and levels, and social struggles that have as their exclusive object the powers that circulate within civil society and that determine inequalities, exclusions and oppressions. It is not a question of deciding whether one should defend or attack the state, but rather deciding whether social struggles should have objectives other than defending or attacking it. This question can also split into certain productive questions, as I will demonstrate below, but in itself, it is an unproductive question. The question, already discussed above, as to whether power should be taken or suppressed is related to this question, but it is broader. The question of the seizure or the extinction of power can assume two forms, depending on whether it influences the state or civil society. That is, it is possible to be in favour of taking power (in civil society) and against the inclusion of the state among the objectives of social struggle, whether to defend it or to attack it. The problem is to know whether this position, being logically correct, has any practical historical consequence.

The unproductive character of the question concerning the relevance or irrelevance of the state has its origins in the fact that, the state being a social relation, that relevance or irrelevance cannot cease to be the result of social struggles that in the past did or did not have the state as their objective. The modern capitalist state does not exist outside its relationship to civil society. The two, far from being external to one another, are the two faces of social domination in capitalist societies. This question of the relevance or irrelevance of the state is an unproductive question because its polarising potential is the other face of its falseness. That is, the state is always relevant, even though this is the result of its pre-eminence in struggles that are premised on the state's irrelevance and that, by confirming it, help to advance the social causes. In order to neutralise its polarising potential, I suggest the following level of indecision or state of suspension: social struggles may have either the state or civil society as their privileged object, but in either case, unprivileged powers always affect the results of the struggles, and are affected by them.

PRODUCTIVE QUESTIONS

I move now to a discussion of productive questions, that is, questions whose discussion may result in a depolarisation of pluralities that today constitute the thought and action of the left.

The state as ally or as enemy

Unlike the unproductive question of the relevance or irrelevance of the state, this question of the state as ally or as enemy is productive precisely because it does not assume the state's relevance in an abstract manner. It gives it a specific political content. The transformations that the state has experienced throughout the twentieth century, whether in countries of the centre or those liberated from colonialism, and the contradictory role that they played in processes of social transformation, have given historical and practical consistency to this question. The experiences of different countries with respect to the social struggle of parties and social movements are very rich and varied, and it would therefore appear that they are not susceptible to being reduced to a general principle or recipe.

The World Social Forum is today an eloquent manifestation of this richness of social struggles, given that movements and associations with the most diverse relations with the state congregate within it. The possibility of constructing a depolarised plurality within that sphere is based precisely on the fact that the majority of movements and associations refuse to take a rigid or principled position in their relations vis-à-vis the state. Their experiences of struggle demonstrate that while the state can sometimes be an enemy, it can also be a precious ally, particularly in peripheral or semi-peripheral countries (e.g., in the struggle against transnational impositions).

If in some situations, confrontation with the state is justified, in others collaboration is advisable, and in still others a combination of the two is appropriate (as in the brilliant example of the strategy adopted by the MST in Brazil).

The conception of the state as a contradictory social relation creates the possibility of contextualised discussions regarding the position that a certain party or movement has to adopt toward the state in a particular social area, in a specific country and in a precise historical moment. It also allows for a comparative evaluation of the diverse positions assumed by different parties or movements in different areas of intervention or in different countries or historical moments. This in turn makes it possible to recognise the existence of different strategies, all of which are contextual, and none of which is free of risk or, above all, susceptible to being transformed into a general principle. This is what depolarised pluralism consists of.

Local, national and global struggles

The question of the relative priority of local, national and global collective actions is today widely debated, and the diversity of left practices on this question is also enormous. It is certainly the case that the theoretical tradition of the left was moulded at the national level. Traditionally, local struggles were considered less important or seen as embryonic forms of national struggles to the detriment of international objectives. For its part, internationalism was in practice always a demonstration of the priorities of national struggles and interests. It was the national level that prevailed in the formation of leftist parties and unions and that continues to structure their activism to this day.

In the second half of the twentieth century, above all beginning in the 1970s, the appearance of two new social movements caused the local level of social movements to acquire an importance that it had not previously had. The organisational tradition of the left prevented the full exploration of the emancipatory potential of the articulation between local and national struggles. The construction of the Brazilian PT has been perhaps where this articulation has been achieved with greatest success.

Beginning in the 1990s, and above all with the emergence of the Zapatistas in 1994 and the World Social Forum in 2001, collective actions at the global level acquired an unprecedented visibility. The co-ordination tasks between the different levels of action became, therefore, more demanding, implying at the same time local, national and global levels.

On the other hand, the field of concrete experiences of struggles at different levels expanded enormously, and as a result fostered contextualised debates about different levels of collective action, their relative advantages, organisational demands and possibilities of articulation. That debate is still under way and is one of the most productive, above all with respect to the specific instruments of co-ordination among the different levels of action.

The World Social Forum unites social movements and associations with different conceptions of the relative priority of the distinct levels of action. Given that the WSF is itself a form of collective action at the global level, many of the movements and associations that take part in it have until recently had little experience of local and national struggles. Nevertheless, they all see in the Forum the possibility of expanding their levels of action, attributing very distinct priorities to the different levels. If for some the global level of the struggle becomes ever more important as the struggle against neo-liberal globalisation deepens, for others the WSF is only a point of encounter or a cultural event, which while useful does not alter the basic principle that the 'true struggles', those that are really important for the well-being of populations, continue to take place at the local and national levels. There are other movements and associations that systematically incorporate into their practice the local and national levels (the MST) or the local, national and global levels (the EZLN). For the great majority of movements, the distance between these levels does not do justice to the real necessities of the concrete struggles. In contemporary societies, the different levels of social and political action are ever more interrelated. In the most remote village of the Amazon, the effects of hegemonic globalisation and the ways in which national states are implicated in those effects are clearly felt. Although each concrete political practice is organised according to a determined level, all the other levels must be involved as a condition of success.

The wealth of experiences of social struggle in this respect is therefore enormous, and makes contextualised and productive debates possible. The possibility of the appearance of depolarised pluralities in this sphere follows from the fact that, in the light of recent experience, it makes ever greater sense to give absolute or abstract priority to any of the levels of action, thereby opening space for appreciating the coexistence of social struggles at distinct levels and the variable geometric relations among them. The decision as to which level to privilege is a political decision that must be taken in accordance with concrete political conditions.

Institutional action or direct action

In contrast to the reform versus revolution question, the question of the choice between institutional or direct action is a productive one to the degree that it is discussed in practical contexts of collective action. It is a matter of knowing whether it is necessary, in the concrete conditions in which a given struggle or collective action is carried out, to privilege the use of legal means or political work within institutions and dialogue with power holders or, on the contrary, the use of illegal methods and institutional confrontation. In the case of institutional action, it is necessary to distinguish between action in the sphere of state power (national or local) and action in the sphere of parallel power, especially through the creation of parallel institutions in areas not penetrated by the state. Parallel institutionality is a type of hybrid collective action in which elements of direct and institutional action are combined. In the case of direct action, it is necessary to distinguish between violent and non-violent action, and in the case of the former, between human and non-human (property) objectives.

These courses of action have costs and benefits that can only be evaluated in concrete contexts, and which, obviously, call for different types of organisation and mobilisation. What in general might be said about one or the other type of collective action is not sufficient for deciding which course of action to take in specific contexts. The context is not limited to the immediate conditions for action, but also involves surrounding conditions, especially the existence (or not) of a representative regime (democracy, even if it is low intensity) and of a system of public opinion. Institutional action is better suited to taking advantage of contradictions of power and divisions among elites, but it is susceptible to co-optation and to the erosion of gains, leaving aside the difficulty of maintaining high levels of mobilisation, especially given the asynchrony between the rhythm of collective formulation of demands and protests, on the one hand, and the judicial or legislative rhythm, on the other. Direct action is better suited to exploiting the inefficiencies of the system of power and the fragility of its social legitimacy, but it has difficulties when it comes to formulating credible alternatives and it is susceptible to repression, which if excessive can jeopardise mobilisation and the very organisation itself. While institutional action tends toward co-ordination with political parties, so long as they exist, direct action tends to be hostile toward that co-ordination.

The possibility of depolarisation with respect to this issue is supported, once again, by the richness of political struggles of the last 30 years. Today, that richness is condensed in a very eloquent way in the World Social Forum, which brings together movements and organisations with very diverse experiences of social struggle. If many of them privilege institutional actions, many others privilege direct actions. But the most significant, in terms of its depolarising potential, is the experience of movements and organisations that, in distinct struggles or in different moments of the same struggle, resort to both types of action, the MST once again being an eloquent example. Despite not being physically present at the Forum, the EZLN opened a horizon of convergent possibilities in this field and today exercises a strong (though not very well known) influence among social movements, especially in Latin America. In the struggles of the EZLN, it is possible to discern moments of direct action (uprising), of institutional action (San Andrés accord, open meeting in the Mexican Congress), and of parallel institutional action (*caracoles*, councils of good government). Once the conditions are created for systematic evaluations (see below), this vast experience has all the conditions for bestowing credibility to the formation of depolarised pluralities.

Struggles for equality and struggles for the respect of difference

The issue of the relative priority of struggles for equality and for the respect of difference is a relatively recent one in the theory and practice of the Latin American left. It emerged during the 1970s and 1980s, when the feminist and indigenous movements erupted on the scene, followed somewhat later by the LGBT (Lesbian, Gay, Bisexual, and Transgender/ Transsexual) and Afro-descendent movements. Organised on the basis of identities that have traditionally been discriminated against, these movements challenged the concept of equality that had prevailed among the social struggles of earlier periods, a concept that was centred on the idea of economic class (worker or peasant) and that was hostile to the recognition of politically significant differences among popular classes. If in general these identity-based movements questioned the importance of class inequalities, they stressed the political importance of inequalities based on race, ethnicity, gender and sexual orientation. According to these movements, the principle of equality tended to homogenise differences and, therefore, to obscure the hierarchies internal to them. These hierarchies are translated into discriminations that irreversibly diminish the opportunities for the personal and social fulfilment of the discriminated. Operating exclusively on the principle of equality, it is not possible to achieve anything more than a subordinate, deforming inclusion. To prevent that, it is necessary to consider the recognition of difference as a principle of social emancipation as significant as that of equality.

Creating a connection between the principles of equality and recognition of difference is not an easy task. But within this domain, the diversity of social struggles of the last three decades has also allowed for the formation of depolarised pluralities. Certainly, there are extreme positions that deny the validity of one of the two principles or that, while recognising the validity of both, give total priority to one of them. Instead, the majority of movements attempt to find concrete forms of co-ordination between the two principles, even while giving priority to one of them. This situation is evident in the union movement, which was founded on the principle of equality, but where there is a growing recognition of the importance of ethnic and sexual discrimination and there exists a positive disposition toward the organisation of identity-based movements around concrete struggles. It is also evident within identity-based movements, above all the feminist movement, with the growing recognition and politicisation of internal class differences.

In this arena, the conditions are created for the formation of depolarised pluralities and, once again, the WSF offers ample space in which opportunities for building connections and coalitions among movements with different conceptions of social emancipation can be generated. Mutual knowledge is a necessary condition for reciprocal recognition. Advances in this arena do not result from an abstract discussion between the two principles, or between radical positions, but rather a discussion of concrete options concerning the configuration of concrete struggles, which commit the movements without obligating them to basic changes in their cultural-philosophical concepts or fundamental politics.

CONCLUSION: A LEFT WITH A FUTURE

Focusing on questions and problems that have a direct impact on the conceptualisation and execution of collective actions – what I have called productive questions throughout this chapter – is a point of departure, but it cannot be a final destination. The depolarised pluralities that appear when the work and discussion focus on productive questions translate into a new type of action. These are actions that must respond to productive questions and issues and that can even provide multiple responses according to the variation in political contexts in different places and at different times. It has to do with actions that are complex, consciously heterogeneous, and sufficiently flexible to accommodate distinct rhythms, time frames, styles and levels of action. Complexity, internal heterogeneity and flexibility are the modes by which depolarised pluralities are translated into the sphere of action.

The conceptualisation and execution of those actions must be undertaken by organisations that are related to them. Of course, it is known that the conventional organisational forms of the left are hostile to plurality and depolarisation. For that reason, those organisations must be profoundly transformed and, if necessary, substituted or complemented by others. In other words, the new type of action calls for a new type of organisation. It calls for organisational forms that are inclusive, internally complex, heterogeneous and flexible. The characteristics of this new type of organisations should be the priority topic of discussion in the construction of a left with a future.

BIBLIOGRAPHY

Aguirre, R., de Sierra, G., Iens, I. and Charbonnier, B. (1992) *Informe de una encuesta a vecinos sobre descentralización, participación y centros comunales zonales*. Montevideo: CIEDUR.

Albó, X. (2002) *Pueblos indios en la política*. La Paz: Plural-Cipca.

Álvarez, S. (1998) 'Latin American Feminisms "Go Global": Trends of the 1990s and Challenges for the New Millennium', in S. Álvarez, E. Dagnino and A. Escobar (eds), *Cultures of Politics, Politics of Culture*. Boulder: Westview Press.

Álvarez, S., Dagnino, E. and Escobar, A. (eds) (1998) *Cultures of Politics, Politics of Culture*. Boulder: Westview Press.

Archila, M. (2001) 'Vida, pasión y ... de los movimientos sociales en Colombia', in M. Archila and M. Pardo (eds), *Movimientos Sociales, Estado y Democracia en Colombia*. Bogota: Universidad Nacional de Colombia.

Archila, M. (2003) *Idas y venidas, vueltas y revueltas: protestas sociales en Colombia (1958–1990)*, Bogota: Icahn/Cinep.

Archila, M. (2004) 'Encuestas y protestas', *El Espectador*, November 19–25.

Arendt, H. (1993) *La Condición Humana* (The Human Condition), Barcelona: Paidós.

Avritzer, L. (2002) *Democracy and the Public Space in Latin America*. Princeton: Princeton University Press.

Baierle, S. (1998) 'The Explosion of Experience: The Emergence of a New Ethical-Political Principle in Popular Movements in Porto Alegre', in S. Álvarez, E. Dagnino and A. Escobar (eds), *Cultures of Politics, Politics of Culture*. Boulder: Westview Press.

Baiocchi, G. (ed.) (2003) *Radicals in Power: The Workers' Party and Experiments in Urban Democracy in Brazil*. London: Zed Books.

Baiocchi, G. (2004) 'The Party and the Multitude: Brazil's Workers' Party (PT) and the Challenges of Building a Just Social Order in a Globalizing Context', *Journal of World-Systems Research* X(1).

Barberán, J., Cárdenas, C., López Monjardín, A. and Zavala, J. (1988) *Radiografía del fraude: análisis de los datos oficiales del 6 de julio*. Mexico: Nuestro Tiempo.

Barrett, P. (2000) 'Regime Change, Democratic Stability, and the Transformation of the Chilean Party System', *Journal of Interamerican Studies and World Affairs* 34(3).

Barrett, P. (2001) 'Labour Policy, Labour–Business Relations, and the Transition to Democracy in Chile', *Journal of Latin American Studies* 33.

Barrett, P. (2002) 'Regime Change and the Transformation of State-Capital Relations in Chile', *Political Power and Social Theory* 15.

Bartra, A. (1985) *Los herederos de Zapata: movimientos campesinos posrevolucionarios en México (1920–1980)*. Mexico: era.

Bartra, A. (2001) 'Sur: megaplanes y utopías en la América equinoccial', in A. Bartra (ed.), *Mesoamérica. Los ríos profundos*. Mexico: Instituto Maya.

Bartra, A. (2003a) 'La llama y la piedra: de cómo cambiar el mundo sin tomar el poder, según John Holloway', *Chiapas* 15.

Bartra, A. (2003b) 'Descifrando la treceava estela', *Observatorio Social de América Latina* 12.

Bartra, A. (2004) 'Las guerras del ogro', *Chiapas* 16.

Bartra, A. (2006) 'El estado de la elección', *Memoria*, México, Centro de Estudios del Movimiento Obrero y Socialista, No. 208, pp. 9–14.

Becassino, Á. (2003) *El Triunfo de Lucho y Pablo, o la derrota de las maquinarias*. Bogota: Grijalbo.

Bellingeri, A. (2003) *Del agrarismo armado a la guerra de los pobres, 1940–1974*. Mexico: Casa Juan Pablos.

Bergamino, A., Caruso, A., de León, E. and Portillo, A. (2001) *Diez años de descentralización en Montevideo*. Montevideo: Intendencia Municipal de Montevideo.

Blanco Muñoz, A. (1998) *Habla el comandante Hugo Chávez Frías*. Caracas: Cátedra Pío Tamayo, Universidad Central de Venezuela.

Blyth, M. (2002) *Great Transformations: Economic Ideas and Institutional Change in The Twentieth Century*. Cambridge: Cambridge University Press.

Bobbio, N. (1995) *Derecha e izquierda: razones y significados de una distinción política*. Madrid: Taurus.

Bobbio, N. (1996) 'La izquierda y sus dudas', in G. Bosetti (ed.), *Izquierda Punto Cero*. Barcelona: Paidós.

Boix, C. (1998) *Political Parties, Growth and Equality: Conservative and Social Democratic Economic Strategies in the World Economy*. Cambridge: Cambridge University Press.

Bonfil Batalla, G. (1990) *México profundo: una civilización negada*. Mexico: Grijalbo and Centro Nacional para la Cultura y las Artes.

Boron, A. (2000) *Tras el búho de Minerva: mercado contra democracia en el capitalismo de fin de siglo*. Buenos Aires: Fondo de Cultura Económica.

Boron, A. (2001) 'La selva y la polis: interrogantes en torno a la teoría política del zapatismo', *Chiapas* 12.

Boron, A. (2002) *Imperio & Imperialismo: una lectura crítica de Michael Hardt y Antonio Negri*. Buenos Aires: Consejo Latinoamericano de Ciencias Sociales.

Boron, A. (2003a) *Estado, capitalismo y democracia en América Latina*. Buenos Aires: Consejo Latinoamericano de Ciencias Sociales.

BIBLIOGRAPHY

Boron, A. (2003b) 'Brazil 2003: ¿los inicios de un nuevo ciclo histórico?', *Observatorio Social de América Latina* January.

Boron, A. (ed.) (2004) *Nueva Hegemonía mundial: alternativas de cambio y movimientos sociales.* Buenos Aires: CONSEJO LATINOAMERICANO DE CIENCIAS SOCIALES.

Boron, A. (2006) 'The Truth about Capitalist Democracy', in L. Panitch and C. Leys (eds), *Socialist Register 2006: Telling the Truth.* London: Merlin Press.

Bosetti, G. (ed.) (1996) *Izquierda Punto Cero.* Barcelona: Paidós.

Bourdieu, P. (1999) *Acts of Resistance: Against the Tyranny of the Market.* New York: New Press.

Brysk, A. (2000) *From Tribal Village to Global Village: Indian Rights and International Relations in Latin America.* Stanford: Stanford University Press.

Caballero, A. (2004) 'Centro izquierda', *Semana,* September 20.

Caetano, G., Buquet, D., Chasquetti, D. and Piñeiro, R. (2002) 'Estudio panorámico sobre el fenómeno de la corrupción en el Uruguay', Montevideo: Instituto de Ciencia Política (ICP).

Calloni, S. (2006) 'Festejos y críticas ante el pago adelantado de Argentina al FMI', *La Jornada,* January 4.

Calvetti, J., Gorritti, P., Otonelli, G., Pizzolanti, A., Varela, P. and Zapata, S. (1998) *Análisis sobre los concejos vecinales.* Montevideo: Intendencia Municipal de Montevideo.

Camejo, Y. (2002) 'Estado y mercado en el proyecto nacional-popular bolivariano', *Revista Venezolana de Economía y Ciencias Sociales* 8(3).

Campbell, H. (1976) *La derecha radical en México, 1929–1974.* Mexico: Secretaría de Educación Pública.

Canzani, A. (2000) 'Mensajes en una botella: analizando las elecciones de 1999–2000', in *Elecciones 1999–2000.* Montevideo: Ediciones de la Banda Oriental.

Cardoso, F.H. (1982) 'La democracia en las sociedades contemporáneas', *Crítica & Utopía* 6.

Cardoso, F.H. (1985) 'La democracia en América Latina', *Punto de Vista* 23.

Carr, E.H. (1946) *The Soviet Impact on the Western World.* New York: MacMillan.

Carvalho, C.E. (2003) 'El gobierno de Lula y el neoliberalismo relanzado', *Nueva Sociedad* 187.

Castañeda, J.G. (1993) *Utopia Unarmed: The Latin American Left After the Cold War.* New York: Alfred A. Knopf.

Castañeda, J.G. (2006) 'Latin America's Left Turn', *Foreign Affairs,* May–June.

Cazés, D. (1990) 'Democracia y desmasificación de la Universidad', in S. Zermeño (ed.), *Universidad Nacional y Democracia.* Mexico: Porrúa.

Ceceña, A.E. (1999) 'La resistencia como espacio de construcción del nuevo mundo', *Chiapas* 7.

Cervantes, J. and Gil Olmos, J. (2003) 'El jugoso negocio electoral', *Proceso* 1391.

Chavez, D. (2004) *Polis and Demos: Participatory Municipal Governance in*

[275]

Montevideo and Porto Alegre. Utrecht: Institute of Social Studies (ISS) and Shaker Publishing.

Chavez, D. (2007) 'Hacer o no hacer: los gobiernos progresistas de Argentina, Brasil y Uruguay frente a las privatizaciones', *Nueva Sociedad* 2007.

Chavez, D. and Carballal, S. (1997*) La ciudad solidaria: el cooperativismo de vivienda por ayuda mutua*. Montevideo: Facultad de Arquitectura de la Universidad de la República and Nordan-Comunidad.

Chavez, D. and Goldfrank, B. (eds) (2004) *La izquierda en la ciudad: gobiernos progresistas en América Latina*. Barcelona: Icaria.

Chernick, M., and Jiménez, M. (1990) *Popular Liberalism and Radical Democracy: The Development of the Colombian Left, 1974–1990*. New York: Columbia University and NYU Centre for Latin American Studies.

CND (1995) 'Los desafíos de la CND: propuestas de la Presidencia colectiva a la Segunda sesión de la CND (Convención Nacional Democrática)', *Chiapas* 1.

COPRE (1988) *Proyecto de reforma integral del Estado*. Caracas: Comisión Presidencial para la Reforma del Estado (COPRE).

Coronil, F. (2004) 'Chávez y las instituciones', *Nueva Sociedad Separatas*, August.

Corporación Latinobarómetro (2006) *Informe Latinobarómetro 2006*. Santiago: Corporación Latinobarómetro.

Costa, A. (2003) 'El gobierno de Lula. ¿Una nueva política exterior?', *Nueva Sociedad*, 187.

Cueva, A. (1976) *El desarrollo del capitalismo en América Latina*. México: Siglo XXI.

Dagnino, E. (1998) 'Culture, Citizenship, and Democracy: Changing Discourses and Practices of the Latin American Left', in S. Álvarez, E. Dagnino and A. Escobar (eds), *Cultures of Politics, Politics of Culture*. Boulder: Westview Press.

Dávalos, P. (2005) 'De paja de páramo sembraremos el mundo: izquierda, utopía y movimiento indígena en Ecuador', in C. Rodríguez-Garavito, P. Barrett and D. Chavez (eds), *La nueva izquierda en América Latina: sus orígenes y trayectoria futura*. Bogota: Grupo Editorial Norma.

de los Campos, E. (2001) 'La recesión económica es una prueba de fuego para la descentralización'. Montevideo: unpublished document.

Denis, R. (2001) *Los fabricantes de la rebelión: movimiento popular, chavismo y sociedad en los años noventa*. Caracas: Primera Línea-Nuevo Sur.

Díaz-Polanco, H. (1988) *La cuestión étnico-nacional*. Mexico: Fontamara.

Díaz-Polanco, H. (1990) *Etnia, nación y política*. Mexico: Juan Pablos.

Díaz-Polanco, H. and López y Rivas, G. (1994) 'Fundamentos de las autonomías regionales', *Cuadernos Agrarios* 8–9.

Dowbor, L. (2003) 'Brasil: tendencias de la gestión social', *Nueva Sociedad* 187.

Doyenart, J.C. (1998) 'El 73 por ciento de los montevideanos considera que la ciudad está mejor que hace 10 años', *Posdata*, January 23.

Duzán, M.J. (2004a) *Así gobierna Uribe*. Bogota: Planeta.

Duzán, M.J. (2004b) 'Los "swingers" de la política', *El Tiempo*, March 8.

El Tiempo (2003) 'Editorial: Adiós a los minipartidos', *El Tiempo*, June 26.

Elías, A. (ed.) (2006) *Los gobiernos progresistas en debate: Argentina, Brasil, Chile, Venezuela y Uruguay.* Buenos Aires: Consejo Latinoamericano de Ciencias Sociales.

Ellner, S. (2004) 'Hugo Chávez y Alberto Fujimori: análisis comparativo de dos variantes de populismo', *Revista Venezolana de Economía y Ciencias Sociales* 10(1).

Ellner, S. and Hellinger, D. (eds) (2003) *La política venezolana en la época de Chávez: clases, polarización y conflicto.* Caracas: Nueva Sociedad.

Elorriaga Berdegué, J. (2003) 'De negociar con el gobierno o dialogar con la sociedad', *Rebeldía* 3.

Equipo Proceso Político (1978) *CAP 5 años: un juicio crítico.* Caracas: Ateneo de Caracas.

Escárzaga, F. and Gutiérrez, R. (eds) (2005) *Movimiento indígena en América Latina: resistencia y proyecto alternativo.* Puebla: Benemérita Universidad Autónoma de Puebla.

EZLN (1994) 'Segunda declaración de la Selva Lacandona', in Ejército Zapatista de Liberación Nacional (ed.), *Documentos y Comunicados.* Mexico: era.

EZLN and Gobierno Federal (2003) *Los Acuerdos de San Andrés.* Mexico: Biblioteca Popular de Chiapas.

Fals Borda, O. (2004) 'Cómo elaborar un cemento ideológico para Alternativa Democrática'. Bogota, unpublished document.

Favaro, O., Arias Bucciarelli, M. and Iuorno, G. (1997) 'La conflictividad social en Neuquén: el movimiento cutralquense y los nuevos sujetos sociales', *Realidad Económica* 148.

Ferro, J.G. and Uribe, G. (2002) *El orden de la guerra: las FARC-EP entre la organización y la política.* Bogota: CEJA.

Filgueira, F. and Lijtenstein, S. (2006) 'La izquierda y las políticas sociales: desafíos y encrucijadas', in Instituto de Ciencia Política (ed.), *El primer ciclo de gobierno de la izquierda en Uruguay: informe de Coyuntura.* Montevideo: Instituto de Ciencia Política (ICP).

Foucault, M. (2001) 'El sujeto y el poder', in H.L. Dreyfus and P. Rabinow (eds), *Michel Foucault: Beyond Structuralism and Hermeneutics.* Buenos Aires: Nueva Visión.

Fraser, N. (1993) 'Rethinking the Public Sphere: A Contribution to the Critique of Actually Existing Democracy', in B. Robbins (ed.), *The Phantom Public Sphere.* Minneapolis: University of Minnesota Press.

FSP (2002) 'Plataforma del frente social y político'. Bogota: Frente Social y Político (FSP).

FSP(2003a) 'Realidad y visión: presente y futuro del FSP,' in VV.AA, *Ponencia presentada al Segundo Consejo Nacional de Dirección FSP.* Bogota: Frente Social y Político (FSP).

FSP (2003b) 'El Frente Social y Político saluda el nacimiento del Partido Polo Democrático Independiente'. Bogota: Frente Social y Político (FSP).

Fung, A. and Wright, E.O. (eds) (2003) *Deepening Democracy: Institutional Innovations in Empowered Participatory Democracy*. London: Verso.

Galeano, E. (2004) 'Aguas de octubre', *La Jornada*, November 1.

Garay, L.J. (2002) *Colombia: entre la exclusión y el desarrollo. Propuestas para la transición al estado social de derecho*. Bogota: Contraloría General de la República.

García Linera, A. (2004) 'The "Multitude"', in O. Olivera (ed.), *¡Cochabamba! Water War in Bolivia*. Cambridge: South End Press.

García, Miguel. 2000. 'Elección popular de alcaldes y terceras fuerzas', in *Análisis Político* 41, pp. 84–97.

García-Peña, D. (2003) 'La candidatura de Lucho se decidió en una piscina', *El Espectador*, December 8.

Garza Toledo, E.d.l. and Rhi Sausi, J.L. (1985) 'Perspectivas del sindicalismo en México', in J. Alcocer (ed.), *México, presente y futuro*. Mexico: Ediciones de Cultura Popular.

Garzón, L.E. (2003a) 'Entrevista: Lucho Garzón – alcalde de Bogotá y líder de la izquierda colombiana', *El País*, November 15.

Garzón, L.E. (2003b) 'Uno no hace cambios arrasando' (entrevista con Lucho Garzón), *Semana*, November 3.

Garzón, L.E. (2004) *Lucho: soy un polo a tierra. Conversaciones con Salud Hernández-Mora y Bernardo García*. Bogota: Oveja Negra.

Gaspar, R., Akerman, M. and Garibe, R. (2006) *Espaço Urbano e Inclusão Social: a gestão pública na cidade de São Paulo 2001–2004*. Sao Paulo: Instituto São Paulo de Políticas Públicas and Editora Fundação Perseu Abramo.

Gaviria, C. (2003a) 'Uribe es un retórico de la acción' [interview], *Revista Credencial*, August 5.

Gaviria, C. (2003b) 'Descartamos la vía armada' [interview], *El Tiempo*, September 19.

Gaviria, C. (2004a) 'Entrevista a Carlos Gaviria' [interview], *Contravía 10*.

Gaviria, C. (2004b), Intervention in the Conference 'The New Latin American Left', Madison, University of Wisconsin-Madison, 29 April.

Gentili, P. and Sader, E. (eds) (2003) *La trama del neoliberalismo: mercado, crisis y exclusión social*. Buenos Aires: CLACSO.

Germani, G. (1965) *Política y sociedad en una época de transición: de la sociedad tradicional a la sociedad de masas*. Buenos Aires: Paidós.

Goldfrank, B. (2002) 'The Fragile Flower of Local Democracy: Participation in Montevideo', *Politics & Society* 30(1).

Goldfrank, B. (2006) 'Los procesos de presupuesto participativo en América Latina: Éxito, Fracaso y Cambio', *Revista Chilena de Ciencia Política* 26(2).

Golinger, E. (2006) *The Chávez Code: Cracking US Intervention in Venezuela*. London: Pluto Press.

Gómez, E. (1999) 'Uruguay Report: menos pobres, más marginados', *Social Watch Annual Report 1998*. Montevideo: Instituto del Tercer Mundo - Social Watch.

Gonzaga, L. (2003) 'Brasil, una funesta apertura financiera', *Nueva Sociedad* 187.

González, L.E. (2000) 'Las elecciones nacionales del 2004: posibles scenarios', in *Elecciones 1999–2000*. Montevideo: Ediciones de la Banda Oriental.

González, M. (1995) '¿Sencillamente vecinos? Las Comisiones Vecinales de Montevideo. Impactos del gobierno municipal sobre formas tradicionales de asociación'. MA thesis. Rio de Janeiro: IUPERJ.

González Casanova, P. (1965) *La democracia en México*. Mexico: era.

González Casanova, P. (1981) *El estado y los partidos políticos en México*. Mexico: era.

Gorz, A. (1964) *Strategy for Labor: A Radical Proposal*. Boston: Beacon Press.

Gutiérrez, F. (ed.) (2001) *Degradación o cambio: evolución del sistema político colombiano*. Bogota: Editorial Norma.

Gutiérrez, F. (2003) 'La radicalización del voto en Colombia', in G. Hoskin, R. Masías and M. García (eds), *Colombia 2002: elecciones, comportamiento electoral y democracia*. Bogota: Ediciones Uniandes.

Gutiérrez, F. (2007) *¿Lo que el viento se llevó? Los partidos políticos y la democracia en Colombia, 1958–2002*. Bogota: Editorial Norma.

Hardt, M. and Negri, A. (2000) *Empire*. Cambridge, MA: Harvard University Press.

Hardt, M. and Negri, A. (2002) *Imperio*. Buenos Aires: Paidós.

Hardt, M. and Negri, A. (2004) *Multitude: War and Democracy in the Age of Empire*. New York: Penguin.

Harnecker, M. (1995) *Forjando la esperanza*. Santiago de Chile and Havana: LOM Ediciones and MEPLA.

Hernández, I. (2000) *El clan Salinas*. Mexico: Seri Editores y Distribuidores.

Hill, J.T. (2004) 'Testimony of General James T. Hill United States Army Commander United States Southern Command Before the House Armed Services Committee'. Washington: United States House of Representatives.

Holloway, J. (2000) 'El zapatismo y las ciencias sociales en América Latina', *Chiapas* 10.

Holloway, J. (2001) *Cambiar el mundo sin tomar el poder: el significado de la revolución hoy*. Puebla: Universidad Autónoma de Puebla.

Holloway, J. (2002), *Cambiar el mundo sin tomar el poder*, México, Universidad Autónoma de Puebla.

Holloway, J. (2004) 'Gente común, es decir rebelde: mucho más que una respuesta a Atilio Boron', *Chiapas* 16.

Hoskin, G., Masías, R. and García, M. (2003), 'La decisión de voto en las elecciones presidenciales de 2002', in G. Hoskin, R. Masías and M. García (eds), *Colombia 2002: elecciones, comportamiento electoral y democracia*. Bogota: Ediciones Uniandes.

Huber, E. and Solt, F. (2004) 'Successes and Failures of Neoliberalism', *Latin American Research Review* 39(3).

Hurtado, J. (1986) *El Katarismo*. La Paz: Hisbol.

ICP (ed.) (2006) *El primer ciclo de gobierno de la izquierda en Uruguay: Informe de Coyuntura*. Montevideo: Instituto de Ciencia Política (ICP).

INE (2004) 'Estimaciones de pobreza por el método del ingreso – año 2003'. Montevideo: Instituto Nacional de Estadística (INE).

Izarra, W.E. (2004) *Reforma o revolución*. Caracas: Centro de Estudios e Investigación de la Democracia Directa.

Jarquín Gálvez, U. and Romero Vadillo, J.J. (1985) *Un pan que no se come*. Mexico: Ediciones de Cultura Popular.

Jessop, B. (1990) *State Theory: Putting Capitalist States in their Place*. Pittsburgh: State University Press.

Kagarlitsky, B. (2000) *The Return Of Radicalism: Reshaping the Left Institutions*. London: Pluto Press.

Klachko, P. (1999) *Cutral Có y Plaza Huincul: el primer corte de ruta*. Buenos Aires: PIMSA.

Knoop, J. (2003) 'El Brasil con Lula. ¿Más de lo mismo?', *Nueva Sociedad* 187.

Kohan, A. (2002) *¡A las calles! Una historia de los movimientos piqueteros y caceroleros de los '90 al 2002*. Buenos Aires: Colihue.

Laclau, E. (1978) *Política e ideología en la teoría marxista*. Madrid: Siglo XXI.

Laclau, E. (2004) *The Populist Reason*. London: Verso.

Laclau, E. (2006) 'La deriva populista y la centroizquierda latinoamericana', *Nueva Sociedad* 205.

Laclau, E. and Mouffe, C. (2001) *Hegemony and Socialist Strategy: Towards a Radical Democratic Politics*. London: Verso.

Lander, E. (1996a) 'Urban Social Movements, Civil Society and New Forms of Citizenship in Venezuela', *International Review of Sociology* 6(1).

Lander, E. (1996b) 'The Impact of Neoliberal Adjustment in Venezuela 1989–1993', *Latin American Perspectives* 23(3).

Lander, E. (2002) 'El papel del gobierno de los E.E.U.U. en el golpe de Estado contra el presidente Chávez: una exploración preliminar', *Observatorio Social de América Latina* 7.

Lander, L.E. (2003) *Poder y petróleo en Venezuela*. Caracas: Ediciones Faces-UCVand PDVSA.

Lechner, N. (1988) *Los patios interiores de la democracia: subjetividad y política*. Santiago: Fondo de Cultura Económica.

Lehmbruch, G. (1979) 'Liberal Corporatism and Party Government', *Comparative Political Studies* 10(1).

Lehmbruch, G. (1984) 'Concertation and the Structure of Corporatist Networks', in J. Goldthorpe (ed.), *Order and Conflict in Contemporary Capitalism*. Oxford: Oxford University Press.

Leys, C. (1989) *Politics in Britain: From Labourism to Thatcherism*. London: Verso.

López Maya, M. (1995) 'El ascenso en Venezuela de la Causa R', *Revista Venezolana de Economía y Ciencias Sociales* 2–3.

López Maya, M. (2004) 'Venezuela: democracia participativa y políticas sociales en el gobierno de Hugo Chávez Frías'. Paper presented at the Latin American Studies Association (LASA), Las Vegas, October 7–9.

López Maya, M. and Gómez Calcaño, L. (1989) *De punto fijo al pacto social: desarrollo y hegemonía en Venezuela (1958–1985)*. Caracas: Fondo Editorial Acta Científica de Venezuela.

López Maya, M. and Lander, E. (1996) 'La transformación de una sociedad "petrolera-rentista", desarrollo económico y viabilidad democrática en Venezuela', in P. Gaitán, R. Peñaranda and E. Pizarro (eds), *Democracia y reestructuración económica en América Latina*. Bogota: Universidad Nacional and CEREC.

López Monjardín, A. and Sandoval Álvarez, R. (2003) 'Las amables telarañas del poder', *Rebeldía* 3.

Luxemburg, R. (2004), 'Social Reform or Revolution', in P. Hudisy and K.B. Anderson (eds), *The Rosa Luxemburg Reader*. New York: Monthly Review Press.

Mainwaring, S. (2001) 'Prefacio', in F. Gutiérrez (ed.), *Degradación o cambio: evolución del sistema político colombiano*. Bogota: Editorial Norma.

Mainwaring, S. and Scully, T. (1995) *Building Democratic Institutions: Party Systems in Latin America*. Stanford: Stanford University Press.

Maneiro, A. (1971) *Notas negativas*. Caracas: Ediciones Venezuela.

Marconi Nicolau, J. (2001) *Dados Eleitorais do Brasil (1982–2000)*. Rio de Janeiro: Instituto Universitário de Pesquisas do Rio de Janeiro (IUPERJ).

Marof, T. (1926) *La justicia del Inca*. Bruselas: Librería Falkfils.

Marof, T. (1934) *La tragedia del altiplano*. Buenos Aires: Claridad.

Marques, R.M. and Mendes, A. (2006) 'O social no governo Lula: a construção de um novo populismo em termos de aplicação de uma agenda neoliberal', *Revista de Economia Política* 26(1).

Martel, A. (1993) 'Metodologías de estimación de la pobreza en Venezuela'. Paper presented at the COPRE-ILDIS seminar on 'Metodologías sobre la Pobreza en Venezuela'. Caracas, February.

Martínez Verdugo, A. (1971) *Partido Comunista Mexicano: trayectoria y perspectivas*. Mexico, Fondo de Cultura Popular.

Masías, R. and Ceballos, M. (2001) *Confianza en las instituciones: principales rasgos y algunos determinantes. Una aproximación a la década de los noventa en Colombia*. Bogota: CESO.

Melucci, A. (1996) *Challenging Codes: Collective Action in the Information Age*. Cambridge: Cambridge University Press.

Mendoza, P.A., Montaner, C.A. and Vargas Llosa, A. (2007) *El regreso del idiota*. Barcelona: Grijalbo.

Mercadante, A. (2006) *Brasil Primeiro Tempo: Análise Comparativa do Governo Lula*. Sao Paulo: Planeta.

Mertes, T. (2002) 'Grass-Roots Globalism: Reply to Michael Hardt', *New Left Review* 17.

Meyer, J. (1973) *La Cristiada 2: el conflicto entre la iglesia y el estado. (1926/1929)*. Mexico: Siglo XXI.

Mides (2006) 'Perfil social de la población incluida en el PANES'. Montevideo: Ministerio de Desarrollo Social (Mides).

Moguel, J. (1987) *Los caminos de la izquierda*. Mexico: Juan Pablos.

Mommer, B. (2003), 'Petróleo subversivo', in S. Ellner and D. Hellinger (eds), *La política venezolana en la época de Chávez*. Caracas: Nueva Sociedad.

Moreira, C. (1998) 'La izquierda en Uruguay y Brasil: cultura política y desarrollo político-partidario'. Paper presented at the LASA (Latin American Studies Association) 1998 Congress, Chicago.

Moreira, C. (2000) 'La izquierda en Uruguay y Brasil: cultura política y desarrollo políticopartidario', in S. Malloy C. Moreira (eds), *La larga espera: itinerarios de las izquierdas en Argentina, Brasil y Uruguay*. Montevideo: Ediciones de la Banda Oriental.

Morquecho, G. (1994) 'Tambores de guerra, tambores de paz/ entrevista al Sub-comandante Marcos', *Cuadernos Agrarios. Nueva época*, 10, pp 164–80.

Müller Rojas, A. (2001) *Época de revolución en Venezuela*. Caracas: Solar.

Munck, R. (2003) 'Neoliberalism, Necessitarianism and Alternatives in Latin America: There is no Alternative (TINA)?', *Third World Quarterly* 24(3).

Naim, M. (2000) 'Washington Consensus or Washington Confusion?', *Foreign Policy*, Spring.

Navarro, A. (2003a) 'Estoy en el lugar correcto en el momento correcto' [interview], *El Tiempo*, November 9.

Navarro, A. (2003b) 'Entrevista de Hernando Salazar a Antonio Navarro' [interview], *El Tiempo*, December 28.

Navarro, A. (2004) 'Entrevista a Antonio Navarro' [interview], *Contravía* 10.

Negri, A. (1994) *Insurgencias: poder constitutivo y el estado moderno*. Madrid: Libertarias-Prodhufi.

Oliveira, F.d. (2004) 'The Duck-billed Platypus', *New Left Review* 24.

Oliveira, F.d. (2006) 'Lula in the Labyrinth, *New Left Review* 42.

Olivera, O. (2004) *¡Cochabamba! Water War in Bolivia*. Cambridge, MA: South End Press.

Oporto Ordoñez, V. (2002) *Triunfo de los vilipendiados*. La Paz: Ediciones Centro de Investigaciones de Trabajo Social.

Ortega, M. and Solís de Alba, A.A. (1999) *Estado, crisis y reorganización sindical*. Mexico: Itaca.

Oviedo, L. (2001). *Una historia del movimiento piquetero*. Buenos Aires: Rumbos.

Palacios, M. and Safford, F. (2002) *Colombia: país fragmentado, sociedad dividida*: Bogota, Norma.

Panizza, F.E. (2005) 'The Social Democratisation of the Latin American Left', *Revista Europea de Estudios Latinoamericanos y del Caribe* 79.

Papa, G. (2003) 'Uruguay: certezas, posibilidades, programa', *Brecha*, November 9.

Parker, D. (2001) 'El chavismo: populismo radical y potencial revolucionario', *Revista Venezolana de Economía y Ciencias Sociales* 7(1).

Parker, D. (2003), '¿Representa Chávez una alternativa al neoliberalismo?', *Revista*

Venezolana de Economía y Ciencias Sociales, 9(3), September–December.

Parra, M. and Lacruz, T. (2003) 'Seguimiento activo a los programas sociales en Venezuela: Caso de los Multihogares de Cuidado Diario, Informe final'. Caracas: Centro de Investigaciones en Ciencias Sociales (CISOR).

Paz, O. (1979) *El ogro filantrópico: historia y política 1971–1978*. Mexico: Joaquín Mortiz.

PDI (2003) 'Plataforma Política'. Bogota: Polo Democrático Independiente (PDI).

Pearce, J. (1999) 'Peace-building on the Periphery: Lessons from Central America', *Third World Quarterly* 20(1).

Pearce, J. and Howell, J. (2001) *Civil Society and Development: A Critical Exploration*. Boulder: Lynne Rienner.

Pedrazzini, I. and Sánchez, M. (1992) *Malandros, bandas y niños de la calle: cultura de urgencia en la metrópolis latinoamericana*. Valencia: Hermanos Vadell.

Peralta, M.H. (2004) 'Un futuro gobierno progresista bajo la lupa "radical": entre la duda y la esperanza', *Brecha*, March 12.

Pereira, M. (2004) 'Con el Senador José Mujica: esta izquierda es la que hay', *Brecha*, February 27.

Pérez, G. (2004) 'Pálido fuego: Hannah Arendt y la declinación de la figura del trabajador en las sociedades contemporáneas', in F. Naishtat, F. Schuster, G. Nardacchione and S. Pereyra (eds), *Tomar la palabra: estudios sobre protesta social y acción colectiva en la Argentina contemporánea*. Buenos Aires: Prometeo.

Pérez Alfonzo, J.P. (1977) *Hundiéndonos en el excremento del diablo*. Caracas: Lisbona.

Pérez Arce, F. (1982) 'Itinerario de las luchas magisteriales', *Información Obrera* 1.

Petkoff, T. (1969) *Checoeslovaquia: el socialismo como problema*. Caracas: Domingo Fuentes.

Petkoff, T. (1970) *¿Socialismo para Venezuela?* Caracas: Domingo Fuentes.

Petkoff, T. (2005) 'Las dos izquierdas', *Nueva Sociedad* 197.

Petras, J. (1999) *The Left Strikes Back: Class Conflict in Latin America in the Age of Neoliberalism*. Boulder: Westview Press.

Petras, J. and Veltmeyer, H. (2006) *Social Movements and State Power: Argentina, Brazil, Bolivia, Ecuador*. London: Pluto Press.

Petro, G. (2004) 'Hacia adelante está el poder' [interview], *El Espectador*, September 19.

Pizarro, E. (2001) 'La atomización partidista en Colombia: el fenómeno de las microempresas electorales', in F. Gutiérrez (ed.), *Degradación o cambio: evolución del sistema político colombiano*. Bogota: Editorial Norma.

Pizarro, E. (2004a) *Una democracia asediada: balance y perspectives del conflicto armado en Colombia*. Bogota: Norma.

Pizarro, E. (2004b), 'Eduardo Pizarro: Colombia está caminando hacia un esquema de tres bloques de partidos politicos,' *El Tiempo*, 5 September.

Polanyi, K. (1995) *La gran transformación: los orígenes políticos y económicos de nuestro tiempo*. Mexico: Fondo de Cultura Económica.

Polo Democrático Alternativo (PDA) (2003) 'Agenda para un pacto social 2003–2006: Propuesta alternativa al plan de desarrollo del gobierno de Álvaro Uribe', Bogotá, mimeograph.

Portes, A. (2003) *El desarrollo futuro de América Latina*. Bogota: Instituto Latinoamericano de Servicios Legales Alternativos (ILSA).

Portillo, A. (1991) 'Montevideo: la primera experiencia del frente amplio', in A. Ziccardi (ed.), *Ciudades y gobiernos locales en la América Latina de los noventa*. Mexico, D.F.: FLACSO, Instituto Moray Grupo Editorial M.A. Porrua.

Przeworski, A. (1985) *Capitalism and Social Democracy*. Cambridge: Cambridge University Press.

Raby, D. (2003) 'Revolución en el caos', *El Colombiano*, January 6.

Ramírez Gallegos, F. (2006) 'Mucho más que dos izquierdas', *Nueva Sociedad* 205.

Ramírez Sáiz, J.M. (1986) *El Movimiento Urbano Popular*. Mexico: Siglo XXI.

Rankin, A. (1995) 'Reflections on the Non-Revolution in Uruguay', *New Left Review* 211.

Restrepo, L. (2004) 'Algo grave pasa en el colombiano' [interview], *El Tiempo*, March 5.

Revueltas, J. (1962) *Ensayo sobre un proletariado sin cabeza*. Mexico: Logos.

Roberts, K. (2002) 'Social Inequalities without Class Cleavages in Latin America's Neoliberal Era', *Studies in Comparative International Development* 36(4).

Robledo, J.E. (2004) *Por qué decirles no al ALCA y al TLC*. Bogota: T.R. Ediciones.

Rocha, J.L. (2004) '25 años después de aquel 19 de Julio. ¿Hacia dónde ha transitado el FSLN?' Paper presented at the International Conference on the Origins and Prospects of the New Latin American Left, University of Wisconsin-Madison, April 29–May 3.

Rodríguez, H. (2001) 'A 10 años de gobierno progresista en Montevideo', *La República* April.

Rodríguez-Garavito, C. and Arenas, L.C. (2005) 'Indigenous Rights, Transnational Activism, and Legal Mobilization: The Struggle of the U'wa People in Colombia', in B.d.S. Santos and C. Rodríguez-Garavito (eds), *Law and Globalization from Below: Toward a Cosmopolitan Legality*. Cambridge, Cambridge University Press.

Rodríguez-Garavito, C., Barrett, P. and Chavez, D. (eds) (2005) *La nueva izquierda en América Latina: sus orígenes y trayectoria futura*. Bogota: Grupo Editorial Norma.

Rodríguez Lascano, S. (2003) '¿Puede ser verde la teoría? Sí, siempre y cuando la vida no sea gris', *Rebeldía* 8.

Rother, L. (2004) 'Tiptoeing Leftward: Uruguayan Victor's Moment of Truth', *The New York Times*, November 2.

Rubino, S. (1991a) 'Una realidad tétrica: la Intendencia Municipal de Montevideo', in C. Perelli, F. Filgueiray S. Rubino (eds), *Gobierno y política en Montevideo*. Montevideo: PEITHO.

Rubino, S. (1991b) 'Los habitantes de Montevideo: visión de la Intendencia en una coyuntura de cambio', in C. Perelli, F. Filgueiray and S. Rubino (eds), *Gobierno y Política en Montevideo*. Montevideo: PEITHO.

Rueschemeyer, D., Huber Stephens, E. and Stephens, J. (1992) *Capitalist Development and Democracy*. Chicago: University of Chicago Press.

Ruiz Hernández, M. (1999) 'La Asamblea Nacional Indígena Plural por la Autonomía (ANIPA)', in A. Burguete Cal y Mayor (ed.), *México. Experiencias de autonomía indígena*. Ciudad de Guatemala: Grupo Internacional de Trabajo sobre Asuntos Indígenas (IWGIA).

Sader, E. (2001) 'La izquierda latinoamericana en el siglo XXI', *Chiapas* 12.

Sader, E. (2002) 'Beyond Civil Society: The Left after Porto Alegre', *New Left Review* 17.

Sader, E. (2004) 'O PT e o Governo Lula', *A Cofraria*, May 18.

Sader, E. (2005) 'El movimiento social brasileño se aparta de Lula', *Le Monde Diplomatique*, January.

Sader, E. and Gentili, P. (eds) (1999) *La trama del neoliberalismo: mercado, crisis y exclusión social*. Buenos Aires: Consejo Lationamericano de Ciencias Sociales.

Sánchez, C. (1999) *Los pueblos indígenas: del indigenismo a la autonomía*. Mexico: Siglo XXI.

Sánchez Rebolledo, A. (2004) 'Democracia en apuros', *La Jornada*, April 21.

Santana, E. (1989) *Mesa redonda consecuencias sociales del cambio urbano de Caracas*. Caracas: Fundación Instituto Internacional de Estudios Avanzados.

Santana, P. (2003) 'El nuevo mapa político: el referendo y las elecciones regionales y municipales,' *Revista Foro* 49.

Santos, B.d.S. (1999) *Reinventar la democracia*. Madrid: Sequitur.

Santos, B.d.S. (2003a) *La caída del Angelus Novus: para una teoría social y una nueva práctica política*. Bogota: Instituto Latinoamericano de Servicios Legales Alternativos (ILSA).

Santos, B.d.S. (2003b) 'Globalización y democracia', *Memoria* 174.

Santos, B.d.S. (2005) *El Foro Social Mundial: manual de uso*. Barcelona: Icaria.

Santos, C., Iglesias, V., Renfrew, D. and Valdomir, S. (2006) *Aguas en movimiento: la resistencia a la privatización del agua en Uruguay*. Montevideo: De La Canilla, Montevideo.

Sarmiento Anzola, L. (2001), 'Gobernabilidad, gestión pública y social', in Fescol, ed. *La otra política*. Bogotá: Fescol, pp. 15–62.

Schuster, F.L. (1997) 'Protestas sociales y represión a la oposición política'. *Informe anual de la situación de los derechos humanos en la Argentina*. Buenos Aires: CELS.

Schuster, F.L. (1998) 'La acción colectiva en la era del desempleo'. Internet publication. Available at: http://econ.udg.es/~josepm. Universidad of Girona.

Schuster, F.L. (1999) 'Social Protest in Argentina Today: Is There Anything New?', in J. Muñoz and J. Riba (eds), *Trebal i vida en una economía global*. Barcelona: Ediciones Llibrería Universitaria.

Schuster, F.L. (2004) 'Las protestas sociales y el estudio de la acción colectiva', in F. Naishtat, F. Schuster, G. Nardacchione and S. Pereyra (eds), *Tomar la palabra: estudios sobre protesta social y acción colectiva en la Argentina contemporánea*. Buenos Aires: Prometeo.

Schuster, F.L. and Pereyra, S. (2001) 'La protesta social en la Argentina democrática: balance y perspectivas de una forma de acción política', in N. Giarracca (ed.), *La protesta social en la Argentina: transformaciones económicas y crisis social en el interior del país*. Buenos Aires: Alianza.

Schuster, F.L., Pérez, G., Pereyra, S., Armelino, M., Bruno, M., Larrondo, M., Patrici, N., Varela, P. and Vázquez, M. (2002) *La trama de la crisis: modos y formas de protesta social a partir de los acontecimientos de diciembre de 2001*. Buenos Aires: Instituto de Investigaciones Gino Germani (IIGG).

Scribano, A. (1999) 'Argentina "cortada": cortes de ruta y visibilidad social en el contexto de ajuste', in M. López Maya (ed.), *Lucha popular, democracia, neoliberalismo: protesta popular en América Latina en los años de ajuste*. Caracas: Nueva Sociedad.

Scribano, A. and Schuster, F.L. (2001) 'Protesta social en la Argentina de 2001: entre la normalidad y la ruptura', *Observatorio Social de América Latina* 5.

Semana (2003) 'Luis Eduardo Garzón: el hombre del año', December 28.

Semo, E. (2003) *La búsqueda 1: la izquierda mexicana en los albores del siglo XXI*. Mexico: Océano.

Sen, J., Anand, A., Escobar, A. and Waterman, P. (eds) (2004) *The World Social Forum: Challenging Empires*. New Delhi, Viveka Foundation.

Seoane, J. and Taddei, E. (eds) (2001) *Resistencias mundiales: de Seattle a Porto Alegre*. Buenos Aires: Consejo Lationamericano de Ciencias Sociales.

Stedile, J. (2002) 'Landless Battalions: The Sem Terra Movement of Brazil', *New Left Review* 15.

Stedile, J. (2007) 'The Neoliberal Agrarian Model in Brazil', *Monthly Review* 58(8).

Stiglitz, J. (2002) *Globalization and Its Discontents*. London: Penguin.

Stiglitz, J. (2006) *Making Globalization Work*. New York: W.W. Norton.

Stolowicz, B. (ed.) (1999) *Gobiernos de izquierda en América Latina: el desafío de cambio*. Mexico: Plaza y Valdés.

Subcomandante insurgente Marcos (2003) 'La treceava estela: cuarta parte'. Mexico: Ejército Zapatista de Liberación Nacional (EZLN).

Superville, M., and Quiñónez, M. (2003) 'Las nuevas funciones del sindicalismo en el cambio del milenio'. Montevideo: Departamento de Sociología de la Universidad de la República.

SUTERM-Tendencia Democrática (1975) 'Declaración de Guadalajara. Programa popular para llevar adelante la Revolución Mexicana'. Mexico: SUTERM-Tendencia Democrática.

Svampa, M. and Pereyra, S. (2003) *Entre la ruta y el barrio: la experiencia de las organizaciones piqueteras*. Buenos Aires: Biblos.

Tarrow, S. (1998) *Power in Movement: Social Movements and Contentious Politics*. Cambridge: Cambridge University Press.

Tavares, M.H. (2003) 'Los desafíos de la reforma social en Brasil: continuando con el cambio', *Nueva Sociedad* 187.

Taylor, M. (2006) *Neoliberalism and Social Transformation in Chile*. London: Pluto Press.

Tello Díaz, C. (2003) 'La abstención', *Proceso* 1394.

Tilly, C. (1990) 'Models and Realities of Popular Collective Action', *Social Research* 52(4).

Tischler, S. (2001) 'La crisis del sujeto leninista y la circunstancia zapatista', *Chiapas* 12.

Torres Rivas, E. (2007) 'Nicaragua: el retorno del sandinismo transfigurado', *Nueva Sociedad* 2007.

Touraine, A. (2006) 'Entre Bachelet y Morales, ¿existe una izquierda en América Latina?, *Nueva Sociedad* 205.

Ungar, E. (2003) '¿Qué pasó en el Senado de la República?', in G. Hoskin, R. Masías and M. García (eds), *Colombia 2002: elecciones, comportamiento electoral y democracia*. Bogota: Ediciones Uniandes.

Urrutia, M. (1991) 'On the Absence of Economic Populism in Colombia', in R. Dornbusch and Sebastian Edwards (eds), *The Macroeconomics of Populism in Latin America*. Chicago: University of Chicago Press.

Valencia, L. (2002) *Adiós a la política, bienvenida a la guerra: secretos de un malogrado proceso de paz*. Bogota: Intermedio.

Valero, J. (2004) 'Agresión extranjera contra la democracia venezolana'. Testimony of Ambassador Jorge Valero befote the Permanent Council of the Organization of American States (OEA-OAS). Washington, March 31.

Van Cott, D. (2003) 'Cambio institucional y partidos étnicos en Suramérica', *Análisis Político* 48.

Vargas, G. (2003) 'Feminism, Globalization and the Global Justice and Solidarity Movement', *Cultural Studies* 17(6).

Veiga, D. (1989) 'Segregación socioeconómica y crisis urbana en Montevideo', in M. Lombardi and D. Veiga (eds), *Las ciudades en conflicto: una perspectiva latinoamericana*. Montevideo: CIESU and Ediciones de la Banda Oriental.

Velasco, M.L. (2000) *Propuestas desde la izquierda al candidato de la transición, Vicente Fox*. Mexico: Raúl Juárez Carro.

Veneziano Esperón, A. (2003) 'La participación en la descentralización del gobierno municipal de Montevideo (1990–2000): evaluación de 10 años de gobierno de izquierda y algunas reflexiones para América Latina', *Documentos IIG* 110.

Vera Herrera, R. (ed.) (2001) *El otro jugador*. Mexico: La Jornada.

Vigorito, A. and Amarante, V. (2006) 'Pobreza y Desigualdad 2006'. Montevideo: Instituto Nacional de Estadística (INE).

Vila Planes, E. (2003) 'La economía social del proyecto bolivariano', *Revista Venezolana de Economía y Ciencias Sociales* 9(3).

Vilas, C. (2005) 'La izquierda latinoamericana y el surgimiento de regímenes nacional-populares', *Nueva Sociedad* 197.

Villalobos, J. (2004) 'Entre la religiosidad y el realismo político', *Semana*, December 20.

Wacquant, L. (2001) *Parias urbanos: marginalidad en la ciudad a comienzos de milenio*. Buenos Aires: Manantial.

Wacquant, L. (2004) *Deadly Symbiosis: Race and the Rise of Neoliberal Penality*. London: Polity Press.

Wainwright, H. (2005) *Reclaim the State. Experiments in Popular Democracy*. London: Verso and Transnational Intitute (TNI).

Wainwright, H. and Branford, S. (2006) *In the Eye of the Storm: Left-wing Activists Discuss the Political Crisis in Brazil*. Amsterdam: Transnational Institute (TNI).

Waksman, G. (2003) 'El congreso del Frente Amplio: la confrontación entre utopía y realidad', *Brecha*, December 26.

Wallerstein, I. (2003) *The Decline of American Power*. New York: The New Press.

Weber, M. (1982) *Escritos políticos*. México: Folios.

Weffort, F. (1984) *Por que democracia?* San Pablo: Brasiliense.

Winn, P., and L. Ferro Clerico (1997) 'Can a Leftist Government Make a Difference? The Frente Amplio Administration of Montevideo, 1990–1994', in D.A. Chalmers and C.M. Vilas (eds), *The New Politics of Inequality in Latin America: Rethinking Participation and Representation*. New York: Oxford University Press.

Womack, J. (1969) *Zapata y la revolución mexicana*. Mexico: Siglo XXI.

Wright, E.O. (2004) 'Taking the "Social" in Socialism Seriously'. Paper presented at the Annual Congress of the Society for the Advancement of Socio-Economics (SASE).

WRM (2006) 'The Botnia Pulp Mill Project Intends to Profit from Climate Change'. Montevideo: World Rainforest Movement (WRM).

Zavaleta, R. (1983) 'Las masas en noviembre', in R. Zavaleta (ed.), *Bolivia Hoy*. Mexico: Siglo XXI.

Zavaleta, R. (1986) *Lo nacional-popular en Bolivia*. Mexico: Siglo XXI.

Zibechi, R. (2003) *Genealogía de la revuelta*. La Plata: Letra Libre-Nordan-Comunidad.

INDEX

Note: political parties and organisations, where indexed here (those mentioned only in passing are not indexed separately) are done so under their local name and not its English translation or their acronym. Please consult the list of acronyms and other terms on pp.viii ff. for alternatives.

Frente Sandinista de
Liberación Nacional
(FSLN, Nicaragua), 31
Frente Social y Político (FSP,
Columbia), 129, 140
Friedman, Milton, 247
Frondizi, Arthur, 160
Fuerzas Armadas
Revolucionarias de
Colombia (FARC),
131–2, 137
Fujimori, Alberto, 235

G
G-8, 183
G-14, 60
G-20, 60
Gaitán, Jorge Eliécer, 131
Galeano, Eduardo, 19, 125
Gallegos, Ramírez, 39n5
Galtieri, Leopoldo F., 161
García, Alan, 18
Garzón, Angelino, 142,
151, 152–6
Garzón, Luis Eduardo
(Lucho), 134–5, 139,
140–5, 148
Gaviria, Carlos, 134, 139,
140, 142, 145, 147, 150,
151, 157n5
genetically modified (GM)
crops, 43
resistance to, 54
global movement, 11, 15,
237–8, 267–8
globalisation, 58, 151,
210, 232–3, 236
struggle against, 93, 268
Goldfrank, Benjamin, 109
Gómez, Enrique, 135–6
Gorz, André, 24
Gramsci, Antonio, 8, 28,
235, 238–9, 251
Group of Twenty, 183
Guadalajara Declaration,
190
Guatemala, 137
guerrilla forces in, 6

guerrilla organisations, 6,
101, 194
in Colombia, 17,
132–3, 149–50
see also armed conflict
Guevara, Ernesto 'Che', 261
Guido, José M., 160
Gutiérrez, F., 138, 153
Gutiérrez, Lucio, 30

H
Haiti, 59, 91, 183
Hardt, M., 13, 238
Hayek, F. W., 239
health policies, 57, 87,
108, 114–15
Hegel, G. W. F., 238
Helena, Heloísa, 62, 68n4
Hill, James T., 91
historical materialism, 8
Holloway, J., 13, 33–4,
203, 264
housing programmes, 108
Howell, J., 15
human rights
campaigns for, 101,
168–9
concept in Venezuela,
80–1
culture of, 42
organisations, 15, 105,
179
promotion of, 252
violations in Uruguay,
111, 116–17, 119
hunger, battle against, 156,
235

I
identities, multiple forms
of, 237
Illia, Arturo, 160
inclusion, process of, 81
see also exclusion
indigenous movements, 2,
3, 10, 13, 194–5, 203,
219–20, 231n3, 236,
238, 261, 270

indigenous people, 216
in Bolivia, 221–2, 229,
230
in the left movement,
12, 221
indianismo, 14
indigenous government
community structures,
227
mobilisation of, 3,
135–6
rights for, 80, 196–8,
203, 206
inequality, 139, 149, 163,
172, 181
efforts to decrease, 23,
48, 88, 139
impact of policies in
Argentina on, 165, 181
impact of policies in
Brazil on, 51, 55–6,
65–6
and political
dividedness, 94
in Uruguay, 114
various sources of, 2–3
in Venezuela, 10, 72–3,
94
see also equality
inflation, controlled in
Brazil, 51
informal economy, 7, 33,
110, 139
infrastructure, state role in
creation, 88
Institutional Revolutionary
Party (PRI, Mexico), 28
institutional vs direct
action, 269–70
Inter-American
Development Bank
(IADB), 123, 247
international capital
efforts to attract, 123,
125
impact of, 20
incursion of, 58, 89
see also financial

sector, foreign direct
investment
international financial
institutions
conditions imposed by,
74
impact of, 20
see also International
Monetary Fund,
structural adjustment
programmes, World
Bank
International Monetary
Fund (IMF), 20, 53, 57,
74, 75, 90, 116, 172,
192, 232, 234, 245, 247
Internet as tool for
organisation, 74
Israel, attitudes to, 91
Izarra, W. E., 81

J
Jiménez, Marcos Pérez, 69

K
Katarismo, 219–20
Katarista movement, 221
Keynes, John Maynard/
Keynesianism, 239, 241,
245, 250
Kirchner, Christina
Fernández de, 182
Kirchner, Néstor, 10, 18,
25, 26, 35–6, 92, 121,
163, 165, 171–2, 176,
178, 181–2, 234, 246,
252
Köhler, Horst, 57

L
labour
code, 56, 63
conditions,
precariousness of, 7,
110, 236
law reform, 75, 115
mobilisation, 169, 177,
190

see also trade unions
labour policy
in Argentina, 165
in Brazil, 55
in Mexico, 208–9
and social rights, 173
in Uruguay, 115–16
Laclau, Ernesto, 78, 249
Lagos, Ricardo, 18
Lancandon Forest,
declarations of, 203
land tenure, reform
of/struggles over, 43,
55, 88, 108, 188, 190,
216, 230, 233
landless rural workers, 11,
12
Lara, Rosalío José
Castillo, 98n4
latifundio, 230
Lechner, Norbert, 14
left
in Argentina, 171–8
attitude to democracy,
248–51
attitude to social
movements, 177–8
in Bolivia, 215–19
'Bourbon', 18
carnivorous vs
vegetarian, 18
divisiveness of, 162
gap between theory
and practice, 255–9
governments of, 2,
35–6, 42–68, 76–89,
99, 104–10, 113–27,
155–6, 163, 172,
176–7, 234
historical challenges
for, 251–4
in and against
government, 22
international
revitalised, 11
lefts (plural), 15
multiple forms in
Mexico, 214

new *see* new left
objectives of, 13
'old', 5–6
'old international', 7
in opposition, 251
plural, 178–9
'popular', 6
pragmatic and utopian,
214
'reformist', 6
social and political, 101
social base and
electorate for, 152–4
'two lefts' thesis, 18
typology of lefts, 178
unification in
Colombia, 146–8
vs right, 5
see also communism,
new left, socialism
Leninism, 12, 28
decline of, 8
lesbian/gay/bisexual/
transexual movements,
208, 270
*Letter to the Brazilian
People, A*, 46–8
literacy projects, 87
local government, 13, 26,
36, 155, 209
in Brazil, 19
and indigenous
community structures,
227
as launch pad for left,
36
local governance in
Bolivia, 223
in Montevideo, 36,
103–10
by non-left parties, 46
by parties of the left,
43, 103–10, 143
see also neighbour-
hood councils/
assemblies
lockouts, 116
López, Alexander, 140